Sweeping Away the Sand

A Novel

To my cousin,
Lois
I hope you
enjoy the read.
Tjaakje Heidema

Tjaakje Charlotte Heidema

References from the Bible are taken from the King James Version.

"Sweeping Away the Sand," by Tjaakje Charlotte Heidema. ISBN 978-1-60264-069-6 (softcover); 1-978-60264-070-2 (hardcover).

Library of Congress Control Number on file with Publisher.

Manufactured in the United States of America.

Dedicated to my family:

to all those who went before
to those who will come after
and to those who were unrelated.

Contents at a Glance

Annotated Table of Contents

Chapter 6: Ann Unpacks

January, 1948, Heidema family trip to America on the *Nieuwe Amsterdam*. The arrival in Hoboken, New Jersey and the train ride from Hobokan to Bozeman, Montana with only $10 left in Jan Piet's pocket. First visits to Monkey Wards and Snappy Service with Uncle Bill. Living on Main Street in Manhattan. Jan Piet says no to Ellensburg, Washington and the Four by Four Church. Pieka, Stientje and other immigrant friends, all are gone

Chapter 7: Polishing Silverware

Ann and Arlyce's special bond formed in Holland. Ann's view on social issues. Arlyce's adventures abroad. Arun calls Steven, "Pa". Succession of mothers and mothering. Pat's list of things to do in Seattle. Steve and Pat's backyard

Chapter 8: Prolastin at North Office

Downtown Phoenix in rush hour traffic. Alpha-1 Deficiency and Prolastin explained. What emphysema is about. Waste in America. Going against the Holy Spirit

Chapter 9: Anil's Meditation

Anil studies Krishnamurti's words. Varieties of beliefs in India

Chapter 10: Homemade Pan of Soup

Pat's ceramics . Sophia and Tjaakje forgot the Drostes. Lupus explained. Pat's overall plan for the family gathering. Tjaakje remembers details about her father. The Van Bergen stories. *"Vitzen Leirn"* and *"Tuddebekje"*. Father and daughter-Sows and piglets, Tjaakje's most precious jewel

Chapter 11: Doc Sandi's Errands on Christmas Eve

Doc Sandi euthanizes Gretchen. Benji understood German commands. Modern veterinary practices. The Warehouse Theatre. Relay for Life. Sandi's errands, meals, cross-stitching and movies. Herbie's shower. River rafting, scuba diving and kayaking

Chapter 12: Jesus, *Sinterklass,* and *Maveli*

Preparation of the Christmas dinner. Ann modeled her new dresses for her dad and still does for her children. Arun's "umbootie". The birth of Jesus according to the gospel of Luke. Steven's prayer. *Sinterklass* or St. Nicholas. King Maveli and the story of *Onam* . Roy Rogers and Gene Autry. Mittens or gloves

Chapter 13: *Sjoeln*

The Knottnerus and Kimn brothers. The shuffleboard, the wood disks and the competition. Anil's uncanny ability in *sjoeln* .

Chapter 14: After Bowling

Kenmore lanes and hotdogs in the parking lot. Snow and icy roads. Sliding off the viaduct outside of Bozeman in the Model A. Jan Piet walked the Lo Line and Ann learned to drive. Doug drove up to Northshore Summit and Sophia made a snow angel

Chapter 15: Three de Vries Brothers in World War II

Prologue   Ann and Tjaakje discuss what makes a good movie

Jan   Ann's oldest brother. Klaas and Pieterke de Vries, father and mother of eight, owned the farm, *Sasmaheerd.* Klaas died in 1937. Jan ran the farm then was replaced by Tjaard. May 10, 1940 Nazis invaded and Holland surrendered. The Swastica. Ties between Germany and The Netherlands. The Thirty Years War. Anti-Semitism in Europe. Hitler's view of the Jews and his exterminist practices. Queen Wilhelmina on the BBC. Hollanders rebelled; Germans clamped down. *Sasmaheerd* family offers free milk. A ride to Thesinge in a horse drawn buggy with illegal goat meat. The ver Kooien family. Jan and Jant's hiding place. Corruption and collaborators. Jan arrested and sent to concentration camp. Jan released

Tjaard   The natural born farmer and partier. Tjaard's shame. Time in the labor camp. De Vries family lost *Sasmaheerd.* Ann's memories of her childhood home

Piet   Ann's youngest brother. Member of the Knuckle Brigade as the resistance fighter, Han, at the age of 19. Failed attempt to free prisoners at the *Weteringeschans.* On the run in a marriage carriage. Stealing weapons from a police station. Life of an undergrounder, a man of many disquises. Overstretched Elastic Syndrome. Recovering in Aroza, Switzerland. Piet's two families. Comparing notes as children of the underground

   Epilogue   Disillusionment and emigration. Aftermath of war. Untold stories

Chapter 16: Breakfast in Bed

The family room serves as the Cok's bedroom. Sandi stuck in Yakima. Sophia provides Room Service. Steve and Pat's volunteer work

Chapter 17: Tjaakje Interviews Ann

Ann, the oldest member of the choir. First born of Klaas de Vries and Pieterke Oudman on the farm *Italie* in Winsum, Groningen. Meals of *stamppot en soepenbrij*. Anje's favorite hired man. Little sister Martje. Teacher's pet and milking cows by hand. Anje's life as a young woman in Baflo. Meeting Jan Piet Heidema in Thesinge. Selling grain to the highest bidder at the *Beurs*. Pat recalls the neighbors in Thesinge. Anje nursed a Huisman boy. Pat had stomach aches to stay home from school but paid a price. Rats from the canal. Anje's engagement and wedding

Chapter 18: Puzzle Talk

Damage caused by snow in Seattle. One more trip to Holland? "Snowbound: A Winter Idyll". The living room wall hangings, furniture and musical instruments. Steve, Pat, the girls, Tjaakje and Ann's trip to Holland in 1973 . Remembering the familiar odor in the *kelderke*. Ann and Margaret's trip to Holland and Switzerland. The stay with the Lightenbergs on Churchill in '53. All the reasons for coming to America. Jan Siemen Dijk family. Annie Eubel's help with getting visas

Chapter 19: Margaret Takes a Walk

Living in Bliss   Margaret is named after Martje. The tear in the acetabulum. The family going for citizenship before Judge Leslie in the Bozeman Courthouse. Margaret as a spunky kid at seven. Skippy, and Tippy, Sugar and Alvin, Snowball and Olieball and all the rest. Marion Schutter at school and Judy Hess close by. What Margaret remembers of her father.

Falling into the Abyss   Margaret saddened at nine. The move to Churchill. At 16 Margaret began work as a nurse's aide. Fulfilling mother's wish to be a nurse. Inflammation of the kidney. Victims of domestic violence: The years with Rick and Kelly.

Rising again to Redress   G. G., Francis and Doug help Margaret out. Doug and Marge are married. The Langel retreat in Glacier Park. Brandon John is born. Margaret goes to college in Kalispell. Black Cat Base back in Rudyard. The Good Samaritan on 64th avenue

Chapter 20: Opening the Presents

Morning: Pat's Apple Pie Burns Sandi stalled on Snoqualmie Pass. Pat is busy. Going from grade 1 through 10 in five and a half years. Finishing high school in Hull, Iowa. Working for room and board. On to Calvin College. Teaching sixth grade at Manhattan Christian and getting an Associate Degree. Dating and marrying Steven. Sandi arrives

Early Afternoon: A Case for Entitlement Disagreement on how much to spend. Social Security is not enough. Ann's experiences with being frugal. Loaning money to relatives. The debt owed to Uncle Bill. Gardening and canning. Many ways to make money. The ill tempered rooster. Pieka finds chicks in her eggs. Grading potatoes. Debts paid off. Ann worked hard to make it on her own. The disagreement is settled. "Do not go gentle into that good night..."

Late Afternoon: John Is the Man They Call John, the snowbird, at his computer in the Arizona room. Lung transplant a 50/50 proposition. Joyce plays the piano at Sunlife. John's creativity: his photography and woodworking. Christmastime at D 82. John's *liet motif*: keep setting goals. A humdinger of a truck. The visionary sets the course. Bea needs help with her computer. The Honda Elite motorcycle. The illegal Mexican medicine had serious side effects. Steps taken in adolescence led to dairying for a living. Sheila, Leland, Michelle, and Kent. Love of flying. Brother and sister on opposite sides of almost everything. Bitter reflections on family ties. This one and the very first panic attack. Xanex kicks in. John flies home

Evening: *Het Onze Vader* and the Group Picture The Lord's Prayer. Skits that the kids did at John and Joyce's. Gifts exchanged. The group picture. Arlyce gets her foot massage.

Chapter 21: Pancakes to Celebrate

Ann's battle with Job's stocking. What her leg veins have endured. Dr. Coglan, Manhattan's only dentist. Ann wraps toilet paper around her French twist. A tailgate hits the windshield. Wina. Dienie. Trui. Martje: her gifts, her difficulties and her broken engagement. Ann's heartbreaking trip to Assen with pancakes for her sister.

Chapter 22: Epiphanies along the Way

Madona stories. Tjaakje's Hobo Hike with Pioneer Girls. Vacation Bible School in Manhattan and the zippered Bible. Red Cheney and hail. Stacking the hay was a family effort but then the stack burned to the ground. Tjaakje rides the palamino bareback. John got the bigger piece, a moral dilemma. "It is cancer, children. It is cancer". Father's last request. Public profession of faith. Kernels of faith. The short lady at the sausage counter in Shop and Save. Burning my baseball cards.

Chapter 23: As the Kaleidoscope Turns

Uncle Piet Heidema calls from Holland to ask about the Seattle weather. Napoleon wanted surnames: Heide means "heather" and van Bruggen means from the "bridge". Heidema family tree. Jan Heidema and Trientje Dijk, their son, Jan Piet, and their daughters, Tjaakje Fylina, and Fylina. Fylina's brother, Jan Piet, dreams of meeting Jesus on the mountain top. Piet's work with horses. Church services canceled. Anil borrows spices from Indian neighbor. Playing solitaire. Singing around the piano. The Coumar family returns home.

Chapter 24: Recess Time in Between Storms

Mudslides and sinkholes in Seattle. The stress of being back in the crucible of family. A short respite of anonymity in the mall.

Chapter 25: Holland and the Sea

Floods in Seattle. Dike Peace in Holland. The history of building dikes in the Netherlands. How land is reclaimed from the sea. Neap tide, the weak side of the sea. The boy who put his thumb in a dike to stop the water is a myth. The flood of 1953. Counteracting the destructiveness of salt. "Luctor et emergo". Ann is awash between cultures.

Chapter 26: Cool Stories

The one-eyed man with a rifle across Camp Creek. A fake kidnapping. *Vrouw* van Ketten and Anje warn their neighbors after curfew in Thesinge. Jan Piet had a forbidden radio. The noise of the *Luftwaffe* bombers at night. Bombing raids. A search for body parts in the pasture. The German soldier stepped through the kitchen window in Baflo.

Chapter 27: *Ollie Bollen*

On New Year's Eve some of the family go to church the others makes *ollie bollen*. A Dutch tradition, the *schuddeldouk*

Chapter 28: It's CHIPS but It's Not Potato Chips

Arlyce at work. Bone marrow transplantation, allogeneic and autologous, explained. Dealing with layers of bigotry. Arlyce before being a wife and mother was a basketball player, lifeguard and runner. Acting like a Siamang monkey on the way home.

Chapter 29: See You in Mexico

The power outage. Sophia has had enough. The mysterious frog. *Maus* and murder in Rudyard. Signing John's birthday card. Facing losses. Ann receives a video of the events of the last 10 days.

Selected Bibliography

Acknowledgements

First and foremost I want to thank my life partner, Sophia Kellis, for her unwavering support. Were it not for the fact that she helped and encouraged me every step of the way, this book would never have happened. At the start, when I could not believe in myself, she believed in me, and in the ten years that it has taken me to complete this work, Sophia has literally prepared my meals, filled my oxygen tanks, carried my books, and envisioned my success.

"When I imagine playing Tchaikovsky's Concertos in Vienna," she would say, "I am wearing dangling diamond earrings and a tight, ankle-length, black dress." For as many years as I have been writing, Sophia has talked—not just to me but to anyone who would listen—of our being driven around in limos and being wined and dined in the big cities on my book tour. Bless her!

Next, but equally important, I want to thank my family for sharing their lives and the stories of their lives with me. I pray that I have not in any way violated their trust. I especially want to thank my mother for always being eager to explore and for almost always satisfying my curiosities by answering question after question after question.

I thank my aunt, Jant Ruiter-de Vries for coming from Holland and visiting with me in Maine. Her stories helped me to expand on some sketchy information about the extended family. My cousins, Peggy Berry and Phoenix van Hardenbroek helped by correcting numerous errors in my spelling of the Dutch words. I thank them, as well, for their confidence and for sharing their stories. Mechteld van Hardenbroek deserves a huge posthumous thank you from me for her detailed letters. She wrote movingly to me, a stranger, about her work in the resistance movement in the Netherlands.

Sandi Cok, my niece, upon hearing me read one of my stories at a family gathering asked me to "please write more." I thank her

i

for those words of encouragement.

I also must express my sincere gratitude to the women of the book group in Southern Maine. The unique background and fascinating personality that each woman brought to the group stimulated me intellectually, and the soul-satisfying discussions with them about the work of women authors illumed my way. Especially, I want to thank Lois Kilroy for her friendship. She continued, after our group ended, to talk with me about books and about writing. Her courage to do so emboldened my very early work.

Both my brother, John, and friend, Phil Freeman, before their passing, gave me important and timely technical support, and I greatly appreciated the computer expertise and advice of Pat and Claudette Davis.

The able proofreading of my manuscript was done by my friend, Vangi De Masters. Her valuable knowledge, help and encouraging words came and continue to come at just the right time. I appreciated, too, that Vangi introduced me to Sharon Westra who was happy to share the steps of her success in the publishing process.

Over the years in a half-a-dozen states across the country, I have taken up space in quite a number of libraries. I thank all those involved for the invaluable presence of those libraries throughout my life.

Finally, I thank all who dealt with me during these past ten years for their willingness to tolerate delay. My pace is not that of most people and they, by waiting patiently, let me find my own way out of my cocoon. I thank them for that.

A scientist was watching a monarch butterfly emerge from its cocoon. It was such a long struggle, the creature fought on and on with the rough material of the cocoon—tearing, pulling, and struggling, fighting to get out.

"If I only snip this little bit at the top, I could help this creature," he said to himself. And he reached in with his scissors and cut away the last piece of the cocoon.

The monarch went on for a few moments, but seemed to grow weaker, and finally, his wings still partly folded, he fell back onto the table, dead.

The scientist realized he had killed the butterfly by trying to make things easier. Each push by the struggling insect forces lifeblood into those glorious wings, and their beauty in flight comes only after the fight to emerge from the cocoon is entirely finished.

Author Unknown

Chapter 1
Fire on the Rum

Plucked from the nest of extended family at the age of four and a half I have wrapped loneliness around me like a warm colorful scarf on a cold day.

L et me reassure you that you are not alone in feeling depressed as the holidays approach. It is a difficult time for many people," affirmed Anil, the empathic therapist, who was midway in his mental status evaluation of university student, Michael Bowman.

"There is a final coming up in Sociology," the boy mumbled haltingly. "I-I, ah, I don't even feel like studying, you know. To tell you the truth," he said then shifted uncomfortably and blew out some air before continuing, "I-I, ah, have to take a little, ah, some speed just to get psyched enough to care, you know what I mean?"

Michael snuffled. Like guys in a Salvation Army lunch line his chin dropped down onto his chest.

"I might not even, like, make it home next week."

Anil registered the significance of the student's last sentence but decided to let it go for the time being and concentrate instead on the more immediate problems.

"Speed may be causing your depression or at least making it worse," he stated as a matter of fact. "Have you been able to sleep?"

"Nah, don't have time for sleep. Barely have time to eat. I was wondering if, ah, I might need some antidepressants or something, ah, tranquilizer or something maybe."

This was not going to be an easy case. All too often the university students, like starving stray cats in winter, came to the mental health clinic desperate to get prescriptions and an easy fix.

1

Kids knew the terminology and the system in this modern society's drug culture. What they did not know was how to live without the roller coaster thrills of the drugs.

There was a chance, though, that this kid was faking it. Underneath the hip lingo about drugs there might lurk a real depression, maybe even an early thought disorder which might mean a psychosis. Mike, with long, straight, uncombed, oily blonde hair falling down over his face, did not really slur his words but spoke slowly, had poor eye contact and in the confines of his small office Anil could tell from the unpleasant odor that the kid had not bathed for some time. Like the medical category for failure-to-thrive youngsters, this guy had a pale, scrawny look to him that bothered Anil. Plus, the kid had lost a parent in his adolescence. That fact alone would raise a red flag for any therapist. Anil's intuition cautioned him: do not categorize this case prematurely.

The University of Washington Mental Health Clinic, like the Honey of a Ham Store, had been busy since the Thanksgiving break and it was intensely busy now just before the end of the semester. Holidays and finals were huge pressures. Anil was perturbed by the insensitivity of the institution. The exams could come later in January. Why now on top of the holidays? It was too much stress for some kids.

Decisions were too often made on the basis of faculty convenience or economics. The unwritten message was: keep the machines running smoothly. If a few students can't handle it they probably shouldn't be here. After all, the pressures in the university just mirror the pressures in the real world and they need to get used to them to make it out there. Anil had heard the hard-nosed, capitalistic, western culture arguments. He didn't buy any of it.

He sat relaxed and confident in his tilting office chair. His brown, pleasant face, like his midriff, was pudgy and made him look shorter than the six feet that he was. Unlike his naturally athletic wife, Arlyce, Anil struggled to stick with an exercise program. He liked to walk and walked the mile to and from work weather permitting and he also swam sporadically, but his interests were more along the lines of computers, techno-gadgets, spiritual and psychological practices and his own inner workings. His indulgences were food and cars. He liked to cook and to eat and loved the hot new models at the car shows or the latest models that

Toyota or Honda was putting out with their cool Global Positioning Systems. He was wearing a light blue, short-sleeved, oxford shirt open at the collar with khaki Dockers, and black leather Wingtip shoes. His thick, black hair was cut short. It was shorter than usual, although he never let it grow very long, and except for a mustache that curved down the sides of his mouth just past his lower lip, he was clean shaven. That was not always the case either. He frequently had a well- trimmed beard.

"There is something that has been bothering me and I need to ask you a question," Anil said as he leaned forward in his chair to get a closer look.

Mike's left hand shot up to his cheek. He stole a sheepish glance up at Anil.

"I would like to know how you got that injury to your face. It looks painful."

Michael's hand fingered an ugly, dark red, scabbed-over mark the size of a dried prune from the corner of his lip up into his cheek.

"There was this party and we was drinking rum and..."

Anil waited for more. Michael slid down in his chair and played absent-mindedly with a loose thread from the cuff of his shaggy, oversized fisherman sweater.

"I'm listening, Mike, do you prefer to be called Mike?" rather than Michael?"

"Yeah."

"There was a party and there was rum and what?" Anil prompted patiently. He thought the boy had a young look. He was small for his age. His sad eyes were a tired, washed-out blue but with normal-appearing pupils.

"They were flaming rum. They had fire on 'em and I wasn't too smart. I thought I, you know, could drink the fire too, I guess." The ashamed freshman shrunk back into himself.

Anil stole a glance at his watch and realized with a start that the 50 minute hour had already elapsed. He made it a practice to stay within the allotted time, plus, he would be late if he did not end right now. It was Thursday afternoon, December 19th, and Arlyce, a nurse, had to start her shift downtown at four o'clock. He had to be home by three-thirty to take over the care of their one-year-old son, Arun.

This was not a good time to tell Mike that they had to quit. However, there was still the obligatory paperwork to do for the evaluation so he really had only one choice. He had to tell him. Anil sighed as he straightened himself in the chair.

The small, narrow, rectangular space was as much a cell as an office. The plain, institutional woodwork had an old dark walnut stain. At one end was the door; at the other an old double pane window from which one could get a glimpse of Lake Union through the pine trees on a sunny day. The office was tolerable but Anil hoped and planned for better.

"I would agree, Mike, that was not too smart," Anil said firmly. "It looks to be healing all right but you will have a scar to remind you. I am sorry to tell you that it is time to stop. Can you come tomorrow? There is more to talk about and I want to see you again."

"Nah, I can't tomorrow."

As Anil thoughtfully consulted his schedule Mike rubbed his right hand back and forth on his thigh and pumped his foot up and down nervously. The dirty, loose shoelaces below the frayed muddy hem of the enormous black denim pant leg tapped on the tiled floor like a cheap alarm clock in the silence. Anil was not confident that Mike would be back. He hated doing it but he would bribe him.

"How about the next day, can you come on Saturday? I will be in for the morning. Maybe by then I can get you a prescription. I am not a psychiatrist. I cannot write you a prescription but I can talk it over with the psychiatrist. What time would be good for you?"

Anil Coumar had earned his Master's degree in Clinical Psychology at the free-thinking Antioch College in Seattle. He could not prescribe medications because he was not licensed as a physician in the States, but he knew about psychopharmacology and he knew it would be a bad idea to medicate this young man at this point.

He was hurrying the boy and he was also aware of feeling fear. Like a successful quarterback able to sense the imminent breakdown of his line protection even when his back is turned, Anil could sense where this was headed. He made it a point to listen to his body, to his inner reactions and consciousness; they told him a lot about what was going on in a relationship. This kid could go

4

sour on him overnight. There wasn't any concrete reason to admit him at this point. Mike had denied having any suicidal thoughts; however, his denial did not rule out that he had them. It was probably too soon for the boy to feel comfortable sharing such information. Anil broke off his thought process; he had to go. The difficult diagnosis and the sudden time pressure were causing tightness in his chest. He stood up, breathed it out and opened the door to the hallway.

"Saturday? Eleven sound good to you?"

"Yeah, maybe."

The therapist's out-of-the-ordinary parting words were, "Get some sleep tonight, Mike. Don't party, okay?" It wasn't Anil's style to be paternal or directive but the kid seemed so bereft, it had come out before he realized it.

As the young man pulled up on his sagging denims and made his slackened way down the hall, Anil shifted gears. He quickly stepped back into the office, took his seat in front of the computer on the desk and adeptly punched in the instructions to page Arlyce.

Anil Coumar of Indian descent had traveled a long way to get to this point. Thirty-six years earlier in 1960 he had been born an only son in Mahe, Kerala in India. That was a long ways away. To picture this geographically, it may be helpful to know that India is roughly half the size of the United States. It has 25 states and the state of Kerala, which means "the land of coconut trees," lies at India's southern tip hugging the western shoreline lengthwise. Like Seattle it has numerous waterways and both lie between the sea to the west and the mountains to the east.

Unlike Seattle, however, Mahe is a small scale city and the Arabian Sea to the west was more easily accessible. Anil, growing up with his two older sisters on what is known as the Malabar Coast, loved going to the beach to collect shells and rocks. His treasure find had been the vertebra of a whale, "as large around as a steering wheel," he claims. He liked to dream of what laid beyond the horizon and to watch the island fisherman pull in their nets. Inland, somewhere in the 1,000 mile heavily forested, low mountain range known as the Western Ghats, he and his family escaped to find some much needed, cooling shade from the heat.

One of the main reasons why Anil prefers to live life in the northwest of North America rather than in India is that Kerala is near the equator. It has two monsoon seasons and has a tropical marine to rainforest climate. The temperature ranges from 70^0 to 115° with very high humidity. Such conditions are extremely oppressive for humans but ideal for vegetation.

As a boy, he was surrounded by an awesome plethora of trees. There were evergreen, teak, laurel, myrtle, and mahogany trees some of which yielded rosewood, sandalwood and balsam. There were bamboo, mangrove, banana, pineapple and rubber trees. There were trees which produced aromatic spices such as cinnamon, cloves and nutmeg. In fact, India is a leading exporter of spices and seventy-five percent of all the spices that India exports come from the state of Kerala. There were also coconut palms, shrubs that produced tea, ferns, flowering plants, fungi, lichens, mosses and even lush, green grasslands! Can you imagine such fertile soil?

India is heavily populated with humans as well. Anil was one of the billion people that live in the country. In fact, one of every six people in the world today is Indian. As diverse as the vegetation, they speak any one or more of 15 official languages or 5,000 secondary languages. In northern India the ancient Indo-European language group of Sanskrit was formed from a convergence of many dialects. In Kerala the language is Malayalam which is not an Indo-European derivative. It is rather in the Dravidian group of languages that is common in southern India. Anil's family and the surrounding peoples are known as *Malay alee* referring to the "people of the mountains."

Being the only son, Anil was not expected to work around the home. It was Indian custom that everything was provided for him by his sisters, mother, Swayam Prabha, and two live-in servants. His father, Patmanabhin, on the other hand, both favored and harshly disciplined him. As a young person, Anil knew almost nothing of his father's work and progressively spent his summers and as much time as permitted away from home with cousins and friends.

As he approached manhood, he realized that his uncle on his father's side owned considerable land and his cousins worked in their large family business. They stood to inherit a great deal. He, Anil, stood to inherit nothing. Even his own family home was in his uncle's name; his father had never put it in his own name! He began to resent his father for what he perceived as his "spinelessness" and their relationship became strained. As Anil matured, however, he came to understand it all very differently.

He learned that his father had strongly supported the French who had held onto the small province during the British colonization and rule of India. Patmanabhin and his family had, in fact, become French citizens. After Indians gained independence from Britain, as well as France, his father had gone to jail for what others perceived as his leanings towards an imperialist power. Though an active and outspoken community figure during the French rule, he was never again accepted officially into the public political arena.

Anil also learned that his father's allegiance to France had been not so much about wanting to be a European colony as about appreciating their style of governing. He approved of the French economic leanings toward socialism and knew that they strongly complemented the long established collective spirit present in India. To this day Kerala is one of the states that are closely aligned with communal wealth, equitable distribution of land, health care and education. It has its advantages: the state has a 100% literacy rate!

Patmanabhin was deeply committed to the cooperative movement which could provide cheaper rates for all. Having been economically unable to continue after one year of medical school, he had dedicated all future efforts to starting two successful co-op stores for groceries and milk. Consistent with his beliefs, he drew his pension but was not interested in personal accumulation of wealth.

"I have enough. I don't need to take anymore," he would say.

Patmanabhin was a man who put his beliefs into practice, a man of integrity, which, as a teenager seeking an identity, his son could not appreciate. Is there a teenager who can?

Instead of inheriting a business then, his son should pursue what he, father, could not: a career in medicine. So, wisely, that was what father encouraged seventeen-year-old Anil to do. Anil, seeing a way out, agreed. He left the western shore of southern India's tip and went over to the eastern shore on the Bay of Bengal to the French city of Pondicherry near Madras. Madras is in the state of Tamil Nadu and is the fourth largest city of India. In contrast to Mahe, Madras is a noisy, densely populated, polluted city.

It is all in the perspective we bring to a situation, is it not? Anil's in-laws, the Coks, struggle to adapt to the explosive growth in Seattle since Bill Gates and Microsoft have brought technology businesses and people to the area. They resent the burgeoning traffic problems. In contrast, Seattle has been, for Anil, an unpolluted, quiet city as well as a cool, refreshing version of the lush green of Mahe. He likes it very much and, when homesick, he makes the trip half way around the globe back to Kerala and back to Mahe to drink in that which is India.

In 1983 he graduated with a medical degree from the Jawarharlal Institute of Post Graduate Medical Education and Research (JIPMER) in Pondicherry after which he sought advanced opportunities in London, Great Britain. He was licensed as a medical doctor and worked in endocrinology research in the Royal Free Hospital. It was there that his research connected him with patients whose diseases had a strong emotional component and he felt himself increasingly pulled in the direction of psychology. He applied to become a psychoanalyst and lay on a couch three times a week to experience the therapy firsthand. As with every one who is pulled in the direction of psychology, he had his own issues to confront. Those issues, for the most part, had their roots in his conflicted relationship or lack of relationship with the complex authority figure, his father, and his more recent guilt for being absent at the time of Swayam Prabha, his mother's, death from complications of diabetes.

It was while at the Royal Free Hospital through mutual friends that he was introduced to, in his opinion, a "beautiful" Caucasian nurse, my niece, Arlyce Cok, from the states. Arlyce had gone to London to get her own geographic distance from family at the time and, simultaneously, to share her knowledge of nursing care for bone marrow transplant patients with the London hospital transplant team.

Anil and Arlyce bonded, lived together, married while in London and moved to Seattle in 1992. His license to practice as a doctor was not accepted in the states and, rather than repeat the arduous educational requirements to be a physician, Anil adapted and enrolled in Antioch College to become a therapist. By searching, traveling and working hard he had gained a family, a respectable career and a home of his own. He was proud of his status and, by rights, could choose to rest on his laurels; however, it was not in his nature to do so. He wanted to have power in his job and to pursue tranquility in his inner journey.

Anil clicked off the computer, left his office, took the elevator down and felt the confusing stress of being a responsible husband, new father and son-in-law as well as aspiring employee who was a minority but not yet a citizen.

Did my own father ever hurry home from work to care for me, his only son? Not likely! What did my father really teach me? At the age of seventeen, I knew nothing about how to care for myself, let alone anyone else. In medical school in Pondicherry I felt woefully unprepared and vulnerable.

I could have chosen to live my whole life, like so many Indian young men of my generation still do, with the customs of our fathers. I could have had a suitable woman selected for me and probably could have received a handsome dowry for marrying a woman from a well-to-do family. Had I done so, I would never have had to deal with shared decision-making, scheduling, laundry, food preparation or diaper changing. But I have not chosen that way of home life or at least I like to think I haven't.

Anil liked being free from confining customs and he wanted to make his beliefs and politics of social equality personal. In other words, he wanted to bring his inherited cooperative politics into his home. Treating a woman, his wife, as a partner, as his equal was a slant on integrity that he was finding so much easier to believe than to practice.

He ran across campus to the parking lot. Short of breath when he reached his car, he vowed to start swimming again. Maybe tomorrow, he thought, I can find a free hour.

Chapter 2
The Langels Reach Mac Donald Pass

There was one, Tante Frouk (who was not a real aunt, we just called her that) in Holland. Tante Frouk called me "lieve scaat" ("precious doll" comes close). I loved that.

Later, on that same Thursday, late in the evening, Margaret, my younger sister by eight years, a not-overly tall woman in her mid-forties, sat intensely focused behind the large steering wheel of the old but well-kept CruiseAir motor home. Her straight, clean, fine hair, the color of wheat, was nearly collar length. The right side was tucked behind her ear; the left was falling forward. Shorter hair at the forehead had been inadvertently brushed up and to one side.

Every now and then this resolutely determined woman leaned forward towards the huge oversized windshield to get a better look at the slippery snow-packed highway speeding by underneath. She was wearing gold wire rim glasses, blue jeans, good quality, beige, Glacier Park sweat shirt, navy down vest and what looked to be fairly new, white, athletic, tennis shoes. From a short distance she was strikingly pretty and tanned with a casual outdoorsy style. On closer inspection of her face, one saw lines and weathering that made her look a good ten years older than she was. Close up, too, one could see that her nervousness was barely contained.

It was nighttime and profoundly dark out. Marge was more than usually edgy. Without breaking her concentration she extended her right arm and with thin, scarred fingers that shook slightly she undid the clip and maneuvered a cigarette from the pack in the nut-brown cigarette case lying on the expansive dashboard. In a continuing, well -rehearsed motion she put the cigarette in her mouth, took the Bic lighter from a slot on the front of the case, lit the cigarette, blew the smoke out and returned the lighter to its slot. Then she put the cigarette in one corner of her mouth and let it dangle there, squinting as the smoke curled up into her narrow set, sky-blue eyes. It was a set of unconscious behaviors, behaviors that had also been so characteristic of our father.

Tall, dark-haired John Peter Heidema, known to his Dutch friends and Mom as Jan Piet, used to have a lit, unfiltered Pall Mall cigarette in the corner of his mouth just like that when he hammered steel on steel on a lousy broken farm implement, or when he hurriedly threw heavy, wet chunks of sod into an irrigation ditch to reinforce a canvas dam or, for that matter, when he emptied a pail of foamy, white, warm milk carefully and slowly into the top of the separator. In almost every imaginable circumstance in which Margaret as a young child had seen him, he had had a cigarette hanging there and he had been squinting his eyes in just that same way.

Smoke in the eyes stings. It hurts and the chemical sludge of tobacco smoke corrodes on the inside. Margaret was only seven when her father died from the effects of his heavy smoking. It had been inoperable bronchial cancer, but like a fuzzy yellow duckling imitating the walk and squawk of its parent, so some of Jan Piet's behaviors were programmed into his youngest daughter.

In modern social sciences it is known as imprinting. The duckling and child never know it is happening and they will keep doing it even if it stings, hurts and kills. Sometimes Margaret wants to quit, especially when her son gives her grief about it, but she pretty much feels defeated before she starts. It is such a powerful addiction and so far the will for her to break the habit has not been there.

Snow and sleet were coming down heavily over Mac Donald Pass as they approached Missoula heading west and Marge, veteran driver that she was, right then was not thinking about anything but keeping the 28 foot motor home on the road. She had decided to take U.S. Highway 12. It is a shortcut between Helena and Missoula instead of having to drop down to Butte on Interstate 15 then up through Anaconda and Deer Lodge on 90 to Missoula. It would save time but maybe it had been a little too late in the year for this altitude of 6,325 feet. Dense, dark stands of pine trees barely visible through the white curtain of steady snow slashed by off to her right. She could not see into the darkness beyond the road on her left. Luckily there had not been another vehicle on the highway for several miles.

They were on the descent of the steep slope and, on the plus side, she was sure that there would not be any wildlife like deer, elk or moose crossing in front of her, like they might have done during the day. Not in this weather. Unlike humans they would have the sense to stay put in the shelter provided by the trees.

The clock in front of her showed that it was getting close to midnight on this and Marge had been tiring. It was the cigarettes that were keeping her hyped up, keeping her awake, alive. Afterwards, she would take something for the headache and sinus congestion which always came with too much smoking and prolonged tension. She had come to expect it. Gingerly Margaret moved her shoulders and neck, tight as a drum and hurting badly. She knew she would have trouble getting to sleep.

Margaret's 65 year old husband, Douglas Langel, was in the back. He is a reticent, slow moving, medium-built man of some kind of Scandinavian descent, Norwegian probably, with English thrown in. Nobody is that sure. He has lots of relations but they no longer talk about that sort of thing. He has a kind, soft face with blondish-gray short, straight, oily hair combed to one side. The slightly stooped, quiet, impervious man habitually pulls his head forward from his shoulders. In the company of others he usually has a quizzical, observant expression on his face.

Just then Doug's ever-present baseball cap was pushed far back on his head. He was dressed in a loose-fitting short-sleeved coverall and dark-colored tennis shoes. He was with ten-year-old energetic son, Brandon, in the middle section of the motor home. The two were jostling back and forth on the couch, Brandon testing his strength, Doug holding his own and letting the boy blow off steam. Colter, a pretty, black, long-haired dog who was part-black lab and part-mutt, was getting into the action too, barking, jumping and running back and forth excitedly.

The foursome had left the rest of their family, a considerable assemblage of rescued stray and wild cats—the number usually hovers somewhere near a dozen—back in small town Rudyard,

Montana. The cats were in the care of Lyle, a longtime bachelor, computer whiz, pathetic housekeeper and family friend.

Catching, neutering and caring for cats have become a family passion and pastime. It is remarkable how all three of these Langels, when home, care for the cats equally. Doug builds special fences and shelters and hauls in large bags of dry food and litter, Marge does the doctoring and keeping the litter boxes clean and B.J. manages the early morning checks and before school feedings. As a more recent arrival Colter, too, though still erratically aggressive, is learning to accept the cat as friend rather than target. His latest trick is to lick the ear mite drops from the ears of an almost-grown kitten. The kitten finds his gesture soothing and affectionate.

Marge probably would do better not to have contact with any animals. She suffers from eczema particularly on her hands and fingers. The eczematous patches dry, harden, crack open and bleed. This painful malady started in her as a young child and has plagued her ever since. It is genetic; our father's younger sister, Fyliena or Lien, had it on most of her body. Margaret, to her credit, has not let the problem govern her heart. She could easily have become a prissy, white-gloved obsessive about it. Though her hands are scarred and sore, she is always closely bonded with her pets and "critters." She loves them and lets them know it. Always has.

Dark-haired, blue-eyed, handsome, husky, young Brandon whose skin color is that of a perpetual tan should have been asleep, given the fact that he had awakened at an unusual early hour; but no way. He was gathering momentum. It was one of his traits from birth. The more tired he was the more hyper he became. They would have to find a place to stop soon so that Marge could quietly, patiently talk him down and get him settled in bed like she had done so often in his life already. If she did not get him to settle down, the laughing would inevitably turn to tears. That was something our mother always said to us when we were kids. Marge, as a mother herself now, knew it to be true. A person getting out of control could get scared, a tickle became a pinch, a word was misunderstood and then, in a flash, playing turned to fighting and crying.

Brandon loved, really loved and got excited by our family gatherings and a family gathering at Christmas time in Seattle was where the Langels were headed in their ungainly CruiseAir at this odd hour and at this odd time of year. The Heidema/Cok/Langel, and now add in Coumar, family gatherings to him were like a noisy stock car race. They were so unlike the small town, quiet rural life of his family in the extreme northern, far ranging plains of Montana. There would be lots of revving of the motors, high-pitched humming and whining on the track, a crash here and there, parts going flying but nobody ever getting really hurt. The public address announcer calling out the plans and times at intervals, snacks continuously available and lots of cheering. That was a family gathering.

Life in Rudyard in Hill County along the Highline, as it is called, three-quarters of the way from Shelby before Havre on U.S. Highway 2 is low key, humdrum most of the time. The plain east of the Continental Divide, Glacier National Park and the Blackfeet Indian Reservation all along the Canadian border is wheat country. Rudyard is one of the many small towns that, like charms on a charm bracelet, hang from the Burlington Northern and Santa Fe train track every six to twelve miles or so. Chester, Joplin, Inverness, Hingham, Gilford, one town not much different from the other. Old and older, gray grain elevators, like long-necked dinosaurs, rising up from the tracks, a few drab retail stores, a café/bar, maybe two bars, a church, a school, a basketball team, a bowling alley, summer dust, a Quonset hut, people bad-mouthing Indians and thirty or more trains thundering by in a day, that is Rudyard and that is Hingham and that is Inverness. But that is not Brandon.

Brandon John or B.J. has known he had been adopted by these two since about the age of six. There had been no desire on the part of Doug or Marge to keep it a secret and so when the time came, Marge told Brandon the facts. It was as if he had always known. He has met and now talked to his birth mother, Sue Olsen. She is a heavy-set, fair-skinned, blonde, blue-eyed daughter of Swedish parents. And, although sometimes late, she always sends him a birthday present.

As for his most likely dark-skinned, dark-haired Brazilian birth father, Gil Batista, Brandon has never seen nor heard from him. Already though, B.J. is checking things out on the Internet. He has a pretty good idea where he could start searching and is pretty sure he will be able to find his birth father some day. If he wants to find him, that is. He might not want to, he says. Being adopted is a big deal, but usually, he says, he doesn't need to think about it. There is even a kid in his class who is adopted too, so it isn't like he is the only one or anything.

Brandon catapulted from the couch onto Doug's back and slid down to the floor where he wrapped his arms around Colter and flailed him about from side to side. The dog, helpless to stop the flagrant indignities, looked pleadingly at Doug. Sorry, but it's your turn, Doug thought, as he eased out of the way and squeezed between the two seats up front.

"Brandon's getting pretty rambunctious back there," Doug said in slowly drawn-out words as he slipped into the large, brown, leather passenger seat next to Marge. Straight ahead the back of a semi trailer-truck swayed dangerously from side to side.

"That guy doesn't know how to drive in these conditions," grumbled Marge. A car with its front-end buried in the snow bank looked abandoned off to the side. They had seen several like that since the sun had gone down and the temperatures had dropped to about ten degrees.

"I'm going to call Uncle Steve and Aunt Pat on the cellular," called Brandon loudly using his most grown-up voice and hoping he sounded official. "Let them know where we are."

"It's too late now, Brandon." Marge's voice had a monotonously measured pace and tone to it. "Better not."

"I imagine the Elmar Campground's another ten miles or so. It's bout three miles after Avon. We can stop there." Doug murmured as he eased his way back past Marge back to B.J.

He took the cellular phone from the boy's outstretched hand. It was surrendered easily. Brandon knew enough right then not to push it. Doug put the phone into his pocket and wrapped one arm around his son's head. With the knuckles of the other hand he rubbed the likeable but testy kid's scalp.

"You knucklehead," he said affectionately, "don't you know what time it is?"

"Yea, I know what time it is," croaked Brandon from the crook of Doug's arm, "time to teach you a lesson." He struggled fruitlessly and decided to try another strategy.

"Let's play another game of Old Maid. Okay, Dad? Or poker? You want to play poker?" pleaded Brandon still in Doug's grip and totally realizing that he was no match for his father's strength.

"Why don't you make that cheese on bread snack? And peel an orange for your mom instead," Doug directed. He let go of the boy's head and held onto him by the back of his shoulders moving him towards the small kitchen area in between the couch and the queen-size bed at the rear. The motor home suddenly lurched to the left and Doug looked quickly back over his shoulder. Marge was pulling out to pass the swaying semi.

Chapter 3
Dennis First, Then Carolers

Sitting at a worldwide loom I have kept my grasp on the many threads (such as Tante Frouk's words) that stretch between my family there and there and there and me here.

There was a sudden, loud knock on the glass, six-foot slider of the 38 foot Mallard park model trailer, causing the thin walls and vertical blinds to shiver in shock. Good grief! Did we within really need another reminder of the flimsy material of our mobile housing?

"Who can it possibly be at this time? It's nine o'clock, for God's sake. Can't they see the blinds are closed?" groused Sophia as she raised her head up off the pillows and sat up on the couch.

Another thing to tend to; it had been that kind of a busy, pressured Friday. Sophia had given her last massage for the week and had taken time to work with Chuck, our neighbor, to replace the automatic timer on the Christmas lights. I, reluctantly, had gone to talk with first, Evelyn down the street and then Wilma next door to get a backup for Figgy's care. Those visits had taken a lot of time. It took diplomacy. I couldn't just blurt out on the landing, "Will you take care of Figgy for two weeks? We're desperate!"

Figgy would not be going to Seattle for the holidays with us and at almost the last hour Sophia's friend, Marlene, who lives in a trailer behind ours, had copped an attitude about taking care of her.

"...you girls are too fussy! What if something happens? I don't want to lose a friendship over a cat! I have to work and I am not going to have time to check on her twice-a-day..!"

Yes, yes, okay, so we are fussy, maybe even too fussy, but have you forgotten that we took care of your Cuddles for three whole weeks not too long

17

ago? We even picked her up from the airport in Maine, in Portland, and she was a psycho case most of the time. Can you come once at least, please, pretty please? I thought that; I didn't say it. Marlene is rarely dissuaded and I had to be grateful for her once-a-day visit.

We had also begun to pack, careful to include the gifts we still had to wrap, and we had sorted out what had to be eaten and what had to be frozen. Anything that would spoil in two weeks in Sophia's makeshift root cellar in the shed had to be brought forward into the refrigerator and so forth. We would not be leaving until Monday afternoon but the weekend would go by quickly. We had finished a late dinner and dishes and were finally able to relax.

I leaned back as far as I could in my new sea mist, Big Man, Lazy Boy recliner and, as I did, a knitting needle slipped silently for what seemed the zillionth time out of sight into a crevice of the chair. I reached way back with my long arm over my head to the left and pulled the curtain cord hanging in the corner.

Figgy, our beautiful and well-cared-for (we have brushed her every single night for the past 12 years; I'd say she is well cared for!) tortoiseshell cat, who had been pressed against my leg fast asleep, now was wide awake and poised to make her escape to her condo. Her safe place, or condo, is an undisturbed, always available, dark corner in the clothes closet of the bedroom at the other end of the trailer. The sliding door to the closet is always kept open and Figgy's comings and goings leave fine little cat hairs on the hems of all our blouses and pullovers. What can you do? A jump on the bed, a quick 90^0 turn to the right, a jump into the two-foot-high closet, a 90^0 turn to the left, all done in a flash of a black tail, and she'd be gone.

Sophia, my partner, a Greek woman in her mid-fifties, had been lying on the couch to my right. In between the recliner and couch was an end table on which was our tiny ceramic Christmas tree with glowing imbedded lights. Newspaper sections were strewn about on the floor. Sophia sat up and irritably pushed buttons on the TV and VCR remotes. Lois and Ned in an intimate embrace on the soap opera, General Hospital, disappeared from the screen.

In so many ways we are polar opposites. Sophia is five feet four inches tall, plump in torso and full-bosomed. She has classic Mediterranean olive skin that is also deeply tanned, somewhat small hands and arms in proportion to her body but strong athletically well-defined forearm, thigh and calf muscles. She has thick, short hair that is salt and pepper in color, facial wrinkles beyond her age and pretty hazel eyes with nice dark lashes and brows.

Sophia's parents, like mine, were immigrants. Though of Greek parentage, Louis Kellis had come from Turkey along with brothers, Tony and Mike, and sister, Mercina. Louis enlisted in the army, fought in W.W.I in France, worked in central Maine's woolen mills and boxed in the ring in his spare time. When he decided to marry, he returned to Greece and was smitten by a pretty young woman on the street of Aegion. Three weeks later he had married Alexandra Charalambopolou and the couple was aboard a ship headed for America. They had four children, one son and three daughters, Sophia being the youngest. When the oldest, Louise, was ten-years-old and Sophia was only five, Louis Kellis died of cancer. Alexandra and the children coped as best they could. The uncles and aunts, the Greek Orthodox church community in Bangor, the Pittsfield neighbors and Pittsfield schools provided a safety net and in spite of poverty, all survived.

For the last fifteen years Sophia has suffered the ever-worsening loss of her mother to Alzheimer's disease. A number of the wrinkles in Sophia's face have to do with enduring this protracted anguish. Alexandra, no longer able to recognize her children, is being cared for in a nursing home in Michigan. Sophia's sister, Helen, looks after their mother. Nightly in her prayers, Sophia asks God to please take her mother home.

A true earth woman, Sophia's passions are massage, cooking, gardening and playing tennis. As a teenager she was an all-around star athlete at Maine Central Institute, a prep school in Pittsfield, Maine. She excelled in field hockey, basketball and softball. At one point she had an awesome .839 batting average! That was unheard of prior to and probably since her time at MCI. She was also the pitcher on the team and still exchanges Christmas cards and memories with the catcher. Her yearbook is filled with accolades, not only from the girls but especially from the guys, the jocks. Not just a tomboy, she twirled around the dance floor with those same guys doing her favorite, the jitterbug, and swinging between the legs of senior, Ronnie Pratt.

In contrast, I was born in Europe with fair and freckled skin tones. I was a whitish-blonde toddler but now have an ash brown color with, as yet, hardly a trace of gray. My hair is annoyingly fine in texture. I am lean and nearly flat-chested. My right side is all the way flat because of a mastectomy and my refusal to deal with a fake breast. Please! I have enough on my plate and don't need to worry about a breast meandering about on my shoulder. I watched that happen to May Sarton, an author, once. She and I were at her house having a scotch and a cigarette before dinner. She was on a chaise lounge and, as she slid down, I watched her prosthetic breast move up. By the time she finished her second drink her breast was riding high. That just isn't going to happen to me. I am six feet one inch tall and I tower over Sophia. Everybody I meet assumes that I played basketball. I didn't. I am an avid television sports fan but, as a participant, I was awkward and slow. I have knock knees; I think that has something to do with it. I could hit a softball but couldn't make it to base fast enough. I was pretty good at volleyball, come to think of it, because I didn't have to run. My mother always told me not to slouch but the older I get; the harder it is not to. My height is mostly in my long legs and what used to be an asset, a calling card, in fact, is fast becoming an embarrassment. "Piano legs," I think they are called, thin at the bottom, not so thin at the top. And, they are piano legs that show they have been kicked and scuffed for 53 years. However, on the bright side, still being somewhat of a swimmer, my upper body strength and appearance is pretty-well toned. I have deep-set brown eyes and am told that I have a great smile (given the circumstances, what else can one do?) More cerebral and creative than athletic I read, write, figure, putter and organize.

Despite the many striking differences between us, it is common for strangers to see us as sisters. And, sometimes it is just easier to agree that we are. Esther, one of our neighbors across the street, thinks that I am Sophia's daughter and, if asked about a husband as Sophia often is, she might just play along and say she is divorced. After all, Soph says, "I almost was engaged three times." That is another difference; I was nowhere close to ever being engaged. It is pretty clear; perceptions of us as a couple are governed by the beholder's comfort level.

What we have in common are three things for sure: a persevering sense of humor (each with our unique brand), stubbornness (not just the Dutch are stubborn by any means!) and left-handedness. The left-handedness, it could be argued, may be irrelevant but the humor and stubbornness are what keep us alive and together.

The two of us met serendipitously in mid February of 1978 on 2 South, a surgical care unit, at Rose Memorial Hospital in Denver, Colorado. Sophia Kellis, R.N. was the busy charge nurse on the evening shift when she received word that Charlotte Heidema R.N., M.S.N. was being admitted for acute abdominal pain.

"Do you know who she is?" Dr. Donald Brown the attending physician asked the staff. "She's the head honcho of nursing at Fort Logan Mental Health Center!"

"So?" Sophia retorted contemptuously.

She wasn't impressed. On her shift everyone, rich or poor, head honcho or bag lady, Jew or gentile, was given the same quality of care and she deeply resented any pressure to do otherwise.

Learning a few days later that I, "the mild-mannered articulate woman who had a master's degree in psychiatric nursing but no common sense," as she described me, did not know the taste of the liqueur Amaretto, she brought a sample in for me in a sterile urine specimen container. At the end of the shift near midnight, propped up in bed, I curiously sipped her Amaretto. Ms. Kellis put up her feet, puffed on her Benson and Hedges cigarette and talked of her dream to own a Mexican restaurant on the coast of Maine.

As the Amaretto potentiated the sleeping pill in me, so this unorthodox charge nurse stirred the heart and soul of this over-achiever. Maine accent, Mexican food, the hint of White Shoulders perfume mingling with cigarette smoke, the disallowed jewelry with the white uniform (Mrs. Brooks, my Nursing Fundamentals teacher, had a fit if we ever wore jewelry!) and the delicious back rub. What a combo! Two years later the two of us went off to Maine. Sophia was emotionally fragile, often depressed and bloated up like a young pregnant hippo from mega doses of steroids for her central nervous system lupus. She was diagnosed a year after we met. She thought she was going home to die. I was abandoning all to go live by the ocean for a while before my newly diagnosed lung disease precluded such a move. In complete denial, the two of us ordered a 5x4 foot, framed, wooden sign for $75.00 that would have painted on it in bold blue lettering against a white background:

Tjaakje C. Heidema

TIA SOPHIA
MEXICAN RESTAURANT

In retrospect it is clear that it was our newly purchased 1920 unfinished, seasonal bungalow with a beautiful view of the Atlantic Ocean that brought out the true mettle in us. We had bought impulsively and soon learned that the house needed everything done or redone. Absolutely everything! And the winter was coming on. There was no heat and little money left. I commuted 70 miles, round trip, weekdays to Southern Maine University in Portland and read thick textbooks under blankets at night to stay ahead of the nursing students. Sophia cleaned up after carpenters, plumbers and electricians. She filled nail holes, painted walls, had the man named Fay, Fay Farrington the carpenter, roto-till her a patch and planted a vegetable garden like her Uncle Mike had taught her to do as a young girl growing up in Pittsfield. Gradually, mercifully, her lupus went into remission.

She enrolled in the South Portland massage therapy school and I planted bulbs, perennials and sweet peas. As we gained a foothold, we canned and froze vegetables, bought a chain saw and cut old wood to burn in the wood stove. We stacked firewood brought in by the cord and hung our clothes out to dry in the crisp sea breeze.

Unfortunately, all was not well with us on the eastern front. Overstepping boundaries, or getting into each other's business, in other words, was a big problem. Did I mention that we were both stubborn? Plus, learning how to manage the vicissitudes of two chronic illnesses on a daily basis was not easy. We had some terribly turbulent times.

In the beginning of 1984, we tried living apart but either one or the other bulked when it came to severing our ties. So, when I was getting chemotherapy in 1987 to squelch the breast cancer and one day just couldn't go on any more, I crashed in Sophia's apartment. The three-year hiatus came to an end shortly thereafter. It was just more practical to live together. As for the turbulent times, we sought help from counselors. Like hurricanes that lose their wallop over land masses, our disturbances too, blowing over newfound wisdom, were downgraded to tropical storms.

I was living midway between my birthplace in the Netherlands and where I had grown up in Montana about 3,000 miles distant from each. I was working hard, scrimping and saving to get ahead like my parents had done. I had cancer and a lung disease. Being nudged toward self- awareness by my new feminist friends in the Women's Study progam at the University, I wondered who am I really and what in the world am I doing here?

One of the first things I felt instinctively important to do was to change my name. From the age of four and a half on I had been Charlotte or Char. That name had been assigned to me arbitrarily by my great uncle, Uncle William Dyk, when we immigrated. Tjaakje to Jackie, maybe, but to Charlotte? Why? What? The name Charlotte had no roots. Saying it had always made my tongue feel strange, kind of thick or twisted; I never liked saying it aloud in class. So, after forty years of being Charlotte, I mustered up the courage and legally took back my original name. I am now officially Tjaakje Charlotte Fylina Heidema. I kept Charlotte in there because I was she for quite some time and it seemed only fair. My father's older sister had been a Tjaakje and her grandmother had been a Tjaakje and who knows how far back the Tjaakjes go. I started using it and discovered that I felt exactly like a Tjaakje.

Then I carved out a few minutes of each day to write in my journal. I wrote about those two distant aspects of my life, Holland and Montana, and why or how I had come to the in-between place so far away from everyone.

As time went on the unused restaurant sign found a home in the garage of Sophia's brother, Basil, and my employment similarly was tucked away in history. Steven Hawking, the renowned physicist at Cambridge, England, as a quadriplegic in a wheelchair can communicate to his class on a computer by blowing into a wand in his mouth but, not nearly as brilliant as he apparently, the University of Southern Maine would not make accommodations for my declining respiratory health. Bitter at first that I was denied tenure I soon adapted and learned to relish my early retirement. Now, along with Figgy, Sophia and I annually go off to Arizona for six months for the winters and back home to our house by the sea for the summers. We chose Sunlife RV Resort, trailer park actually, in Mesa because John and Joyce, my bother and sister-in-law were living here.

Watching the taped soap opera was a nightly ritual and had been for almost eighteen years. Before meeting Sophia, I, the self perceived-intellectual, had scoffed at wasting time like that. Now I appreciate the stress-free 45 minutes. The repetitious reiterations are like mind-numbing mantras that lead to a form of meditation. It is relaxing. In fact, a lot of Sophia has rubbed off on me like that. Sometimes I hardly recognize myself.

As the vertical blind slid to the left the large burly frame of Dennis Hall came into view through the six-foot, glass slider. He was wearing his dark brown jumpsuit and was without either his hat or hair piece. Although the pink of his scalp was still clearly visible above the rim of curly white hair the large bald spot on top was partly covered. Thin, white fluff sprouted there like a dandelion flower gone to seed. Anyone could see his Rogaine treatments were producing exciting results as advertised. On his face there was also more than usual white hair. He obviously had not shaved for several days.

Dennis with ruddy cheeks like those of a pudgy preadolescent was, we could see, beaming with excitement. Sophia pushed open the door and stepped back. He ducked and stepped into the living room simultaneously pushing a small paper sack into Sophia's hand.

"Oh, Dennis, you didn't need to do this," spluttered Sophia.

"I wanted my favorite neighbors to have a, ah, to have something, a, ah, to have one oth-these," stuttered Dennis.

He reached into the sack and pulled out a grayish chunk of thick plastic about the size of a jelly roll. It was a weighted bird, Dennis proclaimed. Also from the paper sack he produced a six-inch length of a pointed dowel that he had painted gray. He excitedly placed the dowel upright on the table. The bird with its wings widespread, tail feathers fanned and with its beak on the point of the dowel, hung there bobbing lightly in space. It had the majestic pose of an eagle but the body of a fat sparrow.

"It only, ah, c-cost me 25C," said Dennis proudly. "I-I thought, since you did such-such a g-good job on the, the dolls, the, ah, the ah. I can't think of the name."

"The kachina dolls," offered Sophia, "the ones that Tjaakje made?"

"Those dolls. I-I thought you could paint this." He turned to me and I knew I looked none too happy. "I h-h-have some at my house; some that-some that I painted."

I managed a tepid smile. Sophia and I are on the cusp of the babyboomer generation; we are twenty to thirty years younger than

Dennis and most of the residents here. Were it not that we are slowed by disabilities I am certain that we would find the pace of Dennis and the others annoying at the least and extremely maddening at the worst. As it is, I believe we are quite tolerant.

Both of us, it also should be noted, were trained as diploma nurses in the early sixties. As such we were indoctrinated, as all women of that time were to some degree or other through religion and education, to value others over self. As student nurses we were taught to stand, give up our chair and move into the background when an upper class student or a doctor entered the room, for heavens sakes. To sacrifice was to live. This, of course, was way before addiction treatment made codependency a concept and way before Helen Reddy forthrightly declared, "I am woman hear me roar." Even though I imagine myself as having been deprogrammed or having deprogrammed myself, rather, from all that obsequious passivity, I still, at times, will show more patience to the friend, the acquaintance or even the stranger, than I will show my partner or myself. It is the same for Soph.

Predictably then, especially that late in the evening, after a trying day, when our mental filters were down, and we were giving Dennis the last scintilla of what patience we had left, it was likely there would be no more for ourselves or each other. Patience, as a positive virtue and not the sniveling kind, is a grounding force. A lack of patience or a lack of grounding can cause a discharge of atmospheric electricity between persons. To put it more simply, you can expect to see some interpersonal lightning flashes and a brief thunderstorm.

A half an hour passed before Sophia could lead Dennis back to the slider. There was still, bless his heart, the sharing of upcoming plans and the holiday hugs to get through. Nearly an hour had gone by before I leaned back to close the verticals again. Figgy, of course, had long ago disappeared.

"I told you we should have bought Dennis and Gwen a gift. Just a little something," fussed Sophia settling herself back on the couch and taking up the clickers. Her voice had a hardened edge to it.

"Sure, blame me why don't you. Why didn't you do something? I hate all this," I fumed in response.

Quick-minded and readily reactive, I am usually the first to vent my frustrations. It would take Sophia a few minutes before she, too, would blow out her pent up emotions.

"Not tonight, Tjaakje, please!" she pleaded adamantly.

She knew that once I got going I would use up a lot of valuable time and energy. Legend has it, and it is so true of me: Dutch peat is like a Dutchman, slow to kindle but very good at a blaze when once started.

"Look at this place! It's full of clutter everywhere. All I do is pick up and try to find places for all this stuff. Do other people like doing this? I sure don't! And I am not painting that stupid-looking bird. A cheap plastic bird he picked up at some flea market and he thinks I am going to spend hours on painting the thing."

"Oh, don't do this. Dennis means well. You don't have to paint it."

"No matter how perfect the coloring I might paint it, it's never going to look like an eagle. It's anatomically wrong. Look at that body! Let's just throw it away right now. It is so ugly! And I don't want to leave all this stuff just lying around here for two weeks while we're gone either? It's a mess! It drives me crazy to sit in the middle of it every year."

I yearn for simplicity; I demand simplicity. Ever since my bout with cancer I have been desperately de-cluttering my life and that of Sophia's. Bookshelves have been emptied and closets stripped. Even my hair is cropped. When I started to lose handfuls of hair from the chemotherapy, I had it cut to a half inch. People said I had a nice-shaped head and looked like a Buddhist monk. I liked the effect enough to keep my hair almost as short ever since.

But, darn it all, I can never get the job done. There is always more clutter, more distractions to plow through. The end-of-the-year holidays present more than the usual and I find it oh, so annoying.

"I just want to finish G.H. Do you mind?" Sophia put down the clickers and picked up a section of the newspaper. "I don't want to hear all this, Tjaakje, okay, please! I'm exhausted and we have a couple of big days ahead."

Sophia's fatigue was usually a symptom of her lupus, though most days she did enough to justify fatigue on its own merits. This day was such an example. Giving the full body massage to a large, stiff-muscled person had taken a lot out of her.

I abruptly and dramatically—living with a Greek, the originators of the great tragedies, having had its influence—I brought the Lazy Boy to its upright position, stood and angrily jerked unsuccessfully at the oxygen tubing that was caught in the chair. Like my older brother, John, I have the genetic deficiency which results in emphysema. At fifty three I am already severely restricted and need supplemental oxygen 24 hours a day.

"I'm sick of you always complaining! What do you want to do about it?" Sophia demanded.

Figgy, the self-appointed matriarch and shepherd of us two, came hurriedly into the room and scooted from one to the other, peeping urgently around our feet.

"Just help me pick up things for ten minutes. Ten minutes. Is that too much to ask?"

"I'm not moving. I'm not doin' one more thing today. Just do it yourself." Sophia turned the pages of the newspaper emphatically and noisily.

Equally noisy and with great fanfare I bustled around and picked up gifts that had come from friends and neighbors. There was pancake mix and maple syrup from L.L.Bean in Freeport, Maine, a gift from Basil, Sophia's brother. Elinor, my friend, had sent a variety of organic, whole grain hot cereals from Pennsylvania. There was Evelyn's annual box of Russell Stover candies, Wilma's plate load of homemade almond Roca and fudge and Louise's still-wrapped gifts. I brought the mailing boxes and wrappings out back in the shed then, breathing ever more heavily, arranged the items at the front of the room near the Christmas tree. The bird with its prop was put back in the paper sack and left guiltily on a back corner of the table.

"At least most of these gifts are all recyclable and not stuff for which I am going to have to find a permanent place," I grumbled.

Satisfied, I settled back into my chair and Figgy jumped up to join me. She had a pouty expression that I assumed matched mine. Before Sophia could finish putting away the newspaper and picking up the clickers, singing could be heard coming from the outdoors. It became progressively louder, moved beyond our trailer a short distance and then stayed the same.

"That is probably the Solos Group," offered Sophia as she walked over, reached into the corner to retract the verticals again and pushed open the slider and screechy screen door that Dennis had pulled shut. She went out on the landing and looked around the corner.

"They are caroling to the shut-ins tonight. It was in the bulletin," she reported calling back over her shoulder. "They've stopped at Martin and Melvina's. Can you hear them?"

"Yes, I can hear them even without the door open. Come on, please, it's getting a little cold here by the door."

"Tjaakje, I think they are coming here now," Sophia called excitedly. "Yes, they are. Quick, come!"

"Great. Now all of a sudden I'm considered a shut-in. Hurrah," I mumbled in a sarcastic monotone.

It has not been that long ago, I thought, *that I was the caroler. Now I am the carolee. Jeepers, what an honor.*

My first time was on a hayride with the Young People's Society back in Montana. We rode through the hills sitting on hay bales on an open wagon and drank hot chocolate from thermos bottles. Spirits soared in the crisp, cold Rocky Mountain air. But now in warm Arizona, as with so many things, the shoe is on the other foot; and, when I take a step in that tight-fitting shoe, I wince with deeply felt pain.

Reluctantly, I put the chair upright again and made my way out to the landing. Figgy thought better of it and went back to her condo. Smiling, happy people of all ages were swarming into the carport and flowed out onto the street. There were quite a number of children, a few even in strollers. Several curious young boys came up to the landing and looked inquisitively at my oxygen tubing. Then they stole a look into the trailer.

"...and may all your Christmases be bright."

Dreams and wishes for a White Christmas, echoed into the night. *Fat chance*, my old scrooge mind mumbled in my thick skull.

People waved and called out cheerily, "Merry Christmas! Merry Christmas!"

Sophia and I returned their greetings.

"Wasn't that just great!" exclaimed Sophia. She clapped her hands and waved enthusiastically. I plastered on a phony smile.

Just then, as one would imagine an angel child on a very important mission, a tiny little girl climbed effortlessly, as if floating, up the short stair steps. Her blonde curls bobbed about her head. She wore a darling, full-length, fitted-waist, light blue coat and on her feet she had turned-over white anklets with patent leather shoes that had a strap across her little foot. Her face glowed with total innocence as she stopped in front of me with thin little arms stretched up. I bent down to receive a hug from this precious child.

Another small girl with dark curls, wearing a navy blue sweater, followed the first child and also extended her arms. She was offering me a small plate of cookies with a shy smile.

"May I give you a thank-you hug?" I asked carefully handing the cookies to Sophia.

The little girl's eyes sparkled as she nodded a big, yes. After the hug she hurried down the stairs, turned quickly to wave and then ran on her tiny little legs to catch up with the departing group.

Colorful Christmas lights blinked on both sides of F Street and I saw the lights reflected in the tears in Sophia's eyes. She slipped her arm around my waist and said warmly, "Come on, Tjaakje, let's go in and finish G.H., okay?"

Once again the descent into darkness had come to an end. It was the winter solstice and light on its own accord was making its way back.

Chapter 4
Pat Sits on Steven's Chair

I am not unique. We are all immigrants who gather threads and weave stories.

Even though it was an hour earlier in the Pacific Time Zone, that same Friday night, my sister and brother-in-law were already in bed. Steadfast Steven Peter Cok, wearing white briefs and a dark red T shirt, was leaning back comfortably on the pillow that was propped up against the headboard of the bed and was reading aloud from the Bible. The gray-white chest hairs showing in the V neck matched his mustache but not the hair that was left on his head. Of that, there was not much, but what was there was pure white.

He finished reading from Ephesians 2 in his soft, rumbly voice, "In whom ye also are builded together for an habitation of God through the Spirit (verse 22)," then he reverently reinserted the bookmark and slowly closed the well-worn book. For a few moments more he pressed the King James Version of the Bible between his long sensitive hands and enjoyed the familiar and resilient feel of the cowhide leather. It always soothed him and especially so at this hour. His chest expanded in a full, deep inspiration as he savored his spiritual calm. It most surely could not be said of most men, but it could of Steven: he is a godly man.

Patricia or Pat, my older sister by six years, Steve's fair-skinned, freckled wife in a sleeveless, navy negligee had been lying on her back. Now she turned to her left side away from him, pulled up her knees and closed her eyes. Her hair in earlier years had been the dark brown color of our father. John, my brother, Marge and I were blonde but Pat was dark like him. In fact, her eyebrows and lashes still are but not her hair. Like Steven's it was white against the white pillowcase.

Steven laid the Bible on the bedside stand, lightly scratched the top of his head which he so often did, softly cleared his throat, checked carefully once more to make sure the alarm was set correctly, then reached around and pressed the light switch attached to the middle of the headboard. It was just one little thing, putting the switch on the headboard, one little thing among many of Steven's innate engineering ideas and projects that were meant to keep life easier and more predictable and thus less stressful. His father, Peter, who wrote letters to his parents in Ohio, which Steven keeps in a shoe box, had written of his three-year- old son, "Steven enjoys himself all day with one thing or another." It is still a truism of the man. Pat, over the years, has come to depend on this from Steven. She is the worrier; he is the fixer. That is just the way it is with these two.

With the light from the street lamps along the cul-de-sac of Court Place filtering through the sheer white curtains, Steve maneuvered his long, heavy-boned, six-foot five-inch frame down along side Pat in their queen-sized bed. In a well-practiced move, thirty-seven years worth to be exact, he turned on his left side, embraced her around the abdomen with his right arm and bent his long legs at the knees under the back of her thighs so she could sit on his chair.

He felt the warmth of her body against his and the extra warmth from the dual-controlled electric blanket on her side of the bed. The Dutch wool blanket weighed heavily on him. She liked all the weight and the warmth. He did not. Later, after Pat was asleep Steve would turn on his right side and inch away from her to his cooler edge of the bed. While sleeping, unlike Pat who could never get enough of the closeness, there was no doubt but that Steve preferred freedom over snuggling.

In the distance off to the left, a frog in bass tones croaked at odd intervals. Persistent rain pattered softly against the windows and off to the right the neighbor's small dog barked intermittently. Neither of the spent couple registered the customary suburban sounds.

The Coks had moved from rural Montana to urban Washington in 1965. Now it was 1996, thirty-one years later. Back then they had felt very mixed about the move. On the one hand leaving rugged, sparsely populated Montana with its plentiful days of sunshine, its wide-open spaces, fertile farmlands and inspiring beauty, even its challenging winters, had seemed utterly foolish. It had been, after all, in rural southwestern Montana in the heart of the productive Gallatin Valley that they had held dear their families and community of believers.

Their first home together had been an apartment in the nearest big city, Bozeman, 20 miles to the east. Shortly thereafter they had moved into their new custom-built home on Churchill. Churchill, in those days, was a tiny unincorporated town on a hill in the center of the Dutch farming community. Churchill was where Dutch immigrants had built their first Christian Reformed Church with its tall, white steeple for all to see at the turn of the century in 1904. Churchill was where ministers, teachers and retired people lived. People did not live in Churchill; they lived on Churchill. In contrast, people lived in Amsterdam, an equally tiny town down the hill two miles away.

The Cok's new home on Churchill with its two-car garage had been built by Al Dyksterhouse as most new homes were in the community. Typical of the houses in the post-atomic bomb era, it included a 12" thick walled, concrete bomb shelter in the basement. Steve and Pat's two daughters, Arlyce, four by then, and Sandra, not quite two, used the cute little room as a play room.

Though in the world at large John Kennedy would be assassinated, the Viet Nam war would be fought and protested and the drug culture would take hold, life on Churchill was the stern reformer John Calvin's version of Camelot. And, like Camelot, "There (was) simply not a spot (better) for ever-aftering than (Churchill)." Steven's income in 1965 was good, the extended families lived nearby, the couple was active in the church and health was taken for granted.

On the other hand, Steven's work in Bozeman in those years was creating for him a window of opportunity facing out towards the west, the Pacific Northwest, away from the community. In the glass of that window of opportunity he saw reflected a vision of his future. He saw himself challenged intellectually with top people in his field, contributing to his profession, helping build a company and making a good salary. All of which, he had been clear, would not be for his aggrandizement alone; that was not his nature. Developing his mind and his abilities would be, first of all, for the glory of God and then for his family. Those were values deeply instilled in him by his mother, the legacy of his father and his church community.

His father, Peter Cok, came from a family with 12 children who all worked on the family truck farm in Ohio. Peter served overseas in the military in World War I and sustained a serious leg injury. Afterwards, he rebelled against working in the muck on the farm and joined his brother Henry who was in Montana. Peter attended and graduated from Montana State College with a B.S. in agriculture and not long after married Agnes Bos—Agnes was a daughter of John and Jennie Bos who were among the original settlers in the Dutch community. Peter and Agnes were active in the Christian Reformed Church and worked hard to acquire a farm in the Valley. As poignantly chronicled in Peter's letters, once acquired, they worked even harder to keep the farm. Steven was born in 1927 and a few years later his sister, Jean, joined him. In 1932, when Agnes was pregnant with their third child, Pearl, and crops were finally beginning to turn a profit, Peter Cok died suddenly of undiagnosed abdominal problems. Agnes had to leave the farm and move to Churchill. She worked long hours in the Amsterdam grocery store and in later years in the hospital laundry department to support her family. With unwavering faith, a love of music and a day-to-day commitment to pulling together and making it through, she instilled in her children the willingness to sacrifice and a lifelong quest for respectability. Steven, a conscientious boy, learned early that it felt good to help out with family finances. He has not forgotten how it felt as a reward to get that quarter every summer for the Fourth of July church picnic.

In Steve's time the Christian High School on Churchill ended after the tenth grade. To continue on through the last two years and graduate in the area, a student had to attend the public school in the town of Manhattan. Steven, though an excellent student, had chosen not to go on after the tenth grade. He had, instead, begun to work. In the summertime he worked on the farm of his Uncle Pete Alberda and in the wintertime in the potato cellars. A few years later Steve was drafted into the army and followed his father's footprints to Europe.

Otherwise unattainable, the military gave Steve at the age of 24 the exciting opportunity to travel. He was stationed at various locations in post World War II Germany and three day passes gave him tours of France, Holland, Austria and, as he puts it, a "look into" Switzerland. Memorably, he told me, while in route to see Hitler's retreat in *Berchtesgaden* and the *Oberomegau* Passion Play; he became sidelined by a sudden attack of appendicitis. He was initially treated in a dispensary then driven to a hospital in Salzburg, Austria, in an "army truck with square wheels on a very rocky road. It felt that way anyway", Steven likes to say with a grin when he tells the story.

Always, as far back as he can remember, he was intrigued by the workings of electricity. In the army he chose and was approved to be a mechanic on self-propelled weaponry. The field of electronics, thereafter, became his life's work. An added bonus to what he had been learning in the army was that he was able to take the test and earn his general equivalency diploma (GED) from high school.

After two years of service Steven received his honorable discharge and returned home to Montana. He was able to enroll in Montana State College in Bozeman with GI benefits and worked three jobs: the hay mill in Belgrade, the farm of his uncle and across the street from home in Ray Segaar's garage on Churchill. He received his B.S. degree in 1958.

He went on to graduate school at Montana State in electrical engineering and in his late twenties was hired by Donald Weaver, a respected faculty member who had taught at Stanford University, to work in a new electronics research laboratory. This position effectively launched his career.

In 1960, he was given his master's degree with honors. Shortly thereafter, a nucleus of the graduate students from the laboratory including Steven and a close associate, Floyd Erps, organized privately. They formed a company of their own and called it Montronics. In 1961 they found a location and set up shop in a build-ing on West Main in Bozeman. The fledgling company specialized in precision frequency generation and measurement as well as producing precision instruments for marketing.

Montronics grew quickly. An initial thirteen employees jumped to fifty in three years and immediately came to the attention of John

Fluke in Seattle. It was at this juncture in Steven's career that the aforementioned window of opportunity to the Northwest opened. Fluke had built up his own company, Fluke Manufacturing, along similar lines as Montronics. He had almost three hundred employees and was looking to expand his interests. Before corporate raiding and buyouts were even a part of business jargon, Fluke had bought out Montronics. In the two years that the company remained in Bozeman he gave engineers at Montronics and their wives a free train trip to Seattle plus a week's lodging and expenses to view the Fluke operation. Then, as had likely been planned all along, John Fluke shut down Montronics in Bozeman and transferred it to Seattle.

Steven had known that Montronics had needed a stronger resource base and he had seen those resources at Fluke. What realistically, he wondered in those days, could he do in Bozeman when Montronics ended? Along with two other engineers Steven decided to transfer.

Of course, it had helped in Steven and Pat's decision making to know that First Christian Reformed Church of Seattle was at 147 and 25th streets and that Watson Groen Christian School was right next to it. They were assured that would have a somewhat familiar community of believers in Seattle too. So, to the disappointment of us in the extended families—I remember it well—Steven, Pat and their two little girls moved away from Churchill to the big Puget Sound city of Washington.

In their souls and in their spirits, Steve and Pat had wavered and wondered as to whether they could survive weeks on end of gray Seattle skies, seemingly constant rain and drizzle, congested city traffic and long commutes on freeways. It had all been overwhelming at first, but, as the days and weeks went by they discovered, to their surprise, that their desperate need for sun was an acquired hunger, an addiction, soon broken. This must have been because in both Steve and Pat's genes there lay dormant their cultural familiarity with the weather patterns of the *nether lands,* the low lands or the *hol lands,* the bog lands.

The low countries—one of which is the Netherlands where Pat was born and from where Steven's grandparents emigrated, and the other two are Belgium and Luxembourg—in northwest Europe have a western boundary of 1100 miles of open connections to the

North Sea. The *Noord Zee* (North Sea) is always restless and cold, and sometimes, when whipped by forceful gales into frenzy, it is unpredictable and treacherous. Its moods dominate the weather of inland Holland similar to the Pacific Ocean's dominance on the weather of the northwestern United States. In one sense Steve and Pat and the girls had left home when they had left the community high up in the Rocky Mountains but, in another sense, when they moved to the city built at sea level they were also coming home.

Hot chocolate, lamps on, sometimes all day in every room, and a crackling fire in the fireplace of the cozy family room of their first, modest home in Shoreline on 188th street helped the Cok's cope with their new circumstances. In 1967 they received the sad news that Agnes was very ill with acute leukemia. She died at the age of 60 after only a few days of knowing her diagnosis. She is greatly missed.

On the wall in the hallway of the second story of their second, more upscale, home now in Kenmore, just outside of Steven and Pat's bedroom, hang all the family pictures. Graduation pictures of Arlyce and Sandi and a grandchild attest to the fact that Steven and Pat have not only survived in their new Seattle setting; they have thrived.

In his thirty years of service, 1965-1995, at Fluke Manufacturing Steven was awarded five United States patents for electronic refinements in frequency detection. In lieu of the actual patents, which he had assigned over to the company, Steven was given certificates of excellence in which he, the inventor, was given recognition for his "significant technical contributions to the progress of the company". The five certificates are proudly framed and displayed on the wall of his in-home office. Now, at 69, Steven is retired.

Pat, ten years younger than Steven, though it would be financially feasible, is not ready to retire. Initially, after the move to Seattle and when the girls were in school, she worked for seven years at the Anderson Nursing Home. Then she joined her college friend, Bern Alberda, in establishing his new medical practice. She continues working part-time in the now much enlarged, private pediatric practice.

"Did you remember to set the alarm a half-hour earlier than usual?" Pat worried from her side of the bed. "I have to clean the downstairs, get groceries and I want to go to the Starbucks at Northgate before we go to the airport. I can't find that mug for Lottie's (my nickname from my Charlotte days) Christmas present anywhere."

"I remembered," murmured Steven nuzzling her neck. He kissed the soft, clean-smelling skin softly and tenderly. Steven liked to bury his nose in her this way after her nightly bath. The touch and pleasing fragrances gave his ever-calculating mind a chance to relax. His hand moved slowly over her rounded abdomen.

"I have to sleep now or I'll never get it all done tomorrow," she protested as she determinedly shifted her position.

Even after her relaxing bath Pat could feel the chronic tightness and pain in her neck and shoulder. Was it Fibromyalgia or an old injury to a cervical vertebra? What was it? An MRI had shown the area to be normal. Of one thing she was certain; her hormones had a major impact. But was estrogen replacement therapy and forced menstruation until she was eighty the answer? Heavens, no! She would not accept that.

It was strange how she was having difficulty. Steven usually had those kinds of problems. He had for years been ever so slowly losing the muscle mass and strength in his shoulders. Rheumatoid arthritis, which has brought its unrelenting painfully crippling fires to his younger sister Pearl's joints, was touching his now, too, but thankfully without the fury. A couple of years ago he had had one of his knee joints scraped. He would never complain but she knew it still bothered him. She worried about Sandi's complaints too, her long hours standing over the operating table. Was Sandi having early signs and, now, she herself too? How aggravating! She must not dwell on any of it. Not now! She was so tired; why could she not go to sleep?

The older twosome were both tired, exhausted really. For 14 days they had tended to their nephew, Keith, Pearl's oldest son, and his wife, Peggy. Keith, 40 years old, was waging a valiant fight against a deadly astrocytoma, a malignant brain tumor. Months before, he had undergone first surgery in Billings and then the highly touted gamma knife radiation procedure in Seattle. There had been some reversal but slowly the disruptive symptoms were recurring.

As a threesome, Peggy, Steve and Pat, had schlepped from one office to another, from one medical department to another, with Keith, a big guy, in a wheelchair. Pat had tried her level best to help the couple, non-medicals, to sort through the divergent opinions of two ego driven doctors, one a neurologist the other a neurosurgeon. One advocated more surgery, the other did not. The calloused arrogance had infuriated Pat. Why could not the doctors talk to each other and come to a reasoned conclusion? The young people were like fish out of water. Help them, for Pete's sake!

The whole while the medical drama had been unfolding, the devoted aunt and uncle had worked hard to understand and be patient with Keith's slow, garbled speech, plus keep ahead with regard to serving meals in or eating out, schedules, etc. It had been a tremendous strain. And it had all happened in the face of the holidays with us six family members coming to stay at their house! In fact, our mother, Ann, was due to arrive at the airport that Saturday afternoon.

Along with exhausted, Pat felt confused and old. It was too much; her mind refused to settle. From his steady breathing and heavy weight against her back she could tell Steven was falling asleep. She moved to get up and go to the bathroom another time; Steven turned. When she lay back in bed, her mind insisted on reviewing as to how exactly she had gotten herself into this frenetic pace.

I've done it again! she thought disgustedly. *What is the story this time?*

In my beleaguered sister's defense it must be said that Keith and Peggy's visit had not been in the works when the upcoming holiday gathering of our family had been agreed upon. Keith and Peggy's stay had been of an emergency nature. The family gathering plans had emerged earlier than that, back in the fall. It had been in October to be more exact. Steven and Pat had gone to Montana to be with our mother who was to have a bladder biopsy. The couple had stayed in the basement of their original custom-built home on Churchill which is now the home of our brother and sister-in-law, John and Joyce Heidema. That was never easy. She always felt strange in that setting. An intruder in her own home, it was weird.

When the Coks had moved from that home in 1965, they had rented it out to Joe and Cora Bos for a few years but then the Boses moved out and Mom had moved in. Mom likes to refer to it as "the family home" and she worked very hard to maintain the three bedroom house, two-car garage and large lawn. At the age of 70, though, in 1983, it all became too much for her.

John and Joyce, meanwhile, had been developing and operating their Plain Vista Dairy a few miles to the south. John had been having more and more difficulty keeping up the hard physical labor and had been thinking the fully grown and married sons, Leland and Kent, could take over the work of the dairy.

Eventually, it had all come together. John and Joyce had bought "the family home" on Churchill and mother had moved into her own apartment in the retirement home just 200 yards away.

Though the changes signaled waning health and strength for our mother and brother, the event of the move from what I heard—I could not attend—had been a fun time for the family. The women tried on Mom's 1960's wigs with a lot of laughs. The guys packed and unpacked with an impressive display of skill and strategy and John shuttled back and forth to town for food and errands.

Thereafter, John and Joyce had completely remodeled the home. On the main floor there was John's office in place of one bedroom; the small sitting room was now a master bath connected to the master bedroom. There was the almost unrecognizable remodeled dining room and kitchen, the new brick patio and the additional garage space for the boat and woodworking shop.

But, to Pat, despite all the changes, it still was in some way her home. She had a right, well, not legally but genetically or squatter's rights maybe or sentimentally. All right, not really.

On Steve and Pat's first evening on Churchill back in October Mother had made a surprise announcement. They were sitting at the table in her retirement apartment having a bowl of soup at the time.

"Now, I have something else to tell you, too, yet," Mom had started.

"Oh, dear, I don't like the sounds of this," Pat had lamented.

It was obvious that this was not the first time Pat had heard this type of introduction and knew sort of what to expect.

"After the doctor works on my bladder tomorrow, then another doctor wants to work on my knee next week. I would like you to be here for that too, Pat, but that may be too long, heh, when you have to work."

Pat's premonition had been correct. She seriously had not liked the sound of it and, immediately after the bladder procedure, had set about finding out more information. That is something pretty clear about Pat. Having worked all those years with doctors, she is in no way intimidated by them. I admire that. After talking with the doctors, she consulted with Margaret and me. The end result was that the arthroscopy had been indefinitely delayed. Future events bore out the fact that it had absolutely been the right decision.

Mom had been naïve—all of us had been—about the impact of general anesthesia on an older person. In 83 years the only time she had spent a day in the hospital was when Margaret, her youngest, had been born on April 22, 1951. Her other three babies were born at home in Thesenge in Holland. She has enjoyed remarkably good health with the exceptions of the degenerated macula in one eye and the bothersome area from a varicose vein on her leg. Neither of those two kept her off her feet. The fatigue after the anesthesia for the bladder procedure, however, knocked her for quite a loop. She would not have been ready for another invasive procedure in just a week.

"If she has to have knee surgery in the near future where do you think we should have it done, here in Bozeman or in Seattle?" Pat had asked me in a telephone conversation at that time back in October. Sophia and I had not yet left for Mesa; we were still in Maine.

I responded spontaneously with, "How about having it done in Seattle over the Christmas holidays! We'll all pile in with you and that way I can help out too, unless of course that would be too much for you and Steven? You probably have plans don't you?"

Pat recalled our conversation now as she continued with her bout of insomnia. It was a knee jerk reaction, she recalled with some regret.

I agree: it had been a knee jerk reaction. Without a moment's hesitation Pat had taken me up on the suggestion.

Honestly, Pat thought, *up until that conversation with Lottie, I had been having anxious thoughts about Christmas. It will be Steve's and my very first Christmas shared with Arlyce and Anil.* Facing that fact was enough to set off a hot flash in her. She heaved a frustrated sigh as she tossed and turned in the bed. Steven was snoring lightly.

Anil had been reared in a different religion, and, although he did not practice any organized religion, at least not that Pat knew of, he had beliefs that were different from her and Steven's beliefs. Initially, when they had met him, I was told by all participants, there had been painful discussions for both parties. Krishnarmuti, who was he? She and Steven didn't have a clue. Krishnarmuti certainly was not in the Bible.

The first couple of years that Anil and Arlyce had lived in Seattle, all involved had mutually avoided the Christmas and Christ's birth situation. Steven and Pat had spent time with us in Arizona and Sandi had joined her parents there.

Now, there was Arun, the loving, nonjudgmental, precious, mixed-race grandson. He was a year and nine months old. Arun loved his grandparents and they loved him. This year he was old enough to be excited by the upcoming festivities. Steve and Pat were staying in Seattle and Arlyce and Anil were participating in a holiday dinner and gift giving at the Cok home.

I just want to rest but it is way too late to back out, Pat thought. *I remember saying to Lottie, 'All coming here is a great idea!' I still believe that.* She signed heavily as the approach-avoidance desires pulled her first one way then the other. *Having lots of people around will be a good thing. I like parties. The more the merrier in my opinion.*

Like the familiar weather patterns of The Netherlands winning her over to the Northwest, so too *feestviering* (feasting and merry-making) would win out in Pat's internal debate. Partying runs in Pat's blood. As she regressed in thought, she recalled some passionate characters in the large, extended deVries family on our mother's side.

Oom (Uncle) Tjaard and Oom Hein and Tante (Aunt) Dienie, they knew how to have a good time. The Heidemas on Dad's side were a smaller group and quieter but all Hollanders know how to celebrate. They had always had music and singing when I lived there.

Pat's mental slide show brought up pictures of village bands playing in parades on the streets of Thesinge, parades along the canals at night, too, with chattering happy people holding flaming torches high, and our father, Jan Piet, in white gloves and top hat sometimes being a judge at these affairs. In the great national holiday every year on April 3rd she and everyone had celebrated the

Oranje Feest, the Queen's birthday. All birthdays and weddings had been loud, joyous occasions.

Our parents and a number of couples—she could still remember them all by name and proudly recited them now, *"Roelf en Diena Oudman, Kees en Fokje Ufkes, Stoffer en Doet van der Veen and Jan Willem en Grietje Havinga"*—had always been very close. Lots of times their merrymaking around her had been punctuated with roars of laughter.

In the warm cocoon of her bed with Steven's deep even breathing beside her, Pat's brain finally churned to a slower pace as it sluggishly flipped through the dusty, old files in storage. Too somnolent to resist the pull, she abandoned reason and floated back in time to the cozy *koamertje ein Thaisin* (parlor in the house in Thesinge—*Thaisin* is in *Gronigs* the familiar Dutch dialect spoken by the people from the province of Groningen.) Begonias, African violets, geraniums and glock zinnias are blooming in pots on the windowsills; beautiful white lace curtains hang at the windows.

The *koamertje* is where neighbors, friends and relatives come to have a cup of coffee. *Opa en Opoe Heidema* (grandpa and grandma) who live just down the street on the other side of the school, come in mid-morning. They have cream and sugar in their coffee and they have a slice of *koek* (a traditional Dutch, heavy, brown, dried fruit and spice bread similar in kind to fruit cake) while they talk.

In midafternoon, people gather to have a cup of tea. Each tea drinker, especially the men, add heaping spoonfuls of sugar to their tea with the *zilveren theelepeltje* (silver tea spoon half the size of a measuring teaspoon). Neither a wedge of lemon nor milk is added as is common with the British. In Holland tea is served with sugar and accompanied by cookies, or perhaps the delicious almond pastry, *banket.*

And again, in the evening after dinner, maybe after a church or school event, folks gather in the *koamertje.* There is coffee again with a *chocolaatje* and before bedtime the grownups enjoy a small glass of whiskey or *jenever* (gin). *Advocaat,* bottled eggnog with or without gin, is a special treat. For drop-in guests at Christmas time, *brandewijn met rozijnen* (brandy with sugar and raisins or apricots fermented for a number of months) is served in liqueur glassware and eaten with an even more tiny, recently polished *lepeltje.* The guests joke about the difference between *boerenjongens en boerenmeisjes* (the drinks for the men and the women; the women's is sweeter).

The rust-colored *pluchen tafelkleed* (plush tablecloth) with its geometric designs—remininiscent of 16th century tapestry designs— is alternated with the handmade lace tablecloth. There are delicate, fancy, colorful china cups and saucers. The rest of the china and silver are kept in dark oak cabinets and proudly displayed through the sliding glass doors of the cabinets. Larger pewter pieces such as teapot, creamer and sugar bowl on a silver etched tray are kept brightly polished on the top of the cabinets along with black and white family photographs and some classic old, deep blue and white delftware.

Nostalgia comforts and softens Pat's anxieties. It is as if at that very minute the adults are talking, laughing and singing downstairs in the *koamertje*. Spoons are clinking against teacups, the aromas of good coffee, spices and brandy hangs in the air. At last, like a warm blanket being tucked around her back and shoulders by her favorite aunt, *Tante* Wina, benevolent sleep comes to enfold Pat in her embrace.

Chapter 5
"Deivame"

It is a known fact that humans, like animals, see and hear selectively. Yet I think, like most humans, that, this fact does not apply to me. I think that my story is the truth.

At eleven o'clock Saturday morning Anil hurried into the elevator and pushed the button for the third floor. When the doors opened he instantly spotted Mike slouched in his chair in the small waiting area. He was in his same set of clothes.

"Come on along, Mike," Anil said his tone of voice unwittingly reflecting the relief that he felt about the student being there for his scheduled appointment.

Anil led the way to his office, flipped the light switch and put his briefcase on the floor next to his desk. He was dressed more casually for the weekend. He had on denim jeans, a short- sleeved white pullover and white athletic shoes.

"Did you talk with the psychiatrist?" asked Mike in a flat tone of voice. He was still standing, barely inside the doorway.

"No, I didn't. Not yet." Anil's reply was unequivocal. He pulled out his chair, sat down and then motioned towards the empty chair. "Please, Mike, sit down. Let me explain my thinking."

Mike hesitantly sat down towards the edge of the chair.

Anil explained, "When I thought it over I knew that I did not have enough information to give the psychiatrist. You have told me that you are feeling down. That you are not sleeping and from the looks of you I'd say you are not eating that well either. You have been using amphetamines and alcohol to speed yourself up and slow yourself down, but you haven't told me anything about why you are behaving this way."

"I think I need some medicine, that's all."

"Come on, Mike, I'm on your side here. You're not telling me anything. Do you have a relationship with a girl or someone?"

"Nah."

Mike pushed himself to the back of the chair.

"Do you want one?"

"Nah, too complicated."

"Tell me about your parents. Father?"

Mike fidgeted in the chair then coughed. Anil waited.

"My dad died a couple of years ago."

"Yes, you mentioned that on Thursday. What was your relationship with him?"

"We weren't close or nothin'. He had too many things going on, you know."

"Mother?"

"She's all right. I don't have many problems with her. Didn't used to anyway."

"Brothers and sisters?"

"Yea. Sisters. They're older."

"So, you grew up more like an only child?"

"Yea, I guess."

"Did you grieve the loss of your father, Mike?"

"Whaddaja mean?"

"Did you feel sad, angry? Did you cry? What was it like for you?"

"He wasn't around that much. We didn't have stuff in common, you know. He thought I was a screw-up most of the time. I didn't care what he thought."

Anil knew in his theoretical files that loss brings with it anger and resentment. When prolonged, these feelings get in the way of taking the deceased person inside us through memories and similarities with the dead person. And he knew that as humans we always carry the baby experience with us, wanting and getting or wanting and not getting. With the not getting comes the feelings of frustration, rage and longing.

Death of a family member means not getting. And with the not getting come the primitive feelings. If those feelings are not owned as part of oneself, they are usually projected or viewed as coming from someone else. In the case of loss the anger can even be

45

viewed as coming from the dead person and that anger is taken in instead of the memories and similarities. Rage that someone we loved has died becomes rage directed within at ourselves. Possibly rage at ourselves for still being alive. And sometimes suicide presents itself as a solution to this psychic dilemma. Anil was quite aware that a high percentage of adolescents and children who commit suicide have experienced the loss of a parent. Their emotional immaturity makes it difficult to process the intense grief reaction (Frankel and Kranz 70-73).

Mike had self-destructive behaviors and he was minimizing his feelings about his father's death. However, it would not help Mike to tell him these theories and facts. In the silence Anil reflected on his own experience.

My father died last year; I have times that I feel sad and of being quite alone. I loved my father but there were also many things that I did not like about what he did and things that I did not agree with. Now it has all ended and I don't know what to do. Sometimes even though I have a wife and new son, a new home, I just feel empty. I don't sink into anything. I get impatient and I just want to get on to the next thing.

Taking note of these thoughts he cleared his mind and sat in silence. It was his preference to be with the client in a non-judging way and to be aware of the questions and feelings that arose. As he reacted physically to his earlier thoughts he felt the restless irritation. Then he spoke.

"It is possible to forget about the past by always wishing for the future. Like maybe I am thinking the next person who walks into this room is going to be more interesting than you and maybe the next guy needs me more or maybe I'm thinking about where I am going to have lunch and what I am going to do next week. And you are thinking about the relief you will get from some medication.

"It is tempting to move into the future in our thinking to get control," he said, as he drew out three sections on a sheet of paper and labeled them Past, Present and Future. He pointed to Future and continued, "but by doing so we really give up control. Then we feel anxious. The fact is this, Mike: this is all we have, you and me, in this moment, in the present. How you and I handle this moment is our business, our work to do. And, right now, I'm thinking that you are not treating me very well. You're here to get drugs from me and I'm not a drug pusher. I'm a therapist."

"Yeah. O.K. Whatever. Are you like, you know, like going to talk to the psychiatrist? You said you were going to."

Mike has just shown a refreshing bit of feistiness, thought Anil. *That may be a positive sign.*

"To be truthful with you in this moment, Mike, I told you that I would talk to a psychiatrist about getting you a prescription in part because I wanted you to come back for another appointment. It wasn't a good thing to do." Anil paused and then saw the similarity and said, "And so I think I did not treat you that well either."

"Yeah, you said you would."

"I made the decision to wait. How about you? Are you going to let me be a therapist instead of a drug pusher?"

"Yeah, I guess." Mike had a hint of a grin on his face. It was another positive sign.

"Okay, let's talk about your going home for the holiday," urged Anil. "Last time you said that you might not make it home next week. I think that possibility is something to explore. Would you agree?"

"I guess."

"Yes or no, give me a clear signal. 'I guess' leaves it up to me to make the decision for you. Do you want to talk about the decision to go home for the holiday or not?"

"Yeah."

"All right, good, let's talk about why go and why not go. Start with why go. Give me some reasons why it would be a good idea for you to go."

Mike slouched down in the chair, there was a long pause and then he said, "Like, you know, I need a break from this place, I guess, and my mom wants me to be there."

"How about why not go?"

"She's still got all his stuff around of my dad like he's not really dead or something, you know, sort of creepy like. She wants me to be something, you know. Like I can't just hang and stuff. She wants me to do things with her like I'm her stupid husband or something." Mike was not as bland as before. His voice just then had some disgust in it.

"Maybe she wants you to be more grown up than you want to be," volunteered Anil.

"Yeah, maybe."

"When a parent dies there are changes, Mike. You may want to stop them from happening but you really can't. So what I am thinking is that you have not processed your feelings about your dad and his dying and then you are faced with going from one set of expectations and pressures here at school to another set at home and it all feels overwhelming to you."

"Yeah."

Anil had learned in working with the students that stresses pile up. They come from home, school and friends and, at this time of year, exams and holidays. Holidays focus on idyllic relationships and for many realities in comparison can be depressing. Peer relationships for many late adolescents are filled with awkwardness, feelings of inadequacy and low self esteem. There are traumas of rejection and abandonment, isolation and loneliness. Kids try to fit in and risk failure. The accumulation of day to day stresses can make it difficult for kids to bounce back. An event that otherwise might seem trivial becomes a major disaster. Add to the mix a tragic loss of a parent and a kid lacking courage and confidence can reach a breaking point.

"And you hype yourself up or numb yourself not to feel all the pressure. You tell me if I have this right."

Mike was silent. Anil did not press him and the two sat in silence for almost ten minutes.

Finally Anil spoke. "Tell me the truth, Mike, did you come here just to get medication or did you come here maybe to get some help facing these pressures without needing drugs?"

"I could get whatever I wanted from somewhere."

"The drugs you mean?"

"Yeah."

"I am not going to get excited about that fact, Mike. Life is full of choices. Your choice to come here is much more interesting to me. I hope it becomes interesting to you, too. I think I understand better what it is you want from me."

Anil sensed that it was time to stop and a glance at his watch confirmed it.

"It is time to stop again. If you decide to go home when would you leave?"

"I don't really know." Mike was back to his insulated manner, mumbling his words and looking down. "Maybe late on Monday."

"Could you come in early on Monday then? Next time we can get an early start on facing the pressures directly."

"Yeah, okay."

Mike pushed himself up from the chair and headed for the door. Anil followed him.

"Try to get some food and sleep between now and then, all right?"

The guy must have showered. He did not smell as bad but the sweater and pants looked like they were worn 24 hours a day every day. Anil would let it ride. He walked out to the desk with Mike and made the appointment.

Anil reflected on the session. He had not heard any evidence of a thought disorder but Mike was clearly depressed. Now the question was whether or not the depression was more than the normal student's reaction to death, holidays, relationships and exams, more than the normal reaction to life's difficulties in general. He couldn't tell and the fear nibbled at him again.

Anil had a sudden urge to go home. He wanted to be held. He wanted Arlyce to hold and comfort him and it was not a sexual thing. The suddenness of the desire startled him. He ducked into the men's room to avoid the banter of the office staff and then went back to his office. He felt excruciatingly vulnerable.

Another client was due in 15 minutes. Arlyce would be going to the folks' house to see Grandma. He really should not bail out right now. As he faced realities, sadness and emptiness gradually replaced his longing for nurturing. He sat and looked out the small window.

It was hard to be a mature adult. The demands of Arun were constant. Arlyce was busy, preoccupied. So was he. It was hard to find time for just the two of them and it was almost impossible to have time alone. It was hard like Mike had said, '...just to hang.' He still felt all the conflicts and pressures that had come with buying the new house, the many knotty details, the tensions with his supervisor and in-laws and then his father dying.

He was grateful that in his late twenties, precipitated by his mother's sudden death in 1988, he and his father had talked about their problems and resentments. Anil flashed back to when he had been sitting at his father's bedside towards the end. His education and training as a doctor had helped him at the time to distance the ugliness of a body dying but now he cringed slightly at the visual memories.

I felt so helpless, he recalled. Again, there it was that slight sensation of tightness in his chest.

His father had not regained consciousness after the stroke. *I saw a response in my father's body when he heard my voice. He knew I was there.* He had been glad of that as he had sat alone by his father's side, gently cleaned away the blood from his bleeding nose and told him that it was all right to go.

A couple of hours after midnight he had died and when Anil reached the family home he had been startled to find reporters already there. By six a.m. the national news from Delhi was announcing Patmanabhin's death!

How could I not have known? Anil agonized. *I had been gone from home for a long time; for twelve years and I did not know that my father's communal contributions had gained national recognition.*

Anil had not been the one to do it but he was aware that his father's body after the death had been carefully washed and then anointed with sandal paste and blessed ashes. It was then dressed for the cremation.

Then I learned that years earlier my father, in preparation for his eventual death, had paid a cousin to perform the nukhagni (the duties of the cremation ritual), Anil recalled sadly. *He had not trusted that I, his only son, would come home to India to do my duty. That made me very sad. I wish he would have asked me; I could have assured him that I would come home.*

Going up in flames, his father believed, as many do in India, is the quickest way to release the spirit from its physical state and from any remaining links to life on earth. The pyre had been prepared with wood in the backyard of the family home. With only males present and reciting funeral words in Sanskrit Anil, along with cousins, nephews and a priest, had carried and placed his father's body on a base of leaves. He had confidently touched the fire to the wood and leaves and circled the pyre three times. Throughout the night he had visited the fire several times and had listened to the unforgettable, explosive sounds as his father's bones and skull splintered into pieces. He could still hear them in his mind.

After five days his sisters had gathered the remains and kept them in the garden. Anil had promised to return to India to take those remains to a local sacred mountain and release them into the waters of the river.

At some level he knew that he missed his father. He missed knowing that his father would be in Kerala when he went back there. He missed his father's eyes looking at him, Anil, his only son. Anil missed his hands, his voice, especially his voice. He missed him, and he was envious of the attention his father had given to others and he was angry at his father for leaving him with still so many mixed-up, frustrated feelings.

Anil put his face in his hands and let the tears of disappointment surface. Never again would he be able to see or hear either of his parents. Anil drew in deep, sad breaths as he touched his buried feelings about having become an emotional orphan. He squeezed his eyes shut. He wanted to eat, to run, to drink a lot, anything, not to feel these feelings of loss and responsibility. He totally understood Michael's wish to avoid.

"Deivame (Oh, God)," he sighed aloud. *"Deivame."*

The fifteen minutes had elapsed and he sat back to quiet himself. He was the next generation and, despite the fact that at times he fell prey to uncertainty, he like Patmanabhin wanted to make a difference in the lives of individuals, in this culture and in this country. He rose to open the door for his next student.

Chapter 6
Ann Unpacks

Regardless of what I think, it is believed by some, perhaps by many, that most autobiographical material is fiction.

Six rooms make up the second level of the Coks' home. The master bedroom with attached bath and Steven's office are to the right of the stairwell. Sandi's bedroom, Pat's sewing room, now doubling as Arun's nap room, and a second bathroom are to the left. Sandi's bedroom serves as the guest room. It is filled with dark heavy Mediterranean style furniture and odd family keepsakes such as the thimble and silver spoon collections.

In this room my mother, Ann, whose name I will use most of the time in lieu of Mom, *Moeke* or Mother, finished putting her clothes on hangers and hanging them in the closet. She looked up. On a shelf above her head were a couple of eight inch plastic horses—a bay and the other a pinto—two pairs of life size wooden shoes, a fan and assorted boxes and bags. A few hours earlier Steve and Pat had picked her up at SeaTac airport. The flight had gone well; she was glad of that. She had not known if anyone else of the family would have arrived but now she knew that she was the first. That pleased her.

Although still hearty and looking good at eighty-three, with her professionally styled but not colored hair and neat appearance, it could not be denied that Ann was slightly more stooped and somewhat more fragile-appearing than just a few weeks before.

It was not just that she had lost almost ten pounds after her recent bladder stretching and biopsy. She could afford to lose even more weight than that. But, the anesthetist never explained the pain in her chest in the recovery room and the invasive procedure, her first ever, had taken more out of her than anyone expected. The impact of it all, seemingly, had stunned her at some deep level and anyone who knew her well could tell that she was more vulnerable.[1]

Ann stepped back a step to survey the results in the closet and to visualize her various outfits for the next almost three weeks of her stay.

"Not too good, Annie", she said reprovingly to herself in her distinct Dutch accent.

As she repeated her name, "Ann," she realized that it still seemed so strange for her to address herself as Ann. In her mind she always has been and was today, Anje. But in America she must be Ann.

"Anje, Ann; Ann, Anje", she said.

She felt the difference in her soul as she repeated her two names. *Ann is tired and old now,* she thought, *but Anje is, as she always has been, happy and full of life.* She paused to reflect. Yes, she had talked to one of the kids that she would have wanted Anje not Ann to be inscribed on her half of the tombstone. It was too late anyway. The other half already had her husband's name, John P., on it, not Jan Piet. Even if it is in America, Jan Piet and Anje, that's how it was in the beginning; that's how she would have liked it in the end. She regretted that mistake.

Which child did I tell? I can't remember. Pat? Tjaakje? I should have written it down maybe but, och, there is never enough time and for me it is difficult to write things in English even after I have been learning now for how many years?

Ann picked up a cream colored soft pullover from the bottom of the suitcase and fingered it in her large hands. She looked back into the closet and saw all the summery short-sleeved blouses.

"Annie," she said, more firmly to herself this time. (No one called her Annie in the family but herself.) "What were you thinking?" She spoke aloud. "It is not going to be so warm in Seattle in December. Warmer, *ja,* than Montana where it is now well twenty below with so much snow but not so warm. It is winter in

---

[1] It was later surmised that Ann likely had suffered her first pulmonary embolus while under anesthesia. She had complained of severe chest pain in the recovery room and was more weakened than the bladder procedure warranted. A few months after this trip to Seattle she survived several life-threatening pulmonary emboli and was hospitalized for a week.

Seattle too. Dumb, *ja*, your mother can be dumb sometimes, children."

Ann laid the remaining items on the bed and closed the bright pink Samsonite suitcase. In doing so, she remembered that I had bought the suitcase on sale for her many years ago in Denver.

"It was a little too pink then and it has stayed a little too pink," she said ruefully. "But it has lasted me a good long time. On that point, Tjaakje, you were correct."

You will be here soon, too, Ann thought, *you and Sophia.*

Ann bent down and pushed the suitcase under the hanging clothes that Pat stored in the other half of the two-door closet. Then she emphatically closed the door to that half, determined that she would not start thinking until necessary about having to go back home alone in three weeks. Shaking her head and sighing deeply, Ann took one last disparaging look at her clothes in the other side of the closet. Then she closed that door, too.

Ann, more stooped when no one looked on, moved carefully in between the bulky, padded, wooden love seat and the foot of the queen-sized bed which had heavy posters. There was little room to maneuver. She made her way to the side of the bed and sat down on Pat's fancy brown velveteen, and beige lace, puffy bedspread to see what surprises her jewelry travel pouch might hold. She hoped that she had done her jewelry all right at least. As she went over her necklaces she began to go through the dates, the events and the mathematics in her head.

How long have I, Anje, been in America? she questioned herself. *In 1948, in January, ja, on January 23rd myself, I was 35 years old, Jan Piet, my husband, he was 39, my family, Pat, 10, John, 7 and Tjaakje, 4, boarded the "Nieuwe (New) Amsterdam" of the Holland America Line in Rotterdam. The ship was so big; I thought nothing could happen to that. Then we said the good byes. The boat leaving the shore; we were all standing there with many other passengers waving goodbyes to the families waving goodbyes to us. I remember that I was wearing the gold pin in my dress that had been made from Grandma Heidema's gold watch.*

Jan Piet had to stay in a room down the hallway with the men. The children were with me. The first time we could go to dinner, I smelled the food; all I could do was quick, find a door to get out again! Pretty soon I was so seasick. I was never sick like that before. They said we should go up on deck for fresh air but it didn't help much.

Sweeping Away the Sand

We had a bad storm on the ocean, I remember. Some portholes on the first floor blew out and the cold water was washing in as the boat swayed and went up and down. I get sick thinking about it. What were we doing there?

"Hai, *toch* (good grief)," she uttered aloud. "That was terrible."

The ship was a few days late because of the storm, too, coming into Hobokan, New Jersey. I remember sleeping on the floor that night, after we landed, in the Christian Seaman's Center. Till the next morning a man was calling out for the Heidemas. The Heidema family was then put on the train to Bozeman, Montana.

There we were. We had only one ten dollar bill left. That is all the money we had! We were on the train a day, a night, another day and another night and then still one more day. And we could not say a word in English!

"Hai, hai, hou durven wie dat toch?" (My, my, how did we dare to do it?)

Then we heard the porter call, "Livingston!"

We thought, close to Bozeman maybe? We got ready, put the kids' coats on, we too. Luggage we had with us ready. It took about a half day yet! It was very bad weather, snowing and snowing and a few feet on the ground already. It was beautiful through the mountains and all the snow! So much snow! I have never seen so much snow!

Finally, on 4 February, 1948, we got to Bozeman, Montana. It was very good to see Uncle Bill Dyk at the depot. Uncle Bill Dyk was the only face we recognized in this strange world.

That year, 1948, in Montana the snow came up to the telephone lines and it was so cold! Ah, it was so cold. Ann shivered at the memory of it.

After the ontmoeting (meeting) in the fresh air of Montana Uncle Bill decided he was going to take us to "Monkey Wards," the store for "overshoes." We didn't know what he was talking about! Jesse Lucas was working there then and she still remembers when we all came in for those overshoes. She is over 80 now and we talked about it when I met her last week.

From there we went to "Snappy Service," a place for a "hamburger." What did we know of a hamburger? Nothing! We were all very tired and hungry so the first hamburger did taste good. And then on to Uncle Bill's place. There I experienced my most disappointing moment in my life! Uncle Bill's wife, Jenny, stood behind her cook stove in her kitchen and she did not welcome us in. No smile on her face! "Och, Och." I was so shocked and wondered, what are we doing here?

I think she was not happy that Uncle Bill brought in another family while they had already a good-size family. I could see that too. They had twelve children. Thirteen really, but a boy of sixteen had died a few years before. Somebody showed us our rooms and, being so tired, we fell in bed and to sleep we went.

Next day they showed us the house on the Main Street in Manhattan and we moved in. Lots of cleaning up to do but we know how to work. Bathroom floor had many different colors of linoleum with holes in it, enz. (etc.) "Och, ja, and getting groceries. I could not say a word of English. *Ik was toch zo verlegen! Ik zalt noit vergeten (*I was so confused! I will never forget it)."

I could see from some pictures what was in the boxes so I picked out some things and brought them to the front. They put them in a box and said, "Do you want them delivered?"

I had no idea, "Ja, tou moar *(yes, go ahead),"* I nodded my head yes. I did not know what they asked. All of a sudden my groceries were gone and there I stood with empty hands. What now? So I come home with nothing. But then soon my groceries come too; so I learned then what they were saying to me.*

From that day on our lives in the U.S. started.. I learned soon that God behoed ons (God provides for us), and our God was the same here in America as in Holland. Later that year in the fall, maybe, Uncle Bill took us to his brothers, Harm and Bert, in the state of Washington to Ellensburg. They thought we could maybe live there.

Some of the Dyk brothers, Harm, Bert, Bill and Sam, I think, had left the Christian Reformed Church for the Missionary Alliance Church. "Four by four,"*they called it. I never know why though. They wanted people to know about Jesus, their savior, but otherwise were not so strict. They thought that Armageddon was really going to happen soon. We didn't think that. We thought it goes on all the time with good and evil.*

Jan Piet and me, we went to the Gereformeerde Kerk (Reformed Church) always two times every Sunday. We were used to singing Dutch Psalms and not all other kinds of songs in church. Dominees (Ministers) preaching from the catechism every Sunday. We did not dance or play cards either and we prayed before and after every meal and we read the Bible with every meal. Oom Bert did pray; I must say that. He prayed on and on and on.

We did not work or go to stores on Sundays. So then when we stopped with the families in Ellensburg to buy ice cream on Sunday, Jan Piet said, "This is not my church. I do not want to live here!" *We went back to Montana.*

"Now it soon will be 1997. Nineteen ninety-seven!" she exclaimed aloud.

Then it is forty-nine years. Next year, 50 years. We have been here forty nine years already and so many holidays with the children. But without Jan Piet. Jan Piet died in 1958 already. That is then almost 40 years ago. We would have been married for 60 years if he would be alive. He was in America for only nine and a half years.

Ann sighed and tried to straighten what she called her weak back. It was bothering her more and more.

The girls, when one of them see me, always tell me to stand up straighter, she recalled, *but that is not so easy anymore, girls.*

"Maybe," she sighed, "there will not be too many more holidays for me. Who knows? Do the children know that I am old now? I am old, children, I am old, I tell them."

They say they are getting old, too, but they don't know how old feels. I can feel it now. Aach, it's not too bad but I can really feel now that I am getting old.

"Kom aan nou, nait meer zoesen," she reprimanded herself, *"verstand der es goud bie* (Come on now, no more wasting time, keep your thoughts on what you are doing)."

"The jewelry is fine. I can do something right yet," she affirmed as she slipped an additional ring on her middle finger.

She squeezed "Our Daily Word," her meditation guide supplied by the Christian Reformed Church, and her diary onto the bedside stand. There was not much room next to the large lamp base and the clock.

"The numbers on the clock are too small anyway," she grumbled. "I will not be able to see them from the bed. Even with my watch on, without my glasses I will not know what time it is."

The last item for which she must find a place was her white satin neck pillow. This she propped against the thick headboard. For a moment she felt pulled to lie down with her pillow. She was tired and could easily sleep for a few minutes if she lay down but she didn't have time.

"Too busy. Always too busy," she fussed angrily as she went into the bathroom to add a little hair spray. "*Dat* is why my *bloezen binen verkeerd* (blouses are wrong)."

"Are you almost done up there?" Pat, her firstborn, called hurriedly from the bottom of the stairs. "Arlyce is going to be here with Arun any minute!"

"*Ja, ja*, almost. I'll be right there."

There had been so many things to do, so many arrangements

to make. And it was almost Christmas Day now, such a busy time always. She was glad that she had done her cards early for a change.

Marion Drew had wanted help with just one more bath, please, please, and then Marion had insisted on treating her to dinner out. She couldn't refuse, of course. They both loved to eat and to have company while they ate.

John doesn't like it that I go to town so much. I always say that it costs just as much to buy groceries and make a meal. And cooking for just one person is not so easy either.

Fannie had agreed to do Gertie's vacuuming but had not been happy about it. Fannie had already taken over Gertie's laundry and was finding it more of a job than what she really wanted.

It had not been a problem to find a replacement for turning the retirement home lights on and off nor to lead the exercises in the Care Wing. But she must not let those jobs go too often. She did not want to lose that little bit of extra money. It was always nice to treat herself and another, too, sometimes.

Ann returned to the bedroom. She had decided to change her blouse. Finished with that, she added a couple of last touches to her temporary new home. The twelve-inch square of blue netting, which would be used to preserve her hairdo when she maneuvered the pullover over her head, was tucked behind the picture frame on the dresser with the large mirror. The rain bonnet was laid on the unusual gray and black, life-size, ceramic typewriter that Arlyce had given Sandi when they were kids.

A necklace would look nice with this blouse, she decided. She walked around the end of the bed again, this time familiarizing herself with the sharp corner on the bed frame. She felt it with her hand and told herself to protect her bad leg and not bump into that tonight. The troublesome leg ulcer, although healed now, could open so easily. She still had to get up two or three times at night but that was so much better than it had been. Ann did not want to think back to the time before the procedure. That had been awful. So much pain and she couldn't go anywhere without worrying about where to go to the bathroom.

Ann sat down to file a few pesky fingernails. She just had not had time enough to get everything done at home. Just before she left Montana she had taken a quick two minutes to say goodbye to Jim De Jong. He had not been well. She would have to remember to call Shelly, her granddaughter, to ask about Jim in a week or so. Maybe he or someone would be gone when she got back. *It is always someone's funeral it seems.*

Gone, so many friends are gone now. Pieka is gone. Pieka was always so down to earth, such a good person. After Jan Piet died I could always go there for a cup of coffee or a bowl of homemade soup with canned peaches. Pieka always had a pan of soup ready. And the children loved Pieka. When Pieka was at the farm once, we had been canning or something, peaches maybe, and Pieka all of a sudden made up a poem about Meindart Noot. Meindart would do some irrigation work in the summer times for us and he loved to talk. Oh, how he loved to talk, especially in Dutch at lunch time. The children laughed so over what Pieka said. How did that poem go again?

> *"Meindart Noot*
> *Hai brook zien poot.*
> *Murgen gait zien kat dood;*
> *Hai wot begrov'n in Middel Sloot."*
> (Meindart Noot—
> pronounced as note—
> Broke his pote (leg).
> Tomorrow his cat will croak
> And be buried in Middle Slote— canal).

Not so many years ago I had been taking care of Pieka some of the time and I was with Pieka that night when she died of that Lou Gehrig's disease in her own bed at home, Ann recalled sadly. *Everybody still misses Pieka. Me too, I still miss her.*

Al, Pieka's husband, had so many operations there was almost nothing left of him. He is gone now too.

And dear, eccentrisch (eccentric) Steintje is gone. And her talking parakeet, Davie, is gone too. There is nobody to feed oatmeal to the wild cats on Churchill in the wintertime, nobody to have a TV dinner with on Sundays and nobody to talk Gronigs with anymore. Most of the immigrants who came after the war are gone. Mrs. Douma, always with a hat on, is long gone. Vrouw Flikkema is gone. "I never could get along with that one. She did not like me either." *Biede olle (both old) Kimns are gone, but enough about that sad subject.*

One more look in the mirror. Ann winced with pain as she hurried around the bed and into the bathroom. That knee was bothering her today. Getting that x-ray of her knee from the doctor sure had thrown a wrench into things. It had taken some quick talking to get Dorothy, her grandson Kent's wife, in the right frame of mind to take her to town again yesterday.

Dorothy and she had already been in Bozeman on Tuesday to buy the new, black, polyester pants. Her old ones were starting to be a disgrace. She didn't always see the problems so well anymore and she had finally taken a good look at the pants. She had been ashamed. They were terrible, all ballie with snags everywhere.

"And now Pat says that it is an x-ray of the wrong knee! How can that be?"

"Mom, Arlyce is here and she is ready to help you polish the silverware. Are you ever coming down?"

"Ja, ik kom der aan (yes, I am coming)," Ann called back. She felt a little irritated as she hobbled down the carpeted stairs, careful to hold on to the railing.

"Polish the silverware on the first day I am here! Now I have to work on this end," Ann fussed aloud. *"Wel, wel, nou nog mooier. Drie en tachtig en, ik vertel je, ik krieg en hekel aan't waark! Dat zee mien moeke din ook toen zai zo old was.* (Eighty-three and, I tell you, I am beginning to hate to work. That is what my mother said too when she was this old.)

"What are you saying?" asked Pat from the foot of the stairs.

"Nothing, dear. Nothing," Ann replied as she made it to the landing and paused to study the familiar *kapstock* (the antique Dutch oak hat and clothes rack) and the old brass Dutch dinner gong. *Did Pat get those from me? Must be, but I can't remember for sure.*

Chapter 7
Polishing Silverware

On the other hand it has also been said that most fiction is autobiographical.

G randma, did you have a good trip?" asked Arlyce in a perceptible caring tone of voice as the two ended their welcoming hug and Arlyce bent down slightly to look directly into her grandmother's face.

Arlyce, Steven and Pat's oldest, in her middle thirties is an expressive, tall, attractive woman. She was wearing ankle length black leotards, Reeboks with hosiery socks and a gray and white, brushed wool, Scandinavian-style car coat. "A five dollar garage sale find! Can you believe it?" Arlyce was fond of saying about the coat. She had come directly from her weekly aerobics class, her island-spice, light auburn hair swept up on top of her head, her finely featured face glowing.

"Yes, dear, I had a very good trip, just fine. Thank you," Ann gave sincere emphasis to each word to match the tone set by Arlyce.

The two stood facing one another at the base of the stairway holding each another's hands. Ann, who used to be 5'8" but had shrunk several inches, looked up squinting with her bad eye in the poor lighting of the hallway to get a better look at the face of her granddaughter.

"And how are you, my little girl?" she asked.

"I'm fine. *A 1-i-t-t-1-e* bit busy but fine." Arlyce accentuated the word *little* with a high pitched prolonged sound and made a wry smile. Then she laughed, "Well, you know how it is, Grandma."

"Ja, dear, are you fine?" Ann reached out and put her wrinkled hand on the pale cheek of Arlyce's thin face. "It's not so easy having a-one-and-a-half-year-old. I know."

"Let's go into the kitchen, Grandma. Mom wants us to polish the silverware while we have a talk. But first we'll have a cup of tea. I am so ready for a cup of tea, how about you?" Arlyce led Ann by the hand straight away through the hallway into the kitchen.

"Oh yes, dear, me too! A cup of tea would be very good," rejoined Ann.

Arlyce and Ann had forged a special bond in Holland a few years earlier. It was during the time that Arlyce was living with Anil in London. Arlyce had told her parents about her living arrangements, and, predictably, Steven and Pat had expressed their strong disapproval on all counts—Anil was not a Christian, he was from a strange culture (who knows what he might do?) and living with someone prior to marriage was a sin, period. This had left Arlyce to fend for herself. Not long after, Ann had gone to Europe to visit relatives in Holland. Arlyce, yet wishing to be forthright, which was Anil's preferred style as well, and still hoping for some family inclusion, risked even further rejection when she chose at that time to introduce Anil to her grandmother. With no small amount of trepidation the twosome had traveled from London to Groningen, the northernmost province in Holland and the largest city in the province.

For that first meeting Ann, Arlyce and Anil had sat at the kitchen table of Ann's niece and namesake, Anjenette. Anjenette is the second youngest daughter of *Tante* (aunt) Wina, Ann's youngest sister. Anjenette had excused herself but *Tante* Wina and *Tante* Dirkje, Ann's sister-in-law had stayed. Arlyce, holding a severe image of her grandmother in mind at that moment, had feared the absolute worst. Her heart, she told me in retrospect, skipped a number of beats in its galloping pace as the subjects of an interracial relationship and of living together outside of marriage surfaced. "It hurt in my chest to breathe and I seriously wondered if I would live through the ordeal," she recalled.

Interestingly, and quite likely, the setting may have had something to do with the surprising outcome of that talk. After all, *Tante* Wina has five grown children who were or are always, in some way or other, exploring the options available in the coupling and uncoupling of consenting adults. Petra at that time was unmarried, had a son and was living with a man who was not the son's father.

Klaas had married a divorced woman with two children, Erna was gay and living with Cobie, her woman friend. Klasien was married with two children and Anjenette was single and living alone. *Tante* Wina loved and loves each one, unconditionally.

Maybe too, in addition to her youngest sister's role modeling, the surprising outcome was favorable for Arlyce and Anil because Mom knew all about the disorienting pain of rejection. Not many years before she had dealt with the stern, uncaring, self-righteous church elders who had first denied her permission to divorce her second husband and then denied her right to the sacrament of communion. Callously unheeded then had gone her painful pleas for tolerance. I know all about how that goes because I went through it, too. Those same elders were on the brink of publicly excommunicating me from the Christian Reformed Church when, thank God, I was finally able to convince a pastor in Denver to quietly transfer my membership and then to drop it.

Maybe, to get back to my hypothesizing as to why my mother showed an extra measure of compassion to Arlyce on that day, it was Ann's desperate need to be loved and accepted just as it was Arlyce's need. For instance, Ann may have curried the young couple's favor as she did while in their presence in Holland and then, sometime later in the presence of Steven and Pat, she might have back-peddled from her previously stated position and taken on the opposing view. She had been known to do that; in fact, if I remember correctly, she did do some of that in this case. Who in all truthfulness has not? Principle is not always Ann's driving force and neither is it always our own. Like hot lava below the earth's crust, primal motivations—such as the desperate need to be loved—lie just below our carefully constructed layer of principles. The heat or the pressure for expression can cause shifts in the firmament. Sometimes, but not necessarily, these shifts will be accompanied by steam, eruptions and great upheavals.

Or maybe—as long as I'm theorizing, I'll add one more—Ann, as a person, as an intelligent woman, deep down has paradoxically, always been more broad-minded and practical-minded than what her religion sanctions or what her children and grandchildren can fathom. There are no broad vistas of that being the case but there have definitely been glimpses of this probability throughout her life.

I, for instance, remember such a glimpse when she and I were visiting in Holland together. We were riding the fast Euro train through the flat fields of Friesland. My mother, in the course of a not uncommon, one-sided conversation, shared her liberated view on the topic of birth control.

Intermingled with talk about Friesland's beautiful pinkish-purple fields of *heide* (heather) and the *wit and rode bont koeien* (white and red-banded cows as opposed to white and black-banded cows which were Ann's favorite), she waxed on about how single girls and married ladies, too, if they wanted to nowadays, should be responsible and use birth control.

"They should take care of themselves and if I had anything to say about it," I remember my mother saying from her soapbox, "I would have them sell birth control from vending machines everywhere."

In regard to social issues, this expressed view of hers was certainly more in line with the liberal reputation of the Dutch as a permissive, socialist country than it was with the conservative reputation of the Dutch as a community in Montana. It was not what I had heard growing up there, anyway. I remember sitting next to her as the train jostled us about, looking out at the cows and wondering if I could risk telling her about my personal situation. I was in 1973—the year of that trip--one of those single girls she was talking about. It was still a long time before I would awaken to the fact that I had sexual interests that did not require birth control and I was struggling with what to do sexually with the men in my life. Frankly, I could have used one of those birth control vending machines. But I did not trust her enough to tell her so; I never have trusted her enough to tell her much of anything.

Dad told me one Sunday morning that Mom was in the hospital and I had a baby sister. I was eight-years-old but she had not told me she was pregnant. Maybe that set a precedent. In the next couple of years I could not tell her that a grown son of friends of the family had groped my little budding breasts nor that a second cousin twice my age attempted intercourse in the straw stack during a game of hide and seek. The pain had been terribly intense and I had wriggled away from his hold just in time, I think. I'm not really sure. I could not tell her about that.

School chums lingered in Churchill's grocery store where Mom worked. Kids, who were terrified to approach their parents with the truth, like a pregnancy out of wedlock, for instance, appreciated Mom's tolerance and acceptance. I was envious of them. Years later, when I did tell her that I had been raped and threatened with a knife and asked her to come be with me, she told me I should not have been with "such a man." I was very sorry I had told her and encouraged her to go back home after a couple of days. I said I was fine. She and I have never discussed my sexual orientation. She is appreciative of Sophia sharing my life and she relates to us as a couple; I think she knows, but we will never speak of it.

The most obvious reason—and I know that I risk beating the whole idea of theories to death now as I go on, but I promise this is the last one—as to why Mom may have supported Arlyce's relationship with Anil—would be that she was expressing unconditional love. Wow, what a concept! I imagine some of you are saying, "That, Tjaakje, was a no brainer." If you are, it is probably because you are forgetting that I had to leave my grandparents in Holland at the age of four. I haven't known that kind of unconditional love from a grand-parent; and in our family, growing up, I thought love was conditional.

Anyway, whatever her reason, on that day in Groningen with Arlyce and Anil, my mother adopted an accepting and forgiving attitude. Good for her! Grandmother, much to Arlyce's relief and Pat and Steven's chagrin, reached across the table, accepted and embraced Anil and, in so doing, endorsed Arlyce's relationship with him. In so doing their bond was insured.

Little laughing boy, Arun, the sole progeny of that relationship, with Pat in pursuit came running from the family room into the kitchen. He paused only a second to look at Ann and then ran to Arlyce holding up a small Matchbox car for her to see.

"*Pa, Pa,* umbootie," he chimed excitedly.

"Is *Pa* coming, Arun? He calls Dad *Pa* because he can't say Grandpa," Arlyce explained to Ann. "And umbootie or the car means that he is going to play with the car on the train track with *Pa.* I'm his interpreter these days," she laughed gaily.

"Isn't that cute, Pat? He calls Steven *Pa.*" Ann was trying to catch Pat's attention.

"Yes, I know," replied Pat who had veered off towards the left and with her back turned was busily pouring tea into cups at the stove.

"Would you like some juice, Arun?" asked Pat solicitously. "Arlyce, would you cut some slices of *koek*, please."

Arun pronounced *Pa* the Dutch way like a sheep bleating, *baa*; and, like the way Pat and everyone in our family addressed our dad. Not like *paw*, the American way. Of course, Pat noticed and thought of it; she would have to have been numb not to. *Pa* had been one of the first words her grandson had spoken and most likely the pronunciation touched her deeply every time she heard it. It was such a precious link and certainly her father would have enjoyed hearing it come from this great-grandson.

This is where I think Pat was coming from when she sidestepped Mom's point. She frankly did not want to underscore the preciousness with her mother. As it says in the Bible, "...Mary kept all these things and pondered them in her heart (Luke 2, verse 19)." This was a keep-it-in-your-heart-pondering kind of thing. More than likely, had she responded to Mom, Mom would have talked about her perfect marriage and her loss of her life's partner, not about Pat's special connection with and loss of her father. Mom is unwilling to acknowledge that the two are different. That the loss of a father is very different from the loss of a spouse and that, no matter what age, we still might like a word of support from her.

For instance, Pat could have responded with, "it is cute when he says *Pa*, isn't it? It reminds me of Dad when Arun says it and so it is kind of sad and sweet at the same time. I still miss him, you know."

And Mom could have said, "Of course you do, dear. I know that. He loved you very much."

On the other hand, Pat would probably say I am being silly and that she never would think of such a thing. Besides, the important issue for Pat was that there just was not time to get into sentimentality with her mother. She had to get Mom and Arlyce to work on the silverware. Doug and Marge and B.J. would be coming right around dinnertime.

"Is Mrs. Doubtfire going to babysit this afternoon, Arlyce?" Pat asked. "You should see their babysitter, Mom; she takes right over like Mrs. Doubtfire did in the movie."

Arlyce stood eating loose crumbs from the *koek* oblivious to time or silverware and watched Arun's tiniest of reactions to Grandma. Grandma was trying to win his trust and Arun was seriously considering it.

Unlike Pat, her mother, who submerged herself totally into her roles and projects, Arlyce had a way of standing aside and curiously observing herself in a process. Nowadays she was particularly intrigued by her self as an independent, confident, not-so-confident, frazzled working mother and wife of the nineties. In some ways motherhood to Arlyce was an amazing, exhausting, heart-expanding adventure to be savored. In other ways it was restricting, stifling and, in being so, annoying at the least, maddening at its worst. Women of her generation were finally free to admit that truth of motherhood.

In her personal life Arlyce had survived the loss of her first love, the trauma of a bad love, and a devastating rift with her parents. And like the hardy snowdrop pushing its way through ice and snow to be the first to bloom in spring, Arlyce had both survived and toughened as a registered nurse in the often chilling, spirit-dampening reality of bureaucratic medical practice. With skill and persistence she had carved out a niche for herself in bone marrow transplantation and she used this niche as a springboard from which to reach the rest of her aspirations.

Before marriage, for instance, she hiked the 150 miles of the Anna Purna Himalayan Circuit of Nepal with her friend Medo. And another time the two bicycled through communist-ruled Yugoslavia, passionate Italy, ancient Greece, Paris and London. This animated, romantic soul bravely and often naively sought beauty in ordinary life and in peoples of all ages and colors. She ate of their food and drank of their wine.

Quite literally, Arlyce put herself into international scenes depicted in posters and reveled in her freedom to do so. It were as if she enjoyed amazing herself. In awe she had often said, "I'm really doing this. I can't believe it! I'm *really* doing this!"

But, of her many and varied life experiences, none had prepared her for the depth of emotion that she would feel mothering a child. A healing, unconditional love has been pouring forth from her inner being. This has been awesome to her, a process, indeed, deserving of joyous mindfulness and devout reverence.

"Yes, Mrs. Doubtfire is going to baby-sit. Arun loves her."

In the days of her mother, and more so in the days of her grandmother and great-grandmother, it had been thought that children were to be rigorously shaped and molded into decent human beings. Total depravity, born and conceived in sin was a cornerstone in their fundamentalist and child-rearing beliefs.

For the succession of mothers preceding her, Pat Cok, Ann Heidema, Pieterke deVries, Martje Woldering and Anje Kolhorn and the others, it had been about the end product, about being acceptable in the sight of God and the community. Would this child be accepted into heaven? That was the bottom line, to be with them in eternity.

Arlyce, in contrast, has likened her responsibilities of motherhood to those of a gardener, one who carefully fashions a flower garden from an untamed border. She did not, for example, want—in a no-turning-back fashion—to pull on a far-reaching root of an annoying weed. She might destroy an—as yet—undiscovered flower. An intensely orange and delicate California poppy perhaps or a wild blue lupine might never bloom if she were to emphatically impose her will. And if she were not careful in digging a hole to plant the new perennial, she has thought, it could result in a damaging cut to the tulip bulb that she planted last fall.

That was the adventure in the nineties, was it not? Focusing on the moment, taking risks, finding balance and bandaging the blisters, it was all about the process and not so much about the end product.

Steven came in from the garage and within a minute *Pa* and Arun were on the floor in the family room fitting together sections of the silver train track. The three women sat at the kitchen table having a second cup of tea.

"Let's go over the list of things that we can do while everybody's here, okay? I have a list going for B.J. and one from Lottie." Pat twisted to reach, felt the pain, but pressed on. She selected a piece of scrap paper from the several lists near the telephone and a stubby little pencil. Arlyce and Ann began to polish silverware.

"I asked Lottie for her list. She said they wanted to go to Discovery Bay somewhere between the Olympic Mountains and the Straits of Juan De Fuca. There is some kind of women's trailer park out there, I guess, near Seguim."

"Seguim, I don't think I have been there, have I, Pat?" Ann was always eager to explore something new.

"No, I don't think so. It's a little too far for now, I think. We'll probably scratch that off the list. The other things on Lottie's list are things we can probably do. She wants to have tea at Queen Mary's Confectioners."

"Oooooo, HMQM, Her Majesty the Queen Mary, I like that idea," crooned Arlyce.

She had discovered and totally fallen in love with the elegant little storefront restaurant on Ravenna Street near the University of Washington. Upon entering the intimate space the first time, it had been as if she had taken a step back into the English countryside. Lace covered the windows and tables; pleated floral fabric lined the high walls. Both the lace and fabric richly complemented bold, dark-wood paneling and moldings. Each patron received her (the patrons were mostly women) own flowered china tea pot and was encouraged to linger over delicious offerings such as chocolate cake with amaretto mousse, German chocolate cake with apricot-coconut icing, marbled very berry cheesecake and fresh fruit torts.

"*Ja*, that sounds good to me too, Arlyce," affirmed Ann.

"Lottie would also like to go to the Northgate Mall and have a latte at Nordstrom's along with everybody shopping for last minute stocking stuffers. We'll have to do that Tuesday. Marge, when I asked her for her list said, 'Whatever,' like usual and I've made a list of what I thought the guys could do with B.J.: Museum of Flight, Science Center, Seattle Center, bowling and ferries. I don't think he is old enough to tour the Boeing plant yet. He has to be a certain age for that."

"That sounds like some good things, Mom."

"Oh, yes, Tjaakje said that Sophia would like to see some snow! Sophia has not seen snow for five years and she misses it. I thought some of us could go with her up to Snoqualmie Pass to meet Sandi when she comes down. There is plenty of snow up there. I think we're supposed to get a storm later in the week but it'll just be rain, I suppose."

"What is the weather now really?" Ann turned to get a better view of the outdoors. "Look, girls, there is the sun! It is beautiful weather in Seattle!"

Ann put her hands up and clapped them together one time

then held them together fingers pointing upward in a prayerful pose, "I am so happy to be in warm Seattle and not in cold, cold snowy Montana. I can't tell you how much. I love it!"

A six-foot glass slider next to the kitchen table and a window above the sink allows people to look out onto the Cok's large deck and down into their expansive back yard. Pat and Arlyce stood to look out. Pat was at the sink and Arlyce next to Ann. As they watched, the shy Seattle sun hid behind a cloud.

There was a six-foot-high wooden, cedar fence along the three sides of the yard and there was little indication that the fence abutted other homes and yards. This back yard, though annually exacting its price of hard work from the Cok twosome, was a peaceful world unto itself. Huge wavy, lined flower beds, now dark, empty and resting, followed the fence line. Along the inner aspects of the flower beds was a healthy lawn of grass, green even in wintertime. In the middle of the grass there were more beautifully landscaped, elevated flower beds and a number of very tall fir trees roughly formed a circle. Large hanging branches filled the sky forming a canopy over the center space of the circle and giving it a shaded, quiet, somewhat sacred quality.

Right then, with all looking and as if blessing a shrine, determined sun rays again broke through needles and branches to spread holy, dappled light upon the earthen altar.

"Beautiful!" exclaimed Ann. "Seattle is beautiful!"

Pat was the first to regain perspective. "Come on you two," she exclaimed, "you have to finish the silverware. Arlyce, you'll have to go to work soon and, Mom, we have to go shopping!"

Chapter 8
Prolastin at North Office

The bottom line is this: though we may have shared a moment in time, my memory and my truth, be they fact or fiction, will likely differ from yours.

In moderately heavy traffic at nine o'clock in the morning I steered Le B, the ice blue, eleven-year-old, four-door Chrysler Lebaron with its sun-damaged vinyl top, through the wide curve off Superstition Freeway onto eight-lane Interstate Highway 10 heading northwest. Instantly, as I completed the curve, hundreds of thousands of tons of 18 wheelers coming from Tucson, traveling at speeds of 65 to 75 miles an hour, barreled down on me. I flipped on the left blinker, worked my way into the middle lane of the beginning-of-the-work-week, fast-moving flow, and felt the tension like a large beetle crawl up my neck.

Years ago, back when I was driving back and forth on Interstate 90 between Denver, Colorado, and Bozeman, Montana, to visit family, I considered trucks and truck drivers my allies. They symbolized freedom and good will. Plenty of times I had seen a smiling male reach up for a couple of pulls on the big horn to give me a friendly hello in passing.

No wonder. In those days, the mid-sixties through the seventies, along with being indiscriminately open and friendly, I had sexually-appealing, shoulder-length, artificially highlighted, blonde hair to go with my then shapely long legs and miniskirts. "A real tomato", brother John would have said, had I not been his sister. He liked describing attractive women that way. I, on the other hand, was totally oblivious to the fact that my appearance drew male attention; I really honestly thought the truck drivers were friendly.

In those days I was as naive as a green tomato still hanging from the vine.

Now, thirty years and more than thirty lessons later and in the over-fifty club, I am but one of the millions upon millions of invisible but no longer oblivious women in the world. I am a woman dear brother would probably describe as a "cow" or a "dog". That's okay. I have been known to call men pigs too. At least it all stays on the farm, so to speak.

A few weeks ago during one of Sophia's and my explorations of the desert south of Mesa near Florence, Arizona, home of the state penitentiary, we ran across a prison work crew decked out in their bright orange coveralls. Heavily armed guards were supervising the work. At the sight of us two women, whistles, cat calls, hoots and hollers chorused forth. Lusting men waved both arms high up in the air.

"When was the last time you heard that, Tjaak?" Sophia asked and laughed.

"Those guys must be from death row!" I responded.

Not that we long for the bygone testosterone attentions, we don't. Each of us is only too happy to have emerged from the onerous groping years still an independent woman. There were experiences beyond groping of more malefic molestation that, when mentioned, bring out the fire in our eyes. All of it has left us wisely wary of most men.

These days, truck drivers not only do not honk but, it is clear to me that they want me to get the hell out of the way. Holding my ground, I realize with each trip out on the freeways, takes more and more effort.

As I maneuvered the car through the twists and turns of I-10, the desert sun high in the eastern sky was already piercingly hot. I would not have needed the dark green, crewneck sweater over the short-sleeved, white, polyester blouse that I was wearing except that I wanted the veins in my hands to be fully dilated when I got to the Pulmonary Associates Office. I figure there is no sense in having the nurse poke me twice if I can help keep it down to just one. These veins have to last for my lifetime.

Lavender slacks and white Nike Air tennis shoes with white anklets made up the rest of my outfit. Almost always, I dress comfortably these days. I honestly can not remember the last time I have worn a dress or skirt. Either would require nylons and a bra and I just won't be bothered with those anymore.

Planes were arriving and departing that morning as every morning, seemingly nonstop, on the black tarmac of the busy Phoenix International Jetport off to my right. To my left, over the downtown skyscrapers, hung the loathsome, brown cloud made up of auto exhaust fumes, last night's fireplace and wood stove burning, a good helping of Los Angeles smog carried on the easterly weather pattern and, worst of all, dust particulate from wind and the frenetic development going on in the desert valley. The wintertime temperature inversion was pushing the carbon monoxide level treacherously high and people like me with lung problems were being urged to stay indoors.

With a deep breath of relief I exited I 10 off to the right onto Squaw Peak Parkway. There were not as many big trucks on the parkway and the highway was laid out straight north to south. I relaxed a little, reached over to the passenger seat for the Gatorade water bottle and took a long drink of water. Then I picked up the hand grip exerciser and started squeezing, another gimmick to encourage my veins to pop out.

I have been receiving the biological product, Prolastin, intravenously for seven years already! First it was every other week, now weekly. Prolastin, pooled plasma with a high concentration of the antitrypsin enzyme, is given to slow down the abnormally active breakdown process in my lungs.

Alpha-1 Deficiency started with a single gene mutation in one individual in northern Europe. This spontaneous mutation or defect, known as the Z allele in the chromosomes, thereafter, was passed on to offspring. Eventually, when two offspring (cousins probably) who each carried the gene, came together an MZ, SZ or ZZ was created. John and I are ZZs which have the greatest deficiency. In us, the glitch in the programming of the cell causes the liver to hold onto rather than to let go of or to secrete a particular protein. Proteins of a certain makeup are called enzymes. There is variation in the enzymes and the specific enzyme that is held back in our livers is the antitrypsin enzyme. The anti- enzyme is needed to act against or, more correctly, to hold in check the actions of another enzyme, elastase. Without the anti- enzyme being secreted from the liver into the blood stream to limit the elastase, it (the elastase) not only destroys mucus material in the lung airways, which is its normal purpose, but goes on to destroy the vital lung (alveolar) tissue. So it is that we lose more and more functional lung tissue. Less and less tissue surface means less exchange of oxygen and carbon monoxide.

The first individuals to have the condition were likely to have been told by the medical professional of the day that he or she did not have enough "elastic in his lungs". That early on diagnosis did not refer to the elastase enzyme, since they did not yet know it existed, but rather to the fact that stale air got trapped in the dead spaces in the lungs leaving them always hyper inflated. Later they would have been told that they had "unexplainable premature emphysema." Now we are told that we have chronic obstructive pulmonary disease (COPD). The diagnosis is a catchall for emphysema, asthma and chronic bronchitis all of which become factors as the lung destruction occurs.

John learned of his condition in his mid-thirties. It was a good five years before I discovered that my tiredness was physical and not mentally based. I had convinced myself that it was the demanding director of nursing job at the state psychiatric hospital that was draining my energy. I had not even noticed that I was short of breath with exertion. My gynecologist was the one who noticed and referred me to an allergist who pinpointed the diagnosis.

Ironic, but totally unrelated, was our father's early death from lung cancer, the bronchial type. Father and brother, both stricken with lung disease, I had unconsciously and mistakenly concluded that respiratory problems were associated with the males in the family. Denial is such an interesting thing, is it not?

Each of us siblings, John and I, unaware of our genetic vulnerability, had previously been a smoker, John starting in his teens and me in my mid-twenties. How stupid was that? I was old enough to know better. Like unfair taxes being heaped on the poor inevitably leads to fires in the streets, so smoking in each of us inflamed an already existing process that could not again be extinguished. The condition shortens the life span of nonsmokers. A former smoker can expect to lose as much as an additional ten years.

I have seen emphysema as a nurse and as a patient. As a nurse, I was trained to hide my feelings but, as most people, I felt it all: the exasperation with the afflicted person's all-consuming slowness, the wish to withdraw from their struggle to breathe and the repulsion at the sounds and ugliness of the end stage. Even as a professional I shared in the human tendency to blame the patient for their plight. Clinically detached, I focused—although there was little that I could do—on the breathing, the actual sound and quality of it: wheezing, congestion, retraction, that sort of thing.

As a patient I have learned that emphysema is not only about breath and the shortness of it. It is about so much more: the progressive crippling weakness in all of my limbs and the persistent accessory muscle pain and tightness from their overuse. Both of which, in order to keep at maximum strength and flexibility, require exercise and the devotion of an athlete. As such, I take on the challenge. I walk, swim and work with weights.

Emphysema is about learning to move slowly and safely in a fast-paced world, to stay behind a line and be content there. That is the biggest challenge, of course, to be content there.

For the most part I am content with the slower pace; in fact, earlier, in the fast lane, when a slower pace seemed out of reach, I craved it, dreamed about it. Naturally observant, thoughtful and reflective, slow is more my nature. I remember one time as a kid on the farm I slowly, painstakingly cut grass that had grown up through the fence, one small 3x3 wire square at a time. (That was long before the days of the weed whacker.) I was sitting on the ground totally engrossed and even though I had to suffer through being called lazy by all the members of my family, I knew that pace was me.

Yet, welling up through my soul and causing conflict with the slow pace are my idealism and passion. I have intense, powerful emotions. Even in good times it takes effort to balance my two natures. In hard times, much to my repeated disappointment, when I do not have the energy or the discipline, I can be overcome by emotion.

Emphysema brings with it inevitable down times. Times when I so miss the challenge of helping people, being with colleagues and friends, having intellectual exchanges and playing, running and working hard physically. Tears overflow with those big waves of loneliness and loss. And, as I witnessed living by the ocean in Maine, a thick sea wall can get tiny cracks in its blocks of concrete from the force of the relentless big waves, so too I can get cracks in the core of my resolve to keep going with dignity. The cracks some day could signal the beginning of the end. I need to keep a close watch and I need to patch the cracks as soon as possible to keep the sea of despair from rushing in and engulfing me.

Emphysema also, I am learning, is not about getting a free pass and being treated with compassion. It is about being isolated and seeing most people in a not-so-good light. I see adults (children I can understand, they are curious) rudely staring at me or, the opposite, quickly looking away. I watch those who crank their nose up a notch or two and deliberately act as if I and my disease are beneath them. As if they are never going to get themselves into this kind of a mess.

Ever thankful for the exception to the rule to offset these cold never-a-hair-out-of-place-I-am-better-than-you-are kinds of people, I am discovering that there are strangers, truly rare, exceptionally kind, warm individuals who, without hesitation, look right through the trappings of oxygen tank, cannula and pursed lip breathing, right into my eyes and soul and smile at me. Always unexpected, always sudden, the jolt of goodness from those unique spirits is like a huge, normal breath. It refreshes every cell in my body and I have learned from them how it is best to be in this world.

Cruising north on the parkway that Monday, I followed an old, beat-up pickup with three Latinos jammed into the small cab. The truck bed was filled to overflowing with palm tree fronds tied down with ropes. Sonoran Desert shrubs, lemon bottlebrushes (the lemon referring to the aroma from its leaves, not its red flower), white and pink oleanders and vibrant red bougainvilleas, or tissue paper plants as they are called, intermingled with small trees such as the Palo verde, mesquite and desert ironwoods in the median strip. The purple buds on the prickly pear cacti were swelled.

It sure doesn't look like it is going to be Christmas anytime soon, I thought. *Not during the daytime at least. Nighttime is a different story. Phoenix and all the neighboring cities are lit up like the strip in Las Vegas. It seems to me every year at this time that the cities flaunt all their electricity made from the dammed-up, used-up Colorado River. As if the people in the states are shamelessly, arrogantly thumbing their noses at the people south of the border.*

It wasn't just the excess of lights that annoyed me that day. It was the Christmas trees. Only two days before Christmas and still there was a lot half full of formerly beautiful trees back on Higley Street. The long dead trees, (I've seen truckloads of trees being hauled south in early November, haven't you?) had been on the lot for three weeks baking in the hot desert sun. It was the same in numerous other such lots. I could not help but think of the trees as sacrificial lambs for the Christmas slaughter. Bah humbug! I grumbled inwardly.

Malls are growing at cancerous rates in the Phoenix area and holiday shoppers are going bonkers. They act like robots used to drive up the economy. Buy! Buy! Buy! Don't bother to fix it. Vacuum cleaners and VCRs are disposable. Just buy a new one!

Unlike little Wells, Maine, which is ahead of its time with its state of the art trash distribution center, people in Mesa don't even recycle yet! All of our trash is dumped into a huge landfill right on the bank of the Salt River. A few years back it rained for seventeen days in a row and the river washed out parts of the landfill. Trash bobbed in the water all the way to the Baja. People wonder if trash will ever deteriorate in the desert climate. No one knows!

As I made my way into the right lane and slowed, I recalled that it was my father who had started me thinking about waste in America. I remembered him always saying that in the "old country" even land along the railroad tracks was put to good use but in Montana there was too much of it. People did not appreciate what they had.

Reeling in my thoughts and memories, I took the Northern Avenue exit, then made a right onto 7th and eventually a left at Hatcher and 3rd. I pulled into the parking lot of the large medical office building across the street from Lincoln C. Hospital in Glendale, the suburb north of Phoenix.

Every week, since John has no longer wanted me to ride with him, I thought, I have driven these same 65 miles round trip and every time I am reminded that Prolastin and all the other medical advances are part and parcel of the same aggressively consuming society that I was just muttering about. How can I complain about so much and benefit from every aspect at the same time?

Truth is I am a square peg in a round hole in terms of culture, religion, and social norms. Ever since my adolescence dawned, I have felt that things do not fit together for me very well. Do they for others?

Only one poke, one hour, the infusion went smoothly. On the

way back home the Fiesta Mall shoppers were backed up for miles causing bumper to bumper delays on the Superstition. I noted with some degree of irritation that Sophia and I would have to allow more time going the other way to the airport in a few hours.

Traveling during the holidays is demanding enough, I remember thinking as I inched Le B along, *and being ambivalent about the season and about going makes it so much harder.*

I always think it's great to be with family. I inevitably feel a special energy and excitement but that same energy and excitement usually stirs up a lot of painful stuff, feelings and memories I mean.

At one fifteen when I finally exited onto the Higley Street ramp and turned left, I remembered a Christmas time at Steve and Pat's house when they still lived on 188th in Shoreline. I had just dissolved into sobs for no apparent reason. I was as shocked about it as everyone else.

I waited at Southern Avenue for the red light to turn and recalled another incident when I was thirteen years old. I remembered exploding and deliberately giving my feelings, my anger, a voice.

"Dishes! I always have to do them! Why always me? I'm sick of it! And, I'm sick of you always..."

Like the cantankerous heifer that would break through barbed wire fencing to get to greener grass, I had broken through Mom's controlling rules. I paid for it dearly, too. Mom gasped, looked scared and took a step backwards before making the unforgettable accusation.

"You have a look in your eyes that I have not seen in the others. There must be something wrong with you. You be careful! You are going against the Holy Spirit!"

It said in the Bible somewhere, of course I had looked it up and found it, that there was no forgiveness for going against the Holy Spirit. That ecclesiastical barbed wire indictment that Mom put on me that day tore a hole in my psychological fabric and the healing of that hole, I don't mind saying, left a sensitive scar.

I have a scar about that incident, I thought, as I turned left off Higley onto U street of Sunlife, *like Figgy has her scar on her back from, Fred that mean, neighborhood bully of a tomcat that the Stanley's had.*

There must be some nerve endings in the scar tissue that get irritated because every now and then Figgy goes for her back with her teeth like she just wants to tear that scar out of her back.

78

I pulled into the carport of F-66, shut down the engine and gathered my things. *Figgy had to wear a lamp shade collar for the longest time,* I remembered, *and cantankerous heifers used to get a three to four-foot pole or two-by-four tied to their necks to keep them from going through fences.* "Now, I'm tethered to this plastic rope," I muttered aloud, as I pulled my tubing free from where it had caught under the seat.

I walked up the three steps to the trailer and could not help but see the flashback of the little children coming up the steps towards me. *Oh, God, if only life could stay that innocent.*

It really would be best to go into the next couple of weeks not wanting to tear the scars out of my psyche. I should hold on to the gifts of those little girls and of Prolastin as if you, Great Spirit, in your infinite wisdom, have sent them especially for me. That might quiet these touchy nerves. But, like a white Christmas in Mesa, it ain't gonna happen, my mind burbled on. *I know myself better than that. Doubting Thomas, you say? Yes, that would be me.*

I stepped into the cramped living room and saw Sophia and the readied suitcases.

"What took you so long?" she asked.

Chapter 9
Anil's Meditation

When I would ask my brother details about the past he often said, "That is so long ago and so much has happened. I can't remember that far back."

U pon Anil's arrival at the clinic in Seattle on that Monday morning, December 23rd, he learned that Mike was a no-show. It could mean a number of things but it was not productive to speculate. That is how it went with these kinds of kids. They would disappear back into the woodwork from which they had come. Some would disappear forever. Others would limp along propped up by various institutions and most others, with a few years of maturity, would emerge to become functioning adults. It was probable he would never know which would be Michael's fate.

Anil had a free hour. He could go for a swim, he could work on the clinic web site on the Internet or he could take an hour for reading and meditation. He chose the later. From the bookshelf he took his well read book of meditations entitled, *The Book of Life: Daily Meditations with Krishnamurti.*

Krishnamurti, Anil recalled, *said, "Why do you want to be students of books instead of students of life? Find out what is true and false in your environment with all its oppressions and its cruelties, and then you will find out what is true ... The story of mankind is in you, the vast experience the deep rooted fears, anxieties, sorrow, pleasure and all the beliefs that man has accumulated throughout the millennia. You are that book (Krishnamurti vii)."*

It was December 23rd and the entry for that day was "Meditation" but Anil's eye strayed across the page to the entry of the next day and so he read:

Sweeping Away the Sand

Know the Whole Content of One Thought

Not being anything is the beginning of freedom. So if you are capable of feeling, of going into this you will find, as you become aware, that you are not free, that you are bound to very many different things, and that at the same time the mind hopes to be free. And you can see that the two are contradictory. So the mind has to investigate why it clings to anything. All this implies hard work. It is much more arduous than going to an office, than any physical labor, than all the sciences put together. Because the humble, intelligent mind is concerned with itself without being self-centered; therefore it has to be extraordinarily alert, aware, and that means real hard work every day, every hour, every minute ... This demands insistent work because freedom does not come easily. Everything impedes—your wife, your husband, your son, your neighbor, your Gods, your religions, your tradition. All these impede you, but you have created them because you want security. And the mind that is seeking security can never find it. If you have watched a little in the world, you know there is no such thing as security. The wife dies, the husband dies, the son runs away, something happens. Life is not static though we would like to make it so. No relationship is static because all life is movement. That is a thing to be grasped, the truth is to be seen, felt, not something to be argued about. Then you will see, as you begin to investigate, that it is really a process of meditation.

But do not be mesmerized by that word. To be aware of every thought, to know from what source it springs and what is its intention that is meditation. And to know the whole content of one thought reveals the whole process of mind.

Anil straightened himself, took several deep breaths, closed his eyes and began his meditation. Gradually his thoughts like waves settled down into the ocean of thought and the ocean grew calmer with each breath in and out. Soon his mind and body achieved the same level of relaxation.

In the verdant oasis of Anil's youth, along with lush varieties of vegetation, grew nearly as many varieties of beliefs. They were symbolized in his environment by the many differing architectural structures of temples, churches, mosques, monasteries and synagogues.

India has for 3,800 years been a nation of great evolving spirituality. As far back as one can know, there had been an ancient, surprisingly advanced, agricultural and trading culture in India known as the Indus Valley Civilization. Around 1500 B.C.E. Aryans, who were early or prehistoric speakers of the Indo-European language—not who were a race or descendants of a common ancestor (if Aryan Race is used for example, as it was by the Nazi's, it is incorrect and used strictly as a political term), began to extend out from Europe to the east and south. One of the warrior branches migrated through Russia, entered Asia and crossed the Himalaya Mountains into India. Once settled in India they quickly propagated their structure and religion on the many diverse indigenous tribes of India; however, unlike what so often happens with an occupation, the Aryan ways did not wipe out the previously existing civilization and cultural heritage of the indigenous tribes. Instead, reconciliation between utterly different religious practices resulted in an amalgamated, inclusive, adaptable faith. (Interestingly, the much heralded Greek culture and the vast Greek pantheon of gods also developed from a synthesis of Aryan civilization with that of the Aegean and Minoan peoples.)

Sindu (Indus) is the Sanskrit name of a river in northern India. The people from that area came to be known as the Hindus and thus the name of the adapted religion as Hinduism. Hinduism is regarded as having existed forever; it has no identified founder and evolves with time. Titles for gods such as *Brahma, Vishnu, Shiva,* (these three main gods are considered the trinity) *Durga, Ganesh and Hanuman* would lead one to think that Hinduism is polytheistic. Yet, all the gods are believed to be the many attributes of a single supreme power which created and organized a constantly changing universe.

The soul or *atman* is believed to long to experience and rejoin the creator. To do so, it must free itself from the physical body through a series of reincarnations. The soul's progress depends on *karma* or the weight of a person's good or faulty actions. Salvation is reached by following a course of action in which each action is offered as a sacrifice to God. Ultimately then, it is believed, the soul will be freed from the cycle of reincarnation.

Sacred Hindu hymns or texts evolving as the *Vedas,* the *Upanishads,* and the *Bhagavad-Gita* state that humanity was created from an entity called the *Purusa,* whose body was torn apart by the gods. His mouth became the *Brahman* or priests, the highest group. His arms became the *Kshatriya,* the warriors, his thighs the *Vaisya,* who are the artisans and merchants, and his feet the *Shudra* who are the servants. By setting up the caste system as their social structure, the people believed they were reproducing the divine order of life.

Approximately a thousand years later an Indian prince, Siddhartha Gautama, became profoundly disturbed by all the poverty and suffering that he saw around him and decided to search for the meaning of existence. He became a religious beggar and one day sat under a tree resolving not to move until he had solved the mystery. He came up with four noble truths: all of life is suffering, the cause of suffering is desire, the end of desire leads to the end of suffering and the means to end desire is a path of discipline and meditation. Siddhartha came to be known as the enlightened one or the Buddha. The path following these truths spread through parts of India and became known as Buddhism.

Indian trade with the Middle East brought early contact with monotheism and Judaism. Some accounts in Kerala, as a matter of interest, relate that King Solomon's court received spices, ivory and peacocks from India. Also, settlers from Israel, it is thought, may have fled from Jerusalem by sailing down the Red Sea and across the Arabian Sea to the east to India settling on its southern shores.

From these exchanges the people of India learned about Abraham, the Semite, his descendants and a belief in a single God whom they called *Yahweh.* It was believed that *Yahweh* had made a direct covenant with Abraham, blessed his nation and bestowed laws through revelations. In the Jewish tradition there are two written accounts of such revelations from *Yahweh.* There is the law including the Ten Commandments which are in the five books of Moses kept on a scroll called the *Torah* and the commentaries are called the *Talmud.*

Sometime after, the Indians learned about a tiny sect in first-century Palestine and about another new religion that was emerging in that area. In fact, there are actually records of a Thomas, an early apostle of this new religion, having been in the state of Kerala and bringing with him stories of the life of a Jesus. Some of its followers believed that this Jesus was not only a prophet but the hoped-for "Messiah" sent by the Father God, *Yahweh*. This "Messiah", the Christ, the light, the "anointed one" had come to bring salvation to the entire depraved human race. Members of the devout group in the second century composed five gospels of these stories which followers believed had been directly inspired by their God. These are contained in the book called the *Bible*, in the New Testament. Members of this new religion came to be called Christians. They wrote and preached that the Christ had risen from the dead and ascended into heaven to take his place in the divine trinity, God the Father, the Son and the Holy Spirit. Believers promise heaven for those who confess their wrongdoing, ask for forgiveness and believe in their salvation through Jesus. Christianity over the years spread into and was particularly embraced by the peoples of Europe.

In the 1500s Moguls from central Asia, known as ancient Persia or modern Iran, invaded India. The Moguls brought yet another religion to the Indian peoples known as Islam. Islam means submission to God, and adherents to Islam worship the same single God of the Jews or Judaism. Instead of *Yahweh*, they call this God *Allah*. The Prophet Mohammed received and recorded his revelations from *Allah* in the book known as the *Quran*. He accepted the prophetic roles of Abraham, Moses and Jesus and added his Five Pillars: reciting the profession of faith, praying five times a day, giving alms to the poor, fasting and abstaining from dawn to dusk for the month of Ramadan and making a pilgrimage to Mecca at least once during one's life if possible.

Attempting to encompass all the traditions and faiths present in India, Sikhism began. Sikhs were inclusive—they still are—and as such are unusual. They even believe in the equality of men and women which the others do not.

For centuries the Portugese, the Dutch, the French, the British, and the Moguls fought for superiority in India. All were trying to corner the lucrative European spice trade. In the mid 1600s the

British joined with Indian tribes to get the upper hand and to remove the Moguls from power. They were successful. However, the religion of Islam stayed in the hearts and minds of many of the Indian people and the British stayed to rule.

So it came to be at the start of the twentieth century that the people of India were a melting pot of religions and politics. Post World War I embitterment over inequality of the Brits and *natives*— as the Brits referred to the Indians—however, soon sparked revolutionary actions from Sikhs and Muslims, and the Amritsar massacre in which British soldiers fired on unarmed men, women and children turned millions more into anti-British revolutionaries. The next year, in 1920, Mahatma Gandhi launched his *satyagraha* (clinging to the truth) campaign and by 1947 India became once again a self-governing country. Today they are the world's largest democracy.

Krishnamurti in this setting had been born in the city of Madras and educated abroad. In England he became a member of the Order of the Star which incorporated aspects of Buddhism and Hinduism and emphasized the mystical nature of the divine. He later defected from this group and began teaching and advocating a way of life and thought unconditioned by the narrowness of nationality, race and religion.

Anil discovered the work of Theosophy and Krishnamurti in London. And, "...the story of mankind ... all the beliefs that man has accumulated throughout the millennia" swirled in his blood. He sat in meditation in hopes of building from all that intellectual and inspired knowledge a limitless and timeless perception.

The free period passed quickly. He resumed normal sensations with several deep breaths, movements of his hands and feet and opened his eyes. Having for a short hour thrown off the heavy yoke of theological and political history, he felt lighter and brighter. He stood, stretched and went to meet his next client. At the reception desk the secretary handed him a pink slip message. He stopped to read: "Mike taken to Emergency Room. Attempted suicide? Maybe overdose? Caller would not give name."

Chapter 10
Homemade Pan of Soup

No matter what has happened in my life, I can remember things "that far back" as if they happened yesterday.

"Hi!" "Merry Christmas!" "I'm so glad you made it!" "Merry Christmas! Welcome to the party!" "Hello, everybody!" Those in the Cok family room swarmed to greet Sophia and me as we entered from the garage entryway.

"Your lights look great driving up! The whole hill is lit up! It's great! That train a couple houses down is amazing," chortled Sophia happily.

"When did you guys get here?" she asked of Marge as the two hugged.

The Langels had arrived early that afternoon, Marge replied. They had stayed in Missoula part of Friday and Saturday to do some shopping so they had been later than expected. Their motor home was situated in the driveway in front of the third bay of the three-car garage. It would continue to be their living quarters.

Steven, Doug and Brandon had been hanging out at Seattle's Flight Museum for the afternoon before going to SeaTac Airport to get Sophia and me at about half past six. After work, downtown Seattle traffic had been heavy; it was now half past eight Monday evening.

"How was your flight?" inquired Pat as our cluster moved to the right into the kitchen and then shifted to clear a path through which Steven could pass with the suitcases.

"I had a really bad headache," I reported as I sat down on one of the high-backed wooden chairs around the table. "It was too soon after my infusion, I think."

"You were probably dehydrated," surmised Sophia. "You know that airplanes are terribly dehydrating."

"I know. It feels better now. I had two ginger ales and water on the plane," I said, happy to relax at last.

"This woman," Sophia began, "took us in an electrical cart from the gate to an area not far from an escalator and told us that someone with a wheelchair would be right there. Nobody ever came! It was so crazy. Then all of a sudden there was B.J. with the portable oxygen and we decided to go without the wheelchair. It's a good thing we didn't give her a tip!"

"You could have given it to me, Sophia," interjected Brandon standing closely next to her to compare his height with hers.

"Did you like the museum, B.J.?" asked Pat as she lifted the lid of the pan simmering on the stove.

"It was all right," answered Brandon none to enthusiastically.

"Come on you guys. The soup is hot. The rest of us have eaten already," announced Pat.

"Tonight you'll eat in the kitchen but from then on we'll have all the meals in the dining room, okay? I think that will help to keep people out of this congested area," Pat directed.

Unrehearsed gaps in life frighten Pat and she works hard to keep chaos at a minimum. In the family her tendencies are put to good use. Though often drawing heavily on the supporting cast, she is, without a doubt, the time-honored chairwoman of family logistics.

The guys and Sophia joined me and seated themselves around the kitchen table. Ann pulled up an empty chair as well. Marge helped Pat serve the soup.

It has become a tradition in the family to have a big pan of homemade soup ready for weary travelers. It is always either a chicken rice and vermicelli soup or beef meatball and vegetable tomato soup. This evening it was the chicken soup. It was usually served, as it was that Monday night, December 23rd, with bread and cheese, and a dish of canned peaches for dessert.

"You look in pretty good shape, Lottie," Pat said to me as she took a bit of a rest while we ate.

"You know what she did once, Sophia?" Pat asked. "She came home for Christmas one year and she was so skinny. She said, 'Oh, don't worry. I haven't eaten very much lately. I bet I'll gain 10 pounds in just a few days.' So, I bet her that she couldn't do that and, by gummy, she did! I had to buy her a $50 pair of boots. That was the bet. I couldn't believe it!"

"I can believe it," responded Sophia. "Tjaakje doesn't bet unless it's a sure thing."

Hanging on the wall behind the kitchen table, I noticed, was a large ceramic representation of the front of a typical Seattle apartment building. It was several stories high. Each small apartment was in some way decorated with a miniature Christmas decoration. It was so like Pat to have something like that on her wall.

She had poured her creative talents into ceramics for a number of years when her girls were younger. She never had a kiln of her own but did her own firing at a ceramic shop. Twelve-inch statues of Swiss Peter and Heidi, a couple of her favorite characters from the <u>Heidi</u> books, were on the family room mantel. Above the fireplace on the Heidema dairy in Montana where Leland and Lisa, John and Joyce's son and daughter-in-law, live with their four children hangs one of Pat's complex ceramic facades of an old-time barn. It has a truck parked in an open garage, a cart and milk cans in front of it, trees to the side, a silo and a windmill coming from behind. There is even light coming from the inside of the building. The detailed painting was perfectly done.

"How is John?" asked Ann of me.

"John is John," I answered tartly. Actually, I realized, a bit more tartly than I had intended.

"What is that, Lottie?" asked Ann puzzled by my offhand remark.

"He's all right. He was riding his scooter and that means he was feeling pretty good," I reassured her, knowing that the earlier remark had make its point with the other adults in the room.

Others knew what John being John meant these days. It meant distance. We all worried about him and hoped that he was feeling good, but we were held at arm's length and didn't know whether to blame him or ourselves for it. Mom blamed his medicine.

"What were your roads like for you guys?" I asked, addressing Doug and changing the subject.

"Not too bad. Just a couple of bad spots," he answered, handing B.J. a knife. B.J. licked the butter from his index finger and took the knife. "Pretty cold," said Doug.

"Oh, no!" I gasped suddenly, covering my mouth with my hand.

"What?" asked several voices in unison startled by the sudden note of despair in my voice. "What is it?"

A person using oxygen probably should know better than to shock a group like that without cause. I forget about it sometimes.

"We forgot the Drostes!" I groaned.

"And the pillow of miniature marshmallows? We had it all ready to go. Oh, Tjaakje, how could you?" accused Sophia.

"What do you mean, how could I? I wasn't the only one packing," I countered defensively.

"What is a Drostes?" asked Ann.

"Hot chocolate, I think." answered Marge.

"Thank goodness," said Pat. "I thought it was something serious."

"Sophia bought this huge bag of marshmallows that looked like a pillow. Shucks! We had it all ready to go."

"I did bring the foot soaks," Sophia volunteered, "and I am going to give everybody a foot massage."

"And I will give everybody a shoulder massage," joined in Brandon. "Are we going to make coupons for everybody's stocking like we did before, Sophia?"

"We'll see,"

"So where are we all going to sleep?" continued Sophia who was exhausted.

Sophia had not had her nap. Her muscles had stiffened from sitting during the two hour flight and the nearly hour-long car ride from the airport. Daily physical exercise, low stress and a nap being vital for her to keep the wolf at bay, this day had been a bust in all areas.

Lupus is the Latin word for wolf. And as the wolf is ravenous and unleashes his fury on live prey, so the disease lupus can similarly flare when the body is vulnerable. Sophia always has a certain amount of muscular soreness, weakness and fatigue but by maintaining a vigil, also like the wolf, she has learned to endure, be courageous and to survive. Her flare-ups over the years have become less and less frequent.

I lay down for a nap every day, too. Our prescriptions for an extension on life are really the same and when the two of us are in sync, the efforts of one inspire the other. To recoup from this trying day and the hectic days preceding it, we needed to rest and get into a better rhythm. It wouldn't be easy with a busy schedule ahead.

"Well, you, Sophia, are going to be on a pullout in my sewing room upstairs at the end of the hallway to the left," Pat dictated. "It's a small room next to Mom's room. Lottie, we put you in our bedroom. We are going to sleep down here in the family room on the couch."

"Really? How come Mom isn't in the sewing room and Soph and me in Sandi's room? Then you could have your own room," I asked feeling guilty about my good fortune.

"Oh, why, Pat?" Ann chimed in. "Shall I sleep here on the couch? You two should stay in your room!"

Neither of us argued our case strongly and the arrangements went forth as planned. It was agreed everyone would turn in early since Pat had to work for a half day in the morning.

"I'm sorry, Langels, but you won't be able to watch TV into the night," said Pat tersely. It was true, when school hours did not determine the schedule, and even then sometimes, the Langels enjoyed being late sleepers and late risers.

"Why, Aunt Pat?" asked Brandon. He had been talking with me and had only heard the last words.

"We have a TV in the motor home. That won't be a problem," offered Marge.

"I think they should just close our office on Christmas Eve Day," Pat protested. "No mother wants to come in with a kid for anything routine. But can you believe it? We actually have two physicals scheduled for the morning. All right, does everybody know what's going to happen this week?"

"Not really," said Marge.

"You either? Me either," said Ann reaching over to put her hand on Marge's.

"Tomorrow, Sophia and Tjaakje will unpack and then Sophia will go with Steven to buy groceries for the Christmas dinner. I thought we'd order a pizza for supper. Arlyce and Arun will probably visit. The guys can go to the Science Center for half of the day if they want."

"There's a good movie on television tomorrow night," I

interjected. "We've been seeing it advertised. It's 'The Christmas Box' with John Boy Walton in it. I think it's a Hallmark movie. That might be nice to all watch after the pizza."

"Here is the overall plan," followed Pat. "On Christmas Day we will have a big meal in the early afternoon during Arun's nap. Arlyce and Anil will be here but we won't open the gifts until Saturday when Sandi can be with us. She would like us to wait. She can get away on Thursday but not before. So, on Saturday we'll have another big meal in the late afternoon or evening for her sake and then we'll open the gifts. How does that sound? Is that okay with everybody?"

"Sounds good, Pat, thanks. I have to go to bed now. My head is full of *phoo-iz-ee*," Sophia said as she decisively pushed back from the table. She had reached the end of her day's rope.

"*Phoo-iz-ee!* What is *phoo-iz-ee?*" laughed B.J. standing by Sophia's side and pressing against her.

"It's noise in my ears from flying." Sophia wrapped her arm around B.J.'s waist.

"What kind of a word is that?"

"It's Greek. *Tha peso amesos. Poo ine i tooaleta?*" Sophia rattled off quickly.

"*Ja*, it's Greek to me too," chimed in Ann.

"What did you say? What did you say?" persisted Brandon.

A prepubescent boy steeped in television and computers, Brandon was on the brink of understanding almost everything about everything. There were precious few years left in which he could still be enjoyably teased about what he didn't know.

"I said, you are pressing against my divine left and it hurts!" Sophia stood up and started collecting her dishes. All but B.J. laughed heartily.

"Your what?" urged Brandon not at all sure of what he had just heard.

"Oooo, rigor mortis is setting in!" complained Sophia as she extricated herself from B.J. and took some stiff legged steps. "I have to go to bed, good night everybody."

As Sophia disappeared into the hallway to the stairs, Steve and Doug headed for the newspaper and television in the family room. Steve sank gratefully into his recliner and elevated his tired and aching knees. Doug, always relieved to end a situation in which there were a number of conversations going on at once, took the couch. I scraped and stacked dishes where I was sitting. Marge brought them to the counter and Pat put them into the dishwasher. Ann sat by watching us three daughters.

"I guess we will all go to bed then," said Ann reluctantly. She would have liked to prolong the evening, stay up to play a few games of tile rummy but the young people were tired. She was a little bit tired too. Maybe it would be better.

"I'm going up too," I said. *"Wel to rusten* (good night), everybody."

Mom came over to kiss me.

"Good night, dear, I am so glad that we are all here and that you made it safely."

"Me too!" I said emphatically and then headed for the hallway.

In the front entryway I removed the micro-nasal cannula that I use in public from around my ears and disconnected it from the portable oxygen tank. I removed a regular, quieter, but larger and more noticeable, cannula from its wrapping, put the prongs up to my nose, brought the two sides over my ears and then down under my chin and connected it to the 50 feet of tubing that was attached to the 100 pound reservoir of liquid oxygen. That finished, I started slowly up the stairs.

When I approached the landing at the top of the stairs I paused to catch my breath and looked up at the collection of pictures on the wall. Specifically, I looked at our father in his twill, charcoal-colored Sunday suit, white shirt and red, white and navy tie.

I see him six-foot-four inches tall, dark brown, short, straight hair parted on the right side and combed to the side, circular bald spot on the crown of his head and thinning in the front, large ears, narrow set, intense, brown eyes—that I fondly recall held a twinkle when teasing—a tight little smile, clean-shaven, large hands and feet, handsome enough and lean; I remember him best, though, back on the farm near Manhattan in the Gallatin Valley of Montana. There *Pa* wore his denim bib overalls, faded, olive-colored shirt with sleeves rolled up to the elbows and the old sweat-stained, felt hat. Memories of him and my relation to him, are like intertwined strands of DNA and RNA, that spiral through every fiber of my being.

He would start out with clean clothes on Monday morning but every week the overalls would get filthy with grease and dirt. He had two pairs, I remember. If he had to make a trip into Manhattan or Bozeman or someone was expected to come to the farm, Mom would make him put on the cleaner pair.

Though Dad scrubbed his hands often and vigorously with the rough Lava soap and a firm brush in the back porch he had a hard time getting his fingernails clean. Grease from working on machinery and dirt was usually ground into his cuticles. I remember the feel of his big, thick, calloused hands. It was not often that I felt those hands and more often than not it was only when he wanted me to move out of the way or show me how to do something. He was, after all, not a man who was openly affectionate with me after a certain age but for whatever reason he touched me, I welcomed it.

Without the hat his bald spot and forehead were pale; in contrast, the rest of his sharply-featured face was deeply sun-tanned and his hands and forearms were a dark reddish-brown. I can easily visualize him, sleeves rolled up, standing in one of the fields in late spring, when the green grain crop was no more than six inches high, under the big blue sky of Montana surveying the subtle elevations and low lying areas with his naked eye and plotting where to dig the ditches for the flood irrigation. He was a thinker a lot of the time.

His body under the clothes was buttermilk white. He looked weird in the swimming pool the time or two we would go to Bozeman Hot Springs after haying the alfalfa or combining the grain in the summers. But so did all the other Dutch farmers look weird who happened to be there on those Saturday nights.

He preferred his corn flakes soggy but without a lot of milk. With one elbow on the table he would lean close to his full bowl, start on one side and eat his way across. He would scoop the soggy spoonfuls methodically into his mouth one after another and then wipe his mouth with his fist.

Like most men from Holland he liked a lot of sugar in his tea, not quite as much in his coffee; and cream in his coffee, not his tea. If he was in a hurry he would pour portions of the steaming hot beverage into his saucer where it cooled more quickly, raise the saucer to his lips and noisily empty it.

He prayed aloud in Dutch before any of us could eat and, without fail, after the meal he read aloud from the Dutch Bible at noon and the *Groot Vertelboek Voor De Bijbelse Geschiedenis,* the oversized white, black and yellow children's Bible storybook in the evening. I loved the poetic sounding words that rolled so effortlessly from his mouth: *goedertierenheid* (mercifulness), *trouwhartig (faithful)*, *onze lieve Heer* (our dear Lord), *geschiedenis* (story), *schuilplaats de Almachtig* (hiding place of the Almighty), *beschikker* (disposer) and so many, many more.

For the most part I did not know the meaning of the words and saw instead colorful unrelated images of their literal translations in my mind. For instance, *trouhartig,* became a trusting deer; *Beschikker,* a lime-green frog. It didn't matter that I didn't know the specifics; I just liked hearing him read out loud.

When he finished reading, Mom, usually with sweat on her brow, wisps of hair flying loose from its roll at the temples, and print apron encircling most of her body, would nudge one or two of us kids to stop nibbling, to fold our hands and to close our eyes. Then with all our heads bowed and hands tightly clasped he prayed aloud again, always in Dutch.

Sometimes on Sundays, when Al and Pieka would come for coffee, Dad and Al would wrestle good-naturedly, but seriously too, on the lawn. They would act like a couple of young guys for a few minutes, their wives fussing and worrying but also laughing.

I remember riding to the Bozeman Livestock Auction with him. The stanchions would have been put on the truck and the cattle in the back would struggle to keep their footing as the old Chevrolet truck lurched forward or swung abruptly to one side. I loved, still do, the hypnotizing tempo of the auctioneer's delivery. Hours would go by and I never tired of it. I could tell from the body language and the energy level of my father and the men sitting around in the uncomfortable seats if the prices were hopping or sluggish that day. If they were good, maybe as much as 24 cents per pound, *Pa* and I would go to Snappy Service for a greasy hamburger and a piece of cherry pie afterwards. That was the best. If the prices were bad we would go right home without much of anything being said.

In the evenings he liked to smoke his cigarettes and read from the Dutch newspaper in his easy chair in the living room. I remember sitting perched on one arm of the easy chair with John on the other while *Pa* read aloud the cartoon strip of the adventuresome but not so smart *Van Bergen.* There were also the little books: *De avonturen van Van Bergen. V.B. gaat op jacht, V.B. gaat uit vissen* and *V.B. krijgt een fiets (V.B.* goes hunting, goes out fishing and gets a bicycle). *Van Bergen* was like the migrant Mexicans who came to work on the farm in the summertime. Mustachioed, with gleaming white teeth and laughter, Jesus and Alois drove the tractor through the barbed wire fence and right into the ditch. After a while in the evenings dad would fall asleep in the chair, sometimes nodding and fighting it, sometimes snoring outright. He would have to wake up for us to kiss him good night.

Some evenings in the wintertime he and Mom would practice skits to do on a stage in front of guests at weddings: *"Vitzen Leirn"* (learning how to ride a bicycle). Mom in an old ladies' crocheted, black head scarf wobbling on a two wheeled bicycle with Dad hanging on for dear life. The other one, I can't remember the name in Dutch but it meant pants too short. In the skit Dad had to stand on a chair with trousers up to mid calf and red flannel underwear to his ankles. And the short play where the husbands wanted the wives to call them *"Tuddebekje"* (something like sweetie pie)." My parents were very funny and they were fearless. As bumbling immigrants they were making fun of themselves and of people in general. That is typical Dutch humor. They always had the audiences in stitches.

I hold one particular memory in my heart like it is my one and only precious jewel. It was of a night before bedtime that I went with *Pa* to check on the sows who were giving birth in the far-away pig barn. He was wearing his worn, heavily lined, hip-length, button-up, denim jacket with the huge pockets and his old felt hat. The yard light didn't reach past the railings by the cow barn but we could see with the moonlight reflecting from the snow. As we stepped over frozen chunks of cow manure with my hand in his big one, I could make out the dark forms of pigs or cows off to our side and the stars overhead.

There was magic in the air as we stepped into the pig barn. The heating lamps in one corner of each sow's wooden pen let off a cozy, warm, reddish-yellow light like so many tiny, friendly, little gas-fed fireplaces. There was the metallic smell of blood and birth, and oats mixed with soured milk. The airy space reverberated with sounds of contented sows rhythmically grunting and piglets noisily nursing. The little, pink creatures squealed and oinked vying for position.

Father and daughter as one, we approached each pen very quietly. In a couple of pens the piglets were heaped in a pile under the warm lamp and the sow was fast asleep on a bed of clean straw a few feet away.

There had been times when the situation was not so tranquil. I had seen piglets flattened and stone cold-dead from having been accidentally laid on by a tired, heavy sow. A birthing sow, too, can be dangerously feverish, and inexperienced sows, in the rage of the fever, can kill some of their own piglets. I once witnessed a young sow angrily toss a newborn piglet across the pen with its drooling mouth. Then, when the instincts brought the piglet back to its mother's nose, I watched the crazed sow rise up on her front hoofs, snap her drooling, jagged-toothed jaws around, and with one bite cut the newborn in half.

Pa always had to work very hard to keep the young away from that type of sow. I would stand by, helpless—the deadly fangs could clamp down on his arm as easily as a piglet. I feared for his very life. During those times the sounds were deeply disturbing to me and to the other sows. They became irritable and restless, the piglets noisy and demanding, and the human heart racing and hurting from too much adrenaline.

Dad, too, could be impatient and rough as if in a fever. There were too many demands on his time and strength. His mind stretched too far too long to grasp the business and language of America and of farming on a large scale. He had dark, brooding moods sometimes and he could be sullenly silent and stern for days.

But that night, the night that is my dearest jewel, there was a palpable spirit of tranquility and accord in the barn and in my father's heart. That night he leaned his hands on the top rail of the enclosures and just soaked up the contentment. I can still see the soft, warm light reflected off his angular, bronzed and peaceful face. He spoke tenderly to some of the old, veteran sows and reassuringly to the new. He spoke softly to me that it was time to go back to the house. He took my hand again after he had closed the door.

"I'm so glad you're here, Tjaakje!" B.J. bubbled as he came up the stairs behind me and stood on the same tread with me. He wrapped his arms around my waist.

"So am I, Beej. It's so good to see you again," I confirmed as I held on to him and the two of us made our way up the remaining few stairs as if we were Siamese twins.

"I love you," Beej said.

"I love you too, Beej, very much," I responded.

Chapter Eleven
Doc Sandi's Errands on Christmas Eve

Remembering and forgetting, like seeing and hearing, I think, are complicated processes. Reasons for each can be as much political as personal.

With its last breath the dog's small chest expanded fully, deflated slowly and then was perfectly still. My niece, the self-respecting, strongly built, tall, handsome young woman standing by her side, saw the pulse of the heart flutter for a few more seconds and then nothing more.

"That's all, Gretchen, that's all," she murmured.

Doc Sandi, as she is known around town, or "Handi Dandi Dr. Sandi", which is on her designer license plate, stroked and smoothed the dog's sleek head and silky ears one last time.

"We gave it a good try, didn't we, girl?"

Then she reluctantly yet resolutely turned away and stripped off her tight-fitting latex gloves.

Sandra Cok, second daughter of Steven and Pat, had first witnessed and performed the euthanasia of an animal as a student at the College of Veterinary Medicine at Washington State University (WSU) in Pullman, Washington. At first she had been awed and shaken by the responsibility. It was so irrefutably final! To do it, a person had to give up the thinking of possibilities and solutions and just call it quits. Not an easy thing to do when you have a sharp mind that loves to solve a puzzle and win at cards like Sandi does. She thrives on the challenge of making the differential diagnosis from a complex set of test results and observation of symptoms, not on putting an animal to sleep.

Sandi, as a young woman, had been clear about wanting to work with animals, but unclear about just how to do it. Should she pursue care of sick animals or get into the field of training animals? I remember that she toyed with the idea of training dogs for the blind for a while. She would have been good at it. As a kid, she taught Benji, the family's devoted little cocker terrier mix, to do tricks and, a lot like her father—always thinking, always perfecting—Sandi even practiced her foreign language requirement while playing with Benji. She gave her commands to him in the polite German form: *Sitzen sie, Legen sie, Bleiben sie, Kommen sie and Sprechen sie?*

With a mind like hers, however, she needed to pursue something more difficult, something more worthy of her God-given talents or so her parents had thought at least, and, in the long run, so had Sandra.

After ten years in the business, she is very good at working with dogs and cats. Maybe someday, off in the future, she might try another area of specialty like marine mammals, she says. She had that as a dream too and really enjoyed the student clinical placement at Sea World in San Diego, California. But, for now, she is content where she is.

Experience has taught Doc Sandi to be toughly realistic. No more squeamish or conflicted hesitance as she handles the mundane and the extreme in the practice. Hand-in-glove with experience and realism has been the challenge of incorporating advances in veterinary science and technology. Treatment of pets keeps pace with that of humans and the clinic works in tandem with the university to incorporate the latest.

A certain percentage of owners bear the expense of going the extra mile. For instance, more and more owners are willing to take their "disc dog" over to the University for magnetic resonance imaging (MRI); in fact, the machine at the vet school is better than the one at the human hospital; so the people from Yakima go to the vet school too! The "disc dog", also like a person, gets surgical disc fenestration or laminectomy. One owner had three back surgeries done on her dog at WSU. The dog would become paralyzed and then respond time and again to the surgery. Sandi has sent over dogs for total hip replacements, heart valve replacements and pace maker implantation. She has dogs that have hemi-madibulectomies or hemimaxillectomies (half of the jaws removed). Cost on such interventions can run $1,500 to $3,000.

She had an owner that had three rottweilers. The first dog, Scud, had a bicipital tendon transfer plus a ruptured cranial cruciate repair done at two separate times at WSU. The second dog, Tank, had a total hip replacement. The third dog, Sassy, had at least five surgeries on her hock for an OCD lesion, fracture repair and the last two to try to fuse the joint because the fracture would not heal. So that was at least eight orthopedic surgeries!

She has cats that get radiation treatment over a several-month period for thoracic masses. One cat was followed up with a surgical thoracic exploratory. She has cats that receive radiation for facial squamous cell carcinomas.

Many owners give multiple medications and injections of insulin daily. Some use bottled water, cook special foods and build special carts for paralyzed dogs. Some will not go on vacation because they do not want to leave their pet. Some take them along everywhere they go.

More often than not, however, expenses to the owner determine the amount of treatment a pet receives. That is a fact of life in her line of work. Most people would not have allowed her to go as far as she had with Gretchen, the sweet little dachshund. She had so hoped for a better outcome because she really likes both the owner and her dog. Kim Kerr is one of her dedicated pet owners.

That is sadly not always the case. Some people do the perfunctory things to care for a pet but there is no bond of love. Some people have the love but no instincts for the job. Doc Sandi has little patience with either. Discipline is love; that is how she grew up. Work hard, do the right thing. What is so difficult about that?

Then there are others who abuse and neglect their animals with blatant lack of concern. Like the man she had heard about in the news who had buried his German shepherd's puppies alive in an empty lot. The mother dog had escaped from her yard, found where the puppies had been buried and dug them up in time for them still to be breathing. The authorities had charged the man with only a misdemeanor and brought the brave shepherd family to a clinic. Kinder folks had offered them their home. That had been a heartwarming ending at least. So many others were not. She had witnessed her share of cruelty and had learned not to dwell on that end of the spectrum for long.

"Okay, that's the last for me," Doc Sandi announced with great animation to the technician who was carrying the limp dog out of the room to the crematory. "I'm on call tonight and tomorrow, Christmas Eve and Christmas Day. I'm off on the day after, Thursday, and heading for Seattle on Friday morning for five days. So that means I'll see you in a week, Peggy. Have a Merry Christmas!"

"Hey, Sandi, did you sign out the sodium pentobarbital?" Peggy called back over her shoulder.

"Of course," Doc Sandi sang out.

"Okay, then, have a Merry Christmas!"

"Merry Christmas!"

Sandi did a quick check in the mirror as she washed and dried her hands, then ran her long fingers through her short, dark blonde, curly hair. Her contacts were bothering her again and her brown eyes were irritated. She wanted to take the contacts out but decided to wait. She took off the light blue smock under which she was wearing comfortable, khaki-colored chinos, a sage-colored, short-sleeved pullover and short-cuffed white socks and tennis shoes. All were recently laundered. She tossed the smock into the laundry hamper and then the confident veterinarian in her early thirties strode through the hallway out to the reception area. She looked over the few people waiting there and spotted Kim. The devoted soul was there as she had said she would be and Doc Sandi with long strides crossed the room. She lowered herself somewhat gingerly onto the hard bench feeling the painful tension in her neck and shoulders as she did so.

Like sand in an hourglass, repressed emotions, sadness, frustrations and the rest have been silently dropping there in her body for years already. It comes with the territory of being a single woman and having to bear the pressures alone. I know; I've been there. Plus, all the hours and hours she stands bent over the too-short operating table working with her hands in small spaces are taking their toll. She should swing her arms up and around vigorously like a windmill every hour or so to move the toxic build up along, but there are all sorts of shoulds in life. She just cannot get to them all. Who can?

Sweeping Away the Sand

It will be so good to have a break, she thought, *I need to rest.* She blew tired air out of her lungs. *Maybe Sophia can give me a massage.* Just thinking about it made Sandi eager to move things along.

"It's over, Kim," she said evenly, matter-of-factly.

"I gave her the injection a couple of minutes ago. I am so sorry we couldn't save her. As you know, autoimmune hemolytic anemia can be a fatal disease. We could have gone on with more therapy and other heroics but, we really don't know if that would have helped either."

"Thank you for what you did," the downcast young woman said fighting back tears. Her chin quivered uncontrollably as they both stood up. "I sure will miss her."

"I know you will," murmured Sandi compassionately.

The grief-stricken owner turned away and started for the door.

"Thank you for trying, Doc," she said once again into her tissue.

She wavered and for a second, had trouble getting hold of the door handle and then was gone.

Kim had not wanted to see Gretchen die. Some owners hold the pet while it is injected and stay in the room with their dead animal a long time, some more than an hour, and then they refuse for years afterward to ever go in the same room again with another animal. Sandi has gone to owner's trucks and homes to euthanize an animal. Some pretend not to care saying, "$60? It's just a cat!" or "She's getting old anyway." That is a popular line. But then, those people will spend fifteen minutes trying to decide how to handle it and cry when they realize it is really dead.

Purposely oblivious to the remaining people waiting with their pets (Dave, her boss who owned the clinic, had said he would pick up the last few) especially the street woman who had brought in another near-dead, young kitten, Doc Sandi walked towards the reception desk.

Why doesn't that woman get herself cleaned up and get herself a job, she thought angrily. *We can't be treating every stray she brings in here and then doesn't take care of.* Having thought it, she brushed it away and, in her eagerness to leave, she practically shouted to the receptionist.

"I'm out of here; I have errands to do and I'm hoping that the stores won't be closed yet! Have a Merry Christmas!"

One last quick stop at Dave's office to confirm her schedule

(Dave was the boss, not a partner; Sandi never wanted administrative responsibility) and Doc Sandi was out of the door and into her dark cranberry Ford Explorer, the one commonly referred to at the clinic as Doc Sandi's Eggplant Mobile. The sun was setting and it was already getting dark out.

Yakima is on the southern edge of the Columbia Basin in central Washington State. It lies east of Washington's famous mountains, Baker, Rainier and St. Helen's, as well as east of the national forests, Gifford, Pinchot, Wenatchee and Okanogan. The Yakima Indian Reservation and the Yakima Training Center skirt its boundaries and the sage desert areas in between are broken up by vast apple orchards. It is not too cold in winter, hot and dry in summer.

Here Sandi has just enough distance from her family in Seattle to give her breathing room and much needed independence. She is very close to her parents and speaks to them almost daily but any closer and she would feel smothered. As it is, she has few secrets; unlike her sister, Arlyce, Sandi is not one who breaks the rules.

The Yakima Veterinary Clinic is on Yakima Avenue about 5 miles east of her home. She drove westward down busy, brightly-lit Main Street and waved at a woman behind the wheel of a police cruiser. The officer was a friend with whom Sandi had been allowed to ride one night a while back. That had been interesting.

Sandi has a lot of acquaintances and friends around her town; she keeps herself involved. Sometimes, she can not immediately remember in what context she has met someone; there are so many. In addition to the veterinary practice, which involves connections with all the clinics in the surrounding area, she is involved in a number of community efforts. Not shy by any means—you certainly could not call a person shy who at the bidding of a flight attendant had stood up in front of a plane full of passengers on a Southwest Airlines flight and sang aloud the "Twelve Days of Christmas" without a glitch or who recited "Prinderella and the Pransome Hince" to audiences at the drop of a hat!—she is a deacon at the Summit View Christian Reformed Church and chairperson of its Activities Committee. Under her leadership it is not unusual to have church members fanned out in Yakima on "Road Rallies". Scavenger hunts really and they are looking for remote things like glo-in-the-dark Band-Aids.

A week earlier Sandi had been the producer for the play, "Cheaper By the Dozen", at the Warehouse Theater in Gilbert Park. The Warehouse Theatre is, as the name indicates, an old fruit warehouse donated by a family to the city of Yakima for the purpose of enhancing the arts. It seats 232 people. The Warehouse Theatre Company, formed in 1946, is run by a volunteer board and all plays, usually five each year, are put on by volunteers. Last year, Sandi did the light design for "Babes in Toyland". She has also done props and managed the stage crew. Not aspiring to be the chief star in the constellation, she much prefers the back stage work to acting and producing.

Every year, in addition to the church and theater work, Sandi makes a deliberate, personal sacrifice. She collects pledges and takes part in the 24-hour Relay for Life marathon to raise money for the American Cancer Society. The event takes place on the west side of town at Zaepfel Stadium, which is part of Eisenhower High School at the busy intersection of 40th Avenue and Tieton Drive. Every single year, with a sincere prayer in her heart and a magic marker in her hand, Sandi writes names, her grandfather's name, John Heidema, as a memorial, my name as a survivor and about 30 or more other names of cancer-afflicted people on separate, small, white paper sacks and puts sand and a votive candle in each. She places the sacks in line with all the other luminaries along the oval track and, at the appointed hour, lights the candles. Over 5,000 luminaries line the track and as the sun sets each name is movingly read aloud over the public address system during the special luminary ceremony.

Then she walks the laps, four laps per mile, mile after mile, through the hours of the night. She calls out encouragement to the others on the track. It is often windy and cold in the month of May, and there have been times that the sprinklers on timers have gone off. Wet walkers have had to dash around, throwing upside down garbage cans over them until they could be shut off. Or pranksters have taken wheelchairs and have had to be chased.

In 1993, her first year, she raised about $500. Each year after, she has almost always doubled the amount that she raised by sending out more letters and more letters asking for sponsorship. The event raised $125,000 in 1995 and it is her goal to get the award for the highest amount raised by an individual.[2]

Sandi serves on the Relay Organizing Committee, works in the retail booth and has arranged continuous entertainment on stage for the 24 hours. Afterwards, she stays to clean up; then, 32 hours from start to finish she fells exhausted into bed.

She has met men, many men, some pretty interesting, in her assorted activities. She has locked arms and waists with lots of them on square dance and contra dance nights but the tall, good looking Mr. Right, that she romantically imagines, is still a stranger far across the crowded room. The yearned-for companion has not stepped forward. Will he ever?

Her mother had thought Dirk was a good enough candidate. He had even traveled to Europe with the family but Sandi didn't want "good enough"; she had not been in love. She liked Craig but it had not felt right with him either. Both guys are married now and she is happy for them. They are good friends.

Of course it bothers her and of course she is lonely but her attitude is positive. There is no point in letting grass grow under her feet, in other words. There are too many things to do, places to see and people to meet. She will determinedly go on shaping and living her life without a companion until God deems otherwise. If it is His will for her to have a mate, it will happen. This she believes with all her heart.

Sandi veered off the main course a few blocks and turned into the parking lot at Craft Warehouse. It was five thirty on Christmas Eve and, phew, it was still open. She went in and picked out a couple of unpainted miniature ceramic houses, gifts for her two aunts, Margaret and me. They would be additions to an ongoing collection. When possible, family members will paint houses together. *The houses for the aunts are not part of the name exchange but, who would complain?* she reflected. *It is tradition.* This prompted her to burst out in a spirited rendition of the "Fiddler on the Roof" song, "Tradition, tradition!"

The skies were dark when she swung into her regular Shell gas station to fill the Explorer for her trip over Snoqualmie Pass on Friday morning. She most surely did not want to leave that until the last minute. Having paid and wished the owner happy holidays, she

---

[2] Sandi achieved this goal in 2003 when she raised in excess of $5,000!

continued on to Albertsons, her favorite grocery store on 40th by the track.

Yes, they were still there! She was relieved. She took two white, stuffed bears from the shelf, added a few food items to her cart and then extended more happy and merry wishes as she checked out. This had been kind of fun. Everyone was so friendly and cheerful. The bears were for B.J. and Arun. They were still kids and did not come under the changing names category. Besides, they were pretty special to her, she could make another exception.

Errands finished, she continued on to the West Valley Country Club, her protected-but-not-gated community off Tieton Drive. As she did so, she mentally rehearsed the parameters of the next few days and her wish list of activities.

For dinner, she thought, *I'll have a chef's salad.*

Salad was a frequent item on her limited menu. She also loved pizza and breakfast out but cooking is just not Sandi's thing. She can, to which her friends and family can attest, put on a fancy meal when she puts her mind to it. For instance, she makes a great prime rib. She packs a top grade of beef in rock salt and when it comes out of the oven it is done to perfection. She serves it with *au jus,* a bit of horse radish, a green salad with berries or citrus slices and a raspberry vinaigrette dressing, warm roll and butter. Mmmm. Perhaps, to top it off, a pecan tart for dessert. Her German pancakes are scrumptious, too. After such cuisine quests might rightly assume that it is a case of Doc Sandi hiding her candle under a bushel.

Normally, she zaps a frozen chicken in the microwave or boils some eggs and has a chef's salad (bought ready-made at the grocery store) to eat throughout the week. She thinks it is her preference and is still a few years away from acknowledging that cooking for oneself on a consistent basis is one of the hardest things to do in life.

I'll sleep in and take time for a good run in the morning, she continued in thought, *and I'll have a delicious cross-stitch time and finally finish up Aunt Margaret's present.*

The pattern, which Margaret had begun, was an idealistic or sentimental piece based on James Herriot's *All Things Bright and Beautiful* and had been a present at the time of her graduation from vet school. Its value now, to be sure, lay not in sentiment as much as in promising Sandi the satisfaction of tying up a loose end.

While cross-stitching I'll watch once again my favorite holiday movie, "It's a Wonderful Life," with Jimmy Stewart, and I'll catch up on my videotaped programs. Last week's episodes of "E.R.", "Diagnosis Murder", "Dr. Quinn, Medicine Woman" and "Touched by an Angel" are all waiting for me. If I run out I'd like to replay a "MacGyver" episode.

I'll put all the presents in a box along with the wrapping paper and ribbon and leave the actual wrapping of the last presents until I get there. It is more fun that way.

Thursday, she decided, *I'll let Herbie have a shower, while I clean his cage. That will be his Christmas present.* Amusing herself, she smiled at the idea.

Herbie, her peach-faced lovebird, when showering, for those who have not had the joy of seeing this in person, stands on a little piece of a dowel at the bottom of the sink and wets his green and blue little feathers in a tiny trickle of warm water from the faucet. As if oblivious to his captive state and as if on a Pacific Island, Herbie stands proudly in his personal waterfall and spreads his wing and tail feathers in the stream. Go ahead. Imagine a tiny palm tree and a tropical breeze and you see the little fellow of the parrot family bathing in bliss. This colorful and loyal Lilliputian has been with the Doc for all of her professional days. He does not leave the shower until he has pristinely preened each little feather with his beak.

After Herbie is completely dry and settled in for the night I'll take him and Baxter to the clinic, she concluded.

Baxter, her German long-hair golden retriever cross—who is not golden but coal black—was born in 1991. His love-struck father, the German long hair who belonged to a school classmate, had climbed over an eight-foot fence of the dog kennel to befriend mother, the golden retriever, and thus Baxter. Like his owner he is well known in Yakima. He has had a role in "Hello, Dolly!" and "Cheaper By the Dozen" and has donated blood several times to dogs at the clinic. One such time he received, in gratitude from an owner, a fresh sirloin steak "which he was kind enough to share with me," says Sandi. Boarding her pets at the clinic is a perk of the job, a handy service for her jaunts out of town.

Oh, yes, she remembered, *I have to get the slides ready. Maybe I can do that tonight.*

Her most recent outing had been a kayaking trip along the coast of Espiritu Santo Island in the Sea of Cortez off Baja, Mexico. The trip, a tantalizing side attraction to earning veterinary continuing education credits, was one of many such that Sandi has taken. She has scuba dived in Hawaii and Florida and river rafted down the Middle Fork of the Salmon River in Idaho. River rafting, more than scuba diving and kayaking, have stirred her pioneering spirit. Navigating the wild Lochsa or the Main Salmon takes courage, strength and commitment to teamwork. Sandi has discovered to her deep satisfaction that she has all three. Good attributes to have learned about and tucked under her belt. Inevitably, she will need them even more later in life. Everyone does, you know.

Sandi is, in my opinion, a pretty typical Yuppie, a young urban professional, in this regard. As such, she is barely conscious of the fact that she lives a privileged life. Yet, she knows instinctively, as do most Yuppies, to seek out risky or extreme adventures in which to test her strength. There are, after all, neither more continents to discover nor prairies to settle; nonetheless, her test to survive will come, as it will for others her age, and she will be ready.

On Friday morning I'll have a quick bowl of cold cereal and get an early start, she thought.

Thanks to the vigilance of Steven, she has chains and flares in the Explorer. Snoqualmie can be tricky. And she has her new cellular phone.

"Oh, boy," she sighed deeply aloud as she waited at a red light and observed a cozy Kincaid-type house. Smoke was curling up from the chimney and Christmas lights blinked on roof edges. "I wish the on call was over already."

She was on call for 36 hours and people gave pets stupid things to eat on holidays. She might even have to work nonstop; it had happened before. If so, she would be too exhausted to enjoy her day off. She hoped not. She did not want to go home to the family in an irritable frame of mind.

Sandi saw in the headlights and street lamps, as she drove through the entrance to the club, that it was beginning to snow. A light dusting had been predicted for the night. After a short way on 76th Avenue, she slowed, waved to the man across the street, pulled into the driveway and then eased into the garage of her dark three-bedroom, ranch-style home. Baxter started his excited barking. Herbie, too, peeped and chattered his welcome.

"I'm almost on vacation!" Sandi called to both as she let Baxter out of his kennel and opened the door to the house. "Too bad for you guys, huh? Guess where you'll have to go pretty soon?"

She laid down her things and embraced Baxter who was leaning against her legs, being too well trained to put his paws anywhere they didn't belong, and ruffled his coat.

"Merry Christmas and sorry! But, hey, you two, here I am now!"

Chapter 12
Jesus, Sinterklass, and Maveli

Losing the people of my life, I have learned, is inevitable. Losing their stories, I decided, is not.

At two o'clock in the afternoon of Christmas day, Steve stood at the kitchen sink. He awkwardly leaned his upper body towards my right as he simultaneously tipped carefully the large china platter that held the roasted 24-pound turkey and waited for the tasty brown juices to flow into the two-quart sauce pan that I was holding. I was squeezed into the right angle corner between Steve at the sink and Anil at the stove and barely avoided bumping Anil's elbow as he lifted the lid of the six-quart stainless steel pan. Steam rolled out from the boiling potatoes. Giblets and neck stood cooling in liquid in another pan at the back of the stove. The microwave at head- level above the stove beeped every few seconds.

"Quick, stop, Steve, it's starting to slide!" I yelped, frantic at the prospect.

Steve straightened the platter in the nick of time and moved it and his operation to the right of the sink. He had already organized his workspace: another platter, a bowl, a large spoon and the electric knife. He began by cutting the string around the bird's legs and spooning the stuffing from the bird's cavity. Anil moved around me and took his pan of potatoes to the sink to drain the liquid.

"I'll take some of that liquid, Anil," I said hastily. Then I set about extracting giblets and neck from the broth and cutting them into small pieces to add to the gravy.

"The microwave is beeping, Pat," Steven repeated calmly a

second time.

Pat having just taken a bowl of previously cooked and sweetened cranberries and various relishes from the refrigerator was arranging the relishes on a dish at the island counter. As if shifting into high gear in response to Steven's words, she hurriedly went to the pantry and reached for a jar of sweet pickles, calling as she did so.

"Sophia, the microwave is beeping!" Then, "Arlyce, will you get the bread out on the table? That needs to be sliced. And get the basket and cloth, please, to put it in."

Sophia opened the microwave door and pulled out the blue and white corning ware casserole dish with bare hands. She set it on the stove top and stirred the corn.

"This will need to be redone," she protested. "I just can't imagine how long it's taking! Some of the corn is still frozen! The directions said to zap it 8-10 minutes and I've done it 20 minutes already."

Sophia was handling the vegetables as usual. Her specialty, however, is cooking fresh vegetables prepared Greek style with olive oil and lemon juice or vinegar, not multiple packages of microwaveable frozen vegetables. She even digs dandelion greens from the earth in springtime and cooks them.

"Marge, your sweet potatoes are done!" Pat called loudly as she moved me towards the sink and bent to look into the oven glass door.

"Okay, I'll be right there," answered Marge.

If Sophia was the Veggie Queen in the family and she was, then Marge was the Duchess of Laundry. She could often be found in the little laundry room that was between the kitchen and family room across from the garage entranceway. Unobtrusive and meticulously neat, Marge collected and returned laundry to every bedroom. Towels used once in the morning would magically be back on the shelf fluffy and folded by evening.

On cue, as if a model in a fashion show, Ann stepped expectantly through the hall doorway into the kitchen. Blondish-grey hair swept up in a French twist, she stood holding herself erect with arms slightly away from her sides and one foot in front of the other. Slowly, she pivoted from side to side.

"Ooo, how nice you look, Grandma!" exclaimed Arlyce, who

was the most fashion-conscious of the kitchen audience. "I love that dress!"

"You do, dear? Thank you!" crooned Ann affectedly beaming with the hoped for complement.

"Lovely, *Moeke*, you're really dressed up! Where did you buy that?" asked Pat barely stopping her industrious orchestrations.

"Very nice, *Mom*," I called over my shoulder after taking a quick look. It was critical that I not take my eyes off the bubbling gravy just then.

"Merry Christmas, everybody!" called Ann grandly as Sophia, Anil and Marge chimed in with their approvals and Merry Christmases.

The belted short-sleeved dress was predominately black background with an off-white print in rayon fabric. It had an off-white organdy vee-shaped and vee-necked bib that dipped almost to the waist. There was white thread embroidery of curving flowery lines throughout the bib and inch-long, off-white, dew-drop shaped tassels around the border. A white insert across the base of the vee-neck covered her cleavage. The area of her delicate skin above the insert was nicely filled in with a double strand of crystal beads. Patent leather pumps and small crystal earrings completed the elegant look.

A few years ago, when some family members were in Mesa for the holidays, Pat and I took Mom shopping for a dress in Anderson's at the Superstition Springs mall. I remember that she stood in front of the three full-length enveloping mirrors pivoting in just the same way, her eyes and face alight with the thrill of the moment.

"My pa, *Klaas DeVries,* liked to have his girls dressed nicely when we went out to be around people in *Baflo,*" she had reminisced. "At home when we would have a new dress, my father always wanted us to show him. *Martje* and me, his two girls then, we would stand in front of him and turn *en* so and he would say how nice we looked."

We caught a glimpse of the younger *Anje's* radiant face in the mirrors as she reflected on that memory. It was filled with the purest of delight.

"Okay, Mom," directed Pat, "you can sit at the kitchen table here and slice the bread. Do you have it ready, Arlyce? Tell her how to do it."

"I've sliced bread before, Pat. But you tell me how to do it okay, dear," said Ann as she seated herself with yet a bit of flare.

"Oh, Grandma, how nice you look," Arlyce interjected once again as the two communed about nice-looking clothes and ways to slice the bread.

"Brandon, is the table set and ready to go?" Pat pressed urgently as the two boys passed through the kitchen. "It won't be long now before we eat."

"I set it, Aunt Pat. I'm taking care of Arun now," Brandon asserted confidently in reply.

He and Arun were in the family room mostly, working little cars around the train track on the floor. Every few minutes Arun ran through the crowded kitchen into the hallway, rounded the corner to his left and came to a stop in the living room. Brandon followed not far behind.

"Umbootie, umbootie," Arun kept saying as he held up Matchbox and Hot Wheels cars for B.J. to see.

"Yes, I see umbootie, Arun. It's a car. Car," Brandon repeated. He was showing a keen interest in the active little fellow.

We adults had been unsure how Brandon would react to competition; after all, he had enjoyed the undisputed attention of this half of the family for nine whole years. It is a good thing, you know—when you think about it—that youth can surprise us grownups. We need the little jolts to remain open to possibilities. Brandon was not fazed in the slightest by competition. He was marvelously gentle and patient with the younger boy, and we were pleased and fascinated.

"I am so afraid, Pat, that one of the little boys will trip over Tjaakje's tubing," Ann pointed out.

It was a valid point. My oxygen tubing snaked through the hallway and laid twisted and bunched up in places on the kitchen floor.

"I was worried too and I've been watching them," rejoined Pat. "They're doing all right so far. Douglas, what are you doing?"

"Nothing."

Doug was standing a few feet beyond the table in the other doorway to the living room. He had been surveying the scene from what he thought would be a safe distance.

"Well then, Doug, will you check to see if Brandon set the table and if there are enough chairs for everybody, please?"

"Arlyce, how do you think I am doing?" queried Ann. She was unaccustomed to slicing a large round loaf of bread with a hard crust. In order to avoid unmanageably large slices the bakery had included a slicing diagram. It showed somewhat complicated angles.

"Mom, do you think Grandma is slicing the bread the way you wanted it?" Arlyce was arranging the bread in a basket.

"Look at the directions it gives," instructed Pat.

"It doesn't matter. Just do it whatever way you want. Have you gone to that Golden Harvest bread store in Mesa yet, Soph? I found one here in Seattle. I just love their breads and you can get a free slice without even buying anything."

Anil took his pan of mashed potatoes to the table and gradually added a packet of Hidden Valley ranch dressing. He methodically worked the powder and some butter into the potatoes.

Steven, who would have loved to tackle the prescribed bread slicing-angles, glanced over, but, thinking better of it, put the finishing touches to the platter of turkey instead.

"Tjaakje, are you doing all right? I don't want you to overdo. You probably shouldn't even be here at the stove with that oxygen," said Pat as she eased me to the right again with the back of her forearm. "I just have to look at these pies in the oven a minute. Oh, grief, they're ready! Where is that pot holder?"

"I'm hot, that's all," I puffed mopping my brow, unable as always to distinguish hot flash from just plain hot. "The gravy is pretty much ready. It came out good. I'll need the gravy boat in a minute or two."

"Douglas, hand me that gravy thing there, would you? Soph, how's the corn now? Don't forget the peas and onions that you did. Is everybody about ready to go into the dining room? Brandon, Arun is going to take his nap. You can get yourself seated in the dining room."

"Anil, do you want to take Arun up?" asked Arlyce. "He looks a little sleepy. I think he'll be fine. He's had his nummie. You better hurry. I think we're almost ready to eat."

"Brandon, what do you want something to drink? You better get it." said Marge.

I backed away from the stove and used John's favorite Dutch

saying, *"Comedie is der niks bie, en* (Comedy is nothing in comparison to this, is it)?"

"Juist zo, wicht (Exactly, girl)! *Comedie is der niks bie. Dat ze mien Pa ook alltiet (My* dad always said that too)."

"Douglas, here's the gravy. Arlyce, will you bring the potatoes? Okay, let's see. Is the bread on the table already, Arlyce? Marge, the sweet potatoes, where are they? And grab the butter wouldja please. Sophia, are you ready to go? Don't forget the stuffing, somebody."

"I think I'm ready", answered Sophia, "finally! Do you have a pepper grinder?"

"Pepper should be on the table but, no, no pepper grinder. Sorry. Arlyce, will you check to make sure the salt and pepper are on?"

"They are, Aunt Pat," announced B.J., "I put them on. I'm hungry,"

"Okay, everybody, let's sit down. Maybe, you better cover that turkey, Steven, since you want to read first."

Brandon whipped into his chair at the back of the table as people started into the dining room. He was precariously close to the glass of the china closet.

"Be careful, B.J.," cautioned Ann sternly as she took the seat at the head of the table at the far end. Steven sat down at the end nearest to the kitchen. Anil slipped into his chair just as Steven opened the Bible.

"Will he go to sleep, do you think?" whispered Arlyce.

Steven cleared his throat. "I am going to read about the first Christmas from the Gospels, the book of Luke, verses one through eleven," said Steven. He went on to read:

"And it came to pass in those days, that there went out a decree from Caesar Augustus, that all the world should be taxed. (And this taxing was first made when Cyrenius was governor of Syria.) And all went to be taxed, everyone to his own city. And Joseph also went up from Galilee, out of the city of Nazareth, into Judaea, unto the city of David, which is called Bethlehem; (because he was of the house and lineage of David: To be taxed with Mary his espoused wife, being great with child."

Bowls of mashed potatoes, corn and peas with pearl onions each with pats of melting butter on the top, and sweet potatoes covered with softened, browned marshmallows sent steam and their tantalizing fragrances into the air like so much burning incense. Brandon eyed the plate of turkey hungrily, and, as if unobserved, reached out surreptitiously to take a piece that protruded from under the loose tin foil. He had already savored a piece that had fallen on the white lace tablecloth and was eager for more. Doug gave him a nudge with his elbow. B.J. frowned then relented.

"...the days were accomplished that she should be delivered. And she brought forth her firstborn son, and wrapped him in swaddling clothes, and laid him in a manger; because there was no room for them in the inn. And there was in the same country—"

I stole a quick look at Anil and saw his impenetrable expression. The Biblical reading at mealtime was a ritual in the Cok home as it had been in our immediate family and in Anje's family before that. *Anil is probably resigned to the fact by now,* I surmised.

"...And the angel said unto them, Fear not: for, behold I bring you good tidings of great joy, which shall be to all people. For unto you is born this day in the city of David a Saviour, which is Christ the Lord."

When he finished reading Steven closed the Bible and said, "Let us pray."

Ann, Pat, Sophia and Steven folded their hands, closed their eyes and bowed their heads. The rest of us sat in some semblance of reverence.

Steven's prayers were always heartfelt and personal. He expressed thanks for making our journeys safe and for allowing us to get together as a family at this special holiday time. He thanked God for health enough for everyone and for the abundance that lay before us. He acknowledged God's valuable gift of his Son and asked for protection of the family members who could not be present. He asked for God's caring for those less fortunate and finished with, "We ask this in Jesus' name. Amen."

Sophia, a Greek Orthodox, crossed herself, repeated, "Amen," and then tucking a napkin in under her chin pronounced, "Let's eat!"

Anil offered a toast of good health with his Martinelli's sparkling apple juice and everyone carefully clinked one another's stemware.

"Eet smaakelijk allemaal" (enjoy your meal one and all)," added Ann.

"Oh, shoot. I forgot the cranberries!" Pat jumped up.

Fine china bowls and platters with a soft gray rose pattern were passed around and matching plates were filled. There was a cacophony of clinks, tinkles, "Umms", "Scrumptious", "So good", "I'll put that over here", and "Delicious!"

When things settled I, sensing or projecting—I knew not which—some emotional undercurrents and group tension, briefly debated whether or not to make a suggestion. Sometimes, I now know well enough, putting my ideas forward leaves me skating on thin ice. But that has not always stopped me from taking risks in my family and it wouldn't today either.

"It might be kind of fun," I proposed, "if we talked about Christmas experiences or traditions that we were a part of in the past. Like St. Nicholas Day in Holland, Mom," I prompted.

"In Holland Christmas is a religious day and the next day too. Two days," said Ann curtly. "We didn't have presents on that day. We would go to church and sing in the choir *enzovoort* (et cetera). We would really celebrate the birth of the baby Jesus. Then we would have a meal together."

"Wasn't there something December 5, *Moeke*, St. Nicholas day?" asked Sophia. "Tjaakje and I used to do something a little special on that day. Why did we ever stop, Tjaakje? We should get back to it."

"You know this too, Sophia? Yes, December 5 was *Sinterklaasavond* (St. Nicholas Eve) and the next morning there would be presents. But that was not Christmas day."

"There is quite a story that goes with St. Nicholas," I reported. "I think you would like it a lot, Beej; it's about body parts floating in brine and stuff."

"Gross!" said Brandon. "Tell me!"

"Three students stop at a country bread and breakfast type

place for a night's sleep. While they are sleeping the wicked landlord goes through their belongings and finds that they are carrying lots of money. He robs and kills the threesome and cuts them into pieces. To not be discovered, he puts the pieces in a big tub of brine (Ebon 55). I suppose he was even going to sell the pieces for pickled pork."

"*Och* no, Lottie, that's not so," mom remarked irritably. In her opinion I come up with the most sacrilegious and unnecessary material. She may have a point.

"Yes, I read the story. From afar St. Nicholas had a vision about the killings and went there. When the wicked landlord fell on his knees and begged for forgiveness, St. Nicholas made the pieces of bodies go back together again. The sons threw themselves at his feet and he blessed them. Santa Claus, by the way, has at times been called Old Saint Nick and he may have started in Holland."

"*Nee maar! Dat heb ik nooit eerder hoord!* (No, never! I have never heard that before!). Have you, Pat?"

"What is brine, Tjaakje?" inserted B.J.

"No, I never heard anything like that!" declared an equally astonished Pat.

"Salt water, it acts as a preservative." I mouthed back to B.J.

"Tell us what you remember, *Moeke,* and Lottie, you keep still," Sophia ruled. "Pass the bread, would you please, Steven."

"Well, on December 5 on *Sinterklaasavond* (Saint Nicholas Eve) the children, we too when we were children, we would put carrots and hay in wooden shoes for St. Nicholas' horse. *Pa* would say, 'Don't you hear him coming?' Sometimes we could hear chains ringing and a voice calling, 'Whoa!' and we would be scared.

"I was scared of him too," asserted Pat.

"Then St. Nicholas would come with his helper, *Zwarte Piet,* (Black Pete)," said Ann.

I broke in with, "Sometimes, in pictures St. Nicholas is on a white horse. He is dressed in embroidered robes glittering with gems and gold. I read that too. He wears a miter on his head, like cardinals in the Catholic Church and he carries a cosier, which is a hooked staff."

"Friends of sailors, and of children!
Double claim have we,

As in youthful joy we're sailing,
O'er a frozen sea!
Nicholas! Saint Nicholas,
Let us sing to thee!"

"I don't even remember where I got that from," I reported but no one heard or cared.

"Hush, Tjaakje. Let your mother talk," exhorted Sophia.

"You are right now, Lottie. St. Nicholas and his partner would ask your parents if you have been good in the last year. *Zarte Piet* would sometimes carry a big sack. Then in the morning on December 6 the hay and carrots would be gone. If you had been good you would get a small present in your wooden shoe, maybe a piece of fruit, an orange or so, with it."

"Did he ever leave you a piece of coal or a switch for a spanking? Didn't that happen if somebody had been bad?" I asked.

"*Ja*, I guess so. But, no, that never happened in our family. They would say that more to scare us and us kids were scared. I remember that. But that was not really Christmas." she reiterated. "We did not have a Christmas tree like we do here. Maybe there would be only one in the town."

"I remember a time in Montana, on Churchill, I think," recounted Pat. "Where you lived in that first house, remember, *Moeke?* The girls were little and John and Joyce were there with their little kids. We were having a Christmas-get together and all of a sudden a perfect looking Santa Claus came in with a big sack and gave the kids all kinds of stuff. It was perfect timing too. Nobody expected it."

"I remember that!" exclaimed Arlyce.

"I don't think we ever knew who that Santa Claus was, did we Mom?" asked Pat. "Pass the turkey around again, Doug, okay?" she instructed in the next breath.

"No, I don't think so. I don't think we ever knew," responded Ann as she took the turkey platter from Doug who was reaching across B.J.'s plate.

"And there was the time when John and Joyce's kids did all those skits," said Pat. "I think that was in the living room of their old house. We need Sandi for this. She remembers that time. I only remember the one of the bum on the park bench pretending to have fleas. He scratches and scratches until everyone else leaves and he can have the bench to sleep on. That's the one we did in Arizona."

"Oh, that was fun!" said Sophia. "Ruth Adams keeps wanting us to do it again."

"I remember a few years ago, well quite a few now, I guess, when we went snowmobiling at John and Joyce's and we had a wiener roast in the snow," offered Marge.

"Oh, yes, and we had our group picture taken with us sitting on straw bales and Kent took the three-wheeler up the hill with Mom in the big inner tube!" exclaimed Pat.

"I remember," added Ann, "Kent said to me, 'Grandma, put your butt in there!'"

Brandon giggled hysterically, "'put your butt—'"

"Brandon, stop it," growled Doug.

"'Put your butt in there, Grandma,' that's what Kent said," Ann restated. "I remember it as plain as day. That was a lot of fun with everybody together."

There was a long pause.

"Did you have any traditions like Christmas in India? Or in your family's religion which was Hinduism, wasn't it, Anil?" I ventured.

"Something to do with giving gifts maybe?" prompted Arlyce.

Anil thought for a few seconds.

"I could tell you the story of *Onam,* the South Indian holiday usually celebrated some time in September. The date on which it is celebrated is based on the lunar calendar. It is like this:

Long ago, in the lush state of Kerala, there was a wonderful, just and kind king. His name was Maveli. He ruled the land well. It was rich and the people were prosperous and happy. There was no poverty. The people of Kerala were so happy that the gods were jealous. They were so jealous that they came up with a plan. They sent one of the gods to Kerala. His name was Vishnu. He came to Kerala as a monk or Brahman. The Indian custom is that you can never refuse anything to a Brahman. The Brahman went to Maveli's palace and asked him for three feet or steps of land. The king agreed. Suddenly, the Brahman became huge and with one step he covered the entire earth.

"Wow!" uttered Brandon with an impressive sounding low

whistle.

"And with the next step, he covered the heavens. He raised his foot for the third step and there was no where left to put it down. So the king knelt in front of him and offered his head. Just before the god stepped on Maveli's head, the king asked for a last wish. His wish was to be given the chance to come back each year and visit his subjects. The god agreed.

So, each year at the *Onam* celebration Maveli comes to visit his people in Kerala. At this time people eat very well, dress up, give gifts or large baskets of fruit and so, decorate with flowers and light lamps.

"How very interesting!" exuded Sophia.

Others murmured their appreciation as well.

"We'll have our dessert later after the naps. Is that all right?" asked Pat.

Everyone heartily agreed as they finished one last small helping of this or that.

"When I was young I loved Roy Rogers and Gene Autrey," recalled Sophia as she pulled the napkin away from where it was tucked under her chin.

They all looked at her curiously; I had heard the story and knew what was coming.

"And one Christmas I was so excited," she continued, "I'll never forget it. I got a little six-shooter! It had little plastic bullets. I loved it!"

Anil threw back his head and laughed heartily at Sophia's childhood memory.

"I don't remember," Sophia went on, "who did it but by the end of the day it was broken. I was so upset. And then, Carl, my step-father, every Christmas would get each of us a new pair of gloves. They weren't gloves. They were mittens. He would put a five dollar bill all folded up in the mitten and fill the mitten with rice."

"Are mittens the ones with or without fingers?" asked Steven.

"Mittens don't have fingers," Sophia declared decisively. "Sometimes he would put the bill in the thumb," she reflected.

She pushed her chair back and announced. "I have to move. Thermogenesis is setting in. I'm starting to get sleepy."

"We're not going to pray again, are we Cok?" Pat asked of

Steven as she rose and began to stack dishes.

"Can we open just one present, Aunt Pat?" Brandon begged as others stood and began milling about.

"Oh, no, B.J., some people haven't even finished shopping yet," contended Pat resolutely as she and others gathered up dishes and moved back into the disheveled kitchen.

"Oh, man," grumbled Brandon. "I have to wait so long yet."

"What make you think there's going to be anything under that tree for you anyway?" kidded Doug.

"And now, what is next on the agenda?" asked Ann.

Chapter 13
"Sjoeln"

Once I committed to putting the stories on paper there was no turning back. I felt it as a duty as much as a whim or a quirk and it was how I chose to spend much of my time. I, as others may, have wondered why the task was so very compelling.

With many hands at work, cleanup after the Christmas dinner took only a few minutes and soon those who napped were oblivious to the determined whirring and swishing of the dishwasher. After an hour and after Pat had emptied and refilled the dishwasher for a second load, family members stirred and once again began to congregate. This time it was in the family room.

"Are you ready for some *sjoeln?"* Pat asked Ann who had dosed sitting up in the living room chair and who was just regaining full consciousness.

"Sjoeln? Ja, zeker (yes, sure)!" Ann responded happily as she pushed herself up out of the chair.

Sjoeln using the *sjoelbak* (shove, shovel or shuffleboard) *is* a game made popular in Holland and is the table top version of shuffleboard, the ground game. There are variations, of course: the target areas are not within a numbered triangle, there is no use of lengthy, pronged, cue sticks, many more disks are utilized and the table top version is much noisier. I will go into the specifics later, but first I want you to know a bit of history of *sjoeln* in the family as I experienced it.

In the dead of winter on the farm in Montana when nearly everything was frozen solid and outdoor work was nigh-to-impossible—it was not unusual to get to 40 or more degrees below

0—a person had to find something to do. So one of those times, in the early fifties, *Pa* made a *sjoelbak* in his tool shed. There was, as yet, no television in our home in those days and cards and movies—as was dancing—were all forbidden by the church; entertainment had to be created. *Pa* was no stranger to these circumstances. He placed his *sjoelbak* on the kitchen table one evening and had *Moeke* call the Kimn and Knottnerus brothers to invite them over for a few games.

Robust, tall Otto and not as robust, or tall brother Ollie Knottnerus often drove down from Big Sandy in southern Alberta, Canada to visit friends, including girlfriends, Minnie and Alice Kimn. Minnie and Alice's brothers, Stanley, the more robust of this pair, and Alex lived with their parents outside of Manhattan. The hale and hearty young men, all in their late twenties, were Dutch bachelors who had recently emigrated from Holland.

Intermingled in the boisterous games of *sjoeln* were coffee, *koek* and bodacious I've-got-one-that-tops-yours, honest-to-God war stories. All of the guys, including Dad, had participated in some way in the resistance to the German occupation of Holland and the Kimn brothers had more stories to tell of when they later had fought as mercenaries in India. From what I could grasp—some was way over my head and some was deliberately coded so us kids could not understand it—there was lots of danger and darkness overcome by daring and narrow escapes.

Pa loved the stories—so did I!—and he loved the elbow in the ribs, can't-you-do-any-better-than-that competition. He always had a sharp analytic mind and had loved his much quieter checkers matches in Thesinge. As a member of the Thesinge Checkers Club he had hosted and even traveled to other towns and villages for checkers tournaments. He didn't often laugh out loud around us kids, but on those nights of *sjoeln* and telling tales with the guys, he did. They all did and we all laughed along, very loudly.

Dad's original *sjoelbak* eventually ended up at John's place but was never used there. Steve and Pat spotted and bought a *sjoelbak* once at a garage sale in Seattle. So, while Pat had been tending the dishwasher, Steven had taken the long trough-like, wooden game board from its storage place behind the family room couch and laid it on the table. Before long teams were chosen and spirited rivalry ensued around the *sjoelbak*.

Sjoeln is played on a six-foot-by-eighteen-inch, flat surface which is probably a three-quarter-inch-thick piece of plywood covered with chalkboard or Formica. There are three-inch-high sideboards and one endboard. At the closed end of the shallow, rectangular receptacle are four cubicles positioned lengthwise. The cubicles are ten inches in length. There is a three-inch-high board across the front of the cubicles.

At the base of this crosswise board are four holes placed at the exact middle of each of the four cubicles. These holes are only a quarter of an inch wider than the size of the round wooden disks used in the game.

The wooden disks are made of oak in order to withstand impact. The disks—or bricks as they are called—of which there are 25, measure two-and-a-half inches in diameter and are one-half inch thick. The shuffleboard is placed on a regular table to give convenient height. Talcum powder is sprinkled on the chalkboard to make it more slippery although that is not necessary for the Formica.

The object of *sjoeln* as to slide, push, shove or scoot the bricks one at a time down the six feet of board through the holes that are entryways to the cubicles. A two-by-one inch board strategically placed across and at the top of the trough twelve inches from the head of the board prevents the player from reaching too far and makes the play considerably more difficult. This crosswise board also provides a convenient shelf on which to stack the as-yet-not-played bricks.

The player scores 20 points when there is one brick in each cubicle, forty points when there are two in each cubicle and so forth with 120 being the maximum score possible. If the player cannot achieve an even number of bricks in each cubicle, then the bricks become worth only one point each.

The player is allowed three opportunities with each turn. After each opportunity the bricks not in the cubicles are retrieved and the player tries again. The score for the turn is tallied only after the third opportunity. To give direction as to which cubicle is in need of a brick, a second person at the cubicle end of the board may stack up the bricks, point to a cubicle and call out instructions such as, "Here, here," or "This one, this one over here," and "Don't forget this one!"

During each opportunity as the disks are shoved towards the end those that do not slide into a cubicle become jammed in front of the holes much like a flock of sheep that are eager to go through a gate. Bricks then must be slid with power to break up a jam and force bricks into the cubicles. This action creates quite a loud, often repeated crashing noise.

To heighten the competition and joviality of the game, it can be played in pairs and teams. With shouts of directions, the racket of the bricks hitting one another, plus cheers and clapping from comrades, the game quickly becomes an exulted raucous event.

Anil quickly took the lead Christmas evening and stunned us Dutch veterans by winning the game outright. It wasn't definite; he could have had a lucky game or been playing "in the zone", as the sports broadcasters might have said, but it looked that evening like he won by using an unorthodox technique. He flicked the brick with thumb and forefinger as opposed to a quick strike of the forearm or an extended shove forward of the whole arm. Some of us tried to use his technique but failed miserably and complained instantly of pain in the forefinger. We had to conclude that Anil had uncanny power and deftness in his forefinger.

It is a skill that may be considered uncanny by us Dutch folks, but it is one that would likely be common to the peoples of India. This should have come as no surprise; all of us had, after all, at one time or another tried to imitate Anil's refined ability to eat with only the fingers of his right hand. It is amazing how he can move any desired amount of food (including elusive kernels of rice) efficiently and neatly from his plate to his mouth with the tips of his fingers and a push of the thumb. You might try it; it is easier said than done. This is custom in India, and as demonstrated by Anil that evening leads to Olympian capabilities in shuffleboard.

After the initial shock wore off, Anil won our loud applause. The little fellow, Arun, too won his share of plaudits. He had to stand on a chair in order to reach the game board. Then he clapped with unbridled joy each time his brick touched another brick at the end of the board.

As the play subsided Pat dialed the familiar Yakima number. "Sandi, we missed you! I told everybody that you would tell us about the skits you and Arlyce did with John and Joyce's kids one Christmas, remember?"

Then she chattered away, filling Sandi in on the details of the festivities. Steven went to the kitchen phone and picked up to listen.

He heard Sandi saying, "I've been watching the Weather Channel. It's snowing more than expected on the pass. It may be closed."

"That's surprising," said Steven.

"I'm glad you're off tomorrow. I hope it's not like that Friday morning," remarked Pat. "They are saying here that we might actually see snow tomorrow. If it's enough to stick on the ground Sophia may have seen her snow. We may not even need to come up and meet you on Snoqualmie on Friday."

"Were you busy today?" asked Steven.

"Pretty busy, I had to go in. Nothing really major and I'd have had to go in anyway to take care of the animals in the clinic. I could handle most of the calls over the phone. I'm going in for the last check now."

"What else did you do?" asked Pat.

"I didn't have a chance to do much. I organized my slides to the Baja and I've been watching 'It's A Wonderful Life' for the zillionth time. I never seem to get sick of it." Sandi had, in fact, watched the movie often enough to know all the dialogue by heart.

"Well, we've got to serve coffee and dessertS; so we better go," said Pat. "Talk to you tomorrow. Enjoy your day off."

All enjoyed a rare lull in the noise and conversation, I think, as we ate our piece of pie. It had been a nice day, lots of work but a nice day. Soon after, Anil, Arlyce and Arun gathered their things and left for home. Pat reminded us that she had to go to work early in the morning, so around ten o'clock we all went off to bed.

Pat fell asleep as soon as her head touched the pillow. Sophia, too. Marge and I, me in my bed upstairs and Marge in the motorhome, lay in bed awake and listened to the obfuscatory croaking of the frog.

Chapter 14
After Bowling

On the other hand, I have not wanted to speculate or to explain why it was compelling. I just wanted to honor the process which kept going on and on and on.

T his doesn't look right," critiqued Sophia as she accepted the change handed to her by Douglas.

Sophia, which means wise in Greek, always keeps an eagle eye on the clerks at cash registers and for good reason, according to her. She often catches mistakes. Usually they are related to advertised and posted sale items, the lowered price of which will not have been entered into the store computer. It is her firm opinion that they are not entered on purpose. Publish the sale, get the people in the store and then charge them the full price. It is an old trick, bait and switch. Most people do not notice the error. This mistake, however, had not turned out to be in her favor.

"I think we still owe him two dollars," she deduced.

"The guy was kind of out of it, wasn't he? Like he hadn't ever worked in there before," I remarked.

"Maybe he owes us some money," offered Brandon hopefully. He didn't bother to take the end of the straw in his Coke out of his mouth as he kept talking. "Maybe we should just keep the money or, even better, you could just give it to me if you want to give it to somebody. Okay, Sophia, Okay?" Brandon pulled the straw out of the container with his mouth and turned his head around. A drop of coke fell on his jacket.

"Brandon, turn around and put the straw back in your coke," ordered Marge in a measured tone.

"No, B.J., that is not right. If we owe him money then we should bring it back," admonished Ann as she wiped away mustard from the corner of her mouth with a napkin. "This hotdog tastes good, don't you think?"

"Umm huh, it is good. We hardly ever have hotdogs," I responded. "This is an unusually long one but not as long as a foot long, is it? I love my latte too. It's much better than the latte I get at The Beanery in the mall in Mesa."

"I think you're right, Soph," said Marge who had also been working the figures in her head.

Marge, Brandon and I were sitting in the front seat of Steve and Pat's Sylvia, their silver-colored, 1989, four-door Oldsmobile Sierra sedan. Mom, Sophia and Doug were squeezed into the back seat. We were parked in a nearly empty parking lot not far from the defunct German restaurant, The Schnitzelbank. One of Seattle's many small espresso stands, this one with hotdogs as well, was behind us.

Our cozy group had just finished bowling a couple of games at Kenmore Lanes. Steve, poor guy, had to leave after one game. Pat called on the cellular phone and asked him to get her from the office. She was finishing early and didn't want to wait for her ride. Luckily, we had taken two cars in case this might happen.

Normally we would have gone for a third game but the bowling alley had been freezing cold and practically deserted. Apparently no one else in the area had thought to go bowling the morning after Christmas. Besides, it was lunchtime, so time to quit.

Doug and Brandon drank their cokes; the rest of us held the hot lattes in our cold hands. Outside of the car it was snowing heavily.

"Can you believe this weather is Seattle? I just can't believe it!" grumbled Ann.

"This is what we wanted to get away from," groaned Marge. "I am already sick of winter and it's only December."

Pat had called from the office earlier when we were still at home to announce excitedly that snow was on the way. "Tell Sophia snow is coming! There are flakes in the air here! We won't have to go up to Snoqualmie. Scratch that off the list!" she had crowed.

And sure enough, even before leaving home the snow had, in fact, dusted the ground. In places it had already been a bit icy and slippery going down hill. Now, a couple of hours later, the area was completely blanketed with snow. Coming out of the bowling alley, we had been downright flabbergasted by the accumulation. Huge chunks of flakes were falling down all around us. It was as if the cloud bank up above had turned solid and was coming down in pieces. The streets were snowpacked. There was not much traffic but, like usual, inexperienced drivers were already spinning out and causing others to swerve dangerously.

"I think it's so beautiful! I don't remember asking for snow like Pat says but I'm glad I did. I've really missed it, you know," Sophia avowed nostalgically.

"Don't forget," she went on, "that I need to pop into a grocery store. I need a little Tabasco sauce to go into the spaghetti that we're going to have tonight. I found Pat's bottle of Tabasco but there wasn't much left and it was all brown. Pat said it might be 30 years old!"

"And then, we better not do anything else but go back up the hill before it gets too bad," advocated Ann.

Old veteran that she was on bad Montana winter roads, with age Ann has lost a lot of her nerve. She still owns and drives her not-very-faded, royal blue, 1973 Nova but not at night and—if she can avoid it—not on icy roads.

"Oh, Sophia, I love spaghetti!" fawned B.J. "I can't wait. I want some right now."

"Do you remember when you and Dad and I almost slid off the viaduct coming out of Bozeman in the Model A in a terrible snow storm, Moeke?" I asked.

"*Och, ja*, that was terrible. Do you remember that, too, Lottie? I can still hear Pa say, *'Hier gaanin wij* (Here we go)!' And I felt us sliding, sliding off the road. We were over the edge! We stayed that night by Meindert and Nellie Noot in Belgrade. Do you remember that? How did we ever get there? I don't remember that part."

"I don't remember that either."

I stuffed my refuse into the paper bag that was circulating and handed it to Brandon. The windows, I noticed, were partially fogged up, creating charming, winter wonderland scenes.

"Pa taught me how to drive in that Model A," recalled Ann. "I can still remember it like it was yesterday. I never had to drive a car in Holland. But Pa got the job to walk the Lo-line canal and the next day he said I had to drive to bring him. It was not far from four corners on the Joe Alberda road, I think, and so just like that, I learned in one day."

"Wow, that must have been scary," Sophia empathized. "Why did your husband walk the canal? That sounds pretty strange."

"He had to make sure that the farmers took what water they had a right to for the irrigation. Sometimes they take too much and rob their neighbors down the line. And then sometimes there would be branches and sticks in the ditch that would get clogged up. He had to clean it out then. It was a hard job. He had to walk a long ways. Westra, he did it too in other years, but he was always on his horse."

"Not long after that you were teaching me how to cut corners with the car," teased Marge.

"No," Ann said, "that was not your mother doing that!"

Doug left the car to pay what was owed, then conferred briefly with Marge and the two switched places.

"Did we owe any money?" asked Sophia.

"Well", mused Doug slowly, "the hotdogs were as much as I thought but somehow I ended up paying only a dollar. It was pretty confusing."

"Should have given it to me," interjected B.J., "then I could get another Coke."

"Will we have trouble getting up the hill, Doug? Pat said that we don't have any snow tires. Did you hear that?" asked Mom nervously. Others, you can imagine, were probably wondering the same thing.

"Nah," replied Doug shaking his head. "This is nothin'. If we get in trouble we have lots of people here to push."

He drove to the grocery store and soon after had Sylvia going up the hill on 185th street.

"Think positive everybody. Concentrate! Visualize us going all the way up," I called.

"You can do it, Doug!"

"We can make it!" chorused the cheerleaders.

"Oh, oh, are we really going to make it?" someone cried.

"Look out for that guy!"

Doug maintained a steady course and gave the other car that

was spinning in the snow to his right a wide berth.

"Hey, Dad, it's a good thing nobody was coming from the other way!" hooted Brandon.

"As long as we don't have to stop we'll be all right," predicted Marge.

"Ooo, that was close!" exclaimed Ann as the rear wheels for a moment swung out to the left just as Doug passed another stranded motorist.

"A little too close, if you ask me."

"Ja, me too, Sophia."

"I'd like to slide all the way down backwards, wouldn't you?" urged Brandon who loved playing the game of uproar with overly serious grownups.

"No. What? Are you totally crazy?" I retorted feigning outrage at the very suggestion.

Doug expertly maneuvered the car over the speed bumps going up to Prestige Heights on 64th to 63rd. He was fortunate not to have to stop at any intersections. Cars all along the way were being pushed or had been abandoned; they were stuck in the snow which was still coming down heavily. At last he reached Northshore Summit, passed the home of Sherwin and Carolyn Van Mersbergen on the corner and pulled into the 192nd Court cul de sac and into the Cok driveway.

"We made it!"

"Good job, Doug! Good job, Sylvia!" we hurrahed gratefully.

"It was the heavy load, I guess." He grinned as we piled out of the car.

"Steve and Pat aren't home yet," observed Ann worriedly. "I hope they didn't get stuck."

"It's a good thing we didn't bowl that third game. We might not have made it another hour from now," I maintained as I maneuvered around to untangle myself from the oxygen tubing.

Inevitably I hog-tie myself getting out of a car. Try as I might, I have not come up with a system that will provide me even a small measure of grace. I am so unlike my brother in this regard. He has every move down and everything just so in a predictable pocket or place. Truthfully, I am more organized when I am alone but, around people, I often become discombobulated. My attention at a critical moment can very easily be pulled in a more interesting direction.

Sophia, with both arms stretched high, was squealing with delight as she ran around like a mad woman in the snow in the driveway.

"Let's make snow angels!" she sang out.

B.J., who was watching her from the open garage, wrinkled his nose with disgust, but before he could make a comment, Sophia put a handful of snow down his neck. He gasped and then went into full attack mode whooping with excitement. Marge joined in the fun and soon snowballs were flying in all directions.

"I forgot how cold snow is!" cried Sophia. "My hands are blue. They're in full Raynaud's spasm. They're freezing!"

"Yeah, well, duh!" said Brandon. "This isn't Arizona you know!"

Sophia went from the driveway onto the lawn area and fell flat on her back in the snow manically waving her arms and legs back and forth.

"Come on, Beej, make a snow angel with me!" she called.

Chapter 15
Three de Vries Brothers in World War II

I interviewed family members, observed, listened, researched, recalled and imagined the rest.

Prologue

The credits rolled onto the television screen and Ann reached for a chocolate chip cookie from the plate on the coffee table. She settled back against the Early American couch, held her cookie up so as not to jar a single crumb loose onto her lap, then made her proclamation.

"Those two don't really belong together."

Hmmm, I murmured; then, paused and thought about it. *The video "Sabrina" is pretty standard fare. There were twists and turns in the plot line, but the destined couple predictably prevailed, and supposedly they will live happily ever after. I thought she would like it.*

"Really, you don't think they belong together?" I reflected using a well-worn psychiatric nursing technique. "Why not?"

I explored the matter with some caution and suspicion as I watched her take a determined careful bite of the cookie and chew deliberately.

"I don't know," said Ann as she worked her mouth methodically to clear it of the cookie and then took a swallow of coffee.

"They are not really in love, I think. Not like two people who know each other and are close. Let's just say it was not my favorite movie."

Ann, in the wintertime on Saturday nights after dinner out at the 4Bs in Bozeman with a small group of ladies, will come back to one or another's place, have some popcorn and settle in to watch a movie on the VCR. "Driving Miss Daisy" is their all-time favorite video and unlike most has received their full approval.

This was not Saturday night, although it felt like it to Ann. It was Thursday night a couple of hours after everyone had enjoyed Sophia's tasty dinner of spaghetti, salad and garlic bread. Even Doug, a careful eater, had heartily indulged.

She and I were sitting on the couch in the family room. We, along with Sophia and Brandon, had watched the movie and the other two had already left the room to find a new adventure. Doug, Marge and Pat had opted out of the movie and were sitting around the kitchen table playing the card game of Hand and Foot. Steve was still on duty doing the shuttle service for his family. Anil had run stuck in the snow earlier in the day and Steve had been asked to take Arlyce to work. Now, in the continuing snowstorm that was shocking all of the Seattle area including the meteorologists who were busily trying to explain why this was happening, he was getting Arlyce from her work in downtown Seattle and bringing her to her home on 105th.

"You know what I have thought would make a great movie?" I queried having decided that it was best to avoid yet another disagreement about what it takes for a couple to be right for each other. We had been there and done that too many times already. Mom, in my experience, unfailingly uses her own marriage as the exclusive template and always maintains an irritatingly smug position of superior knowledge in the area.

I had my legs up on the couch and was propped up against a pillow facing her. I was tired and felt chilled even though I was covered with Pat's cream-colored, hand-crocheted afghan, a gift from who else, my mother. She was sitting at the foot of the couch.

"No, dear," replied Ann reaching for another cookie. "How would I know what you would think was a good movie?"

"I've always thought that a story about your three brothers would make an excellent movie. *Oom* Jan (Uncle John; Jan is not pronounced like Jan as in Janet, but more like *ja* with an *n* sound on the end of it), *Oom* Tjaard (pronounced like you are putting a *ch* sound before saying *aah* and adding a *t* sound at the end) and *Oom*

Piet (pronounced just like Pete). You know, each one handled the war against the Nazis so differently and that affected their lives dramatically and the lives of those around them afterwards, don't you think?"

Without pausing long enough for a response I went on.

"And then the relationship of *Opoe* (a familiar form of *Oma*, grandmother) with each of her sons is so interesting and complicated. It would make a great movie."

"*Jaaa*, maybe so." reflected Ann hesitantly.

She looked straight ahead to the opposing wall and thought of those people and events neither objectively nor dramatically like I, a generation removed, did. Ann was reluctant to let herself be pulled in that direction again. All three brothers, Jan, Tjaard and Piet were dead now and her memories of their adult lives were muddled, bittersweet at best. Yet, despite best intentions her mind drifted back to those times. All of those terribly troubled times.

Jan

W*hen Hitler ordered the Nazi assault on the Netherlands in 1940, Jan, the oldest of my brothers, already had some life behind him,* Ann thought. *Three years before in 1937, our father, Klaas de Vries—Tjaakje's Opa—at the age of 53 (1884) had died so unexpectedly* (he had developed a kidney infection and within a couple days died of uremic poisoning).

Och, och, what a terrible shock to me, to my mother and to all of us eight children in our family! Ann recalled. *Jan, the third child but their first son, born on November 9 of 1918, then barely 20 years old, was all of a sudden expected by our mother to step into his father's shoes and this, for Jan, was not a very easy thing to do.*

Klaas de Vries, my father, was considered a hereboer (a gentleman farmer) *or a dikke boer* (great farmer) *who owned a boerderij mit land* (farm buildings with land).*In landbouwbedrijf* (farming industry or agriculture) *as in other ways of life in Holland there was and still is---but not so much as then—classes of people. The fact that the Klaas de Vries family owned both buildings and land put us into a high class in the dorp* (village) *of*

Baflo in the northern province of Groningen.

As a gentleman farmer, father deVries managed the work of boeren arbeiders (farm laborers who came to work for daily wages) *and three knechten* (servants) *who were full time workers that lived on the farm but in separate quarters. There were also two meiden* (maids) *at the busy boerderij which had been named Sasmaheerd by the earlier owner. Our parents expected all of these workers, plus us children, to work hard. So Mijnheer en Mevrouw* (master and lady) *de Vries were very busy. They did not just work but supervised, made visits and did work in the community.*

Klaas de Vries served as chairman of the School Board in Baflo. It was a very important responsibility in the village. He had other positions too and was a most respected man. My parents owned a De Soto with a yellow stripe around it. I remember it so clearly, Ann thought. *In this fancy auto Mijnheer de Vries chauffeured his wife to her morning coffee or afternoon tea.*

At the time of Father's death the three oldest girls had already left home. Me, Anje, I was married, lived ten miles south in Thesinge and was pregnant with my first child. Martje, the second daughter, my dear sister, was in and out of psychiatric care. Home for Martje was a place of trouble sometimes and she would often stay with friends of the family. And the third, Trui, married to Else Elses, lived not far from the boerderij in Baflo.

If I still had been at Sasmaheerd, I could have helped Jan, she speculated, *I could have helped with the cows especially. The outcome may have been different. But, as things go, Jan was not too interested or had his own ideas of how to do things and he put things off. He just was not suited for the job, especially not at that time in his life.*

He was always, as a kid already, slower than the rest of us kids, Ann remembered. *When we would leave to go to school, Jan would just be getting up. Even his own daughter, Zus, as she had always been known in Holland, or Peggy, Peggy Berry as she is known now living in New Jersey, even she in a visit to Montana not that long ago, had said this of her father.*

"*As a family we were without fail always, always late,*" Peggy had said. "*Dad would putter and putter and putter. Time didn't seem to matter to him.*"

Jan was overwhelmed by the responsibilities. It was hard for him to manage workers who knew more about the operation of the farm than he did. His mother needed him to drive her places; Tjaard, the next boy in line, a teenager, was going off to see girls and sow wild oats instead of sewing barley or hoeing sugar beets like he was supposed to; and Piet, shy, just 14, was not always well. Plus, Jan had his personal life too.

A few years went by and at the age of twenty-three Jan married his girl friend, Jant Ruiter. She had been his classmate for eight years and was best friends with sister Trui. Mother didn't like it at all. Jant was the daughter of Principal Ruiter at the Christian school in Baflo which, by the class idea, was not a good match for a landowner's son. That did not matter at all to Jan. He did just as he wanted.

At the point of their marriage Moeder (mother), Pieterke de Vries-Oudman, even though she could see there were problems, properly turned the operations of the boerderij over to Jan and Jant and moved with her youngest three, Piet, Dien and Wina, into a home in Baflo. Tjaard stayed on the farm with the new married couple. And, as could be expected with young people in those days, Jan and Jant soon had their first daughter, Stijn.

Before too much more time went by, Mother could see that things were not going good. Tjaard was working on other farms because he could not get along with Jan and Jan's management skills were not getting any better.

Mother changed her mind! She made the decision to replace Jan and took Tjaard back under her wing. The two households switched homes. Mother with the younger ones moved back onto the farm with Tjaard. Jan, Jant and child were shuffled off to the home in Baflo with nothing.

Free and forced to find his way in life, Jan first worked selling seed potatoes and grain. Then he began to work with his first love, horses. He was not afraid at all of the large animals. Not like me. I have always been a little afraid of horses, Ann reflected. *He boarded and took grote hengsten* (large stallions, mostly Belgian, work horses) *around for stud service. It became his life's work. By the time Jan left Sasmaheerd in 1941 and began his travels around in the province of Groningen with his horses,* Ann recalled glumly, *the Moffen* (Huns, barbarians, slang for Germans) *were already everywhere in the countryside of Holland.*

These thoughts being a personal reverie for Ann, it was not in her desire to dig through history. But, for the reader to gain perspective, it might be helpful for me to do so. Thus, we go even farther back in time.

For almost a century, from the mid 1800s on to 1940, there was a policy of neutrality in place in the Netherlands. For that reason, in the First World War (1914-18), the Germans invaded Russia, France and Belgium but not the Netherlands. However, Adolf Hitler, who was elected as the new *fuhrer* (leader) of Germany in the late 1920s, had no respect for the Dutch policy. His arrogant recognition-craving ambitions to create *lebensraum das*

Grossgermanische Reich (living space for the people of the Third Reich) made it a very different story in World War II (1939-45).

May 10th, 1940, in the quiet dawn of the promising spring day Hitler's *Wehrmacht* (armed forces) blitzed Holland. Fighter airplanes of the *Luftwaffe* (air force) droned overhead, paratroopers floated noiselessly from the sky, tanks in the panzer divisions chewed up roads and ground troops of the *Waffen SS* swarmed out of military trucks.

Blitzkrieg (Lightning War) was a new military tactic in the world. It was suited for a series of intense, short campaigns in order to avoid a long war. All offensive weapons such as planes, tanks and artillery were brought to bear in a narrow corridor. This corridor would then split the enemy defenses in two and allow tank divisions to penetrate rapidly and attack the rear of the enemy lines. Though brave and resilient, as the troops have historically been for the Dutch, the fighting between the Nazis and Netherland's forces of the interior, the *Nederlandsche Binnenlandsche Strydkrachten (N.B.S.)*, officially lasted only a few days. Ammunition, it was said, had been sabotaged; some of the boxes thought to hold weapons were found to be filled with nothing but sand (Ippisch, p.19). The Germans bombed Rotterdam mercilessly including its hospitals and threatened to do the same to the other large cities. The Dutch military simply was no match for the massive German military and industrial machine. For Holland, a small country, there really was no choice. The Dutch army surrendered on May 14th and the royal Dutch family consisting of the Queen, Wilhelmina, the Princess, Juliana, her husband, Prince Bernhard and their two daughters, Beatrix and Irene, along with a box of the crown jewels and select government members fled to London during the night.

Armed German soldiers of all ages in grayish green uniforms took command throughout the land. Administration was swiftly and efficiently put in place under *Reichskommissar* Arthur Seyss-Inquart and brash, loud officers sporting silver insignias and wearing black-bordered swastikas on their arms took over the governance in every village, town and city. It was not long before the dreaded swastikas, the National Socialist German Worker's Party (NSDAP) or Nazi Party emblem, flew boldly over the Dutch government houses, police stations, court houses, dikes, pastoral canals and timeworn windmills.

The swastika was originally an ancient cosmic sign for the sun and has been found in remains that date as far back as the Neolithic period. Ironically, the name *swastika* or *hakenkruisen* (hooked crosses formed by bending the ends of the arms of the Greek cross at right angles) comes from Sanskrit and means "good luck" and "well being". It had become a well known Nordic symbol as well. However, when Hitler and his followers adopted it, it became the twentieth century's bloody symbol of dominance and hate.

Of the several neighbors of Germany, Holland was richest in strategic supplies. The Germans not only gained the Dutch resources but also her colonial resources of the East and West Indies—Sumatra, Borneo, New Guinea, and Aruba. Their huge supplies of crude oil, rubber, tea, tin, sugar and coffee were invaluable. Holland was also an ideal neighbor in terms of being a strategic location. From Holland the Germans could send rockets into France and across the North Sea into London, and they were able to build defenses on the sand dunes against any amphibious assaults. Like a dark, heavy cloud cover, the dampening realities of war settled over the Dutch people.

After what came to be known bitterly as "The Phony War" in which the Dutch forces relented, the nine million Hollanders wasted little time accommodating themselves to their invaders. For the first couple of years of the occupation business went on like usual.

Germany borders Holland all along its eastern boundary and some of the Dutch thought and still think of Germans as more than neighbors, though Ann and many others never again will. In fact, the sound of a young German male voice speaking German still sends involuntary shivers up her spine and always will. But before then—and some Dutch probably now again—consider the Germans cousins. The Dutch national anthem with its commingling of scripture and history begins with these words:

"Wilhelmus van Nassouwe, ben ik, van Duitsen bloed, Den Vaderland getrouwe Blif ik tot in den dood;..."
(I am William of Nassau, of German blood. To the Fatherland I will remain faithful to my death.)

Duits, Deutsch, Dutch. Emotional, cultural and blood ties exist between the two countries. They not only have a shared boundary; they also have a shared history.

The ancient Germanic (related) tribes, also referred to as the Nordic or Teutonic peoples, are those who originated from the peninsula known as Jutland (modern day Denmark). They were Caucasoid, of tall stature, had a long head, light skin and hair, and blue eyes. They used the Aryan language which, as mentioned before, was the parent language to the future Indo-European family of languages. In the year 101 B.C. a branch of the Germanic tribes known as the Cimbri stepped into history by unsuccessfully invading Italy. The Roman Empire decimated the invading forces. Subsequently, they were controlled and further devastated by nomadic Asians led by the brutal Attila the Hun. By the fifth century Attila was dead, his kingdom dispersed and Caesar advanced the Roman army up the Rhine River. Saint Servatius of the Roman Catholic Church followed the army into the conquered lands.

The Franks and the Goths, two other Germanic tribes, later freed the subjects from the Roman rule. However, the Roman church stayed. Around 500-800 A.D., in the days of Clovis I and Charlemagne, kings of the Franks, and the Saints Willibrord and Boniface, missionaries of the church, the lands were officially Christianized.

Chaotic times followed. Successions of royal families divided regions along new lines every time a new empire replaced an old or when an heir came of age. The Merovingians were replaced by the Carolingians. The Carolingians gave way to the Saxons. Then the Hohenstaufen Dynasty, the House of Burgundy and the Hapsburgs.

Separation of church and state, as it is constitutionally determined in the United States, was not a democratic concept in those days. Religion and politics were intertwined and were a deadly combination. The ruler of the region decreed the church. And the church, threatening excommunication, had a strangle hold on the ruler.

Because of long standing grievances of exploitation against Rome and the Roman Catholic Church, the people were heavily influenced by a fiery, radical-minded, Augustinian monk, Martin Luther, in the early 1500s. In his 95 theses Luther blasted the

Roman Catholic sale of indulgences for the absolution of sins. He advocated instead for the authority of scripture, justification by faith and removal of the medieval popes and councils.

Martin Luther was both a reformer and a skilful politician. As such, he inaugurated the protest movement called Protestantism. By 1529 the new movement was firmly established in some states as the official church while Roman Catholicism remained dominant in others.

Emperor Charles V, a Hapsburg, desperate to preserve classic civilization by enforcing unity of belief, attempted to resolve the intense doctrinal differences. But the political interests of each proved too strong. Charles abdicated his throne in 1553. His great possessions were divided between his brother, Ferdinand, who became Emperor Ferdinand of Germany, and his son Philip. Philip became King Philip II of what was called the *Koninkrijk de Nederlande* (kingdom of the Low Countries), causing the seventeen provinces of the united nether lands thenceforth to become inseparable. Philip II also became the king of Spain.

A French-born scholar, John Calvin, who also repudiated the papacy, joined the reformers. He contributed to the vagaries of history by fanning the flickering flame of providential direction and the notion of a "chosen people." In his work, *Institutes of the Christian Religion*, Calvin set forth the decree of predestination in which God appoints to each soul eternal happiness or woe. His doctrine also advocated a strict social discipline which swept rapidly from Geneva, where he was writing, to the Upper Rhineland and from south to north into the northern lands. Calvinistic churches, Reformed and Presbyterian, were started.

The first German prince to accept Calvinism was Elector Frederick III. In 1563 he authorized the Heidelberg Catechism. And in the United Netherlands, the reformed clergy had a cozy relationship with the House of Orange, a league of nobles involved in the governing of the provinces. The Bible was their source book of stories and comparisons. It was befitting that the trials and promises for ancient Israel in the Old Testament of the Bible paralleled the history of necessary suffering and earned recompense in Europe.

While the influence of the Protestant Reformation was substantial, new Catholic dioceses were also being created. Lands were being awarded to bishops in the United Netherlands by Philip II, from his throne in Spain, and trouble between the two forces was brewing.

Philip's chief ministers were opposed in the United Netherlands by the nobles led by William (the Silent) of Nassau, prince of Orange. This group petitioned the governor, Margaret of Parma, half-sister of Philip II, for religious tolerance. One of Margaret's councilors in response scoffed contemptuously at the petitioners and referred to them as "beggars". The insult backfired. The name, Beggars, was quickly adopted by the growing Dutch revolutionary movement.

Increasing conflicts led Philip to order the Catholic Church to expand its Inquisition so as to include the Protestant heretics—up to this time the Jews had been its chief victims. The Inquisition was a tribunal of the Catholic Church that had widespread powers to expose and to suppress heresy. Though clergy were forbidden by the Church to shed blood, they were able to authorize princes and governors to do so. Penalties handed down from the Inquisition ranged from fines to hanging, to burning at the stake.

Philip sent Alva, his cruelest of military leaders, to uproot the heretics in the United Netherlands on land and he sent the Spanish Armada to subdue the Sea Beggars on the North Sea. Alva's siege of the city of Leiden and the people's resistance led to starvation of the people. The stubborn resolve of the Dutch resulted in thousands of deaths. At the end only a few prevailed. These few are still the Dutch model for bravery, piety and perseverance.

Catholicism against Protestantism, France against Hapsburg, the Dutch against Spain—in what was the Dutch War of Independence—and Denmark and Sweden as Protestant powers preventing Catholic subjugation, all became embroiled in what was called The Thirty Years War. It was an ugly, long, and bloody affair.

The diverse groupings of people in the seventeen provinces of the Netherlands set aside their religious differences and pulled together for the greater good of winning independence. The fighting was intense, but with the German imperial army giving support, the provinces were successful. And, amazingly, the new independent republic offered freedom of worship to all! It was a concept heretofore unknown and untested in the regions of Europe.

What followed was a golden age of prosperity for the upper classes. In the 17th century the lower classes rebelled and asked for help from France. France not only responded but quickly subdued the ruling parties and stayed. Thus the regions of both Germany and the Netherlands were occupied by France during the revolutionary Napoleonic Period. Eventually, with the aid of Prussia, the two countries of Germany and the Netherlands and both the upper and lower classes fought side by side to free themselves once again. This time it was from the rule of France.

By the early 1900s after decades of depression there was finally a time of peaceful productivity and economic interdependence. The machine age was coming. Germany was growing dramatically in stature and becoming the most advanced economic and military nation in Europe. It was a beacon guiding all idealistic German-speaking peoples in to the homeland. In the music and philosophy of the country there were the mythic figures of Teutonic folklore. They told legends of a Master Race and Aryan (noble) supermen.

Of great practical importance along with ancestral, political and religious kinship of the Netherlands and Germany is the reality that the two countries, as neighbors, have relied and still rely on each other as trade partners for many products. To risk the trade status between the two means to risk the economy of each.

Europe was quiet, but there was trouble in the Balkans. The Austro-Hungarians had annexed Bosnia-Herzegovina and the Serbs deeply resented it. On June 28, 1914, while riding through the Bosnian capital of Sarajevo, a Serb fanatic assassinated Franz Ferdinand, Archduke of the Austro-Hungarian Empire. The Austrians declared war on Serbia and the Romanov czar of Russia, Serbia's ally, mobilized his troops just in case they were needed. In turn Germany, Austria's ally in the Dual Alliance, declared war on Russia. France, seeking revenge for its loss in the Napoleon era and bound to the Russians by treaty, declared war on the Germans and so forth and so forth.

The Netherlands had adopted a policy of neutrality which Germany respected, whereas Britain went to war to get Germany out of Belgium. World War I, the Great War, lasted four years, and it blows the mind to think there were six million dead soldiers at the end of it. In 1918 the carnage was over, the victors, the Allies, blamed Germany and the German Kaiser was exiled to Holland.

The resulting Treaty of Versailles stripped the Germans of all their military power and imposed high war reparations. It was a humiliating blow which the young man Hitler and millions of other German nationalists could not accept.

By 1934 Adolf Hitler, a long time, nationalist, far right agitator and National Socialist German Workers' Party (Nazis) leader, had worked his way up the ranks to be appointed the Chancellor of Germany. He quickly quashed all opposition and assumed dictatorial powers as the *Der Fuhrer*. Thereafter, on behalf of the Third Reich, every part of German life was made an extension of the Nazi power and philosophy. Hitler wanted to restore Germany to her former glory, to be the ruler of Eastern and Central Europe and to get revenge for Germany's humiliation. At first leaders of other countries thought it was time that Germany be given her rightful place in Europe again; they tolerated Hitler's strong arm tactics for a number of years. Hitler was allowed to rearm, to re-occupy some of Germany's former colonies and to re-occupy Austria and parts of Czechoslovakia. By 1938, however, it became clear to the other nations that Hitler's march would not stop there; his march towards world conquest had begun.

Because of the aforementioned similarities and interdependence of the two peoples of Germany and the Netherlands, there was a period of seeming passivity and even participation on the part of the Dutch people when the Germans ignored the Dutch policy of neutrality and occupied the country this time around. One hundred thousand Dutchmen actually volunteered to work in the Nazi munitions factories. Another 50,000 joined the *Wehrmacht* and *Waffen-SS* to fight with the Germans against Russia, and nearly a half million showed up at *Nederlandse Unie*, a movement that advocated cooperation with the German occupiers. The largest newspaper, *De Telegraaf*, in Holland was openly collaborationist (MacPherson 123-124).

In fact, it was common knowledge that the prince of Holland, Bernhard von Lippe-Biesterfeld, had direct ties to the New Order in Germany. *Benno,* as he was called by his German friends, had been a uncommonly poor prince in Germany. He had been treated as a royal yet he had little money with which to live the lifestyle. He was frustrated and had been a mediocre student until he attended the University of Berlin. The university was a hotbed of Nazism, and the prince was soon converted. In succession with great passion for his work he became a member of each of Hitler's paramilitary groups. First he was with the *Sturm Abteilung* (the SA, the Storm Troopers) in which he trained to become a Luftwaffe pilot and then the *Sicherheitsdientst (SD)*. The SD was the security force of Heinrich Himmmler's dreaded *Schutzstaffel,* (the SS, the Brown Shirts). Still desperate to find a solution to his financial embarrassment in those days, Bernhard also became an employee and then Secretary to the Board of I.G. Farben, a huge German chemical company which was setting up a private worldwide Intelligence and industrial spy network. One of I.G. Farben's subsidiaries, in fact, produced Zyklon B, the gas which was later used in the death camps! The I.G. Farben works at Monowitz was known as Auschwitz III. There a total of 35,000 prisoners were sent to work of whom no less than 25,000 perished (de Jong 16). Drooling at the prospect of acquiring Holland's shares in Shell oil, it was a banker of I.G. Farben who arranged for Bernhard to become husband to Juliana, the daughter of Queen Wilhelmina of Holland in 1937. After his marriage, though Prince Bernhard had publicly resigned from the company, it was apparent that he was their contact man. His former boss arranged for him to join a bank in Holland that had strong ties to I.G. Farben and from there the Prince moved to one of the Royal Dutch Shell banks. Even though the Prince continued to train as a fighter pilot while in Britain and flew as a British Officer during the war it is commonly believed, though never substantiated, that Prince Bernhard in 1942 wrote a letter to Hitler offering Holland to Hitler in exchange for the ranking position of *Stadtholder* (govenor) (MacPherson 184-189).

Despite heroic stories of Jews being hidden and helped to leave the country by Dutch families—who are known as "righteous gentiles" by the holocaust Martyrs' and Heroes' Remembrance Authority in Israel (Woolf 2)—this practice was not widespread. By making use of three effective weapons: the weapon of fear, the weapon of dividing their opponents, and the weapon of deception the Germans deported 107,000 of 140,000 Dutch Jewish inhabitants in freight cars, most of them to Auschwitz, to be exterminated (de Jong 9). Dutch engineers and switchmen operated the trains! Only 5,000 of the 107,000 ever returned from the camps; thus, over 75 per cent of Holland's Jews perished. According to Dr.

Woolf "this represents the largest percentage of Jews to die from a particular country with the exception of Poland (Woolf 2).

Just as blight ruins the beautiful green foliage of a potato crop, anti-Semitism or hostility towards Jews, is the ugly corollary of Christianity in Europe. Though the one God, *Yahweh,* and the ancient Israelites were revered, the Jews of modern times were not. The Jews not only threatened the European gentiles' folklore of living in an idyllic society of Teutonic order and values in which the lesser races would do their bidding; they also stood in defiant opposition to the Christianity that had become the moral fabric since the Christianizing during the days of the Frankish rule.

The Jews were perceived as having rejected and participated in the killing of Jesus. The often repeated self-imposed (some say false) curse of the Jews is quoted in the Bible in the book of Matthew, chapter 27, verse 25: "Then answered all the people, and said, His (Jesus') blood be upon us and upon our children." The Jews were said to have shouted this curse in response to the Roman magistrate, Pontius Pilate, who was dramatically and sarcastically washing his hands of responsibility for the crucifixion and saying, "I am innocent of this man's blood; see to it yourselves."

"Crucify him! Crucify him!" the Jews, the Christ-killers, were to have shouted (Luke, chapter 23, verse 21). Anti-Semitism has swept through Europe time and time again avenging the blood of Christ and putting it upon the children of the Jews.

By their very cultural existence and their loyalty to Judaism, the Jews, according to Christians, defiled all that was considered sacred. If the Jews, chosen people of God, did not accept Jesus as the Messiah that God had promised, then something was amiss. Either the Messiah was false or the Jews were wrong. Or, if Jews were right, then Christians were wrong. In a land that had brought forth many Christian zealots, Catholic and Protestant alike, the Christians believed—heart and soul—that they were right (Goldhagen 49-50).

Maybe the Jews had been influenced by the Devil himself to kill Jesus. If it were so, maybe they still were tools of the Devil and therefore evil. If evil, then probably evil was in their blood. Maybe the Jew was not the same kind of human. Maybe he was like a bacilli, a vermin, a parasite, wicked, mischievous and clever. In any case, the Jew must clearly be subhuman, a nonperson, and so on and so on went the invective conversations. The bigoted paranoia grew, as it will with prejudice and stereotyping, and, with each telling, the Jews were ascribed more diabolical intent. Soon, evil Jews in league with the Devil were believed by many to be abnormally clannish and therefore linked to communism and Jews were believed to be conspiring to take over the economies of the world.

The first European anti-Semitic excesses took place strangely enough in 1095 when Pope Urban II declared war on the *infidels,* meaning the people who followed the teachings of Mohammad. Kings, princes and lords throughout Europe took up the cross and formed the first Crusade. The intent was to rid the continent and the Holy Land—specifically Jerusalem—of Muslims but along the way the rowdy, hungry-for-blood troops attacked enclaves of isolated Jews. This continued through the centuries of the following Crusades—there were seven from 1095-1270. Additionally, whenever there was stress in the economy, the Jews were blamed. When there was a wave of nationalism, there was an accompanying wave of Anti-Semitism. When there was ecclesiastic fervor in a region, Jews were driven out or forcefully baptized.

Germany had a long history of cruel ambivalence towards the Jews. Because they were marginalized by society, unmercifully taxed while kept out of the job market, the Jews turned to trading goods and money between Asia and Europe. They became local money lenders. German rulers used the enterprising Jew to obtain their great wealth of goods for their court and turned around and taxed the Jews in poverty to get even more.

Adolf Hitler—a man influenced by the likes of philosopher Friedrich Nietzsche who had prophesied that a super-race would evolve, by Richard Wagner the anti-Semitic composer who designated the Germans as the people who would comprise the super-race (Anderson 101-105), by Dr. Leopold Potsch his racist-tainted history teacher (29), by the writings of an extremist, racist, defrocked monk by the name of Lanz von Liebenfels (41-43), by the racist secret Thule Society (16, 72, 125-127) and others—walked onto the political stage of Germany and used the longstanding cultural hatred of Jews to his utmost advantage. In his book, *Mien Kampf,* written in prison before he was appointed chancellor, Hitler revealed his murderous vision:

"Today it is not princes and princes' mistresses who haggle and bargain over state borders; it is the inexorable Jew who struggles for his domination over the nations. No nation can remove this hand from its throat except by the sword. Only the assembled and concentrated might of a national passion rearing up in its strength can defy the international enslavement of peoples. Such a process is and remains a just one (Goldhagen 86)."

Though not a religious man, Austrian-born Hitler thought he was called by God to free and unite the Germans. That meant free them from the *Judenfrage* (Jewish problem) and unite them as a pure race. He claimed to be doing the Lord's work and, with the Nuremberg Laws, he established policies to forbid marriage to a Jew, to remove Jews from government jobs, to order Jews to wear a yellow star of David in public, to separate and ghettoize Jewish populations, to force sterilization and to deport Jews. It was Hitler's dream to return Europe to its beautiful God-given destiny and it was his goal to rid Europe of its blight, eleven million Jews.

With such governmental sanction there sprang-up ever-increasing individual incidences of violence against Jews without reprisal and one night members of Hitler's paramilitary group, the Storm Troopers, erupted *en masse*. They beat and killed Jews in the streets for all to see. Storefront windows of Jewish businesses were smashed. The sound of shattering glass resulted in the night forever being referred to as *Kristallnacht*. Importantly, it took place on November 10th, Martin Luther's birthday. Luther, referred to by Bishop Sasse as "the greatest anti-Semite of his time, the warner of his people against the Jews", centuries before, had railed against the Jews and had in his time advocated the burning of their books and synagogues (Goldhagen 53, 111, 284).

It was not long after *Kristallnacht* that eliminationistic policies in Germany turned to exterministic policies. In fact *Kristallnacht* marked the beginning of the systematic slaughter of the European Jews.

Hitler is often quoted as having said, "What good fortune for governments that people do not think."

Amazing! It is a tragic trait in human society that hundreds, thousands, even millions of people, like sheep, will follow the lead of a powerful, angry, enigmatic man. In the case of Hitler the Germans followed a powerful, angry, enigmatic man with a boundless, annihilating focus.

The worst atrocities of the war were meted out against six million Jews. But that was not enough. Another five million non-Jews lost their lives in the euthanasia program as well; they were the physical and mental misfits, homosexuals, Jehovah Witnesses, Slavic people, socialists, communists and Gypsies (Woolf 2). Can you imagine the staggering numbers that were slaughtered?

Jews were driven with whips into synagogues and the synagogues were set on fire. Those who tried to escape from the building were shot. The German police battalions were under an order called the *Schiessbefehl*. It was a shoot-to-kill order for any Jew that was caught outside of the ghetto which was the restricted area that they had been herded into at gunpoint. There were *Schiesserei* (shootings) when Nazis shot blindly into houses and windows, house after house after house. There were the *Judenvernichtungslager* (extermination camps) for Jews, as many as 10,000—only a few have been made famous, the *Einsatzgruppen* (mobile killing units) and endless death marches leading to nowhere.

Louis de Jong, the revered Dutch historian who had worked in London for Radio Orange during the war and who afterwards wrote twelve volumes about the Netherlands and the war wrote the following:

> "What had been built up in the heart of Europe was a tremendous machinery of destruction, powered by the energy of an evil doctrine making use of the cogs and wheels of every form of official organization grinding millions of helpless and innocent people to dust (de Jong 25)."

Seeming passivity in the Netherlands was just that; it appeared so. But beneath the surface it was something else. Queen Wilhelmina's decision not to allow herself to become Hitler's prisoner was a testimony not to her cowardliness but to her unbroken spirit. Despite the fact that her mother, her husband and son-on-law were all of German descent, the Queen, in her Radio Orange broadcasts on the British Broadcasting Corporation (BBC), called the Nazis, "de *Moffen*" and appealed to her listeners to resist the foreign invaders(de Jong 67). If Britain falls, you shoot me, she is purported to bluntly have instructed her secretary. Her voice on the air waves was clear and vigorous. She characterized the war as a struggle between good and evil. As mother of the people, she was deeply disturbed by the indignities inflicted on her children. Those who had kept their radios against orders (including Jan Piet Heidema) were inspired. They spread the word that the Queen had not given up. German-issued stamps were defiantly put on the left side of the envelope because the right side belonged to the image of the Queen.

Similarities and interdependence of the two countries be damned. Some knew right from wrong and, according to them, what the Nazis were doing was dead wrong. The silent mind-your-own-business Dutch, both military and common citizens, were reacting. Many went on protest strikes and many were risking their lives by getting involved in activities and organizations of resistance.

Leaflets from underground presses sprang up telling the truth of things. Churches, time and again, voiced their indignation in pastoral letters. When Jews were rounded up into ghettos, workers in Amsterdam went on strike. As Nazis clamped down, more Hollanders rebelled. In 1942 organized university students, reading about what Mahatma Gandhi had been doing in India and following his example, in nonviolent disobedience, left classes and shut down the large Nazified Dutch universities of Delft and Leiden. In 1943 all the other schools of higher learning were closed in similar protest. Ten percent of these courageous university students paid for their actions by dying in prisons and concentration camps. Theaters and concert halls, at a similar price to the participants, were closed down.

Dutch men up to the age of 45, 400,000 in all, were forcefully taken to work in German labor camps or conscripted into the German army. Males 45-60 had to work for local forces. Those who resisted were shot or put into prisons. The Dutch hid young men and Jews in their homes and transported them from safe place to safe place.

With the British blockade in effect, the Dutch were wholly dependant on Germany for raw materials which declined more and more. Additionally the Nazis pillaged cows, butter, wool and machinery. A person caught hoarding wool or making use of unauthorized electricity might be given the death penalty. Nazis dismantled workshops and moved them to Germany. They melted down church bells, antiques and silverware for the metal. Hearing this, the Dutch defiantly buried their metal in the gardens, in the church steeples and in fields.

The Nazis confiscated other food items off the shelves and then rationed only some of it back to the Dutch people via food coupons. Coupons and identification papers, in turn, were forged, stolen and distributed to those in hiding by underground workers.

The Germans were paying the wages of the railway workers, but in 1944 after working with the underground leaders, the Dutch government guaranteed to reimburse companies and people who could pay the normal wages for the railway workers; once done, every single worker went on strike on September 17 shutting down the entire transportation system in the country! It was the same day that the Allied Airborne Army landed near the big rivers in the south.

In retaliation the Germans held back food and fuel to the people. Green saplings were cut down for fuel and people existed on next to nothing. Central kitchens in the big cities supplied weak soups of cabbage and potatoes. If an individual could get there they were given a half-liter which amounted to no more than 600 calories. Other sources of food having been used up, it was too brutal for many. In the winter of starvation 16,000 Dutch people died of cold and hunger. Many died along the wayside in search of something to eat. Tragically, to make terrible conditions even worse, neighbor turned on neighbor.

In regard to food, rural people, farmers, especially those in northern Holland were more fortunate than those in cities. They had access to farm products and, though illegal according to the German mandates, distributed products such as milk secretly to their needy relatives and neighbors.

People lined up on a daily basis so that the family and workers at *Sasmaheerd* could fill each pitcher of milk, one per family. Mother de Vries-Oudman kept a list of clients. A hundred clients or more came from all around. Some came by train from as far away as Groningen. She, also, took in a refugee family that had fled from their home in the south of Holland because of the heavy fighting in that area. The ver Kooiens had seven children; their eighth child was born on the de Vries *boerderij.*[3]

There was a time that Anje and Jan Piet put some meat of a butchered goat from *Sasmaheerd* into a cream can and were transporting it from Baflo to Thesinge in the *koetzewagen* (horse-drawn buggy) when a German vehicle had come up and followed them. As she told it, her chest had tightened and her stomach had filled with acid. Quickly, she had covered the cream can with a coat and tried to act like nothing was going on. The vehicle had finally turned off and the heavy weight on her chest had lifted. But fear, that black octopus, had its long, thin, cold fingers wrapped tightly around her heart. And it had stayed. The memory of it lingers still.

My brother, Jan, and his wife, Jant, a brave, simple couple, did their part against the Germans too, Ann thought, as we return to her musings. *As they studied their home in Baflo they discovered a natural hiding place built into it. There was a small space between the framing wall and the inside finish wall of their bedroom with the roof rafters on a slant overtop. A person could crawl along its length, the length of the bedroom; at the end of it there was another space at right angles to it. This was a little bigger. Jan and Jant lowered a straw mat down into the space from the attic. Then Jan made a closure that looked just like a wall at the point of the right angle. If a person shone a flashlight down the first space, and the Nazis did several times, they would never know that the second space was there. Many young men were hidden safely in this secret space by my brother and his wife. But then one day he was caught and sent to Vught.*

Again for a moment, let us expand the picture beyond Ann's recollections. Germans had access to and control of all of the civil records and could learn about the existence and whereabouts of every person. They would summon young men by name by posting notices in public places. They were expected to show up at a certain time and place. The young men were then transported to Germany to work in factories, dig trenches or whatever they wanted them to do. If those called did not show up, they were considered fugitives and became sought after by the *Gestapo, the Geheimestaatspolizei* (Police of the State). The *Gestapo,* when frustrated, conducted

---

[3] In gratitude and remembrance, the ver Kooiens sent Ohma, *Mevrouw* de Vries-Oudman, a centerpiece of flowers for her birthday, April 13th (1887), every year after for 27 years in a row! At her funeral, there was also one last centerpiece from the ver Kooien family.

terrifying *razzias* (raids, roundups) when all the houses in one area were searched.

Young men involved in agriculture, as Jan was, were not routinely conscripted. Their function of producing food was too vital for Germany. Jan, with the attitude that no one was going to tell him what to do or not do, became involved in underground work to get forged food coupons. In one such effort in the winter of 1943 he was one of three men who relayed food coupons to a hiding place for Jews in Groningen. One evening the temptation for the Jewish hideaways to get a breath of fresh air was too strong. One or more of the men went out to the street and when there, revealed that they were able to get food coupons. The listener was very eager to know from whom they were able to get these coupons. One thing led to another and soon the man who had given them the coupons was picked up by the German police.

By no means, reader, were all of the Dutch unwilling partners with the Germans even at this late date. There was a great deal of corruption. Some Dutch people sought to curry favor with their aggressor and possible future governing body, should the Germans win the war. Some saw it as an opportunity to avenge an old grudge against a neighbor or a former business partner. Some satisfied their greed and made profits from selling on the black market or buying abandoned property and plundering homes of captured Jews and political prisoners. And about one and a half percent of all the Dutch continued to give outright support to the fascist racist ideology and efforts. Those people had signed up with the *National Socialistic Beweging (NSB),* the Dutch Nazi party, and they had their own *Grune Politie* (Green Police). These chameleonic characters, the German collaborators, the infiltrators and informants, the *NSBrs,* turned against their own people. Such self-serving betrayal tore at the fibers of decency in families, neighborhoods and communities.

When Jan heard that the underground food coupon scheme had gone sour and that one of their threesome had been picked up, he went into hiding. He did not hide in his own home but in the home of another villager. After a three-day stay Jan's rebellious nature resurfaced. He naively left his hiding place and, wearing his familiar smirk and fearless attitude, went back out onto the street.

Meanwhile, the captured man of the threesome was being tortured in jail. After a few days of taking the abuse, thinking that

Jan had had plenty of time to go into hiding, the man gave Jan's name to the *Gestapo*.

In February of 1943 Jan was picked up and sent directly to a concentration camp. He was kept in Vught, a camp in North Braband in Holland, where prisoners were kept in line with nasty, hungry German shepherd guard dogs.

The Jews were treated the worst but anyone in a concentration camp served as a target. Common German, also common Dutch Nazis, petty bureaucrats, just plain men and women who—given a paycheck, a little power and fervent speeches by their warped leader, Hitler—could use the occasion to act out their own malicious feelings and fantasies. During his seven and a half months in Vught Jan saw, heard, smelled, tasted and touched the heart of darkness.

One day, as was often the case, there was a list read off with the names of those who were to be transported to Germany. Jan heard his name and, fearing the worst, he hid. Where else but between the haunches of the horses in a stable! Several days later another list was read with the names of those who were to be released. Jan's name miraculously was again read off! He could not believe his good fortune!

When Jan came home, Ann remembered, *young sister Wina went running down the street of Baflo calling out to everyone, "Jan de Vries is thoes (home)! Jan de Vries is thoes!"*

Jan was tall, she thought. *Maybe 6'4" or more, Tjaard and Piet too, all like our father, Klaas. Jan was always very thin with sharp angles to his face. The only time that his family, and me too, saw him not so thin was when he was set free from the camp. He was very bloated from the every day meals of just cabbage soup. I was amazed at how he looked. I could hardly believe it was him. But his thinness came back and he looked bad to me for a time.*

Everyone—you too—reader, knows the concentration camp look. We've all seen the pictures: bony, drawn, gaunt and such a desolate look in the deep-set, dark eyes.

I always thought Jan suffered from depression in his life from that, Ann contemplated. *I would see it when I visited back there. I think he had bad memories of his days in the camp. Maybe he dreamed about it. I don't know; he didn't talk to me really. After the war he was slow too but it was different. He sat in a darkened living room too much. But still, his mind was always good.*

As Peggy, who was ten days after Jan's release from the camp, has reported, her father could hardly bring himself to talk about his experiences. She tells a story about growing up with him and about a time when she had been reluctant to eat the food set before her.

"Empty your plate!" he would say.

It was the rule. Peggy rebelled. As a lesson to her, so she would more fully appreciate her blessings, her father told her about his desperate acts to stave off starving to death in the camp.

"I would prop and hold up a dead man's stinking body to make it look like he was still alive" he had blurted out and he had begun to shake uncontrollably, "to get his portion of the rotten food! And what food? A cup of watery soup with worms in it from rotted vegetables! Do you understand? Do you understand what I had to do? To hold up a dead man's body? I did this more than once. And now, you sit here and want to waste good food? You don't know how good you have it!"

Peggy, as she says, was shocked. In her mind's eye she can still see his haunted look and shaking anger as he relived the horror. Tragically, in 1945, when hope of liberation and celebration was on the horizon for the Netherlands, Jan and Jant's two-year-old son, Klaas, named after his grandfather, drowned in a *gracht* (deep, wide ditch) that was at the end of their street. The couple was devastated. Later, two more children, Greetje and Albert, were added to Jan and Jant's family.

The government of the Netherlands after the war sought to honor the efforts of her patriotic countrymen. Jan was awarded a sum of money for his sacrifices but without hesitation he turned it down.

"I did not do what I did for money," was Jan's simple, straight-forward reasoning.

Being the oldest son and so the one to inherit the family farm, Ann reflected, *Jan was very hurt when his mother passed him by and gave the boerderij over to her second son, Tjaard, for what we all in the family said was a song of what it was worth. The handwriting had always been on the wall but things with Tjaard were not good and Jan had still hoped that he could one day be back on Sasmaheerd. Maybe, now that we know everything, it would have been better.*

This thing of Mother, one son over another, was terrible for the whole family but especially for Jan and Jant. It made things hard with bad feelings. I think Jan was bitter about that and I can't really blame him.

But Peggy, even though she knew he resented his mother for her decision and so did she as the granddaughter, remembers him as a loving forgiving man and father who was devoted to his family. A man, she says who never abandoned his *Gereformeerde* Calvinistic faith and who lived each day with such integrity.

Jan and Jant together in Baflo lived quietly into old age until 1990, six years ago now, Ann recalled sadly. Then at the age of 72 Jan lost his hold on a branch, fell from an apple tree and broke his pelvis. In a few days he had complications set in and he lost his hold on life too. I dropped everything and flew to Holland for another funeral of a brother. Jan was the last of my three brothers to go. The other two, Tjaard and Piet, both younger already had died.

Tjaard

Tjaard, the middle son born November 24th, 1921, everybody agreed on it, was a born farmer, a natural, like me, Ann thought. We were like our revered father, Klaas. We loved the out-of-doors, the land, the animals and the challenge of farming. After Jan left the boerderij in 1941 Tjaard became Mother's right hand man and Father's shoes fit more comfortably on this son's feet.*

It was difficult for Ann to think about Tjaard. Of the three brothers she had felt the most kinship with him and of the three he had been the one who most tugged at her heart and eventually the one who had broken it. We shall fill in the gaps of her thinking as needed. First, read a description and then learn the shocking news.

Tjaard was a good-looking, well-built, tall man with brown, tousled, curly hair. He was of two natures. On the one hand, he was pretty much a hard-working, stay-at-home-on-the-farm kind of guy who was most comfortable in his old worn *klompen* (wooden shoes). He liked good food and telling a joke to make family and workers laugh. On the other hand, quite unlike his recalcitrant older brother, Jan, Tjaard was a charmer and a partier. During the war he was in his very early twenties and Tjaard didn't take too much too seriously. He reveled in having a rowdy, good time with his friends in the bar.

In 1945 the resistance and the Allies prevailed. The Germans were driven out of Baflo and all of Holland welcomed the Canadian and American soldiers. Let the bells ring! Let the celebrations begin! But wait a minute. Have you heard? Tjaard de Vries has been arrested by the Dutch police for being an informer! An *NSBer!*

Tjaard de Vries?! What had he said? Or done? About whom? When? For how long? What were the circumstances of Tjaard's acts of treason? Why? How had they bribed him? What had he profited? Was his mother aware? Was she involved?

I believed that he did nothing more than sign up with the National Socialistic Beweging, defended Ann in the privacy of her mind. *But did I know the truth? He had been drinking and partying a little too much, I heard, with his friends in a bar and then signed when he was drunk. Maybe on a Saturday night or so. I think he never really did much of anything else.*

Let us imagine the scenario, reader. Obviously, some people knew that he had signed up with the *NSB* and told others, the police or the resistance people. Everyone kept track of everybody else. A neighbor may have watched from behind their lace curtains at night and told secrets to the Nazis or to the resistance people the next day. A drunken friend may have whispered it for a price. People kept tabs and somebody had kept tabs on Tjaard de Vries, son of the distinguished family who lived on the *boerderij* just outside of town. Someone may have had a moment of sweet revenge or acted out a jealous fantasy against the *dikke boer.* At any rate his proud family was shaken and shamed.

What Tjaard did, whatever it was, was certainly small potatoes compared to some of the greedy, vindictive hate crimes committed in those days. One hundred thousand homes had been destroyed; families had been shattered by death, delusion and deceit. Traitors had to be taught a lesson. In disgrace Klaas and Pieterke de Vries's son, Tjaard, the golden boy with so much promise, the fun-loving brother and nice uncle, had his head shaved by people who took the law into their own hands.

Ann didn't remember; didn't want to remember. *Was he put in a brown burlap sack, tarred, feathered and paraded through the streets along the lines of jeering crowds like many were? If so, I was not there to see it; I was thankful for that,* she affirmed. *He was taken publicly from Baflo by the police and placed in a Dutch labor camp to work in the slikken (mud and mire) by the dike with other traitors. He was there for seven months.*

Tjaakje C. Heidema

Like Jan's imprisonment, nothing much is known or said about Tjaard's confinement. Were his Dutch jailers humane to collaborators or was he tortured? "Sometimes, the camps were staffed by former resistance workers," said David Barnouw, an official at the National Institute of War Documentation, not long ago on Radio Nederland on the internet, "and this was seen as part of the revenge. We know there were beatings, in which rifle butts were used, that people were starved or forced to stay awake, and that 20 - 30 people died as a result. It didn't happen everywhere, but it did happen. Houses (too) were plundered and either kept for the plunderers or sometimes redistributed to families who had lost everything. Around 100,000 people were incarcerated after the war until they could be tried. A total of 400,000 were eventually investigated, and 10 to 15,000 of them were sentenced...The children," said Mr P. K. "of people who were collaborators...share some level of trauma...(they) have the added problem that it is still almost impossible to talk about. Often the children of parents who were wrong feel as if they are wrong, too: they feel guilty of what their parents did."

"The Germans were treated okay in the camps," said one of those children on Radio Nederland, "but what happened to the Dutch - you don't want to know. My father was sent to Westerbork and he was a broken man when he got out. I feel again and again that people don't want to know what happened."

When he had finished his time in the labor camp, Tjaard came back to Baflo to work on the farm, Ann recalled. *He married Dirkje Feitsema, the daughter of a landowner, en familie van stand (a family of "class"), some said for her money, and they had three sons, Klaas, Gert and Johan, and one daughter, Trynie.*

Although some people in the town didn't want to have anything to do with him again, Tjaard still went to town and looked for a good party. Some would say he would go after other women. I don't know about that. He liked and needed his liquor too much. I know that. He was an alcoholic and that is why I hate the stuff. I do not even want it in my house. I only have a little in the house sometimes for to make krentjebrij and the bottle of Mogan David can sit in the cupboard for years, Ann brooded.

As an aside, it must be said that Tjaard's carousing came as no surprise to the old-timers in Baflo. After all, he was the grandson and namesake of the old Tjaard de Vries. That man, too, had liked his drinks and a woman on the side, it had been said.

No matter how firmly religious and how strict Tjaard's mother had been, and she really had been both—some have said to excess—the charming son defied the woman who had given him every chance possible. As the years ticked away he ever more forfeited the spine-straightening de Vries pride for a quick fix. And, of course, as the years ticked away, despite his mother's generosity and his own innate abilities, *Sasmaheerd,* the family *boerderij*—like Tjaard's own body—suffered from ever more neglect.

I could barely stand to see what was happening on the farm in those days when I would go back to Holland to visit, ruminated Ann.

Then one day, on the farm three miles south of Manhattan, Montana in America, I was told that my beloved home and shed and barn at Sasmaheerd had nearly burned to the ground! Some electrical fault, they said on the telephone, and Tjaard's family had moved into Baflo. I could not believe it! She felt again the paralyzing dismay that had swept through her soul on that day.

And then not long after that Tjaard and Dirkje sold the boerderij mit land. Not one in all the children of the new generations in Holland—and there are many, nearly 50 now—not one is involved in landbouwbedrijf, in farming. Not one. It hurts no one more than it does me, Anje (de Vries) Heidema, she thought with no small degree of bitterness. *Alcohol, I hate the stuff. Don't talk to me about alcohol. Only here in Montana in America are children with de Vries blood still on a farm.*

Whenever I visit Baflo I go to the concrete post that still has the name, Sasmaheerd, on it and I remember: The luscious, green grass of the pasture after a rain, the fresh smell of cut grass and clover to make hay and the sweet smell of cow manure carried on a light breeze. I see the black and white Holstein cows quietly grazing and chewing their cud. Off in the distance the koren is op ruiters (grain is up on sticks in a row).

I see the water that flows quietly by in the ditch where Pat as a young girl caught stiegel staatjes (tiny little fish with barbed tails). *And the bushes whose roots are so deep along the ditch they are not afraid to let themselves be swayed about by the strong winds. I see again the birth of the kid from the mother goat. The first birth I ever saw. So amazing! I can see it like it was yesterday.*

Doar is't goud op blaik (There is the laundry spread out on the lawn to dry), *zwart and rode aalbessen ein toen* (black and red currants in the garden) *and the small kruudorens* (gooseberries), *the ones in the back with the little hairs on them. They were the sweetest. In the kelder* (basement) *is the sauerkraut; I didn't like that and in the rain barrel there were eels. For me, for Anje-Ann, Sasmaheerd was and will always feel like home.*

As Ann's mind lingers on those cherished memories, let us face the tragic end of this chapter. In his late forties and early fifties Tjaard became Baflo's town drunk. Time and again he had to be retrieved by Jan from one embarrassment or another. Tjaard's children would call *Oom* Jan: Dad won't listen. Will *Oom* Jan please get him and bring him home? Tjaard, no matter what drunken state he was in, had finally come to the point in his life when he took orders from his older brother.

There were periods of time when Tjaard went on the wagon and did not drink. He would return to the church and family seeking solace. Neither of which ever refused him nor abandoned him. Ann would have long, heartfelt talks with him when she visited. He was unusual that way. She could talk with him whereas she never could with Jan or Piet, and if he had been sober when she left, she would return home to the States hopeful.

"Tjaard has promised me this time that he..." this or that. I remember her saying it.

Tragically, though, he was not able to hold onto a healing forgiveness of himself for very long. He broke all his promises. He and his family struggled near poverty.

On September 22nd, 1978 at the age of 56 Tjaard died of a massive heart attack, Ann remembered. *He was my second brother to go. My third brother, Piet, the youngest, had already been the first to die.*

Piet

Piet, the youngest de Vries son, born on October 16th, 1923, was unlike both his stubborn, yet temperate brother Jan and his likable, but self destructive brother Tjaard. There being a ten-year-age difference between herself and Piet, Ann knew him the least well of the three.

Early on, she remembered, *Piet was frail and in his tender teen years around the time that our father died, he had become quite weakened by a bout of pleurisy. He then had to submit to the tent cure, the open air treatment.*

Mom did not remember much more about Piet's young life when I asked her but *Tante* Jant, Jan's wife—who in her early 80s visited with her daughter, Peggy, in New Jersey and who came to Maine with Peggy to visit with me once—was able to add some information. Piet, she said essentially, was a shy, studious young fellow who was turned off by the contentiousness between his brothers and mother. According to her Piet had no interest in vying for their or his mother's attentions. *"Moeder* (Mother) *de Vries"* had designs on him to become a minister, but, *Tante* Jant said, Piet was not interested in her designs. It was one reason, she said, why he did not get along well with his mother and that he looked forward to being old enough to leave home.

So at 19, looking around for an arena in which to mature, he was provided it by being drafted into the *Nederlandse* military. It is not clear to me what functions the Dutch military had in those days but, regardless, for reasons I also do not know, he was soon dismissed from the military. Not long after, he got wind of the fact that several of his former officers were forming resistance groups. Then, again according to *Tante* Jant, Piet's previous lieutenant colonel personally selected him as one suited to become a resistance fighter in North Holland.

You must understand, reader, in Holland there was resistance to the war with a small *r*, so to speak, in which many such as Jan became involved and there was resistance with a capital *R*. The capital *R* resistance fighters, a significant number of whom were Jews (flying in the face of the myth that the Jews went passively to their deaths) were organized and used force. At first their activities centered on dealing with the many enemies of the country within their own Dutch people, but as the war progressed it included retaliatory strikes against the Nazis.

Piet became a member of the *Knok Ploeg (K.P.,* Knuckle Brigade) from District 11. Wholeheartedly and idealistically, as a late-blooming adolescent will do, he immersed himself in his work. He became an *onderduiker,* someone who went underground and took on a completely different identity. As such he was given the code name of Han.

After the war Piet talked about some of his experiences to a journalist who was collecting stories from men who had worked

Tjaakje C. Heidema

under the oversight of a Commandant Wastenecker. When published, the book, *De Mannen van overste Wastenecker,* had the chapter, *En K.P.er Vertelt* (pp.154-169), about Piet and some of what he had done as Han. I have translated his chapter into English and will share it with you and a drawing of him, which is also in the chapter, but it is necessary, I think, to have some background material, first.

In the early 1940s Gerrit van der Veen, whose part will soon be explained, was a happy-go-lucky sculptor in Holland with many artist and intellectual friends. Together with other groups he and his friends masterminded a plan to destroy the *Amsterdamse Bevolkings* (the register of the citizens of Amsterdam) which contained all the citizens' names and family connections. If successful, the Germans would be unable to trace the identity of people in the underground who carried false identification papers.

Half completed, the plan broke down and most of the group was held in the *Weteringeschans,* a prison for both common criminals and those Germans considered political prisoners. The leader of the plan, Gerrit van der Veen, was free and wanted to free his friends. Piet became involved in an attempt to do just that.

Here is my translation of Piet's words:

At one time there were many men imprisoned in the *Weteringeschans* and they faced execution. In Amsterdam their friends wanted to make an attempt to free them. Because it would be a difficult job help was asked for from District 11. They were asked if they could drum together a group of K.P.ers who would dare to take it on.

Ah, well! It had to be done and we made ourselves available. So that on an evening we went to Amsterdam where we met at a specified address. To that unfamiliar house we came dragging in, all well armed with our *blaffertjes* (barkers-guns) and all with tight nerves.

We were there with about 30 men. While we were sitting in a room upstairs waiting, below on the first floor Gerrit v.d.Veen and others devised a plan. So hours slipped away that we killed by playing cards. We were called downstairs and were given our orders. What each one of us must do, how to handle it afterwards, where to flee if it failed and so forth, and so forth. Until it was four o'clock.

At that moment, one by one, very carefully the front door was opened and then in pairs we left in the direction of the *Weteringeschans* pistol in hand. It was tiresome that there were some Home Guard hovering around because those we had to try to evade. Not that we were afraid of exchanging shots but such an encounter could throw the whole works off from what was really intended.

Everything then stood in readiness in front of the disreputable building. A guard who was in on the plot had left the side door open. Watchmen are posted and then everything is ready for the break in. The door is open!

But as the first K.P.ers go inside, a dog starts barking. That was not planned for. And barely had we realized what consequences the barking could have when the shooting began.

It rains bullets! They ricochet off the walls and splinter window panes. An ear-deafening noise. It seems as if two large groups are exchanging intense firepower in the quiet morning hours.

The noise can be heard in town and the danger becomes greater by the minute. We come to realize that we are not going to be able to free the prisoners. We must go back into town as long as the coast is clear. So spread out fast.

There are still shots made from both sides. Keep walking. Disappear. Already there is the siren of the first police wagon in the distance. And another one! And another one!

Take cover! Leave!

Screeching, the wagons whiz by us.

And when we finally balanced it out, it wasn't that bad. We had a couple who were slightly wounded and v.d.Veen was seriously wounded but no one was missing...

Some time after the failed attempt the *Gestapo* found the wounded Gerrit van der Veen. In retribution the Germans shot him and his friends, who had been imprisoned at the *Weteringeschans,* in the sand dunes. Their bodies lay in a mass grave there.

And then follows Piet's story of the marriage coach. In this segment he refers to himself as "he" or "the K.P.er."

...things had gone wrong in Enkhuizen. Quite a lot of the guys had been picked up and by pure chance the leader had not been with them. He was in the neighborhood of Schagen and knew nothing about the arrests.

Sure there had been some uneasiness before but there wasn't any special reason to expect a raid or such. The arrest of the Enkhuizen group happened on a Tuesday. Saturday thereupon was the K.P.er's birthday and he wanted to spend it with his family.

They lived far off, about 125 miles. Since you never could know what might happen he decided the day beforehand just to go to Enkhuizen to make a couple of arrangements with his team.

The train brought him past Hoorn through De Streek to his place of destination. He walked directly, calmly and quietly to a certain address, went inside and was startled.

"What in heaven's name are you doing here? All the lads have been picked up and our house is being watched!"

Boom! After that first blow sank in he quickly left to the second address. The boss of this business was underground and the advice was: Get away immediately. The S.D. is always searching around. He leaves again.

But he can't, just as he was going to go to another address he heard the piercing sound of the police van. Quickly, through the shop and out the back door with another fugitive.

Race, race! Three crossings! Like lightening he goes to the last address. Bad luck. Not home. But the door is open. When he smells a scent the Kraut will search and track it down. It looks like he is everywhere in all the streets and all the alleys. There is no rescue possible anymore. This must be the end. Well, yes, maybe it will be another half hour or an hour but he will be found.

There it is already happening. Somebody is racing into the house.

"They are looking for you!"

"Escape! Yes, I know. But where do I go?"

All at once the warner has an idea. The neighbor next door has a livery stable. If you...

Fifteen minutes later a marriage carriage is riding through the streets of Enkhuizen. On the high seat sits the underground worker or K.P.er neatly in uniform. In the carriage is the other young fugitive who will be getting his bride in Grootebroek...

Time and again the vans drive by the carriage looking for the K.P.er who is sitting somewhere in hiding. Because he has been targeted. As Enkhuizen already lies far behind him, the cigarette tastes doubly good.

In Grootebroek the K.P.er goes on the train to Heerhugowaard where he finds safe shelter with old acquaintances and fellow workers. He is exhausted and tells only the essentials of his story. Then he goes to sleep well into the next day.

Towards evening of the following day it is discovered that it is his birthday. Bless you! And have many more years! Fun birthday...

He has not been back to Enkhuizen so long as the Krauts ruled over our land. It was too dangerous because the S.D. gang know him now. They had a photo of him and his name and other particular details.

No, it became too hot in West-Friesland. The S.D. was lying in wait day and night. Like a bloodhound who had smelled a scent and then lost it ...

... He was aching to again go to work. Then after some weeks, it is to that point. A friend out of Heerhugowaard came by to him. He must go to work, directly, immediately.

Please, here is a set of false papers, and a false identity card.

A new period of hard and dangerous work followed.

And so the police station on the Overtoom in Amsterdam had

5

a turn. The K.P., insatiable as always, needed weapons and the Amsterdam police had these nice hand-guns that you could so easily carry loose in your pocket.

The place of gathering was not very suitable, a bicycle storage place. There was no other convenient place. The affair was already planned: two K.P.-ers dressed in uniforms of the S.D. would go, further, a citizen working as a detective and the rest...

It was nearly midnight when the company departed. The street is empty because at 11 o'clock everyone must be inside. In front an S.D.er, then a column of twelve of the long column the detective in civilian clothes. So the procession is hauled to the police station on the Overtoom. The bell rings and the cautious agent opens the panel in the door.

"Security Police!" roared the officer in German and he does it well.

He roared further in perfect German: We're here bringing a bunch of undergrounders. Because the damned Hollanders who do not want to work in Germany will learn this time what the German regime stands for.

When one of the underground workers moves he is corrected German-style by the detective. Light. The door goes open and the whole group goes inside. Instantly, the damned terrorists are put against the wall, hands up. He roars further: the whole lot must be securely put behind bars. Understand? The officer understands. Asks if any assistance is needed. He will call for it.

That is not at all necessary; (imagine still more officers, there are already three!...). He thunders some more: the terrorists must be registered and hurry up, okay?

That is the moment. The attention of the officers is distracted and at that same instant the commando thunders, "Hands up!"

As the three police officers look up they see the barrels of three pistols. At that same instant the door opens: a patrol of two officers comes back. They are at once deactivated and offer no resistance.

Then quickly get to work: the telephone is put out of order, cabinets broken open and a couple of minutes later the terrorists disappear with captured weapons and uniforms; the officers are left behind in a cell.

The bicycle garage is quickly reached. The K.P.-ers are satisfied and exuberant, too exuberant because they make a little noise. As a consequence the hubbub penetrates to the second story where the master of the house hangs out of the window and calls down: are there people there? A K.P.-er answers affirmatively but no one comes. It becomes a little tense because any instant everything can be uncovered. There is actually such a nice warning system for the various police bureaus: every 15 minutes there is a telephone report! Fifteen minutes is soon gone.

So, get out of this neighborhood that will be searched soon. But where to?

It doesn't matter as long as it is away from here. Look a second: quick, over the bridge. Very quick!

And just as the bridge is cleared a couple of police vans come charging with sharp headlights.

A dive in a bush that luckily is nearby. The beam of light glides farther along the asphalt, past the row of houses.

The group sneaks farther along. A light is shining somewhere in an upper story. Coolly, ring the bell. Once more. In vain.

A couple of houses further, light again. Ring the bell again. New luck here. The door goes open and the occupant is jolted with fear because he is looking into the barrel of a pistol. Under this threat it is said that they must be let in. And they come inside. Further no explanation is given but for the occupants of the house it is sufficient.

And here is the funny part of the case: man and wife understand the situation and are going along with it. Bread comes on the table and beer. And, it becomes a very sociable night, full of rich adventurous stories.

Early in the morning the company departed with two bags full of pistols.

A night well spent...

Piet was able to stay away from the S.D. but not all of his friends were as lucky. In one risky mission, Ann remembered him telling her, *a group of underground workers walked quietly in a canal in the dark of night holding their weapons above water. But somebody had told the Gestapo of this and they waited for them on a bridge. Shots rang out. In all eighteen Dutch young men were killed but Piet survived. Piet told me himself that he felt so terrible about that.*

Another time, the Germans knew Piet was on a train and were waiting for him to get off at the station. But he had put on a disguise on the train and Piet walked right through their reception committee without being recognized.

Rarely did Piet's family get to see him during those years. It was dangerous for a resistance fighter to be associated with family. Innocent bystanders and families had to endure the brunt of *Gestapo* tactics meant to break the resistance down. For instance, if someone was known to have fed an *onderduiker* their furniture might be burned in the street. If the resistance fighters killed a known German collaborator who was responsible for sending people to horrific deaths, the Germans made innocents pay. The house near where the body was found might be burned, perhaps the people in the house shot to death in full view of their neighbors. If Germans had been killed, uninvolved people might be lined up and murdered. In one such grisly episode 400 Hollanders in the vicinity lost their lives. No questions asked.

Like in Piet's stories Mother too went against the German authorities and hid young men in the barn of Sasmaheerd, Ann thought. *In an unused stall where much old equipment was piled in a dusty heap underneath the boards, there was a hiding place. The boerderij was completely gone over by the Nazis 13 times! Thirteen times!*

No one was ever found. Were the raids because of Piet/Han's work? Did the *Gestapo* know who his family was?

A quiet knock on the door, and Piet/Han, I would hardly recognize him, would stand in the doorway of me, Anje, his oldest sister and my husband, Jan Piet, in Thesinge, Ann recalled. *His normally straight, dark brown hair was sometimes black and slicked back, or it had grown longer and was curly from a permanent. Sometimes he was wearing thick horn-rimmed glasses. The family learned that he had met a woman in his verzetgroep (resistance group). The two were known as Nan and Han and they had become engaged to one another.*

The family learned later too that he had changed his name to Pieter de Vries Maats. Mother was so upset about that. I can still hear her say, "Oh, oh, Piet what did you do that for?"

Piet, in youthful, grateful zeal, had legally taken on the name of a retired sea captain who fulfilled a father role for him. Remember, he was only 19, 20, 21 years old when he was an *onderduiker*. The captain ran a retirement home in Alkmaar which doubled as a safe house for young men on the run. This name change, despite the unusual mitigating circumstances, greatly upset Mother de Vries. She considered it a slap against the proud de Vries name and it angered her. She never accepted it.

I think Piet studied in Switzerland after the war. I am not so very clear on that, Ann thought. *What was it that lady told me again about Piet? I can't really remember it now.*

The lady that Mom was trying to remember was an eighty-year-old physician who lived in Grand Junction, Colorado. In 1992 this lady had made a pilgrimage of sorts to Montana in her camper by herself to find and talk with Piet's sister, an Ann Heidema, on Churchill. Mom had opened her door to a knock and had seen a complete stranger who was saying, "I am from Colorado. I am Mechteld van Hardenbroek and I knew your brother, Piet."

Later over dinner at Perkins, Dr van Hardenbroek, had told a flabbergasted Ann that she, Mechteld, had known Piet during that time in Switzerland and that Piet had a daughter from their relationship. Mom, after a few years of stunned silence in which she had no idea if anyone else in the de Vries family knew of this liaison, told me of Mechteld's visit. I was eager to explore this hot tip, of course, and soon thereafter my correspondence with Dr. van Hardenbroek began. She was equally pleased to hear from me and shared her story in series of letters to me.

"I was a medical student and lifelong sufferer of asthma," she wrote. "I had studied at the University of Utrecht before its closure. I had taken heart from the resistance efforts of the students in closing down the university and involved myself in more resistance work. This put me at odds with my father who stubbornly admired the German military machinery and refused to know what the Nazis were doing to people. He hid me once and convinced the Germans not to search but I could not stay at home. My sister, who had not

169

yet reached 25, along with many of my underground friends, had died in the concentration camp in *Ravensbruck.*"

"I," Mechteld wrote, "had spent time in Switzerland as a teenager to get away from the damp Dutch weather and towards the end of the war, when my asthma was again getting the better of me friends from Switzerland invited me to come."

When their hospitality came to an end, she wrote, she decided to stay in the area and hired on as a maid in the home of a banker in the town of Arosa. While there she learned of the group of exhausted Dutch underground workers who were staying in a chalet above the town.

Han, as he identified himself to Mechteld, looked ill to her. She wrote, "He was very thin, tired, with hollow eyes. He became a symbol for me of all those I had lost."

Onderduikers, she explained, could never talk about what they were doing; it was taboo. Boasters had not made it. All had to be as natural and casual as possible to succeed despite fear and constant stress. This habit, she continued, kept Piet from talking about his thoughts and feelings after the danger was past and it was too much to keep inside.

Piet, she reported, had broken under the strain. Perhaps, with some liquor to soften his boundaries and strengthen his impulses, it may be assumed, he had walked out into the street in broad view singing out to the enemy. He had endangered himself and others by shouting out his identity and secrets. His friends had quickly smuggled him away and then he had attempted suicide. He had been put under strong medication and psychiatric care to prevent another attempt.

Piet, a sensitive, studious young man who had wanted to get away from conflicts, was emotionally bankrupt at that time. He felt empty, disconnected and guilty. His condition, Mechteld wrote, was called the "overstretched elastic syndrome", a common condition of resistance workers. He had pushed beyond the limits and could not recoil. He suffered from survivor's guilt.

"If I had been braver, better trained or smarter, I could have saved so and so." That is how we all felt, she wrote.

The Resistance had connections. A family in Rotterdam who was sympathetic to young men in such distress owned a chalet in Arosa, Switzerland and Piet had been sent there for rest and recovery. In the chalet he lived with a few others who were in the same shape.

"We were a small confused family living in the moment," wrote Mechteld. "We young people had been so often so close to dying and friends had been lost regularly, so many friends, so many dead people. Our Victorian, reserved upbringing no longer made sense to us. Friends slept together as good friends to feel close and not to feel so afraid and devastated, not waiting for a stable future that might not exist again."

Mechteld learned that she was pregnant with Piet's child after she had left Arosa. She was ecstatic. "Life became worth living again! My body and soul resurrected with the advent of new life."

Piet returned to Holland where the liberation and celebrations had passed him by. He was like a fish out of water, and according to Mechteld required further psychiatric intervention to adjust. He may have been institutionalized, although she was not certain of that.

Six months later Mechteld contacted Han and told him of her pregnancy but he said it was "too late". "I never knew what he meant by that," Mechteld wrote. She spoke with his doctor who advised against forcing marriage. Mechteld, who, as she wrote, had "a strong need for independence anyway," took the doctor's advice and made no demands. She named her daughter, Phoenix, as a symbol of life rising from the ashes.

Piet, in the eyes of the country, emerged from the war a national hero. He was given medals, one of which was given to him in person by none other than Winston Churchill, and money. His engagement to Jan, the other underground worker, fell through, but later he married a woman from South Holland by the name of Mieta Grootes. Piet and Mieta settled in Alkmaar, a city northwest of Amsterdam.

Mieta was unlike her sisters-in-law in rural Groningen and her appearance raised eyebrows in the conservative, religious family back home. "Mieta wore bright red lipstick and had long finger nails with bright red nail polish. I remember that as clear as night and day," recalls Peggy. "*Oom* Piet and *Tante* Mieta were quite a couple."

Piet and Mieta through the years remained aloof, somewhat mysterious figures to the relatives up north. He seldom came back to revisit his roots, and when he did make the effort, relations were strained.

In terms of employment Piet first held the position of administrator of a large old people's home in Alkmaar. Was it the home of his revered sea captain? Perhaps. Then with a partner he established a successful private accounting firm. Mechteld wrote that he knew where she and daughter, Phoenix, lived but he never tried to contact them nor did he provide any financial help or child support. He kept their presence a secret of his life.

Though distant, stern and not at all affectionate, he was responsible and a good provider to Mieta and his two other children, a girl and a boy. He supported his children's interests, was on the school board and in community affairs and he was good to those in his accounting office; but, not to himself.

On weekends Piet went alone to a small farm on which he kept a few animals. He did not want his family with him. There in isolation he consumed alcohol to drown the taunting demons. Unlike his brother, Tjaard, however, Piet hid his problem very well. He was, after all, a master of deception.

Oom Piet, as I remember him from when we visited in Holland, was a tall, intriguing, intelligent-sounding man who would have made a good poker player. What I mean is this: he listened thoughtfully, revealed no reaction in his facial expression and was cautious in his speech. Though his black hair had thinned some, he had taken obvious pains to slick it down and comb it towards the back. He still looked reasonably fit, was a smart dresser and showed no signs of illness. I think of him as looking like Pat Riley, the Laker and Miami Heat professional basketball coach: always intense, serious and cool. A worrisome detail was that he kept a very alert, ready-to-defend, Doberman pinscher quivering close by his side.

Drinking to excess made Piet a target for stomach cancer, and cancer was an enemy which this proud patriot could not resist. He died December 3, 1975 at the age of only 52 and his body at his request was donated to science.

What memories and emotions did he and his resistance cronies have to bury with alcohol? How far had this intelligent, sensitive man gone in retaliation? How deeply had he felt the hate and, in feeling such, how close had he come to becoming like the enemy? All questions that inevitably plaque a soldier's heart and mind— assuming that the soldier still has a conscience left when armed conflict ends, that is.

At the time of Piet's death there was a feature article written in a Dutch newspaper about him. It was another glowing tribute to his heroism and national service.

Many years later, Mechteld—who had left Holland and become an American citizen after having worked as a doctor long enough to pay back her medical school loans—contacted Piet's son, Christiaan. Chris agreed to meet Mechteld at his work in the Rijksmuseum where she told him about Phoenix, or Lupijn, as is her nickname. (Lupijn is another wonderfully symbolic name. Lupines are in the pea family which returns nitrogen to the soil. They are used as a transformation crop when land is being reclaimed from the sea). Initial denial by Chris and saying his father could not have done "such a thing" eventually gave way to facts, and Chris accepted that he had not only his sister, Helena, but also a half-sister. "That explains it!" Chris said to Mechteld. "On his death bed my father rambled about Arosa but we didn't know why."

Phoenix, too, following Mechteld's trip, met both Chris and Helena some years later and was welcomed by them as being "family". It wasn't long before they were comparing notes as children of *onderduikers*.

"Do you lie easily?" one asked the other. "You know, don't you, that parents such as ours who were *onderduikers* are proud of children who are secretive and who can lie well."

"Yes, I do! You too? It has been quite a problem in my adult relationships."

"My mother used to smile and say to me when I lied, 'You are such a good little *onderduiker*.' She would be proud of me!"

Chris and Helen shared with Phoenix that there is even an official psychiatric syndrome in Holland that describes certain behavior patterns in those now middle-aged people. Ripples, such as these caused by war in the ocean of humanity, go on and on and on.[4]

---

[4] Dr. Mechteld van Hardenbroek is no longer alive. Lupijn or Phoenix van Hardenbroek with whom I visit occasionally and find to be a soul mate, lives in California. She has a son named Alex who is lean and tall at 6'9"—no surprise here, Peggy's two sons are Al 6'7" and Roger 6'8" and Klaas of *Tante* Wina is 7'—and a daughter named Emily. Emily has a keen interest in dairies and chose as an elective in

Epilogue

J an, Tjaard and Piet, three brothers, my three uncles, were three unique, interesting, very young men with bright futures at one time; however, surviving a five-year-long (1940-1945) war in a conflicted, occupied, small country made them into three tired, old men by the time they reached their middle to late 20s. The wounds in individuals and in the country did not heal quickly. When Hollanders who had been Nazi sympathizers either were not punished or resumed influential political positions in the country, many people were profoundly disillusioned and predicted doom and gloom for the small nation. Many others were outraged and left. From 1946 to 1952 as many as 425,000 people emigrated to settle in South Africa, New Zealand, Australia, Canada and the U.S.

During her return trips to Holland Ann, as the oldest of the eight, acted as a self-appointed emissary. She talked earnestly with each brother. Not about the past, not about the old angst, but about the lives of their other two brothers, about their families, about the health and well-being of their mother and sisters. Her presence sometimes gave the brothers a reason to get together, but when she turned her back and went home to the States, the three drifted ever farther apart. Because of the war each man's heart had been handcuffed to painful memories, and many years earlier the key needed to release those handcuffs had been lost in the rubble of events.

"If I had my health I would go to Holland and interview everybody I could about the three brothers," I dreamed aloud totally unresponsive to my mother's very prolonged hesitance. "I would prowl around in town records and libraries. I would read all the books I could get my hands on. It would be exciting. There are probably lots of stories and facts to dig up."

Mom took another cookie and a bite and then said, *"Tis*

---

her schooling to work on a dairy for a semester. Emily visited with the Heidema family on their dairy in Montana in the summer of 2002.

misschain moar goud das doe dat nait doun kenst! Ik heb ook wel stories dat ik you kinder nait eerder verteld heb." (Maybe it is good that you can't do that! I have stories, too, that I have not told you children before.)

"Really?"

I was nonplussed. She has always done that. Tantalize me with more stories, that is. Other than her standard stories which she repeats over and over, it is like pulling teeth, teeth that have long, twisted roots, some of which cling tightly to the jawbone, to get her to talk more about the days during the war. For me the stories hold great intrigue and excitement. For my parents it was a painful, mostly-to-be-forgotten, hellish ordeal. For instance, Mom has never been able to watch even the first few minutes of "The Diary of Anne Frank". Just the singsong sound of the war-time sirens on television and she goes running from the room.

Why does her generation, why does Mom at the age of 83, still keep secrets about those war days? I fumed internally. *It seems so crucial to me that she tell.*

As a perpetual student of human behavior, I firmly believe that the next generations need to learn about the true nature of the human, of collective behavior and of the things that are not recorded neatly in history books. I believe that it would help us to come to grips with it all.

"Oh, I wish you would tell or write those stories, Mom," I pleaded aloud. "You could tell me and I could write them. We may not have much more time and then those stories in you will be gone forever."

"*Dat is ook zo. Moar van oavnd mout dat moar nait* (That is true. But we better not do that tonight)."

"*Vreselijk* (terrible)!" She always says this as she shakes her head back and forth. I imagine it is to rid her mind of horrifying pictures.

"*Vreselijk, vreselijk! Oorlog is vreseliijk.* War is terrible, children. Remember that! Don't ever wish for war. It is terrible. So terrible."

Chapter 16
Breakfast in Bed

For years, chapter after chapter, as I filled out the stories, I became better acquainted with the members of my family and their histories or herstories, as the case may have been. It was a homecoming of sorts for me.

I 've already been to the clinic to pick up Herbie and Baxter," lamented Sandi into the telephone. "I know I can't get to you guys today. I had already brought them last night but both Snoqualmie and Stevens are closed now so I am not going anywhere! There are lots of people stranded up on the passes."

Steve and Pat were listening on the other end. Pat on the mobile phone, Steven on the cellular. It was early on Friday morning and the two were still in their pullout couch-bed.

The family room looked more like a crowded, unused annex or bunkhouse than their bedroom. The coffee table was pushed against the stonework of the fireplace at the far end of the room. Steven's recliner and the other comfortable sitting chair were pushed up against the round table at the near end. The ungainly *sjoelbak* still lay on the table and some of the matching straight chairs were set against the wall. The queen-sized bed pretty much filled the remainder of the room.

Steve's clothes were draped over the arms of the recliner, Pat's over a straight chair. There were two open cardboard boxes marked "His" and "Hers"; one was on the *sjoelbak* and the other on a straight chair. They cleverly served as transportable drawers. Each had clean socks and under-garments in it.

"Did you have any trouble driving to the clinic, Sandi?" asked Steve in his low morning voice.

"No, the streets had not been plowed yet, but with the

Explorer it wasn't any problem."

"It sounds like you're all settled for today then," said Steve. "In the morning I'll get the reports on the passes off the Internet to see if tomorrow might be a go."

Steven had worked with computers at his job with Fluke Manufacturing for many years; however, he had only recently acquired his personal computer. It was a Leading Edge with a 486 Intel microprocessor. He had the Microsoft Windows 95 operating system and used America on Line (AOL) for e-mail. His software was limited as yet but he had Quicken, Works, World Atlas and the Hoyle games.

For a short while after his retirement, he and the family wondered how he would fill his time. They didn't wonder anymore. What minutes he could steal away from his many projects and errands he spent at the computer in his office on the second floor.

"What are you going to do today, then?" Pat asked.

Despite her second daughter's age, Pat still worried and kept close tabs on her. Sandi reciprocated. She worried about her parents. Every couple of months Steve and Pat drove the 300 miles round trip to Yakima. Sometimes they babysat the pets while Sandi was off on a trip. While there, they built, fixed and maintained everything in sight. It was her first home and Sandi welcomed the help and suggestions.

"I'm going to rest some more. Watch television and cross-stitch. There are still some programs I've taped that I haven't been able to get to. I would like to be there with everybody but I haven't had a couple of days totally off for so long. It's kind of nice really, but I hope it doesn't go on too long," Sandi answered.

"I don't know what we'll do here today," said Pat. "We're stuck. All of Seattle is snowed in with more than a foot of snow. It's still snowing pretty hard. Can you believe it! Nobody can move. On T.V. it shows there is hardly anybody on the freeways even. Cars, buses and airplanes have all stopped. Anil drove to work in Cressie, the Toyota Camry, yesterday and he got as far as 15 NE just off Ravena Boulevard before he got stuck. He left the car right there and walked the rest of the way to work. He was walking in snow that came up to his knees, he said. He didn't have any boots or gloves on!

"The rest went bowling and barely made it back up the hill. Dad is going to have to bring Arlyce to work again this afternoon if he can get out with the pickup. We're saying it is all Sophia's fault. You should have seen her yesterday. She was running around in it like a little kid. She wants to make a snowman today. We won't have to drive her up to the pass to meet you, that's for sure!" Pat reported the news to Sandi quickly and excitedly.

"Oh, Sophia, what's this? Oh, you didn't have to do this!" Pat squealed. "Sandi, you won't believe this! Sophia just walked in with our breakfast. This is too much!" Pat laughed hysterically.

Steven chortled merrily along, the sparse, white hair on his head standing straight up. Pat's hair was flat as a pancake on one side and the rest looked like one of Phyllis Dillard's famous wild hairdos. Her glasses were still laying off to the side on the end table.

"It's about time somebody served you two. I'd say you deserve it. Enjoy!" Sophia proclaimed holding a tray with steaming cups and bowls.

"You two there in bed look like a couple of *leehonas.*"

"Leehonas?" Pat cried as she raised herself up in the bed. "What are *leehonas?"*

Sophia, not always fluent in Greek, realized she had made a mistake and ignored Pat's question. She waited for them to pull themselves up to a better sitting position and then placed the tray on Pat's lap.

Where did that word leehona come from? Sophia wondered. *Mumma used to use it, I think. It just popped out.*

Sophia had not chosen the correct word but she was right about one thing. Steve and Pat deserved a treat. They worked tirelessly for others. In the family, as they methodically eliminated items on the various To Do Lists, they were jokingly referred to as the World Relief Committee. In addition to the help they gave to family members, they volunteered with the Christian Reformed World Relief Committee (CRWRC). In 1994, in Fillmore, California, a city north of Los Angeles hard hit by a devastating earthquake, they had gone door to door to do a needs-assessment for CRWRC. Day after day they had talked to families whose lives were in crisis.

They had been in the thick of it. Motels collapsed on rows of cars. Roadways completely demolished. In their personal living space Pat had hung clothes on a bathroom rod that promptly fell to the floor. On close inspection Steven discovered that the entire wall of the motel had been moved out an inch from the effects of the earthquake. They were now Disaster Area Managers for CRWRC in the Pacific Northwest. Their region covered everything from Mount Vernon, north of Seattle, to the Oregon border.

Through the Mercy Ministries of the Northwest they had been part of a team that painted a church in Quincy, Washington. Steven had done flood damage assessment for the Red Cross and on a weekly basis took his red Toyota pickup around to deliver meals to the homebound for the Volunteers of America food bank. He had served as many as 22 people in one day. Pat, too, had helped out at the Blessed Sacrament soup kitchen downtown Seattle.

By nature Sophia, being a detailed person, noticed such things. To her credit she not only noticed, but acknowledged them and did something in return.

"We're having oatmeal, toast, orange juice and fresh perked coffee delivered to us in bed," Pat chirped into the phone. "I just can't believe it!"

Sophia held up the camera and took a picture of the two, then amended what Pat had said.

"Not just plain oatmeal. It is Walnut Acres organic oatmeal! It's a Christmas gift from Elinor Bethke; you know, she's Tjaakje's good friend in Monte Vista, Colorado. Elinor sent us seven different kinds of organic hot cereals. We brought this one along for you to try.

"I remember having breakfast in bed once in New York City," Pat chattered still on the telephone. "Lottie was with us. She had just graduated from Blodgett's nurses training in Grand Rapids. Mom and Kelly were at the graduation, too, but we had separate cars, and they drove north to Niagara Falls for their honeymoon afterwards. Steve and I took Lottie on a trip to Washington D.C. and New York City. It was a business trip for Steve, so she and I went on tours while he was working. I remember Lottie being so upset that one morning because she had to get up and put her housecoat on so that she could open the door for Room Service. She thought it defeated the whole purpose of having breakfast in bed. We didn't even have to open the door for this Room Service, Steven!"

"No, that's right," concurred Steve. "Mmmm this is good."

"Don't let it get cold now," Sophia mothered. "I'll be back."

"Before we say good-bye, Sandi, I wanted to tell you about this program we happened to watch on T.V. before we all went to bed last night," Pat prattled. "It was all about pigs. It was the funniest thing! Some of the pigs had long tassels on their ears and looked so strange. Some had beards. It was a riot all of us sitting there looking at these weird pigs."

"How funny!" affirmed Sandi.

"We'll just say good-bye for now then, Sandi. Enjoy your day. Hope you can get here tomorrow! Talk to you later," said Pat.

"We'll talk to you again, Sandi," said Steve in a similar cadence.

Even though the two right now looked not at all like a couple of prostitutes (*leehones*) as Sophia had said but rather like two, recently licked, white, long-haired kittens, they were in actuality a matched pair. Like a couple of wizened, old draft horses, they always pulled the load together.

Chapter 17
Tjaakje Interviews Ann

One said about her chapter, "Some was right on and then there were sections in which I did not recognize myself."

I brushed away some crumbs and placed a small microphone in front of my mother, Ann, who was seated at the dining room table. Boxes of cereal, the toaster, the open sugar bowl, remnants left over from breakfast, were still on the dining room table. I could see snow falling steadily through the window at Ann's back. I had requested this morning get-together and Mumsy was happy to oblige.

"So, you can still think of questions to ask me? Don't you have all the answers by now?" she teased.

I didn't mind her teasing because I know deep down she marvels at my persistence. She has told me that she does.

For years, for all of her life almost, she has been asking me for more about my stories, I imagine Mom thinking. *She was only four and a half when we left Holland so why does this girl need to know and understand everything?*

I had written professionally, meaning for my work in nursing—see Chapter Nine in Madeline Leininger's book, *Two World's Blend,* for example—unfortunately, none of my ideas and theories about autism in that chapter hold up to more enlightened ones nowadays, yet there it is in print—but I had never written personally until I had to take some time off from work for my hysterectomy in 1980. (Endometriosis had been the underlying cause of the infection and the acute abdominal pain for which I had been hospitalized in 1978 and two years more of almost constant pain had finally brought me to the point of surgery. You might be curious: no, not once in my entire life have I wanted to give birth or be a mother—maybe it was too much babysitting or feeling too responsible for Margaret at a young age—losing that physical capacity was never an issue for me. And no, I do not think it has anything to do with my sexual orientation; there are many gay women who want to have and do have children.) After surgery I took eight weeks sick leave to recuperate and eight weeks more without pay to have a much needed break from the demanding Director of Nursing job. It was, I think, the first free time of my life. I took lessons on how to do yoga, how to crochet and how to write poems. Prior to the class on poetry I had written a few angry, sackcloth-and-ashes type poems—doesn't everyone?—a few critical entries in my diary in high school—for instance, there is an entry about having to wear a wet girdle to school because I had washed it too late the night before—a very serious, brief article for the Manhattan Christian School newsletter entitled, "Keeping Christ in Christmas", some illogical scrawls about dreams written in the middle of the night for a therapist and a few notes during my trip to Holland in 1973. That was about it. Anyway, the first assignment in my poetry class was not to write a poem but to keep a journal of descriptions and dreams. Ever since, as I have mentioned before, keeping a journal has been a satisfying tool of exploration for me. Then in 1988 when I was forced into early retirement at the age of 45, I suddenly had time again for yoga, crocheting and writing. I didn't much like crocheting so I wrote twenty-four episodes chronicling my adventures with an imaginary moose named Glasnos instead. These I sent to Brandon as letters; he was young enough at the time to believe that Glasnos did, in fact, talk to me. I wrote a number of personal essays, too; one of which to my delight, actually made it into print. I had started to write one such essay about my father, when I was still back in Maine, and to my surprise, really, I found that I needed many more specifics than what I had available to me. Knowing that I would be going to Seattle for the holidays, I had brought my tape recorder and hoped in this morning's interview to get the specifics from Mom. A side benefit, of course, would be that I would get her story and her voice on tape—something I wish I would have done before my father's passing.

"Yup, more questions," I answered, straining to plug the cord into the wall outlet next to the china closet and walking back around the table.

Sweeping Away the Sand

"Always more questions," I puffed, "I don't know that we have much time left."

"We don't, Lottie? What are we going to do pretty soon then?"

I chuckled and seated myself near her.

"I don't mean today, Mom. I mean in our lives. You know, *wie worden der ja nait jonger bie* (we are not getting any younger)."

"*Juust zo, wicht. Wat bis doe toch wies* (That's right, girl. You are so wise)", Ann retorted playfully. "Just remember that your book must be in large print so I can read it."

"I'm glad that you'll want to read it."

"Just so long as what it says is good, I will read it."

Margaret came in and placed a cup of coffee in front of each of us. She smiled broadly, left without saying a word and closed the door behind her. We called out our thank-you's.

"Okay, let's start at the beginning, all right?"

"That is a song, *ja?* 'Let's start at the beginning,'" Ann sang in a thin soprano searching for the correct melody.

I began the song anew and we sang, "Let's start at the very beginning. A very good place to start."

"That's from the 'Sound of Music,'" I informed her as if she had asked.

Naming and labeling the world for my mother, as well as others, is an automatic reflex in me, a habit picked up in the days when we children translated the language for our parents. It is probably why teaching came easily and why I liked it so much.

"You're still singing in the choir aren't you, Mom?"

"*Ja*, I do. Sometimes I think, now I am going to quit, this old lady. But they say, 'No, we want you back.' So I am still singing. I love it but maybe I am getting too old now. I am the oldest one in the choir, you know."

"Good for you! Just keep right on going until you absolutely can't go anymore. Now, it is time to start. No more fooling around. Tell me about when you were born."

"That was such a long time ago, Lottie. Maybe I can't remember that far back."

"Just start, *Moeke*, please. *Ik wil nou nait kwoad worden* (I don't want to get angry)."

It was a warning she had used effectively countless times to keep us kids in line. I enjoyed turning the tables and using it on her.

Tjaakje C. Heidema

"Goud den. ik zal begunnen (Good then. I shall begin)."

Anje cleared her throat with exaggerated seriousness, the beginnings of a smile at the corners of her mouth. She so loved to toy with me, with my patience but she sensed the limit had been reached.

"I was the first-born daughter of my dear parents, my father, Klaas de Vries, born on February 21, 1887 and my mother, Pieterke Oudman, born on April 13, 1887 in The Netherlands. My father was a tall man and always very thin. Mom worried a lot about *Pa*. I remember that every evening before they went to bed Mother would have about one quart of milk on the back of the cook stove for *Pa* to drink before retiring. On his birthday Mother would have *wie ans kiender* (us as children) decorate his comfortable chair with ribbons and she would have always a new shirt for him. He would come in and say, 'Wat is dit nou wier (what is this now again)?' *Dat ze hie altiet* (he always said that).

"Our meals were mostly of *stamppot* (mashed food).

Wais wel (You know), *eerrappels* (potatoes) mashed together with a vegetable such as *wortels* (carrots), *snie bonen* (French style sliced beans), *knollen* (turnips), *kool of boerenkool* (cabbage or kale). *Boerenkool, zeden wie ja altied, was maus moar ik wait echtwaoar nait woar dat woordt vandoan komt* (We always knew kale as *maus* but I honestly do not know where that word came from). Mashed together with the cooking juices, a little milk, *een beetje spek (a* little lard) *een beetje siebel* (and a little onion), zalt en pepper. *En din en worst der boven op* (And then a sausage on top). That is *stamppot* or *hutspot*.

"'*Boescol mit vis. Oka, doka, dat zo is!' Dat zegen wie kiender altiet* (Cabbage with fish. Oka, doka, so it is! That's what we always said as kids)!" Ann threw her head back and laughed aloud. *"Doar heb ik al ver jor'n nait over docht* (I haven't thought about that for years)!

"*En stamppot kin ook wel mit 'n biezunder zuide dreuge appel. Dit is toch zuk lekker eet'n! Dei appels kin ik hier jen Amerikoa nait koop'n. Ik kin ze noeit vien'n. Ik heb wel es zukke appels thoes brochd van Holland. Tante Wiets haar sums wel es 'n podje kloar veur mie om mit te neem'n. Wies wel? Dat hes doe toch ook wel es eet'n? Ik heb die wel es wat stuurd. Die stamppot is toch zo lekker. Ik ken't nog wel pruiv'm!* (And the mashed food can also be made with a special kind of sweet dried apple. That is such delicious food. I can never find them in America. I have never found them. I have brought that kind of apple home with me from Holland. *Tante* Wiets (Aunt Wiets Helliga-Heidema) sometimes has had a small bag ready for me to take with me. You know. You have eaten that, haven't you? I have sent them to you. That meal is so delicious. I can just taste it now!)

"*Stamppot en soepenbrij met stroop* (Mashed food and buttermilk and barley porridge with syrup). We ate that maybe twice a day. *Roggebrood met kornsmeer ook hail lekker* (Coarse whole grain rye bread with a fat spread, very delicious. *Kornsmeer* was made from a special piece of fat from the back of a pig. The fat was fried out and what remained was made into a spread. A little syrup was added for taste.) or *roggebrood* or white bread with butter and cheese and hot milk for breakfast. Once in a while she would have a slice of raisin bread. That was always a treat.

"*Och, wicht toch! ik kin der nait meer over proaten. Ik wor der ja zo hongerig ver* (Oh, girl! I cannot talk about this anymore. It is making me so hungry for it)!"

"Me too!" I chorused. "You'll be happy to know that I brought a quart of canned spiced crab apples to have with *maus* all the way from Maine to Arizona and now to here. I plan to make a meal of it for everybody one of these days."

"Really, Tjaakje, all the way from Maine you brought it?"

"Yup. That wasn't so easy either. The jar is kind of heavy. Sophia hand-carried it in her bag on the plane twice. But continue with your story. You are on a roll, *Moeke*, and I love it."

"Okay, then. *Pa* and *Moeke* were married on January 12th and I was born on the 21st of October in 1913. The day I was born was a day that there was every year a cattle market in Winsum, Groningen. So, from then on I think it was said that Anje was *geboren op Winsumer beestemarkt dag* (born on Winsumer cattle market day).

"Pa had to come home, I guess. They were happy with their baby, Anje. I was named after my father's mother, Anje Kolhorn."

Ann paused and finished her coffee.

"You are doing very good, Mom. Keep right on going. This is wonderful stuff!" I urged as I double checked the equipment.

"*Ja?* You think so?"

She paused, and then continued.

"I don't remember much of my first few years of my life. Pretty normal, I guess. I have a picture of my mother and me when I was,

I think, about three or four years old. She has such a beautiful buckle on her belt in the picture. I always wonder what happened to that. Isn't that silly? But I wonder about it.

"About the first thing I can remember is that I was walking in a furrow in the ground to bring food to the man who was plowing and there were seagulls ahead of me. I did like animals; I know that, the cows *Pa* had, and so forth, and the hired help. I was afraid of horses, in fact, still today. My father had, and my mother did, too, have help in the house. I remember one time. I must have been in the cow barn and fell in the manure. One of the kitchen help took me in to my mother and mother said to the help, *'Je mag nait op her (Anje) pruttelen, hur; zie kont nait helpen* (You may not grumble at her; she couldn't help it).' So, you see, my mother was protecting me.

"After dinner the hired men would take a short nap in the hayloft and my after-dinner nap was spent with them in the hay, too. Jan Mihl, the oldest of the men would pick me up, roll me in his coat and I slept with him. I can remember that so clear; I still can smell the hay and feel the coat over me.

"By then I had a little sister, Martje, named after Mother's mother, Martje Woldring, and before going to school we had to see the doctor for an injection for small pox. I can remember that big, old house so high and the entrance was very impressive to us. So was the doctor. But we did not go to school there. Pa sold the farm, *Italie,* in Winsum. This farm's name is still on the gate in the lane going to the place. I visit this place about every time I've been visiting my family in Holland.

"*Pa* bought the farm, *Sasmaheerd,* in Baflo with more acres of pastureland so we could milk more cows, like always 48 to 50. So this move happened before I started school. Then we found out that the injection for *pokking* (small pox) didn't take and I had to go again. Another big doctor's house and another big doctor. These few things I remember happened before I was five years old.

"The first few years of school, as I remember, were fun. I loved my teachers; maybe, I was the teacher's pet. I was a good student and went through eight grades. Soon there was another sister, Trui, named after *Pa*'s sister, Gertruda. We little girls did our knitting after the evening meal. We would knit our leg stockings. Mother would hide a coin in a little box in the middle of the ball of yarn that made us knit faster to get to it. My father played the organ and we girls sang.

"Besides school I always milked cows by hand out in the open field. I can tell you that I milked nine cows by the time I was nine years old!"

Of all the facts about her life story, Ann was perhaps the most proud of this one. She mimed the hand movements of milking with her long, slender fingers forming a fist first with the index finger and then without pause working all the fingers sequentially and rhythmically into and out of a fist. As she worked she alternated hands without a break between the two.

It was clear to me, Ann relished the movements. Her face glowed with joy as her hands brought her in touch again with the warm, rubbery resilience of the cow's teats, the swishing and flicking of the cow's long tail and the strength and heat of its massive, nurturing body into which she pressed her head. The methodical trance-forming rhythm, swoosh, swoosh, swoosh, swoosh, of the milk going into the foam of the steaming milk in the pail, sent into the young girl's nostrils and soul the rich aromatic fragrances of cow, milk and manure. Was there ever a perfume dearer to her heart? Never!

"*ik geloof dat ik die nog wel hollen kin met deze handen* (I believe that I can still hold you down with these hands)!"

Anne had a gleam in her eye as she gripped each fist tightly, shook them a bit and pretended to have a grasp on me.

"I don't doubt that for a minute, *Moeke*." I laughed good naturedly, remembering very well the will and strength in those two hands.

There had been plenty of times when not any of us kids would have dared to laugh while in their powerful grip. The one-hand, upper-arm hold had left no hope of wriggling free and if punishment came on top of its control, there had been an excruciating, painful pinch of the ear or of the sensitive skin on the underside of the upper arm. Ouch!

"Milking was hard work," Ann continued. "Carrying the wooden milking yoke on my shoulders with five-gallon milk cans hanging on each side with chains and hooks was hard. One time I remember milking a cow on one side and a calf falling into the canal on the other side. And just a little thing, but I remember that there would be frogs and eels in the water in the rain barrel that was our drinking water. We would cook and eat the eels. Can you imagine?

"I remember when I was twelve years old Martje and I went to visit our cousins. We had not been on our own before and I put both butter and jam on my raisin bread. One cousin poked the other and said, '*Nou dut zie der ook nog shem op* (Now she is putting jam on it too yet)!' I was so embarrassed! It was the first time we prepared our own bread!

"Besides milkings, as I got older, I did a lot of babysitting, just at home, being the oldest of eight. Mother had to get out, too, sometime. She would say, '*Anje is ja tuis* (Anje is home).' I heard my mom telling my Aunt Bouwina, too, that I was her best ironer. But then I could not go on for more school. That hurt me very much. Oh, I cried so. I loved school. My parents needed me at home. My sister, Martje, did go past the eighth grade. It was better for Martje to go to school. I could see that too. She was very smart and not so good with house or farm work. She was the only one of all eight who went on to high school. Martje was good, too, with playing the piano. She had lessons. I started the lessons but I did not go on. I did not practice enough and the teacher said I did not need to come back. I was sorry later.

"So I worked and learned how to sew. I sang in the choir and went to Girl's Society on Sunday evenings. I remember, when we came home with friends, Mother would have peanuts on the table."

"You were in Baflo, right? How did you happen to meet Dad who must have been living in Thesinge?" I inquired. "Baflo and Thesinge are how far apart?"

I pressed on, not want Ann to stop talking. I knew many of the memories brought forward her sad and lonely feelings of having had to live so much of her life without her family. It was rare that she would sit still like this to tell the story of her life.

"My mother had a sister, Janna, who lived in Thesinge. She was married to Jacob vander Borg. They had some daughters. Mom would go to visit and Martje and I would go along to visit with the girls. The Heidemas would come there. Mr. vander Borg had a boat on the canal that would be used to deliver grain to the city of Groningen. Heidema was a grain, ah, what shall I say? He would take grain to...I don't know what to say the *Buers* is. It was a place that had to do with grain-selling. He would get bids on the samples and then sell a farmer's crop of grain to the highest bidder. He had to make arrangements to get the grain delivered, too, I think, so he would do business with Mr. vander Borg."

"It sounds something like a commodities exchange and that he was a grain broker."

Like consulting a thesaurus, I scrolled down the words, names and idioms in my mental vocabulary lists that might fit with the description my mother was giving and selected a couple. However, I had not understood the function of the *Buers* very well and now Ann did not understand my interpretation very well.

"*Ja,* I don't know, maybe," she said. "Van Zanten had horses and a wagon to deliver the grain from the farmer to the boat of vander Borgs. I can still see him urging on the horses to get the wagon over the hill."

"Do you remember the first time you saw Dad?"

"Oh, sure, I knew he was Jan Heidema's son, Jan Piet. I can still see him on that boat with grain. *Lange sokken, pofbroek, pet der op* (Long socks, breeches-puff pants just below the knee, soft tweed fabric, golf-style cap—I admit it. I made up the style of cap. It had to be like that, did't it? They did not have baseball caps in those days and the little caps with the narrow brim were for very small boys, I think)."

"How old were you then?"

"I was, *ja, wat zal ik zeggen* (what shall I say?), I was twelve-thirteen maybe. He was born in 1909, you know, four years older than I was. So he was sixteen-seventeen. I would see him when we visited. Just kids, a group of us. Then some time he started to come to Baflo. It was a long way, an hour and a half or so, on bike. He came late at night one time, I remember, and he had a car. The car had a flat tire and he had to push the car over the hill. I can still see him pushing and pushing..."

Nostalgic images of life in Holland receded when Pat abruptly pushed open wide the dining room door. Her white hair still askew, she was wearing a gray sweatshirt and blue sweatpants with fleece-lined beige, slippers and black socks. She was slightly winded.

"Are you two still in here?" she gasped. "It's so busy out here!"

Pat had been getting everyone in sight to pick up ten items that were out of their designated place and put back where they belonged. This form of housekeeping was a longstanding tradition in the Cok family.

"Ja, kom der moar ien, wicht. Ik kin dien help wel bruuken (Yes, come on in, girl. I can use your help)," Ann invited, as she pushed the cereal father down on the table to clear a space. *"Hes ook nog een kopke kovvie? Ik ben nog een beetje dreug (Do* you have another cup of coffee? I am still a little dry)."

"I don't really have time to sit. I shouldn't have another cup; I'm shaky already." Pat quibbled as she turned back into the kitchen. She returned within seconds with a half-full pot of coffee and set it on the table in front of Ann.

"What have you been talking about all this time?" Pat asked as she sank into a chair at the opposite end of the table and put both feet up on another chair. "Phew," she expelled, "I'm sweating; I've been so busy."

"The vanden Borgs in Thaisin. *Kens doe del olle mensen nog wel herinnerin,* Pat (Can you remember those elderly people)?" Ann replied as she poured the coffee into her cup.

"Sure, they lived a few houses from us next to the windmill. And on the other side were the van Kettens who had the bakery.

"Ja, warme bakker (warm baker) van Ketten. I will never forget that one night with her..."

"Then, interrupted Pat, "there was a house where Fran lived. She had T.B. and just lay in her bed in the window for years. I can still see her. On the other side of the windmill and around the corner were the Huisman's: Bart, Dinko, Deno and Hari. They did a lot of *gymnastieken* (gymnastics). They had those rings hanging up. In school only the boys could do the gymnastics. That wasn't fair but I would do them at their place. They would do boxing too. Wasn't Hari one of the children that you nursed during the war, *Moeke?"*

"Och kom, doar heb ik nait over docht veur zo veul joaren al! Ja, twas wel zo. Dat heb ik ook doan ein mien levenstiet. Noa dat Tjaakje 'n joar of zo old was. Vrouw Huisman was zaik of sowat. (Oh, come on, I have not thought about that for so many years! Yes, it was that way. I have also done that in my lifetime. After Tjaakje was a year or so old Mrs. Huisman was sick or something.)

"It was wartime *alles was veranderd* (everything was changed). I was over at their house and the baby boy was crying and crying and his mother was sick and without thinking I said, 'Shall I take him home with me for a while?'

"They said, oh, no, they couldn't do that but then the next

morning Luut Huisman, her husband, came and asked was it still good what I had said? So the little boy came by us and stayed for four, five months and I did nurse him at that time then."

"I always thought that you said that you nursed me for two years?" I protested, obviously disturbed at some core level, though more than a half century had passed, to learn that I had shared my mother's breast with a strange baby. *A baby boy at that; a crying demanding baby boy no less,* I thought.

"I did," avowed Ann, "I always had plenty of milk and you never wanted any other kind. When I gave you cow's milk, you wanted nothing to do with it."

"Still don't," I muttered.

"I remember that in school girls had to learn how to knit while the boys had their gymnastics," Pat continued, still working her own childhood envy issue.

"I remember that I just couldn't get that knitting! Once I stood up to see what the boys were doing and *Juffrouw* (Miss or madam for someone in a position of respect) Dykema, the teacher, slapped each side of my face really hard with her red pencil. I was so shocked!

"I always had stomach aches, remember, *Moeke?*" Pat questioned. "And I wouldn't want to go back to school after lunch. Finally, one day you let me be late and when I got to school, I started right out, like we usually did, to sing the opening Psalm. And you know me, I was singing as loud as I could and all the rest of the kids just recited it! I was so humiliated. I think that cured me of my stomach aches."

"Ja dat loof ik wel (yes, I believe that)," reflected Ann.

"One of my earliest memories," reported Pat, "is having a *portefeuille* (billfold) tied to a string and laying it on the sidewalk in front of our house. Then I would hide behind the bush and hold the end of the string. I don't remember if anything ever happened or not.

"When I was naughty once, Mom, you put me in a dark closet. I remember standing against that long, green, herringbone winter coat for the longest time. And we had a toilet that had a bucket under it and someone would come to empty the bucket. What a job for that person!

"And, ouuw," Pat shivered dramatically and squeezed her eyes shut for a second or two, then continued, "those awful rats! Once, Mom, you moved my little table and chairs set outside and you stepped on a rat! Remember? It went into the sewer and Dad poured some boiling water in there. The rat came running out and you stomped on it with your bare feet and then it went under the chicken house! Do you remember that! Owuuh!"

Mom laughed in astonishment. "*Ach*, no *toch*, Pat! I remember we had rats but I don't think I would step on one with my bare feet!"

"Yes, you did! I remember it as clear as day. Dad would catch rats in traps, they would come from the canals and ditches, I guess. Then he would drown them. I can still hear their high-pitched squeals. I hated it!!!"

Pat shuddered and hugged her body. "I still can't stand the thought of rats or mice either. Ouuw, it gives me the creeps just talking about it. I better get back to work!"

Pat leapt up, hurriedly gathered up the coffee pot and cups and was on her way out of the room, saying as she went, "I hope you two will wrap this up soon. We need to decide what we are going to do with the rest of the day!"

Ann reflexively started to gather herself and I quickly interjected, "Mom, can you just quick tell me about when Dad proposed and about your wedding? Then we'll stop, okay?"

"All right, just a few more minutes then."

"Would you tell me about the time he proposed?"

"*Na*," Ann blushed and smiled, "*Na, dat mot moar nait* (No, I better not)."

"Were you engaged?" I persisted.

"Oh, sure, at nineteen I was engaged and then we were engaged for three years before we married. We had talked about it and I felt that the proposal was coming, shall we just say that? We were married when I was 22 and your father was 26. It was on June 26, 1936."

"Tell me something about the wedding, will you? Please."

"Well, I had on a smooth, silver-gray, floor-length wedding dress that had a short train. I carried long-stemmed, white lilies. White bridal dresses were not always the style. Did you know that, Lottie? Some weeks ago in Ladies Aid we all brought in our wedding pictures and talked about the different styles over the years. It was very interesting. I loved the front of my wedding dress and still always look for something like it in a blouse or dress. Your father wore a *trou pak mit slip jas en swafke stat en 'n hooge hoet* (black pinstripe suit with vest and tails and a top hat). First, we went to the church, and, then the Government house. That is how it was in those days. All of that in Baflo. Afterward to *Sasmaheerd.*

"My father did everything to make it very nice. *Toen tussen akkertjes mos ook haked worden en wit zand tussen peijes. Twas wat. Schuur hadden ze mit kanefas 'n mooi grote koamer van moakt.* (The ground between the rows in the garden had to be raked and white sand was put on the pathways. It was something. They had made a nice large room in the tall shed by using canvas.) There we had the reception.

"There was a very nice program with music and *spelletjes* (skits). The fun lasted until four in the morning. There was liquor, too, at the party and some of the young people had a little too much, of course. They always laughed about this one young man. When he left, instead of driving between the poles along the driveway where *Sasmaheerd* starts he drove around one of the poles."

"And then Jan Piet and me, we went to our home in Thaisin and by five in the morning we were both outside milking the cows in the pasture."

"Really? At five o'clock? Was there any time then for anything else?" Ann laughed teasingly and said, "Further, I am not going to say a word!"

"Did you go on a honeymoon later?"

"No, we didn't do that in those days," Ann said as she stood. "And now, my dear, we must stop. We must get to doing something, don't you think?"

Mijnheer en Mevrouw
Klaas de Vries and Pieterke Oudman

Anje, at the age of three, with her mother

de Vries Family: 1st Row: Trui, Klaas, Wina, Pieterke, Dien
2nd Row: Jan, Anje, Martje, Piet, Tjaard

The three de
Vries brothers

Anje as a young
woman in Baflo

Jan

Tjaard

Piet

Tjaakje C. Heidema

Five de Vries sisters:

Left: Martje

Below L-R: Anje,
Trui, Diennie
and Wina

People lined up to get a portion of milk from Wina de Vries during the war

Sasmaheerd, the de Vries *boederij* in Baflo

Tjaakje C. Heidema

Jan Heidema and Trientje van Dijken (Dyk)

Heidema family L-R Fijlena, Pieter, Piet, Heina, Tjaakje and Jan
Piet

Jan Piet
Heidema
and
Anje de Vries
are married
on
June 26, 1936

Thesinge or *Thaisin*

199

The family picture before emigrating L-R: Jan Piet, Tjaakje, Pieterke, Jan and Anje

A fun trip to the Zoo with cousins before leaving Holland L-R: Wina (de Boer), Hilige (our fun loving maid), Tini (de Boer), Tjaakje, Pia (Pat), Ange, and Jan (John)

The first picture of the family in America with Steintje Bolhuis and Uncle Bill Dvk

Our first trip to Gallatin Canyon in our new American clothes and with our new American names L-R: John, Charlotte and Patricia

First formal family picture in America

Ann and John on a Sunday in
America

Margaret on Tante Lien's
lap. The folks took
Margaret to Holland with
them to introduce her to
the family.

Chapter 18
Puzzle Talk

Another said, "I had no idea you noticed such detail." Mrs. Brooks, my Nursing Fundamentals teacher, would have been proud to hear that. She liked details. When we came to Nursing Arts lab we had to describe every detail we had seen on the walk from the college to the hospital. It was a two-mile walk and there was a lot to see.

I hope, girls, that I can go back to Holland one more time," declared Ann in an upbeat hopeful tone.

Marge, Sophia and I were sitting on folding chairs each at a side of the card table near the center of the living room. The fourth side of the table was pushed up to the short couch on which Pat and Ann were sitting; their backs were supported by thick pillows. All five of our heads were bent forward as we worked on the 500-piece, Cok-favorite, puzzle before us. The picture on the box of the puzzle had some 25 red, gold and green objects and symbols of the holiday. Christmas music was coming from the stereo. It was mid-afternoon.

After the interview with Mom in the morning, I had set about making a big pan of turkey soup. It was simmering on the stove and its tantalizing aroma wafted throughout the house. With a red-leaf lettuce salad and freshly baked bread from the Golden Harvest, we would have the soup for the evening meal.

Outside the snow was still coming down, though at last it was coming down somewhat less heavily. In the span of 24 hours a second storm had, according to the weathermen, dove-tailed with the first and the two had conspired to dump an awesomely uncommon 18 to 22 inches of snow on Seattle and the surrounding region. Already houseboats had been shown on television to be sinking from the heavy weight. Roofs and docks of marinas were collapsing. Part of the roof of a Darigold barn nearby in Bothell had given way. In downtown Seattle in Westlake Park the much-loved, old Carousel built in 1906 had collapsed. Large sections of the Puget Sound area were blacked out and public works could not keep up with the demand. Snow conditions on the streets were treacherous and in the mountains, because of the threat of avalanches, it was becoming more and more hazardous. Resolute holiday hikers were being urged to delay their plans because this was such a major event.

To make matters worse, yet a third storm system, the prognosticastors said, was rapidly gaining momentum in the Pacific. They were predicting that it would dump an untold amount of rain on the absorbent snow.

Despite the worsening road conditions Doug, Steve and Brandon were at the base of the hill on Bothell Way in the pickup to get some propane for the gas grill out on the deck. No one was planning to have a backyard barbecue; don't be silly, not in that wannabe blizzard! No, this was a mission with nobler intent. The primitive provider and protector instincts were stirring in the guys as they sniffed the dangers carried on the prevailing air currents. Like aging, yet proud, bull elks leading and protecting their harems, they were thinking ahead. With a temporary, but probable, power outage event, the grill, the guys had reasoned, would serve as backup for the electric stove and microwave oven. Off they had gone, antlers held high, in search of propane.

Brandon's goal for the jaunt was less about masculine sniffing and snorting instincts and more about pursuing his pleasure principle. He wanted to get some videos. I, too, had seized the moment and given him a short list of movie titles that I thought might be suitable for the whole group.

"If you can get one of these, I had told him, we might convince all of them to watch it after dinner."

While listening to me, Beej had held his mouth like he was pressing his tongue up in a sore back tooth and moved his eyes around so as not to look at me straight on. Clearly, he had listened with half a mind. In the other half he'd been holding on to a not-yet-revealed list of his personal, more important selections.

"I remember one time when I went to Holland I saw this old

lady sitting there," continued Ann. "We started talking and she told me she was 83 years old. I remember that exactly. Eighty-three! Can you imagine? And I thought then, *'Hai, hai, wat dos du toch op padt* (My, my, what are you doing on the path)?' So old and she is going on this airplane? *'Du moest maar thuis blijven, dachte ik* (you should stay home, I thought).' I really thought that. You know, Sophia? She was 83 and she was going to Europe!"

"Yes, I caught that," replied Sophia. "That's amazing. Was she by herself?"

"I don't know that for sure. Oh, you need to get a piece here, you think, little lady?"

Margaret reached across to the other side of the puzzle and picked up a piece. She, after all, had her reputation to uphold. She is the most stubborn and successful puzzler in the family. Margaret, let me tell you, in years past, has sat up well past midnight 'puzzling', which is what we have always called it; she will go on long after the rest of us have gone to bed. If she is determined to finish a section or the whole puzzle, more often than not she achieves her goal. Marge and Sandi, too, another one cut from the same cloth, have over the years put together many puzzles much more difficult than this one.

"Now I am 83 and talking about going to Holland," Ann burbled on. "Sometimes I can't believe that I am that old. Can you believe it?"

"I haven't put a piece in yet. Help me, Tjaakje," whined Sophia. "I am working on this red and gold drum here." She pointed to the picture on the empty box. With an impish, smug grin Margaret handed Sophia a piece and pointed to where it would fit.

I straightened my back and looked up to watch the snow fall silently past the windows for a few moments. It reminded me of the scene created in the poem "Snow-Bound: A Winter Idyll," by John Greenleaf Whittier. The lengthy poem, as I recalled, was about the poet's experiences on the other coast in the family home in New Hampshire.

I fondly remembered how I had come to know that fact. It was during a crackling, cold and frozen winter in Montana and, Miss Eunice Niewenhuis, our fourth grade teacher, introduced Whittier's work to our class. Miss Niewenhuis not only read and discussed the poem for weeks, but she also had our whole class act it out like a play for weeks. Not for a public presentation, but just so that we students would more deeply appreciate the gifts of Whittier and winter.

I remembered sitting with classmates Howard Cole, Marcene Van Dyken, Genevieve Overweg, Jack Bos and the rest in a semicircle up in front of the room all bundled up in heavy coats, shawls and boots. Words, rhythms, pictures and giggles all magically flowed together and I loved every single second of it.

> "Shut in from all the world without,
> We sat the clean-winged hearth about,
> Content to let the north-wind roar
> In baffled rage at pane and door..."

I pushed back from the table a little to ease the strain in my shoulders and, as I was a bit removed from the chatter, my eyes roamed softly around the rectangular living room and took in the rich mixture of holiday decorations, Christianity and Dutch memorabilia.

To my left Pat's three-foot-square quilt hung on the wall above the mantel. The design, done in a variety of fabric patterns of green, red and white, was of a framed wreath. On the mantel by my head I counted eight beautiful and fascinatingly unique wooden soldiers standing at attention on a bed of evergreen branches. Two had white hair; a redheaded one wore a kelly green uniform. Slightly taller because of the furry black headdress was the one that symbolized a guard at the Buckingham Palace; another like Abraham Lincoln was in black uniform and top hat; and still another was considerably shorter than the rest and looked like it might have been a soldier of the American Revolution.

Nine large stockings hung from the shelf of the mantel. Over the years, using bright, colorful fabrics, Pat had designed and sewn the six for her immediate family. Sophia and I had brought and hung our knit ones too. One had the Peanuts character, Snoopy, knitted in it; the other had snowflakes. Large, brown shopping bags from Fred Meyers stood open on the hearth for those that did not have stockings. A name had been printed on each with a black marker.

Sweeping Away the Sand

To the right of the fireplace above the stereo was a familiar cluster of wall hangings. There were a couple of large, hand-painted, delft plates. One depicted old-style sail boats floating on a canal; the other, a windmill on flat land. Along with the plates were a couple of ceramic tiles with written messages:

Want bij U is de	(For with thee
fontein des levens:	is the fountain of life:
in Uw licht zien	in thy light
wij het licht.	Shall we see light.)
	Psalm 36:9

Van het concert des leven	For the concert of life
Krijgtniemand een program	No one gets a program

Also hanging in the cluster with the plates and tiles was one of Sandi's blue-on-white needlework originals. She, I noticed, had creatively designed and embroidered the lettering of a Dutch lullaby (author unknown) and encircled the words with a simple decorative border. In the verse of the evening prayer or lullaby, the child is falling asleep and asks for continuation of God's faithful watch. Pat sang this sweet, soothing song to Sandi, Mom sang it to us and so down through the generations of mothers and children. Translating from Dutch to English unfortunately means the rhyme and rhythm are sacrificed.

Ik ga slapen; ik ben moe.	(I am going to sleep; I am tired.
'k Sluit mijn beide oogjes toe.	I am closing both mine eyes.
Heere, houd ook deze nacht	Lord, hold also on this night
Over my getrouw de wacht.	your faithful watch over me.)

A second verse not shown in Sandi's needlework but sung by the foremothers was:

'T Boze dat ik heb gedaan;	(The evil I have done;
Zie het Heere toch niet aan.	Please, Lord do not count.
Schoon mijn zonden velen zijn;	Clean away my many sins;
Make om Jesus wil my rein	Make me pure for Jesus' sake.)

Other wall hangings that I saw in the room included an excerpt from the Bible known as the Beatitudes, the blessings thought to have been made by Jesus in his sermon on the mountain as reported in the book of Matthew, chapter 5, verses 3-12, and the well-known prose "Footprints in the Sand". There was a representation of the popular *Martini toren* (Martini tower) in Groningen done by Pat in an extra fine cross-stitch, and from the Reijk's Museum a replica of a very old oil painting featuring a primitive style windmill in the dark, gathering clouds of storm.

Continuing around the room from the stereo to the short wall there was a window, and in front of the window stood a magnificent six-foot, fully decorated Christmas tree. From its branches hung red velvet ribbons and colorful balls with pictures of Mother Goose and other nursery rhyme characters on them. Arlyce and Sandi had made those when they were in the Calvinettes at the church. Underneath the tree was a red sled with green runners. It was covered with brightly wrapped presents, the number of which, like the snow, had been increasing steadily the last couple of days. Extra wrapping paper, tape and scissors lay nearby.

The long wall that was opposite the fireplace was flanked on both ends by entranceways, one to the stairway, the other to the kitchen. In between the entranceways was a long couch that matched the short couch on which the "puzzlers" sat. Both pieces of furniture looked new, though modern they were not. Their color was a light grayish-beige with broad vertical bands of a soft-tinted rose and off-green floral pattern. Above the long couch was a large rectangular mirror.

At the end opposite from where the Christmas tree stood there was another window and placed against opposing walls on this end of the room were each a piano and an organ. Steven is musically talented and can play either instrument equally well. He usually does so on Sundays. The organ, I knew, was in its fourteenth year of being stored with the Coks by a neighbor. I took a moment to marvel at that.

What kind of people leaves an organ at a neighbor's house for that long? I wondered.

On the floor next to the piano I saw the black case to Pat's trumpet. *This case, in a point of fact, holds her second trumpet,* I recalled vaguely. *Her first was a gift to her brought back from Holland by Mom and Dad when she was in high school. Boy was she lucky! I remember those squawks and honks coming from the back cement step of the house on the farm for the longest time. It would sound a lot like a passing flock of Canadian geese in early fall. We would tease her about it. Eventually, she figured out how to play the thing and produced sounds that could pass for civilized music. I think she taught herself. She couldn't play it in the school band though. For some strange reason, I remembered her telling us that her cherished trumpet wasn't compatible with American trumpets. She had to get another one that wasn't as good. I think Leland* (John and Joyce's son) *played the trumpet too. I wonder if he still does?*

A mostly-glass, round, two-shelf coffee table—now pushed off in the direction of the tree—was usually in the middle of the room. On the top shelf was angel hair and an artistic centerpiece of deep red, silk poinsettias and five tall white candles staggered for a sacred effect. On the bottom shelf was a small but lovely collection of delftware: a vase, two tea mugs, a miniaturized pair of wooden shoes, salt and pepper shakers, and a covered butter dish. All the Dutch items were laid out on an elegantly displayed whitish-blue silk scarf from India. The scarf, I knew, had been a gift for Pat from Arlyce after her trip to Nepal and the display, I also knew, had predated the introduction of Anil.

Coincidental? Not likely, I thought with some psychological humor, *it was and is a symbol of east joining west. But if I told Pat that she would poohoo the idea.*

Along with the matching short and long couches, there were two also new-appearing, blue-grey, velour easy chairs that were pushed to the side. Usually they were in the place of the tree with an end table and table-top lamp between them. Sheer curtains and green linen draperies that matched the green in the floral pattern of the couches hung at the windows and on the floor was plush, light, grayish-beige carpeting.

The colors in the room are beautifully blended together, I reflected. *I am kind of envious of Pat's knack and resources for this kind of thing. When it comes right down to it, we are really quite different,* I mused on, oblivious to the others. *I just get by with the major focus on comfort like I'm still in college or something. I used to care about appearances, I guess. I went through a phase of wearing makeup and nice clothes, but that's what it was for me, a phase. I went through it, and as my life unfolded, I adapted in a very different way. Actually, I think that I have become more like I was as a kid—loving the outdoors and animals, making things with a saw, a hammer and some nails, throwing a ball, cooking Dutch food, reading books and watching television. Pat has this inordinately neat, always new-like room that is a virtual Christian Reformed shrine. It's sort of like being in the holy of holies of a Jewish tabernacle, I grumbled silently. Well, maybe that's going a little too far. But still, a person can imagine oneself above the fray of humanity in a room like this.*

"I am not going to go to Holland alone again," Ann persisted with the obvious, but futile, hope that she would recruit a volunteer as fellow traveler, "I said that last time. That's too much for me now."

My mother has returned to Holland to visit with relatives quite a number of times. First, she went with Dad, then with her friends, Al and Pieka, once with her second husband and several times alone. Steve, Pat, the girls when Arlyce was twelve and Sandi a ten-year-old and I went with her in 1973.

It was Pat's and my first time back since 1948 and Pat rejoiced at seeing familiarity everywhere. It was quite a different experience for me. Besides the relatives, who were known to me if not by memory at least by voice and manner as told to me by my parents over the years, there was only one thing that struck a cord of recognition. That was all. In the small, cold, cement, cellar room called the *kelderke* just off the kitchen in the house in Thesinge I smelled a familiar odor. I knew, un-mistakably, in that first soul-satisfying sniff that I had been in that small storage room before. The *kelderke* has (I will assume it is still there; I could not bear to write of it in the past tense) one small window towards the ceiling, is some six feet lower than the kitchen, partially underground, and serves as a natural refrigerator—it is the only refrigerator that kitchen has ever had! Women have stored sausages, traditionally prepared foods –like kale, turnip and carrot *hutspot,* French cut beans with nutmeg and puddings with cinnamon—and dairy products in that room for over 150 years. I wish I could step into it now and again to infuse my tired being with that primitive distinctly satisfying aroma.

We six travelers spent a number of days joyously acting like tourists and not just relatives on that trip. We took the fast- moving Euro rail to get to the busy cheese market in Gouda near Alkmaar and after the market visited with *Oom* Piet, *Tanta* Mita and the kids. We toured the dignified delftware factory in where else? Delft. We rented a car to go to the island of Urk to watch the picturesque, costumed colony of fishermen and women.

Steven located a couple of distant cousins in the city of Amsterdam and they gave us a discounted rate at their Cok Hotel. Go figure! We went through the modern Van Gogh Museum and stood by Rembrandt's, *The Night Watch,* in the Rijksmuseum. We walked solemnly through Anne Frank's hiding place and had a boat tour on the foul-smelling canals. We strolled the bustling streets of the city past the square where old women fed self-important, scuttling pigeons, past the famed red light district where women in the storefront windows nakedly displayed their assets and their prices and watched vendors on street corners as business people bought raw herring for lunch instead of hotdogs. First the herring was dipped in chopped onion, then held expertly aloft by the tail and consumed *in toto.* Though a bit squeamish at first, I believe all of us, wishing to confirm our legitimate Dutch pedigree, no doubt, tried it exactly the same way in the safety of our hotel room. Hey, not bad!

The trip was both exhilarating and exhausting, exhilarating in making it happen all together with the relatives and exhausting in trying to understand the *Hoog Hollandse* (High Dutch) that was spoken by almost everyone. Whatever happened to good old *Gronigs?* The dialect is no longer used, they said, and laughed with great hilarity at my four-and-a-half-year-old *Gronigs* words.

All in all, it was a great adventure and great fun. I should have gone back more often when I still could; I so regret that now. Upon return back in Seattle Mom won the award for most weight gained. No surprise there! Every relative she had visited had tried to out-do the last with a little piece of this; a slice of that and a *slokje* (swallow) of something they had just opened, and Mom, being Queen for the Day, was too polite to refuse. Steven won for most weight lost. Poor guy, he had done more schlepping of suitcases than he cared to remember.

Steve and Pat with John and Joyce went without Mom to Holland in 1985. They were part of a tour group that went to a number of countries, but they took time away from the group to visit relatives. John, like Pat, had many memories of special places and people. He especially liked reuniting with his uncles, *Oom* Klaas and *Oom* Piet, and afterward said that he had felt like he was talking to his own father again when he talked with *Oom* Piet. "We cried together," he told me, "several times." It was an important healing experience for him. One that he wished he would have sought sooner.

Even though she had little ability to speak or understand much of any kind of Dutch, Margaret bravely accompanied Mom on a trip to Holland, too, once. That trip included a sightseeing tour of Switzerland, a gift to Mom for her fiftieth birthday from us four kids. By the end of the visit with relatives Margaret was managing well enough. She fondly remembers talking with *Oom* Piet as well.

Margaret has been to Holland twice, actually. The first time was in the dead of winter when she was only two-years-old. Our folks took Margaret along so they could introduce their new daughter to the extended family. We older kids along with Blackie, the milk cow, stayed with family friends, the Lightenbergs, on Churchill for more than a month. That was a trauma and a half on my growing list of traumas by the age of ten. The first had been leaving my bosom buddy, Nutie Apol, back in Thesinge when I was four-and –a-half. The second happened when my father had been yelled at by the Customs officials. I remember peeking out from behind my mother's skirt, watching him struggle to understand what they were saying and being scared they would take him away. The third trauma was being unable to take my Dutch doll to Doll Day—Farm Machinery Day for the boys—in first grade either because I thought they would make fun of her and me or because I didn't believe Doll Day was real and ending up being the only girl without a doll; and the fourth, as I have mentioned before, was getting a baby sister without being consulted.

Not only did my parents abandon me for more than a month when they went to Holland but Mrs. Lightenberg served, way too often, large bowls of tomato soup made from scratch with whole milk and whole tomatoes. Yuk! I didn't like the milk and I hated the skin that formed over the hot milk; plus, I had to eat everything in the bowl. Can you imagine? I gagged on the skins of the tomatoes, too! To top it off I tore a big hole in my inner thigh climbing over a barbed wire fence. My bloodied jeans froze solid into the wound and I didn't even discover it until I couldn't undress for a bath. I had to call Pat. How embarrassing. That meant a late-night trip for the Lightenbergs to Bozeman to the doctor and some seven or nine stitches. The doctor deadened it by putting a needle right down in the middle of the ragged tear! But, and this was absolutely vital to me back then, I did not cry.

Pat, being older and having an easier time of it, learned how to pinch blackheads with Darlene, her new best friend/sister, whoop de do; and John, darn it all, learned the fun of reading comic books with his new friend/brother, Ken. John never let me read even one.

How life affects us differently at different ages and with different likes and dislikes, huh? I once asked Pat if she remembered the soup of Mrs. Lightenberg.

"Tomato soup?" she frowned. "No, I don't remember that."

How is that possible? Did my siblings even know that I existed back then!?

"Why did you come to America, *Moeke*?" asked Sophia.

"Now, my dear, that is a question," answered Ann rubbing her hands back and forth together.

"Wasn't it so that we could get a better education?" pre-empted Pat. "That was always why I thought we came. Or that's what you and dad said at least."

"*Ja*, I guess so. It was after wartime and it had been hard, a hard time. Your dad had fevers from undulant fever from brucellosis after the war and Dad was...what shall I say? Upset? No. Discouraged, I think, is a better word. Pa was discouraged by the hardship of living in such a small country during wartime. The people in *Nederland* had nothing to say, you know. Then *Oom* Bill came from America and talked to your father," Ann recalled.

Willem or William (*Oom* Bill) Dyk, the uncle Ann referred to was my father's uncle. Back in 1904 Jan Siemen Dijk (John Simon Dyk) and his wife, Fylina van Dijken (Fylina Van Dyken) took seven of their eight sons and immigrated to the United States to Montana. Trientje, their only daughter, and one remaining son, Siemen (Sam), were delayed due to illness but followed two weeks later.

One of the eight Dyk boys, Hendrick (Henry), died of the flu at 23. Two of the boys, Harm and Lambertus (Bert) settled in Ellensberg, Washington, and four boys, Bill, Sam, Pieter (Pete) and Arend (Arie), settled in Manhattan, Montana. Jan (John), the remaining son, ended up in the Christian Reformed ministry in Grand Rapids, Michigan. Trientje stayed in America for less than a year. She had left Holland engaged to be married and she had not been favorably impressed with America. She returned alone to Holland where she married Jan Heidema. The two settled in Thesinge and had three children: Tjaakje, Jan Piet and Fylina. Trientje, at the age of only 31, died not long after giving birth to Fylina.

"After the war, you know, one of the Dyk brothers, William, *Oom* Bill, made a visit to us in Holland and he told us stories of America, the 'land of milk and honey' and your father listened," reiterated Ann.

"Didn't you tell me once that Dad had worked for an older woman on her farm in Holland for many years and that she had led him to believe that he would inherit her farm someday? And that when this woman died some cousin of hers, whom Dad had never heard her mention before, came from a city somewhere and claimed the farm? And since nothing had ever been in writing about her leaving it to Dad he didn't have anything to say about it. That he was terribly disillusioned by that?" I volunteered eagerly.

"I never heard that story before. Is that true?" demanded Pat incredulously.

"*Ja*, that's true," Ann answered slowly. "Your father wanted to be more of a farmer. We had a little land, some cows and a horse, Bles, was his name, your father loved that horse, but it was not really a farm. He still worked with the grain market with his father. *Ik kin ze nog wel zain. Elke Moandag Jan Piet mit zien Pa mit al die witte zakjes, monsters* (I can still see them. Every Monday, Jan Piet with his dad with those little white sacks with the grain samples). Then all went into a large sack and on the bike to the city to the *Buers* on Tuesday. *Hie kwam altiedt tuis mit en kopzeerte* (He always came home with a headache). He had his *kantor* (office) in the house and handled some insurance for the farmers, too. What do I say? Worker's insurance?"

"Workman's compensation?" suggested Marge.

"*Ja, kin wel* (could be). No, more than that, I think. For hail and so, too, but hail we didn't really have there. *'Kwijt net nait* (I don't know exactly). *Oom* Piet took over all that business when we left."

"Wasn't he an accountant? That's what I thought," Marge

interjected.

"No, not really I don't think. More of *en boukholer, en...*"

"Bookkeeper," inserted Pat.

"But go back to that old lady, *Moeke*, on that farm that Tjaakje just said."

"Tjaakje doesn't have it right. It was not an old lady. It was an old man. It was Piet Dijksterhuis. *Hou was dat ook nog weer* (How was that again)?" she pondered. "*Orn van Dijken's land...*" Ann was squeezing her eyes shut as she talked and tilting her head upward trying to remember. "Piet Dijksterhuis got Orn van Dijken's farm. And your father worked together with Piet, *die olle oom* (that old uncle). *Ik 'lof wel dat hie en oom waz of zo wat* (I believe he was an uncle or something). I cannot remember that right now. Piet Dijksterhuis always told him that he would get the farm when he died, but all of a sudden then when he did die a cousin or a nephew or something came for the land. Pa was very disappointed."

"I can't believe that you never told me that before," grumbled Pat.

"He thought about the States and talked about it with me. I said to *Pa*," Ann continued, "'if you really want to go to the States, then we take the children and I go with you,'" Ann tightened her mouth and jaw and spoke firmly. "I said it to him just like that. 'Then I go with you,' I said. I left my whole family, you know. My mother and all my brothers and sisters I left them behind."

"How did we get our visas then? I never did know that either," Pat continued questioning. "Not just anybody could come, could they?"

"*Ja,* how did that go? Annie Eubels, you remember her, Pat? She was getting better from tuberculosis. She stayed with us and she had something to do with it. In the last of the war she came to live with us. In the south where she lived people did not have enough food, and she was sick. I don't know anymore how our name came to her. Through the underground, I guess. But later then, after it was all over she helped us to get our papers in order. I don't remember how that all went. She was engaged to Sieger Heys in Zantanen. *"Wies wel* (Did you know), Pat? He was related somehow too to the Sieger Heys here, but how I couldn't tell you."

"No. I didn't know that."

"Was it the right thing? The right decision, girls? I ask myself sometimes. *Pa*, you know, died after not even ten years that we were in Montana. Then I was alone with you kids. Maybe, I should have gone back to Holland at that time. But, Pat, you were already with Steve, almost ready to marry. And John and Joyce the same. I could have gone with just the two younger girls. I wonder, you know. You wonder these things some-times. My family, what is left now, still would like me to come back but, with you kids here, I say, 'No, my life is here,' I stay here now til I die. Right, girls?"

There was a long quiet pause.

"Right," affirmed Marge with a bit of the slow Langel drawl. The rest of us sat transfixed and said nothing.

Like staying away from the badger hole back in the corner of the fields in the alkali patch near the railroad tracks, we girls have avoided talking about this uncomfortable conundrum with Mom forever. Life without extended family, was it the right decision for any of us? A badger, it has been said, can bite clean through a man's leg. "Stay away from there!" had been Dad's strictest order. Sometimes in life, you just know when you're staring down into a badger hole.

"If it doesn't stop snowing soon we might all be here until we die," I quipped uncomfortably.

"You know this is all your fault, Sophia!" teased Pat.

"Yes, and I love it. Don't you love it, Pat?"

"It is kind of different. I would feel better if Sandi was here, I guess."

Car doors slammed and Brandon burst into the house from the garage entrance calling as he did so, "What you guys doing? I got some movies. I'm going to go watch them now, okay, Mom?"

"Hi, Brandon, how are the streets? Is it still snowing?" asked Pat.

"It stopped for a while, I guess," said Doug coming up behind Brandon.

"Oh, I just can't stand it that I forgot the Droste's," I moaned to Sophia. "This would be a perfect time for hot chocolate."

"Arlyce and Anil will come later after we wake up from our naps if they can make it," said Pat. "Shall I ask them to bring eggnog lattes for everybody?"

Sweeping Away the Sand

There was a chorus of yeses and B.J. turned on the charm with, "Oh, yes, Aunt Pat, would you, please, pretty please. I'll give you a neck massage for only fifty cents if you do. And, then please, pretty please, pretty, pretty please, can we open some presents?"

"And, for the winter fireside meet,
Between the andirons' straddling feet,
The mug of cider simmered slow,
The apples sputtered in a row,
And, close at hand, the basket stood
With nuts from brown October's wood.

What matter how the night behaved?
What matter how the north wind raved?
Blow high, blow low, not all its snow
Could quench our hearth-fire's ruddy glow..."

Chapter 19
Margaret Takes a Walk

It is, perhaps, evident from my writing and should go without saying but, I underscore it here: My experiences have shaped my point of view, my beliefs.

Living in Bliss

The snow was 20 inches deep in some places. It covered everything in sight. Shrubs were so much taller, power lines so much thicker. Houses, bundled in their new plush white winter coats, were magically smaller. The multicolored Christmas lights that were meant to be the flames of twelve-inch-high plastic candles along the short driveway were mostly buried. Here and there was a dot of primary color: red, blue, yellow. It looked like someone had placed huge M&Ms on earth's meringue pie before putting it in the oven to bake. The six-foot-high lamp post at the entranceway to Court Place was a look-a-like for *The Cat in the Hat,* the popular Dr. Seuss character. On its head was a tall, white hat slightly off-kilter and covering its neck was a spiraling, red and white turtleneck. The character stretched its neck up out of the snow to survey the neighbor-hood and to its amazement it saw others just like it looking back at him.

Margaret, named after Mom's closest sister, *Martje,* was seeing all sorts of marvels from where she stood on a ladder propped against the motor home. She had opted out of taking a nap and had, instead, set to work with a broom on the roof. She pushed and pushed hard at the weight of snow but soon realized that she was not going to budge it that way. She would have to break the solid mass into pieces.

Sweeping Away the Sand

Car tires whined as inexperienced drivers on Northshore Summit tried to overcome the slippery ice pack with a persistent foot to the gas peddle. At ground level, also not napping, Doug and Steve scuttled industriously back and forth between the house and motor home. The clever fellows, having earlier readied the barbecue grill for cooking, were now devising a way to hook the furnace in the house up to the generator of the CruiseAir. There were reports of sweeping power outages in the suburbs. If it happened at the Cok home, the guys figured the motor home generator would give a little heat, at least, and maybe a couple of lights.

As Marge worked, great chunks of snow fell to the ground with resounding thuds. She swept what was left off the roof, then warily lowered herself down the rungs of the ladder. Off and on she still felt a twinge of pain in her left hip but it was nothing compared to what it had been. Three years earlier Marge had suffered a tear in the cartilage of the acetabulum. This is the inverted cup-shaped, cartilage-covered socket in the lower part of the pelvis. It receives the head of the femur or the thigh bone and it takes a lot of pounding over time. The tear, it was surmised, happened or at least had been aggravated during bowling. The Langels love to bowl; B.J., too, is already quite an accomplished bowler in his age group. Marge, as team member in a Women's League back then, had given it her all. She had given her all plus a little extra; that is how she tackles most things. The doctors scared everyone with talk of "untreatable vascular necrosis," and if so, they said, it means that the vital blood vessels have become unattached from the socket and tissue is dying from lack of oxygen and nutrients. They even mentioned a possible total hip replacement at her young age of 44. They treated it conservatively for a long time, almost two years. Weeks upon weeks of massage and physical therapy, crutches and wheelchair to achieve the condition of no weight-bearing and then six agonizing weeks of rest on the couch, all were tried and endured with no relief. Finally, at the Mayo Clinic in Rochester, Minnesota, the decision was made to intervene surgically, and fortunately a tear with no vascular disconnect was found. Marge has been gaining strength in her hip and in her spirit ever since. Also, the whole experience has given her a new appreciation of physical freedom and capability.

She shoveled away what snow had fallen on the asphalt carport in front of the motor home and then tackled another part of the driveway. When she tired she thought about going indoors but felt an inner tug to first take a walk. The fresh air in the interlude between storms was invigorating and she loved being outside. Why not? She opened the door to the motor home and attached a leash to eager Colter. He bounded out and jumped up, down and around. She playfully threw snow in his direction. He leapt up in the air with abandon trying to catch it in his mouth.

When the initial burst of raw energy from Colter had waned a bit, she guided him through the deep tire track in the snow of the driveway out onto the street. In the street there were more deep tire tracks that circled the cul de sac of Court Place and out to 63rd Avenue. Seattle, not being used to this amount of snow pack, did not have the road equipment to clear even the main freeways. The residential streets would have to wait until they were cleared by natural weather conditions. From the looks of it that was going to take a while.

The magnificently decorated-for-Christmas, four-foot-high train engine, coal car and passenger car on real-appearing tracks in the neighbor's yard was dwarfed by mounds of snow. She paused and held Colter back. There was something so very familiar about that scene. Had she seen something like it? Pictures in history books of early trains crossing the prairie in the frigid weather came to mind. Maybe that was it. The images went on: steam engines puffing up smoke, buffalo herds in the background, Native Americans standing in deerskin and furs next to their tepees.

There is so much shared history in the Heidema family that Margaret did not experience or was too young to remember. Mom, Pat, John and I, have a past rooted in flat, pastoral Holland with its slow-moving canals, windmills and cattails, a stalwart husband and dad, and at least some connection with a large, extended family unit across the ocean. Not her, not Marge.

Judge Leslie in the Courthouse in Bozeman had asked our parents questions, humiliating questions some of them, like in what year was the War of 1812 fought? Puhlease! They had studied for weeks. They knew that in 1953 Dwight D. Eisenhower was the president, Richard M. Nixon the Vice President, John Foster Dulles the Secretary of State and Ezra Taft Benson was the Secretary of Agriculture. In fact, they knew the names of all the cabinet members and Earl Warren, the Chief Justice of the United States Supreme Court. They had memorized the names of the branches of government and so forth. But Judge Leslie, like a cat with a mouse, from his high, pompous bench toyed with them and made a mockery of their stumbling efforts.

Nevertheless, after the nerve-wracking ordeal our parents became what is called naturalized citizens of the United States and so did us three older children. We have our citizenship papers to prove it but not Marge. She, two years earlier in 1951, had been born a citizen, a citizen of the United States, of the west and of trains on prairies, of Sitting Bull and the battle of Little Big Horn, of Black Elk, holy man of the Ogallala Sioux, of geysers erupting into the air and moose standing in the thicket along the Gallatin River in the canyon.

Often, therefore, it is as if Margaret is a stranger in her own family. She could understand most of the common Dutch words that were used in the home but they always felt strange to her. At the age of two she had been made to say her cute Dutch words in front of company. She had performed and said them in the most darling way. After that she hardly ever said Dutch words out loud.

Being eight years younger than I, Marge, especially after all the family upheaval following our father's death, pretty much grew up psychically alone; alone, but yet, with an ever-present and ever-gnawing fear of being abandoned. She is not at all sure that she can survive another grief as intense and, though the youngest, she unabashedly wants to be the next in our family to go.

A quick glance back in time will explain it. Come with me. It is April, in the spring of 1958, and Margaret has just turned seven. In her short, innocent past she has been a bright, blue-eyed, cute-as-a-button, pug-nosed little toddler with short, blonde, naturally curly hair and dimples. Back then she had some terrific facial expressions and was adored by all. Now at seven she has grown to be a cute, spunky little kid with a sprinkling of freckles over her nose. She is alert to every creature and adventure in her magical kingdom.

Skippy's puppies are round balls of happy fur. They wriggle out from under the bunk house when they hear Margaret coming; they lick her face with their little tongues and get the soft oatmeal that is all over their muzzles in her hair. She doesn't care; she runs to climb the ladder up into the warm hayloft where the new kittens are snuggled up to their mother. The kittens' tails are long and their eyes are still sealed shut. They have the tiniest mewing sound and the mother worries so about the one little Margaret is holding in her hand.

She bottle-feeds frisky orphan lambs, Sugar and Alvin. Sugar is all white; she is the smaller of the two. Alvin has a black head. The two are long-legged and wobbly. They lean in to suck the large black nipple or her hand and it does not even hurt. Warm, white slime runs down from their mouths as they drink and their long tails are busy moving every which way. When the bottle is empty, they butt their heads into her. She laughs and she almost falls. Other lambs in the pasture are frolicking in the background.

She watches calves nurse and their tails move, too, but more from side to side. She rides Nancy, the dear, good-natured bay, who is lame with a badly swollen knee but who willingly goes the extra mile for any member of the family. Her sister, that would be me, likes to braid the patient mare's black mane and tail.

And there are the bigger-than-life Belgian draft horses, *Ollieball*, a chestnut, and Snowball, all white. She may not come near them, but she loves them. She likes to smell the hay, the oats and the sweaty horse smell. She likes to listen to them snort and stomp their heavy hoofs on the wooden floorboards, to hear the chains hitting the wooden yoke and the creaking of the old leather before her dad takes off the big harnesses. She likes to see them stand strong and solid.

As all these things take place she is surrounded by a celestial symphony. There are always to be heard the sounds of meowing, mooing, cock-a-doodle-doing, baaing, grunting, barking, whinnying and chattering. There is the occasional cacophony of distress. A pig squeals as he is bullied away from the trough, a cow moos her complaint when she has to wait too long at the barn door, her sister cries in pain when her brother punches her arm. And there is the euphony of contentment. The cat purrs, the ewe murmurs, a sow snores, Dad teases and Mom laughs.

Margaret is also in her first year of school. She has finally joined John and me in our three-quarter-mile walk on the graveled lane to catch the big yellow school bus at the mail box. She carries her lunch pail and is so proud as she walks past those 180 acres that are the entire universe to her: those snowcapped peaks in the distance, those beautiful, encircling mountain ranges, the Saddle and the Devil's slide, those fertile fields of wheat, barley, oats, alfalfa and potatoes. Ghosts of old man White's wild palomino stallions, with their all palomino harems, graze and gallop in the field alongside the lane; and in the vast space and land that stretches in all directions she can hear their pounding hooves.

In the summertime she walks in the other direction on the lane that is dotted with pies of rich fresh cow manure and buzzes with flies everywhere. Past the cemetery and gopher colony she goes. Just up ahead is always busy, happy, part-collie Skippy and by her side is faithful cocker spaniel Tippy. They are going down to the pasture and over the noisy bridge to get the cows. Sometimes now with one of us grown-ups she can even go farther into the pasture to go fishing for rainbow trout in Camp Creek.

Marion Schutter, her girlfriend, lives just a few miles up the road; they are classmates now, and within walking distance lives her second girlfriend, little talkative Judy Hess. She loves to giggle. Dick and the other brown horse are always in the field next to the Hess's driveway. If Margaret stretches way up on her tiptoes she can see Judy's house and the horses through the kitchen window above the sink.

For dinner there are the steaming bowls of boiled potatoes and green beans, the plate of roast beef, the applesauce or the fresh, sweetened, cornstarch-thickened, pinkish-red rhubarb. The white cucumber slices floating in diluted, apple-cider vinegar in the red Pyrex bowl and the *schuddeldouk* (dishrag) being passed around. On Saturday Char listens to the New York Yankees on "The Game of the Week" and on Memorial Day the lilacs are in full bloom.

Margaret feels like she is with her father a lot in those days but in later years remembers him only in snatches: his plowing the ditches in the fields, his burning the weeds along the side of the lane in the fall, his blacksmith work in the shop while she played nearby, going to Manhattan together, his having to be in the hospital because he had a sliver of metal stuck in his eye and his having to wear the oxygen mask over his face "until he dies".

Falling Into the Abyss

A short two and a half years later at the tender age of only nine our little Margaret has become an empty shell, and she is struggling to survive. What a tragic, unforgivable transformation! The symphony has stopped. There is not an animal in sight or a lane to walk. There is no hint of manure, hay or potato harvest carried on the breeze. There is no cat or dog asleep by the door. Why not, for heaven's sake? Not even a cat? No not even a cat. No lamb to feed, no father to watch. Magic and mystery have turned to misery and mundane; heaven has turned to hell. It is obvious that the weight of so many losses has left our young Marge profoundly wounded. She clings to an all-consuming feeling of emptiness as if it were a dirty, tattered security blanket.

In a blur of red velvet, *Oom* Hein and *Tante* Dienie's arguments and their noisy, nosey kids, John and Joyce's wedding has taken place in the snows of December of 1960 and Marge has been moved to a house on the outskirts of chilly Churchill. Ann, Marge's and my displaced and bereaved mother who still wears black on Sundays, and I, her grumpy adolescent sister, are also there. We are coping with things in our own ways. For mom, perpetual work outside of the home and a stoic belief in God's will and the life hereafter, wherein she will reunite with *Pa,* are balms of a sort. For me, her driven sister, achieving good grades in high school and making money for college are priorities. Neither Marge nor I want to risk poking a hole in our mother's armor so we stuff our feelings deeper and deeper. Margaret lays for endless hours in our new sterile home, a saddened lump on the couch. Sometimes her depression draws the ire and fire out of Mom or me; we want her to act normal and don't want to be reminded of what caused her unending grief. She becomes the target at which we throw our pent-up sadness, anger and frustrations. Margaret is much too young and confused to understand such a logical explanation of illogical acts during loss and change. She accepts, instead, our angry outbursts as personally deserved. What self esteem our child Margaret had incorporated as that young innocent in the happy, hard-working family is now completely shattered. In its place she carries undeserved blame and shame into her adolescence.

Sweeping Away the Sand

I leave for college and now Margaret is the only child still with Mom. Margaret has heard Mom speak passionately and frequently—as both Pat and I did—of her thwarted wish to have gone on in school and to have become a nurse, and so at the age of sixteen Marge, too, begins working part-time as a nurse's aide in Bozeman Deaconess Hospital. There she observes one of the bad habits of the nursing staff to be smoking. Smoking is the thing to do when nurses take their breaks. In fact, smokers take a break and nonsmokers are asked to cover the call lights. She gets the picture. Someone offers her one. Subliminally, the aroma evokes her father's presence and she draws in deeply with a slight resulting inner rush. Even Ann says that she likes the familiar smell around the house.

In high school she begins to have acute discomfort in her back and flank. It is recurring and she is diagnosed as having pyelonephritis, an inflammation of the kidney. In the next few years she suffers episodes of such severe pain that medication is required. And she discovers that the combination of pain pills and cigarettes will lift—if but temporarily—the black cloud over her head.

She graduates from high school in 1969 and attempts to walk in the footsteps of Pat and myself at Calvin College in Grand Rapids, Michigan. Her attempt is short-lived. She continues to have bouts of pain and feels lost in this experience away from home. She does not return after her first year.

Listlessly, Marge applies and is accepted into the Montana State nursing program in Bozeman and attends for two years. She goes to Great Falls for part of her clinical work and she goes to bars for fun. In the darkened room, where strangers easily become friends and Schlitz is on tap, she rests her elbows on the sticky beer-wet table. She hears the cue stick strike the pool ball, the ball cracking the triangle of pool balls and Loretta Lynn's voice telling her that she never was promised a rose garden. In the darkened, heavy blue haze of cigarette smoke she is asked or told, rather, to have this dance by a dark-haired, swarthy, stocky young man. The aggressive, defiant male is named Vaughn; he is in his early thirties, and he almost immediately tells her—he brags really—that he is a Vietnam veteran who had been a gunner, a rigger and crew chief on helicopters that picked up casualties in the field. And Vaughn, as Margaret learns later, has old injuries, nightmares and a drug habit to show for it.

In Marge Vaughn finds a winsome, long-haired, blonde young woman who desperately needs to believe. Mostly, she needs to believe that she has worth and that she can make a difference in someone's life, if not in her own. She tries. She gives up on school and does all that she can for four years in regard to Vaughn. It is not enough. Vaughn in turn leads Marge into the world of domestic abuse and deeper into the use of prescription drugs. The two are in and out of hospitals and jobs; they teeter on the edge of disaster and operate just out of the reach of the law.

We in the family instinctively know that Vaughn is bad news—we feel intimidated, too—but also feel stuck. Pat and I during brief visits home think we should do something but do not want to undermine Marge's individuality and choices, and Ann ironically is having trouble in her own marriage.

Five years after Jan Piet's death she married the long-time, middle-aged bachelor on Churchill, Kelly Eisenga, and Kelly has proven to be ill-suited for marriage. Ann's friends, Al and Pieka, had cautioned Ann. Kelly, they said, has black moods that can last for days. But, like countless other women including her youngest daughter, Ann deluded herself into thinking that she would make the magical difference in this man's life.

Taciturn and secretive Kelly has pushed Ann away emotionally and physically. She lives in her home with a brutish stranger and rues the day she decided to marry him. She is miserable. Margaret knows this. She cannot help her mother and her mother cannot help her.

They are both victims of domestic violence, even though it is not called that in those days—there is no mention of such a thing as Battered Wife Syndrome either, and just like victims of incest or rape and cancer patients and racial minorities in the sixties the victims are blamed. They are stigmatized and shunned.

"His threats were intense and they involved a gun," Margaret tells me much later. "I was afraid he would kill me if I told anybody. He regularly inflicted real pain and injury."

Rising Again To Redress

U p north in Vaughn's old stamping grounds, in Hingham and Rudyard, J.J. and Stella, Vaughn's father and second wife, and some of his friends including Doug Langel know Vaughn a whole lot better than do the naive Heidemas in the Dutch community in Gallatin Valley. They know Vaughn had a reputation for temper and trouble long before Vietnam and their concern, bless them, is not as much for their son as it is for Marge. J.J. and Stella encourage Margaret to confide in them and eventually, after one more especially violent episode, Marge goes to them and they shelter her. With their continued support and protection she is able to leave Vaughn and then later to file for her divorce from him. It is here that we will interrupt our glance backward to check on her whereabouts.

As the sun struggled to send a few weak rays through the stubborn Seattle cloud cover, Margaret, ever more grateful to be past those horrendous, battered days, threw snowballs ahead for Colter. His boundless joyous energy was contagious. He made her smile; she felt good. There were other hearty people, mostly children, out on the downward slope of 64th Avenue. Some were sledding. Laughter and shouting rang out over the quiet of the snowy world all around them. It were as if the happy voices came bursting through from another world, a long-ago-past world, before the street had even been built and before cars were being manufactured. No one would have been surprised to see a horse and wagon go by. It was almost possible to hear the snorting of the horse, the creaking of the leather harness and the jingling of the bells. Knowing that Margaret is safe, come again with me and I shall finish with the story of her past.

Doug Langel, a reserved man in his late forties, is living in Rudyard with his parents, Ted and Netes Langel, as he has done all of his life. He takes special notice of Vaughn's new wife. Doug is around off and on and, like Vaughn's parents, Doug has a caring concern for this reticent, self effacing, hard working young woman.

Doug, 20 years older than Marge, has not married. Untreated complications of scarlet fever as a child, have left Doug shy and, for the rest of his life, coping with severe hearing loss. He has been content to work the family farm, tinker with cars, especially old vintage cars, Model T's and A's, and generally make himself useful around the small town of Rudyard where everybody knows everybody.

Margaret stays on in Rudyard after her divorce and works as a waitress in the cafe where Doug comes often to eat. They develop an uncomplicated relationship in which Marge feels safe for the first time in a long time; before much more time goes by Doug asks her to marry him. With little fuss she accepts. They are married and settle into a small home across town from Ted and Netes.

The human being has within it an amazing capacity to heal, and Marge in all spheres, mind, body and soul has a lot of healing to do. So, predictably—because this is the nature of things—once in her new safe surroundings, old traumas, like rocks in a field, begin to work their way to the surface. There are times when she trips and falls and has to be helped back up. There are seemingly endless headaches, hospitalizations, cycles between energized times and depressions, a questionable diagnosis of bipolar disorder, medications and just plain tough times.

Living in Rudyard, that very small town, when she is stumbling through a field filled with rocks is not easy. The people, used to their own and familiar with what Margaret's life has been before Doug, gossip about her past and her problems. Some are downright unfriendly. Netes, as mother-in-law, is cool, too.

Doug's vulnerability is his gut. He endures the rigors and flares of Chron's disease. Sometimes debilitating, sometimes annoying, always to be considered Chron's disease. It drains the stuffings out of a person, and Doug has those times.

There are weeks in the little house in Rudyard when all the struggler can do is to crawl away from the other into a makeshift cave, curl up and lick his or her own wounds. But, through it all with little fanfare Doug sticks by Marge and she with him.

Luckily, she can escape. In the summertime with enormous relief she can go to the Langel retreat. It is a house 180 miles to the west near Apgar and Lake McDonald in Glacier Park. There in the immense stillness surrounded by nature and in the company of the wild she breathes much more easily. She spends endless hours fishing for trout "who," she says, "are smart and who like to fight".

The peace and focus finally allow her to reconnect with what is beautiful in life.

Jack Gladstone, a mixed-race Blackfoot Native American, also comes to the sacred land. He and his ancestors honor The Great Spirit along the shores of St. Mary's Lake. He sings from the heart of the lives of his Blackfoot relatives, their beliefs, their foibles and their struggles. Marge listens and listens to his Native American lore and rhythms. She makes them her own and comes home to rest at the base of her favorite mountain, Heaven's Peak.

Then Sue, a friend whom Marge had met at the Mayo Clinic in Rochester, Minnesota, becomes pregnant after having relations with a student from Brazil. Sue decides to carry the child to term, but does not want to raise the child. She tells Marge who—along with or perhaps because of the rest of her problems has suffered from painful endometriosis—has had to have a hysterectomy and can not give birth to a child. Sue asks Marge if she and Doug will adopt the child, and they say yes.

The baby is born on February 5, 1986 and Margaret is in attendance at the birth. The Langels name their son, Brandon John, and after official requirements are met, the adoption is made legal. Brandon John, B.J., is a magical gift, and an exhausting blur of needs. Marge has good mothering instincts. She has always had it for the lambs, the cats and the "critters" everywhere. She needs to focus now, be consistent, available and reliable for a child, a human child like she herself has been. Of course, there are still steps to be taken to heal, and to learn how to apply such nurturing qualities to herself as well as the child, but there always will be.

After a few years the Langels decide to take a break from Rudyard. Margaret feels the need to grow, to go after some personal goals, and Doug is in a weakened state. He suffered a terrible debilitating bout of the Chron's and underwent major surgery for a bowel resection and colostomy in Seattle; he needs time and space to recuperate.

When Margaret suggested they leave Rudyard for a while, he said what he usually says, "Whatever." He is able to lease out the farm and the small family of three take an apartment in the city of Kalispell. They seize an opportunity and buy half ownership in a Town Pump operation. Marge works at the busy convenience store and attends Flathead Valley Community College while B.J. advances from preschool through kindergarten at the Christian Center. Marge, by stretching herself thin and expecting perfection, excels in all her classes. To our delight she receives special praise from her professors in mathematics; it is a field in which a link to Dad is obvious. He was also very good with figures and enjoyed them. In the spring of 1990 she boosts her self-esteem a bit higher by graduating magna cum laude with Associate Degrees in both Arts and Science.

When it comes time for B.J. to start first grade he does so at the Blue Sky Elementary back in Rudyard. The lease for the farm has run into legal problems and so the Langels must resume responsibility for the 200 acres of crops. Doug, not as strong as before, must find ways to reduce his workload. He participates in the Federal Crop Reduction Program and Margaret cultivates the fallow fields and learns the paperwork. Their operation is officially called Black Cat Base, Inc. and because Doug is now the age at which he can draw social security age, Margaret is listed as its president. Even Brandon, at the age of eleven, drives a vehicle to help out.

And so, we are brought up to date. It was deceptive on my part to preface Margaret's journey with saying we would take a quick glance. A person's life story is, of course, always worth much more than a quick glance.

On the snow-packed hill in Seattle Marge, with her ever vigilant, kind spirit, noticed something amiss with a boy about the age of Brandon. He was facing downhill with his legs out in front of him, but he was sitting still, slumped over on an aluminum disc. Now and then in lackluster fashion he reached behind himself with his arms and pulled himself up the hill a few inches at a time.

"Are you all right?" she asked him. She could she he was near tears.

"I hit the stop sign," the boy haltingly managed to report.

Marge thought the boy was okay but badly in need of attention. "How about if I get you some help?" she offered. "Where do you live? Do you live near here?"

The boy was able to give her directions and before too long she and Colter, like brave Canadian Mounties in frozen territories, found the designated home. She alerted the boy's mother. Then she and Colter stood watch with the boy until the mother arrived to take him home.

Though shy and reclusive, Margaret accepts people the way they are. She would do anything for someone or some critter in need, especially so for someone or some critter she cares about. When it comes right down to it, you can't say that about many people.

"Okay, Colter!" called Marge clapping her hands as tiny pellets of sleet started to come down. "Let's go see what B.J. is up to."

The dog bounded towards Marge and she ruffled his black coat vigorously. The surge of freedom and energy that she had enjoyed earlier had been subtlety replaced by the flow of motherly juices and fatigue. She needed to rest and people would be wondering what had happened to her. As she savored the afterglow of having lived life in the moment, she climbed slowly back up to the Prestige Heights area of the summit.

Chapter 20
Opening the Presents

To look experience full in the face and to allow it to instruct and change me involves a deep trust in the intrinsic value of those experiences.

Morning: Pat's Apple Pie Burns

The tall pine trees on the steep mountain slopes stoically and silently bore their heavy burden of new snow. Sharply banked up, ten-feet-high, compacted snow flanked both sides of the divided highway and, in the median strip, graded snow raised up a good six feet, all but shutting out any sign of the other half of the four-lane highway. Interstate 90 itself, carved out of invisible solid rock in places on the Snoqualmie Pass, was heavily snow-packed, but passable. In this white winter wonderland snow continued to fall and an intrusive black road sign with red digital lettering blinked on and off: "Chains required next four miles".

Traffic was as still as the snow and the trees. Some drivers stood outside of their vehicles to stretch their legs and talk in hushed tones with one another. The driver ahead of Sandi had told her that the authorities had closed the pass shortly after midnight and that he'd slept in his truck at the pullout off the road. When he woke the traffic had been moving; when he was ready to go it had stopped again. He assumed snowplows were clearing away a small avalanche of snow up ahead. It happened often he had said and Sandi knew it was so.

"Sleet," he'd said, "is turning to rain on the other side of the pass and I sure don't look forward to that." Search teams according to the radio had found the frozen bodies of two-nineteen-year-olds at the 5000 feet level. Robert Mattson and Matthew Ichihashi had been missing since Monday morning. The two University roommates, skilled in hiking and climbing, had done it all right, the announcement emphasized. One had left a detailed map with his father of where they were going, plus the youth had worn an electronic homing device. The device had, in fact, led the rescuers right to the site. There was evidence, said the announcer, that there had been a major avalanche in that area.

Old news, Sandi thought. *I heard that tragic story two days ago. The media is really milking it.* She turned the switch to off, flipped out the tape of Amy Grant's "Praise and Worship Choruses" and replaced it with the Andrew Lloyd Weber, "Joseph and the Amazing Technicolor Dream Coat," tape. She sang along with a couple of songs. Sandi knows all the words to songs in musicals; it is just something she expects of herself.

It was Saturday morning, and now that she was seeing the road conditions for herself, she was confident that she would make it through the pass to Seattle. She had weathered this type of situation before; it was just a matter of patience. Tape completed she turned off the stereo. Then, with an ear tuned to the truck in front of her she picked up her paperback from the seat beside her and began to read.

Moonlight Becomes you, the latest mystery by Mary Higgins Clark, was proving to be a good one. Clark had a set formula for obscuring who her murderers were, and usually Sandi solved the mystery a third of the way through a book. So far, though, in this one she had not yet guessed who had done the dastardly deed.

Down below in the city Pat zipped around the Cok house doing a bit of everything at the same time. Her hair was half done up in rollers. Maroon sweats on top and blues on the bottom, white socks, well-worn slippers. Flour from the apple pie that she was making clung to the front of her shirt and there was a streak of it on her cheek.

She put her head farther into the full refrigerator and sorted through leftovers and other foods. Everything was jammed together.

"Oh, no," Pat groaned dramatically, "somebody opened the nonfat eggnog!"

Animated voices in Walton family style rang out from various rooms, "Who opened the nonfat eggnog?"

"Who opened the nonfat eggnog?"

"I didn't."

"I didn't either."

"It was probably B.J.," Marge volunteered. She was at work again in the laundry room.

"It was not, Mom!" protested Brandon vigorously from the living room where he was practicing Christmas carols on his shiny, golden, new saxophone.

Pat had placed herself in charge of the evening meal. There would be a honey ham, mashed potatoes, country peasant bread, vegetables and pie. Between the meal and dessert, she had decided, they would gather in the living room and finally open the presents. Sandi had called in on her cellular just before she had come to the pass where she would lose cellular connection. As far as Pat knew the pass was open though that didn't keep her from worrying. It looked like sleet outside. She wished Sandi would just be there.

"How are you doing?" asked Steven tenderly after he had nearly collided with his frenzied wife in the doorway to the family room. One arm entwined with hers, he placed the other on the side of her face and softly wiped away the flour with his thumb.

"Okay, I guess," answered Pat leaning her weight against him for barely a second then bouncing away as she whooped, "I'm so busy, Cok!"

Truth be told, Pat had been busy since the day she walked down the gangplank onto American soil. In February of 1948 her father took Pat with the customary large bow in her hair and brother, John, in his knickers to the public school in Manhattan. *Pa* pointed to the door with a 1 on it and pushed them towards it. Pat had been in the fourth grade in Thesinge but had no choice; in the new country she started over in the first grade.

Rena Douma and Marie Dyk, a daughter of Uncle Bill, were instructed to take the two odd-looking immigrant children into the school office and to teach them the alphabet. Jennie, another first grader, led them to the playground.

Pat was quick to learn the English language and became the family translator and teacher. Why were the k's silent in knife and know? Shouldn't it be kanife and kanow?

In September of the next school year Pat, skipping Grade 2,

went into Grade 3 for just one week. Then she was advanced to Grade 4 for the remainder of the school year. In the fall she went into Grade 5 with Mrs. Peterson who did not keep her long. She put her in Grade 6 just before semester tests. She passed all of the sixth grade tests except Health.

On Friday in Grade 6 Mrs. Friday was Mrs. Friday and on Monday through a divorce Mrs. Friday had become Miss Finch. The irascible woman put down the law. No one was to call her Mrs. Friday ever again! When a child slipped and called her by her old name she took them off into another room. There she whacked the poor child repeatedly on the hand with a ruler so hard that the class could hear it next door. Pat was careful to avoid the punishment from Mrs. Friday, Oops! From Miss Finch. Isn't it interesting what leaves an impression on a child's mind?

Before the school year ended the family moved from Manhattan to Dick Heys' old house in the Dutch community south of Churchill and Pat had to take the public school bus to finish out her year. In the fall of 1950, only two-and-a-half years after she restarted in first grade, she entered Manhattan Christian in a combined Grade 7 and 8 with Mr. Zimmer. Surprising everyone including herself the intellectually precocious seventh grader answered aloud a question meant for the eighth graders.

When Pat finished the 10th grade which was still all that Manhattan Christian offered, she had been in the States for just five and a half years. She turned sweet sixteen in June, and in the beginning of September left home with fellow students, Jean and Willis Alberda, Don Bos and Betty Leep to attend Western Christian High School in Hull, Iowa.

Even though her absence would cause an emotional strain and her education would cause a financial hardship on our family, our parents, especially *Pa*, had insisted unequivocally that she continue in a Christian school. He had been mortified to have to tell his family in Holland that his children were in public school in their first years in America, and he was not going to allow that to happen again. In person he had taken her to Chambers and Fisher clothing store in Bozeman to pick out a nice dress. Along with Mom the threesome had agreed on a green, two-piece, knit dress that cost $35.00.

Unheard of! Like catching a fish in Perk's Ditch would have

been. Camp Creek, yes—though illegal because of it being in a game preserve—a person could haul a fair-sized rainbow trout out of Camp Creek. But nothing ever came out of Perk's Ditch. And Jan Piet, *Pa,* never shopped for clothes. First of all her father had absolutely no patience for shopping, and secondly she could not believe the huge amount he agreed to pay. She had been deeply touched. Forty years have gone by and Pat still holds onto the knit dress.

In turn, she worked hard to earn money and studied hard to get good grades. Living in the private home of Dick and Grace Dykstra in Hull, Iowa, she did the baby-sitting and housekeeping in partial exchange for her room and board. Not much time was left over for the new boy friend, Sebert Kooima; not much time but just enough for her to have an exciting experience, her first kiss! She carefully recorded this fact in her daily diary, and I gleefully in turn read and broadcasted that fact to the family when Pat came home for vacation.

Remarkably, given the fact that a short time before Pat had not even spoken the English language, in 1955 she graduated as valedictorian of her large senior class! She was also awarded a scholarship for college.

Though her friends all talked about college, Pat had not dared to dream of it. But a scholarship! It was a gift not to be wasted; the family would make allowances. Off to Calvin College, the Christian Reformed Church sponsored, liberal arts college in Grand Rapids, Michigan, she went. It was too late to get into Blodgett's three-year diploma nursing program that was affiliated with Calvin so she started on an assortment of classes to work towards an eventual degree in nursing.

As she had been doing in high school, she worked hard to earn her way in college. She did baby-sitting for two families; one had five children, the other a set of twins. She made the toast and burned her fingers most mornings working on the serving line in the school cafeteria. She wore black and white to set tables and serve for special banquets. She did the laundry and ironed shirts for Wayne and Bern Alberda and Stan Cole. It was a grinding job week after week after week. She worked a regular weekend evening shift in a private nursing home cooking for up to fourteen residents. And, along with all that, she maintained an excellent grade point average.

Sadly and abruptly, in April of her second year her busy and exciting days at Calvin College came to a screeching halt. Her father had been diagnosed with a terminal illness! "You better come home," her mother decreed.

Presto! She took all but her Chemistry final exams. Three weeks early! A few days later she studied for her Chemistry final while cultivating a field on the farm back home back in Montana. Her detailed notes were taped to the wheel covers on the reliable old Oliver tractor. The professor sent the exam but also said she could choose between taking a B+ or taking the exam to improve her grade. She chose the B+.

In the summertime of 1957, as she had already been doing for several years, Pat worked on the farm and as a nurse's aide at Bozeman Deaconess Hospital. She had been hired personally by the Director of Nursing, Mildred Flannigan. As an aside, Millie, as she was known, would go on to hire Marge, Me and Ann—in that order—as well in future years. If asked, one can well imagine what Ms. Flanigan might have said: The Heidemas came and went, each time there was a different one, throughout my entire career. Hard workers all of them; I'd hire 'em on the spot.

Short on teachers for the school year that fall the Christian school board on Churchill approached Pat to teach the sixth grade. At first appalled by the very thought of it, she later relented. The family desperately needed the income. She would pursue her nursing career by taking a child development course during the school year and more courses the following summer in the nursing program at Montana State College in Bozeman.

It was during this challenging year of teaching, studying and coping with our father's ever-worsening illness (she gave him injections of Demerol during a train trip to and from Texas where there was purported to be a cancer cure) that Pat began to take special notice of Steven. She had been aware of Steven over the years because they both attended Young People's Society at the church and he was a cousin of her best friend, Jean Alberda. But, up until her year of teaching, when suddenly she felt ever so much more mature, he had seemed too old for her.

Steven was finishing work on his baccalaureate degree and was planning to continue to earn the master's degree (which he did in

1960) at the time. Like her he was tall, good-looking, hard-working, Dutch, clean-cut, Calvinistic Christian and available. What was not to love?

Their first date came, providentially they would say, on Memorial Day. The Young People's Society was having an outing at Oozel Falls in Gallatin Canyon. Pat needed a ride. Steven offered to take her.

And then, providentially again, no doubt, the fan belt in the old brown Chevrolet broke while Pat was driving it from the school yard. Steven, working at Ray Segaar's garage on Churchill, was there to fix it.

The Young People's Society always met on Sunday evenings after the church service. Immediately after the Young People's meeting was the exciting time. That was when a girl was asked for a date, and the date would be to cruise around in a car together or to go to someone's home for cake and coffee and for singing maybe.

In the beginning of their courtship Pat was not always certain of Steven's intentions. She was pretty much a wreck over the unpredictability, if you ask me. Sometimes he would ask her out and sometimes he wouldn't. Sometimes he wouldn't even go to the Young People's meeting!

Steven, it so happened, was an usher for the evening service. He did his ushering work on the same aisle as was habitually used by us Heidemas. The proximity of the two parties heightened the anticipation of course. After a number of Sunday evenings Pat, in order to ease her uncertainty, concluded that Steven sent signals as to whether or not he would ask her out later. In addition to the presence or absence of a smile and personal recognition, a yellow tie meant yes, the red and blue, no, and the green, maybe.

The yellow tie must have had quite a workout because after a while there were dates not only on Sunday evenings but other times as well. Plus Steven, who had a pilot's license, started to make sweeping flights with a two-person Cessna over the Heidema farm. Every time that Pat heard the approaching sound of a single-engine plane, I remember she raced from wherever she was in the house, slammed the screen door behind her and stood on the cement steps looking up. If the Cessna dipped its wings in greeting, it was Steven and Pat would wave her arms excitedly.

The whirlwind teaching year of 57-58 came to an end and that summer Pat began working on the Montana State nursing program in earnest. She attended classes at Community Hospital in Butte and rode back and forth with Dick DeGroot in his Amsterdam Store produce truck. On the days that there were no classes she worked at the Deaconess in Bozeman for pay. Her father, a patient at the same hospital, died in July.

The next year in 1959 Pat did a psychiatric clinical affiliation at Warm Springs. She took the bus back and forth on weekends when she helped on the farm, worked and saw Steven in the little time she had left. In August of that year, eleven years after coming to America, she graduated with an Associate Degree in Nursing, married Steven three days later and moved with him into an apartment in Bozeman. Phew!

"Come home, come home, it's supper time. The evening shadows fall. Come home, come home, it's supper time..." The familiar song played a few days later on the KGVW Christian radio station request program as the Coks rode leisurely along on Belgrade road. "That song was played for the newly-wed Steven and Pat Cok," crooned the announcer. "It was requested by their sister, Char, who wants them to hurry on home. So, Steven and Pat, the family is waiting for you for supper. You better scoot on home!" That had been 37 years ago.

"Does anybody smell smoke?" asked Marge who had come into the kitchen and stood sniffing the air.

Pat gasped and flew towards the stove, "My pie, my pie is burning. I forgot all about it!" She whipped open the oven door and smoke came pouring out.

"Oh, no, it's ruined! It's ruined!" wailed Pat. "Help me, Cok!"

Steve took up the hot pads. I hurriedly exited from the smoky room, oxygen tubing snaking wildly behind me. Ann and Marge threw open doors to the outside. Brandon, still holding his saxophone with the cord around his neck, witnessed the melee from the living room doorway.

"Is there a crisis here?" asked Sandi calmly walking into the family room from the garage entryway.

"Quick, Sandi," instructed Pat standing wide-eyed in the middle of things, "wave this dish towel over the smoke alarm there by your head to keep it from going off! Arlyce, you do that one. Arun is asleep; we don't want to wake him up!

Sandi, dressed in hooded sweatshirt, down vest and blue jeans, put down her bags and raised both arms waving the towel back and forth. Arlyce did the same at the other end of the room.

"Hi, Sandi! Welcome home!" called Arlyce.

The girls laughed in unison at the familiar antics of their frantic mother.

Luckily, there was no fire. The bubbling apple pie had overflowed and the caramelized sugar runoff on the cookie sheet had begun to smoke. The pie, unaffected, was beautiful.

Early Afternoon: A Case for Entitlement

Aware that the presents would finally be opened in the evening, Ann was itching to do a little last minute shopping. She had not quite finished buying what she wanted for Steven, the person whose name she had drawn for the gift exchange. Doug, despite the fact that the sleet and rain were treacherously icing the snowpacked streets, had taken the trusty Toyota pickup and was out in the nasty weather buying a present for B.J. Ann knew this.

"I could have gone along," she groused, "but no one told me that he was going."

Mom was standing in the kitchen and voicing her frustrations to Pat and me. Like the two women, Mary and Martha of Biblical lore, I was tending to Mother's words and Pat was busy preparing food at the stove. Martha, as I remember, grumbled about Mary not doing the work, but Jesus told her that Mary was doing something more important by anointing his feet with oil. I hoped that I was doing something important; but, in retrospect, I would have done better to get Sophia to do Mom's feet.

"How about making a gift certificate to a bookstore?" I suggested as Mother moved toward the table and sat down. "You can add that to what you already have. That would be nice."

"He had a belt buckle with a train on it on his list and something else too," she stubbornly retorted biting her lower lip. "I should give him something to do with that. I should go shopping, too."

"Just write a check and make a certificate. That's really all you can do at this point, isn't it?" I urged, adjusting the tubing under my nose to stop the hissing noises. I felt irritated with Mom's typical procrastination. Everyone had known their Christmas name and had their suggested gift list for weeks already. *It is so like her to be doing this at the last minute,* I thought.

"Ja, wel. Het spiet mie toch (It disappoints me). I will make the check for $20.00 then," announced Ann pointedly as she pulled her checkbook out of her purse.

"How much did the book cost that you are giving him?" I queried.

I was suspicious that she would be going over the agreed-upon amount. It was another one of her predictable maneuvers.

"Fifteen dollars," she responded tartly.

"Then, you need to write the check for ten dollars. We have a total limit of $25.00, you know."

I was unafraid of stressing the boundaries with her, but also knew from experience, that when I did, I had to pay the emotional price for doing so.

"Well, that is up to me," Mother persisted.

"I stayed in the limit," I stated firmly, "and I assume others did as well. I think it is only fair that you do it, too."

I sucked in air deeply through my nose, then puffed out my cheeks and blew it out steadily and forcefully as if I were getting ready to deliver a crucial pitch in the World Series. What I needed was to have my catcher come to the mound for a conference. Instead, I pleaded with my older sister.

"Pat, don't you agree?"

Why could Ann not have kept the amount of the check to herself? Write the check, slip it in an envelope and let whoever wanted to complain do so after the fact. Simple, you say? Not really. Why not, you ask? I will tell you why not. It is a case of disputed entitlement.

First of all, let me just say that neither Mom nor I wanted to be involved in this contentious conversation; money is a sensitive, painful area in our family. And keep in mind as you read further, you are seeing just the tip of the iceberg.

In the years after Kelly and Ann were separated Steve and Pat helped Ann with her house payments, Doug and Marge paid for a majority of the house and appliance maintenance, and I sent monthly personal money. When Ann moved into the retirement home, our continued financial support, now including that of John and Joyce as well, became more formalized.

Ann's meager social security payments were never enough. Even working regularly Ann had not been able to afford her circumstances. No one expected her to do it alone, and no one begrudged carrying her some, until...until she wanted to be a little more generous. Until she wanted to behave a little more freely. Until she wanted to act richer than she was. Until..., until.

Mother, as you may remember, was the firstborn child of a *dikke boer* in Holland, and she grew up in a culture that had for centuries heavily favored royalty and upper class. That meant she was reared to not only appear decent or nice-looking in public, but to present herself as being *deftig* (distinguished, dignified). She was used to *pronk'n* (preening, showing off), you might say.

On the other hand, when it comes to being *zuinig* (frugal), Ann knows every trick in the book. At one time or another she has darned holes in socks, replaced worn elastic in panties and bras, remodeled clothes that no longer fit and eaten every morsel of an animal that a human can eat. She has eaten the tail, heart, tongue, liver and kidneys. She has washed out pig intestines and then stuffed them to make sausages. She has made and eaten blood sausages which were made from blood, flour, raisins and a sweetener. They, by the way, required hours of stirring and more stirring and then were put into *klont puten* (small cotton bags). She has eaten head stuff, the meat and fat on the skulls. She has gone without sugar and reused a tea bag until the water was clear.

So she is no stranger to cutting costs. She just plain does not like it. And, having raised four successful children and made it through all the hard times, she simply does not always want to cut corners.

Should we children restrict her spending? Should there be a bottom line? How great should our sacrifice be? There is no easy formula. Plus, and I think this has been a major factor, there has been neither cushioning nor confronting from members of an extended family group. A sympathetic aunt or a no-nonsense type uncle, for instance, would most likely have helped along the way.

Our money issues really started in 1948 with our emigration

from Holland. The Dutch economy had been dealt a severe blow by the war, and we were among the many citizens that were leaving the country. Holland could not financially afford to lose the money holdings of these people; so a law was put into effect to restrict the amount of money that could leave the country. Since we could not take the money with us, Dad and Mom, just before departure, gave sums of money to a couple of Mom's neediest siblings. Supposedly, it was given with the understanding that it would be repaid over time and sent to the family in the States. There was no paperwork. Behaving as we often do, human beings will selectively and conveniently forget such family transactions. The relatives did just that, they forgot to pay it back.

Following the east-to-west train trip of our family in 1948, *Oom* Bill loaned our suddenly poverty-stricken family start-up money and *Pa* picked up odd jobs. He worked as a Sheetrock finishing man for Al Dyksterhouse, and he walked the ditch line. In a few years, when the opportunity came, we rented and moved onto Rose White's farm near Manhattan. There were more start up costs and more loans from *Oom* Bill. Not many years passed before the accumulated debt to *Oom* Bill became an albatross around our family's neck. While *Pa* was alive and the family lived on the farm, there was always a lot of stress around having enough money to pay the landlord, Rose White, to pay the interest and a little on the debt to *Oom* Bill and to have enough left over for farm implements, tools, feed, taxes, church and Christian school tuition.

Enough food on the table, blessedly, was never a problem. Mom, with the help of Pat, grew a huge vegetable garden. Many hours each summer and early fall were spent canning—more than a hundred jars at least—of green beans, *snee bonen* (french style green beans), fawn brown *walsa or walske bonen* (fava beans), bright orange, sliced carrots, red cabbage and rhubarb.

Fruit was purchased by the bushel or self-picked and a hundred more quart jars were filled with peaches, pears, apricots, cherries, applesauce and amber-colored crab apples with a whole clove in each apple and a cinnamon stick in each jar. All were colorfully stored on shelving along all of one wall and half of another in the cool, dark, dirt basement.

There were always plenty of potatoes to be gleaned from the crops in the fields. These were also kept in the dark basement in a burlap sack. Sometimes, along side of the potatoes there would be a small wooden barrel of smoked and salted white fish sent from relatives in Holland.

Cows were milked by hand and whole milk and cream were sold. In order to get cream, whole milk was poured into the top of the separator and collected from two spouts as either skim milk, which the pigs loved with their grain called slop, or cream. The worst part of that operation was cleaning the separator and the 100 or so metal discs with soap and water.

Chickens and animals were butchered, whole sides of pork and beef were cut up and frozen and stored in rented freezer compartments in Manhattan Creamery. Whole livers were boiled and sliced cold for sandwiches, and eggs were both eaten and sold.

Egg production, as all activities on the farm, had with it some memorable events. For instance, there was the overly protective, ill-tempered old Leghorn rooster who saw it as his duty to attack every intruder. Whenever one of us approached his flock or his territory—the chicken coop and about 20 feet in front of it—the proud old fellow would get infuriated. With his intense, beady eyes, bright red, indignant head and an even redder wobbling comb atop and ruffed feathers at the neck, he would dramatically tilt his body forward and get a running start in our direction. Then, with wings flapping madly and beak extended, he would launch himself right at our faces. He wanted to peck out the intruder's eyes; there was no doubt about it. With enamel basin in hand in which to collect the eggs, we would intercept the mad fowl's challenge in midair and clunk him over the head. It was a ritual. While the fallen rooster lay on the ground with eyes fluttering, we would quickly feed the chickens, scoop up the eggs and get the heck out of his space. The old fool just never quit.

One such day John hurriedly did the task and mistakenly scooped up the eggs from under the brooding hen that Mom had decided to allow to sit until the eggs turned to chicks. Those eggs were mysteriously missed in the candling process—when an egg is held up to a light in order to see if there are blood spots or other abnormalities in the egg—and not many days passed before Pieka was on the party line: "*Hez mi ja keukens verkaught* (You've sold me chicks)!" It was a while before Pieka would let us forget what it had been like to cut into what she thought would be a soft boiled egg and to find instead yellow fluff, a beak and yellow feet.

Those chicks were a mistake, but the two hundred chicks that came in the mail each spring for four years were not a mistake; they were my responsibility and my tuition for the four years of high school. Raising them, I remember well, was a darn filthy job. Not only did they make a mess in their water, their food and their space, but when they got cold they would pile on top of one another—I could find ten to twenty flattened in the morning. Or they would go through a phase, before they were fully feathered out, when they would peck each other to death. To get them to quit, I had to smear the wounds with some awful-tasting purple paste. I helped to butcher them, too, and sold them dressed as five pound fryers.

Oom Bill, considering it his right, I assume because we owed him, interjected himself into the workings of the farm, especially in the area of cattle raising. It was not unusual to hear Mom say, *"Och, nee, hier komt Oom Bill ook weer ann* (Oh, no, here comes Uncle Bill too again)!

The man took it upon himself to buy cheap animals at the Bozeman Livestock Auction, load them on his pickup with the stock racks, unload them into the corral on the farm and hand the bill to Dad. Sometimes an animal had a cancerous growth on its head, another would be malnourished or diseased in some way—there was always good reason for why animals were sold for next to nothing.

Just so with horses, there was the fiery pinto that freaked out over the sodden bumps in the lower pasture. He bucked until he threw my father farther than he ever could have imagined. *Pa* never got on that horse again; he went right back to the auction. There was the big powerful, too-fast palomino; she stayed for a while but wasn't of much use. And there was Nancy who came to us already lame; she suffered from that bad knee for a lot of years.

Everyone in the family worked hard to earn money. John milked a neighbor's cows and helped with stacking his hay. There were lots of baby-sitting jobs for Pat and me. Some families were generous; others were downright stingy. Baby-sitting for a stingy family meant being there from three in the afternoon until eleven in the evening, getting a good hot meal for older kids and the hired man, doing all the dishes, feeding and diapering infants, putting kids to bed and straightening the house for one silver dollar. One silver dollar!

Baby-sitting for a generous family was so much better. The kids would usually have had their dinner and the dishes would have been done. If not, everything would be ready to go. I would put a couple of kids to bed at eight and have a quiet evening with a snack—they encouraged it—in front of the television. Maybe even snooze—they didn't mind—until 12:30-1:00 a.m. for three dollars.

Oom Bill paid John a penny per gopher tail or magpie beak or egg. Heino Dornbos paid me a half-penny per live night crawler. After dark I would crawl on hands and knees through the wet grass; I would hold my flashlight with one hand and pick the night crawler with the other. Man, those things are fast! Mom would make me quit after a couple of hours. Old Heino, the next morning, would dump the clump of worms out of the five-pound coffee can that I brought in, throw out each of the dead ones that had died overnight and subtract the number from the total. Talk about cheap!

Another way to help the family financially was to participate in grading our own potatoes. In the dark, dank potato cellar with a few low-wattage, eerie, exposed light bulbs dangling over our heads we stood at an elevated table and sorted the potatoes moving along a conveyor belt. Breathing in the stench of potato rot and dirt we sliced knobs off potatoes with sharp blades set into the table in front of us. If the potato was too knobby we graded it a second and put it into sacks at our sides. Rotten ones soaked our brown, cloth gloves with their juice and were thrown into a pile. A tractor with a front loader would at the end of the day haul those away to be fed to livestock. The good potatoes, the number ones, were allowed to go on and were sacked at the end of the table. The new burlap sacks were sewn shut and put on trucks or to be shipped out. When the huge doors to the cellar were open to let in or out a truck, the frigid Montana air rushed in to chill us further; our toes had probably been numb since ten o'clock already. I remember praying for break time to have that cup of hot coffee or tea.

Every member of our family worked hard but even back then there was not enough money to absorb the devastating costs of illness. When Dad was sick, the church stepped in to help with the outstanding hospital bills and when *Pa's* life and dream ended, the animals and machinery were sold off to resolve the debts. At last the heavy weighted albatross was lifted; *Oom* Bill, the uncle who was so full of bluster while keeping close track of figures, was finally out of our lives! Oh, but at what a price.

In the winter of 1960 when John married Joyce the small insurance policy on Dad's life allowed Mom to make the down payment on the two bedroom house on Churchill. She took a job in Jim and Elsie De Jong's grocery store and coffee shop and she baked pies, which she had never done before, poured coffee, stocked shelves, mopped floors and checked out groceries. In a second job she cleaned Doctor William's home and office weekly. And, when I left for college, she took in a couple of school teachers as boarders to help pay the mortgage.

Mom's struggle to be self-supporting was temporarily eased in her second marriage. In addition to Kelly's job with Al Dyksterhouse which brought in a regular paycheck she and Kelly took on the janitorial job at the Bethel Christian Reformed Church. Kelly's stay was relatively short-lived, however, and along with him, out went his paycheck and the church job.

Ann, on her own again, screwed up her courage another notch and carried on. She took a Bozeman Deaconess Hospital course and proudly graduated as a Certified Nurse Aide. She worked full time in the Extended Care Facility at the hospital. Over a year's time, however, she found the work of lifting to be hard on her already painful back; nursing, she realized, was nowhere near as idyllic as she long had imagined. She then went to part-time hospital work, and through her friendship with Al Dyksterhouse became the weekend, evening and night manager at the new Churchill Retirement Home as well. Later on she chose to clean houses instead and did so into her early eighties. The Bacons, the Cowans, the Reynolds and "The National Geographic" photography couple never did not want to let her go. They said she was "the best". True to her Dutch heritage, Ann scrubbed everything in sight. She always washed and waxed floors on her hands and knees. Plus, she did windows! Until they sparkled!

It was not that Ann did not deserve to be more generous and free and to act richer than she was. Along with being born into class with certain privileges, she had, as the investment company, Smith Barney, television advertisement used to say, done it the "old fashioned way," she had "earned it".

Compare Pat's and my reactions in the check-writing scenario then, if you will, to the use of intensives and superlatives in language. A carefully placed and emphasized "very" here, a "most", "absolute" or "best" there can cause the listener to perk up the ears and take note. The use of too many such words, however, has just the opposite effect. The speaker is considered over-the-top, phony, grandstanding.

Just so, in relation to Mom's generous gesture towards Steven's Christmas gift. It was not one of which we daughters took note. There were too many of such, in the opinion of us children. Her claim, that it was up to her, fell on our long-ago deafened ears.

"I think we need to hold to the limit, *Moeke*. We did," emphasized Pat.

Mother angrily wrote the check for ten dollars and pushed it away from her towards me.

"Here. You make the certificate then and say what you want it to say." She pushed her chair back, stood and left the room without another word.

The ritualistic rooster of entitlement had once again been clunked on the head, a small victory for us children. No doubt, before too long it would rise up, dust itself off and prepare to defend a new day. After all, it was all about who ruled the roost, was it not? But, think again, maybe not.

Certainly the rooster of the chicken coop did not like to get clunked. He could just have pranced around the yard being the little king that he was, without taking that thump on the head each time. And Mom could just have written the check without a word and smugly held her head up high when the complaints came after the deed was done.

Clearly, our two roosters, one real and one so-called, were angry and had a need to show it. They had not been born to be stupid. They had been born to be proud. Dylan Thomas, the poet, may have said it best:

> "Do not go gentle into that good night,
> Old age should burn and rave at close of day;
> Rage, rage against the dying of the light..."

Repetitiously irritating as they may be and as ostensibly stupid as they may seem, the ones who never give up on their claims, therein lay our heroes, our role models.

"And you, my (parent), there on the sad height,
Curse, bless, me now with your fierce tears, I pray.
Do not go gentle into that good night.
Rage, rage against the dying of the light."

Late Afternoon: John Is the Man They Call

Far away from the fray in Seattle, in the 40-foot park model on space D-82 of Sunlife Resort in Mesa, Arizona, John sat in his black, high-back office chair and faced the nineteen inch screen of the computer monitor. Even though he had the best and the latest models in equipment, he needed to lean forward closer to the screen to read the data. None too soon apparently, his appointments for cataract surgery at Swagel-Wouton Eye Clinic were set for next month. When he finished reading through a column of figures, my serious-minded brother leaned back for a few moments to rest. He took off his glasses, rubbed his eyes and then, since his pain-filled back had really stiffened up, he pressed his blonde, long-haired forearms down on the armrests to ease the pressure.

When he had been in the hospital in Billings for his bad back some twenty odd years ago, the pain, he told me, had been so bad he had bent the metal of the head frame in a severe spasm of agony. Unfortunately, the two surgeries for his ruptured disc had not been worth the considerable amount of trouble they had caused. That was typically the way it was, John had learned from talking to other guys since that time; disc surgery was always a gamble. Maybe a 50/50 proposition like lung transplantation was.

Only half of single- or double-lung transplants made it past the first year. And maybe half again of those that made it had any kind of quality of life. There were the complications of aspergillis, a fungus, or pseudomonas, a resistant bacterial infection, or of a medialstinal shift going on when the new lung got cramped by the native lung, chronic rejection, drug side effects, the always compromised immune system hassles not to mention he and Joyce having to be away from family for maybe as long as two years in a strange place. He'd known a number of Alphas with the disease who'd jumped on the transplant wagon only to lose their lives after a year or two. He'd keep waiting it out, as he had for 23 years already—he had been diagnosed when he was 34 years old—rather than trade his familiar set of problems for another with those kinds of odds.

The walnut-veneer-over-pressed-wood, self-assembled desk with shelving and pullout keyboard tray at which he sat was set up against the vinyl-coated aluminum, trailer coach wall. The rest of the carpeted Arizona room was at his back. Furniture in the room included a round table with straight-backed, gold, plastic, padded chairs, a cream-colored couch and two burnt-orange easy chairs. Mini-blinds and handmade multicolored valances graced the windows and tastefully blended with papered walls. Vertical blinds hung by the sides of the two six-foot glass sliders.

To John's left, around the corner at the back of the trailer in a bright, sunny area was his wife's sewing machine, and against the wall facing him was the Casio electronic piano keyboard with open sheet music. Joyce, John's wife of 36 years, Peter R. and Gertrude Van Dyken's oldest, was carrying on the tradition of her mother and sister, Karen, who played the piano and organ in the Christian Reformed churches on Churchill. Joyce played the piano for the chapel service in the Activity Hall of Sunlife every Sunday morning during their six-month stay and she was often asked to play for other special musical numbers in the park. Although she did most of her practicing on the regular piano at the hall, the keyboard was handy when she needed to work out difficult pieces. Knowing that her talents had been overshadowed by her mother's and sister's, John took great pride in his wife's playing. He had supported her all along and enjoyed seeing and hearing the results of her increasing confidence.

Taking up the northeast corner space of the room was an indispensable eight feet by twelve feet storage shed that housed the washer and dryer, liquid oxygen reservoir tanks and John's tools. The two walls of the shed that were in the Arizona room had been covered with drywall and wall-papered to match the other walls in the room. Like a house prepared for pastoral visitation, everything was neat and clean; there was nothing extraneous lying about in the room.

To John's right on the other side of the three steps leading into the coach, the oxygen concentrator heaved and wheezed as it ran through a mechanical cycle over and over and over. So much a part of this man's life, the sounds—like white noise—soothed him as did his eleven by fourteen matted and framed photographs of Montana's snowcapped mountains hanging on the walls. There was the one of the majestic Spanish Peaks and another with the puffy, white clouds in the big, blue sky over the Bridger Range. Just visible inside the coach in the bedroom hung another one of his personal favorites. It was of a perfect, red rose blossom, and he had captured it with delicate droplets of dew clinging to the flawless pink petals, deep green leaves and fuzzy stem. This particular photograph hung in that spot as daily proof to the man that he had indeed learned to stop and smell the roses.

It was obvious from these samples that bro had the right equipment, an appreciation of pristine nature and a good eye for photography. When he had looked around, desperate for something productive to do after he could no longer do physical work on the dairy, he had taken both the Basic and Advanced courses in Photography at Montana State University. Along the way he had become an active member of the Camera Club of Bozeman and had won prizes on a number of his entries. He showed his work at the Photo Fair in the mall, at the Winter Fair and some of his landscapes, by his Doctor's request, hung on the walls of the medical building. He had also put together an educational twenty-minute slide show on milk production and had shown it in a number of venues in the state. For a little extra income back home he and Joyce as a team did portraits in their in-house studio and photographed family groups—sometimes large family reunion groups and sports teams—in natural settings. He had hoped to do something similar in Mesa at Sunlife but anymore it was too much of an effort to bring the equipment to Arizona. He usually had his camera and zoom lens ready-to-go, was alert for a good picture and was involved in the Photography Club in the park, but the interest in the park for photography wasn't great any more. In fact, his interest, too, was ebbing. He was moving on.

Productivity at any level being absolutely crucial to his mental well being, he had, also back home, doggedly devised another way for him to work with his hands. He had added a well-equipped woodshop to the garage and had installed a state-of-the-art vacuum system to keep the air clean for his special respiratory needs. In that new shop—as opposed to the old shop on White's farm by Manhattan or the shop on the dairy that he had especially built or the shop in the hanger at the airport that he had rented—he had crafted a bed out of oak for his granddaughter, Breanne. "So that Grandpa will be remembered for decades to come," he wrote in a letter to me. He also had made too-numerous-to-count lawn ornaments, and with his thin-as-a-needle scroll saw blades he had carefully sculpted the heads of alert, antlered deer, elk, horses, eagles, singing birds on tree branches and praying hands and mounted them in redwood frames. One of these hung on the wall of the Arizona room above the couch.

Being thought of as an artist would have been as foreign a concept to him as being called an environmentalist, and yet here was evidence that he was both. His work spoke not only of a drive to be productive but of an inner urge to create and preserve beauty. He loved nature and sought out hideaways in which to observe it. In one of his letters he wrote, "Spring is a beautiful time of the year. The young calves and colts are racing around the pastures as their mothers anxiously watch their every move. The meadowlarks are singing their little hearts out and the robins are busy building their nests. We have a few meadowlarks in our shelter belt and they wake me up every morning. They start singing at about 5:15 AM, and I just love to lay there listening to them in the stillness of the morning before the business of the day starts...something that soothes the mind and heart daily...I thank God for His wonderful handiwork...river, fish, deer, magpie (on endangered species list now), butterfly...God's creation floats along peacefully. I am spellbound really."

The soon to be 56-year-old rubbed his eyes once again and then looked at the bright rays of sunshine coming in through the glass slider. The bright orb of the sun was gradually lowering itself in the western winter sky at 4:15 in the afternoon and in doing so was reassuringly warming the carport. The large-print, round temperature gauge hanging on the outer wall registered a toasty 82 degrees. Parked in the carport was the new, white, Starcraft conversion, Chevy van with its designer JH&JH license plate and its

Armoralled tires. In front of the trailer in the graveled, four-foot space between trailer and sidewalk the ceramic black and white spaniel held its front paws up on the bark of the palm tree and tirelessly looked at the fake bird just out of its reach. Alongside the dog was a black and white, stone-still Sylvester the cat whirligig— obviously, there was not the slightest hint of a breeze in the desert on this day. Accompanying the ornamental dog and cat to the right were the three-foot-high blue, wooden Dutch windmill and Joyce's healthy-looking snapdragons and petunias in the large, clay flowerpot.

Ostensibly, Christmas time in December was the same here as at other trailers. There were strings of lights hung across the front and down the supports of the carport awning, the handrailing of the front steps was wrapped in dark green and silver garland, and a ball of lights made with plastic cocktail glasses hung above a makeshift tree of lights. The tree was creatively attached to the front of the palm tree with bungee cords and spikes. One could see inside through the front slider that there was a large, dark red poinsettia plant, an attractive centerpiece and Christmas cards on display.

To honor the birth of the Christ child, the couple on the previous Friday evening had attended a Christmas choir program at the Grace Community Church. On Christmas Eve Joyce had played the piano for the special Sunlife program and on Wednesday, Christmas Day, for dinner in the Activity Hall the two had dressed in their finery and brought Joyce's much sought-after lemon meringue pies to the table reserved for the members of the Computer Club.

There was, however, a difference from most people in their activities. There was none of the hustle and bustle of last minute preparations and neither of the two had done any shopping for presents. There had been no wrapped packages to be seen and none had been sent. It wasn't that they were ascetic in their religious practices, although their disciplined day-to-day conduct might have appeared so to an onlooker; it was that the gift-giving custom of Christmas had already been observed back in October in Montana. It was always then that the twosome gathered their immediate family along with both mothers, Ann and Gertrude, in their home for a festive dinner and for what seemed to be a generous mountain of presents. Throughout the year especially in Arizona in the many stores Joyce shopped for gifts, mostly clothes, and all items in the spring were ferried home in the van for the post-harvest, pre departure celebration. Consequently, Christmas in December for the couple was not that big of a deal.

They had been snowbirds coming to Arizona for eight years. At first Joyce had wept over missing her brood at holiday time and she felt keenly the sacrifice of her children and grandchildren in favor of her husband. He, on the other hand, emphasized the benefits of the lower altitude, warmer weather and plentiful technology stores within ready reach. So much so, he claimed, that he didn't have time to miss anyone or anything. He was just pissin' up a rope, as guys would say. John also said that he never thought about his dad nor his dad's dying, and that he never felt depressed. That was his style. Defer and deny the demons. Keep a step ahead of 'em. Long before it became a 90's cliché he'd believed that image was everything. Don't let 'em see you're weak, the most primitive of survival strategies.

In his shirt pocket was a small notebook in which were jotted his list of things-to-do. He wrote them down as they came to him and every weekday morning at 8:30 over two ritualistic cups of coffee at MacDonald's—after getting up at 6:00 and having a light breakfast, every weekday morning, of canned, sweetened grapefruit wedges and a cooked egg at home—he set his goals. Then for the rest of the day he went about meeting them.

It was his *liet motif* at the monthly Alphazonie Support Group meetings in Phoenix for which he served as a board member and held the elected post of secretary. "Don't worry about your disease and your future. Set goals. Keep setting goals and keep busy. Keep your mind off your problems. That's what I do and I've been doing it for more than twenty years. The days still aren't long enough for me to get everything done." And, having discovered that he liked to write and was good at it, he wrote this same philosophy in the Alpha 1 National Association newsletter and in many encouraging personal letters to other Alphas around the country.

Though he and Joyce were twice-a-Sunday churchgoers, he disliked the interruptions of weekends. He had to sit around way too much and more often than not eat way too much, and tonight, like every Saturday night of his life, he had to take that dreaded *douche*. *Douche* is the Dutch word for shower; he liked calling it that.

Unlike me he hated to be in water. I remember that he caught me once swimming in the Sunlife pool in a rain storm. He couldn't believe his eyes and erupted, "Have you lost your mind? You're the craziest person I've ever met!"

Right now, brief break ended and Prime Net E-mail in place, he started typing the truck information to his sons, Leland and Kent. With both forefingers he pecked rapidly at the keyboard:

PLAIN-VISTA DAIRY
John Heidema and Sons AG-BAGGERS

1980 International 2574 semi truck
300 horse power Cummins engine
9 speed Fuller transmission
Power steering
Locking power divider
Air brakes and air horn
22 foot TYCROP live bottom silage box
Pto and hydraulics installed with flow speed control mounted on
the back
12,000 lb front axle with 40,000 lb rear axles
Empty weight 29,340 lb
GVW 46,000 lb.

This is our new addition for custom bagging 200'bags...

I worked a long time to locate that humdinger of a truck. They better appreciate it, he thought, as he pecked on.

Next to the laboring concentrator in the corner on FOX, Channel 10 television, Judge Judy, the no-nonsense, high-paid arbitrator was in usual fashion jerking the chains of the day's would-be flimflam artist.

"Look at me! Look in my eyes! Do I look like I have STUPID written on my forehead?" she snapped at the clueless plaintive.

Simultaneously, from the small black boombox on the desktop next to the computer monitor on 99.9, KESZ FM radio, Celine Dion kept stretching her vocal cords as she sang "...my heart will go on and on" in her Titanic oath to the loved one lost at sea. Apparently the non-stop Christmas music that had been playing on that station for a solid week prior to Christmas had now been replaced with easy pop. And every now and then, during a rare still point in the Arizona room, Christian music, "...no heartaches shall come...what a day that will be..." could be heard coming from inside the coach where Joyce was writing a letter to her mother at the kitchen table. Her radio dial was always set on the family station KBIE 89.1 FM.

It wasn't by accident that both radio and television were on at the same time in the Arizona room. It was by design. Brain constantly rapid-firing in multiple spheres suited this intense alpha male the best. He would have liked a CD playing, too. At his real home he had the Prologic Surround Sound, the best, with five speakers, four of which where built into the walls, and a satellite disk, and he kept abreast of news and politics on several networks.

Father and still boss, figuratively at least, although he did kind of know that Joyce and the kids were making decisions that they didn't bother him about, he decided the big money items. He was the seer, the prophet; it was his job to have the vision, to anticipate trends and developments and set the course. John took what information he could from observing and talking with dairymen across the state of Montana, visiting huge dairies in the neighboring town of Gilbert in Arizona and in other states like Texas and California, talking and listening to men hanging out at auctions, sitting at counters in cafes, reading dairy reports on the Internet and in trade magazines and listening to talk radio. He tempered it all with his personal experience, distilled the financial and political implications and had then what he considered a firm grasp on the what-might-happens. More often than not, his predictions had a pessimistic bent to them. If asked, how are such and such? The answer almost always was, "It could be better." That is the nature of farmers, is it not?

After the Agbaggers letter was finished and sent on its way he exited Prime Net and glanced up to the self on which lay his large black leather-bound Bible. He liked to read a few verses everyday and then make some comments on them in one of his files on the computer, but he decided against it and went instead into "My Documents" to continue work on Gertrude's twenty-seven page autobiography. Because he had to scan and sequence old family pictures into the narrative, the job was proving to be irritatingly time-consuming. Computer work often was, but in mastering the new challenges he was far ahead of most.

The phone rang and Joyce called as she approached him, "It's for you. Can you help Bea with her computer?"

"Man, how often does a guy have to tell that old gal what she's doing wrong?" he grumbled as he saved what he had done and put the computer in standby mode.

"I better shake the dew off my lily before I go," he added.

Joyce in well-practiced, unspoken moves took his red and white Darigold jacket from the closet, laid it on the bedspread and stood by waiting for him to say as she knew he would, "Maybe you better pound on me before I go."

He sat on the bedspread at the end of the bed and leaned forward. She bent over him and with both flat hands vigorously percussed his back. His barreled, emphysematous chest needed pounding as many as six times a day. Sometimes Joyce just came over to him and told him to lean forward without him asking; she could hear when he needed it.

He rejected the jacket and, when he reached the Arizona room slider, handed the oxygen tubing back in to Joyce. He walked the couple of steps to his 250 Honda Elite motorcycle and sat down on it. As he turned the scooter around, he was plainly short of breath. He paused briefly and faked making a couple of adjustments on the bike.

Despite medical advice to do so John did not yet use oxygen in public. His lips, ear tips and nail beds showed the cyanosis, but according to his own assessment his body was accustomed to a much lower oxygen saturation level than normal people. "I've adapted over time," was his homespun explanation.

Breathing restored to normalcy, his normal, that is, he headed down D street. A golden eagle soaring in flight was emblazoned on the back of the black storage compartment of the cycle and a "Praise the Lord" sticker was stuck on the fuel tank facing him as driver.

It could be said that John Heidema was the John Wayne of the Sunlife Computer Club. He had been involved in starting the club, had taught classes, still served as a board member and was a busy consultant. He was their symbol of the vitality of computer savvy. Erect in the saddle, so to speak, he was still an imposing six feet three inches and his self-taught, hands-on knowledge of computers was much respected. If someone ran stuck they called on this man.

To not besmirch the American icon—Mr. Wayne's much too hallowed name with unfair comparisons—however, it must be said that John Heidema had forfeited two-and-a-half inches of his previous six feet five and a half inches in height to pride, ignorance and desperation. On the advice of some people with asthma in the community, he had traveled to Mexicalli, Mexico to purchase and ingest some unidentified white pills for a couple of years, and he had felt really great until, that is, his bones started to break from advanced osteoporosis. Darn it all, calcium had been insidiously leeching out of his bones by the steroids that were in the pills and the damage resulted in 11 broken ribs and four compression fractures of his spinal vertebral bodies.

"I practically bought the farm on that one," he put it, when, after figuring it out, he had stopped the medicine cold turkey. That was his way. He had stopped smoking that way too, nothing mamby pamby about this cold-climate kind of guy. How could he have known that his adrenal glands had shut down when his body was full of artificial cortisone? He wasn't a medical type like his sisters were, although he had learned plenty, doctoring with animals his whole life, and knew practically as much as they did because of it. He'd just never run into this kind of thing with his animals.

The sudden withdrawal of cortisone from his body had hit him like a ton of bricks. He had been sure that he was a goner. Clearly, he had not died but he had ended up in a wheel chair and totally without an appetite for months. Absolutely could not eat. His puffed-up, moon-shaped face as a result of the steroids had returned to the rugged lines of the de Vries genes, but his gut still hung on his belt. That hadn't gone away no matter how much weight he had lost. Sure, he was sorry he had ever taken those tricky little white pills but, man, he'd had a couple more good years, he'd felt fantastic, the boys had a couple more years in which to mature into the work on the dairy and all that had been worth something. A guy had to take a risk sometimes. Besides, it was all in the past.

High-dose vitamin D, fluoride and calcium tablets along with his natural testosterone, the presence of which according to him had never ever been in doubt, stabilized the bone situation. The back compressions were irreversible and painful but he was back to about 180 pounds and, when rested, looked good. He had narrow-set, piercing, true blue eyes. His hair the color of ripened grain was always combed and sprayed to stay neatly in place and there was no sign whatever of his father's baldness. He sported a closely trimmed mustache and, of course, when riding his electric horse he did not wear a helmet. Joyce's selection for his clothes were a long-sleeved blue and gray sports shirt, dark gray Lee slacks with blended gray socks and neutral-colored SAS shoes with Velcro closures. His additions were matching silver Cross pen and pencil with small notebook in left shirt pocket, wallet in back pants pocket, pills in container in right pants pocket and tissues in left.

The accessories were a far cry from revolvers hanging from a belt in their holsters, but a western musical theme could well have played in the minds of observers as this urban cowboy went on another mission to rescue a fuzzy-headed oldster lost in cyberspace. "Hi yo, Silver!" Whoops, that was not John Wayne; that was the Lone Ranger. Well, the Lone Ranger analogy would have worked too. Though he is a family man and connected with many people through his business and interests, John is a self-described loner.

A half an hour later, having solved Bea's problem and reinstructed her as to how to stay out trouble, he rode up and down the streets of Sunlife as he did every day when the weather was warm. He inspected the park much like he had always done his dairy herd: he observed the changes, noted the flaws and made a mental list of what needed to be done. Last week he had made it a point to tell administration that the filthy tractor was a heck of an eyesore parked by the sales office, and now he saw that the Mexicans, as he always called them, were keeping the thing parked by the maintenance shed where it should have been all along. To his satisfaction it proved he still had clout.

Milking cows had not been his idea of a satisfying life; in truth, as a kid he had vowed never to do it when he grew up. But life had taken him down that path and, like Jacob in the Biblical dream, he had wrestled with God's angels to squeeze success out of it.

"When Dad died I was supposed to take over," he wrote in a letter. "I wasn't given a choice and I was too young to know what I wanted out of life. I jumped in with both feet and tried my darnedest to do the best job I knew how. I became trapped and worked myself to death. The first years were very trying as I had no one to turn to for advice as to how to do things right."

Neil and Marv Feddes were neighbors and they had helped out some. Their hired man, John MacLees, who was still plowing fields at 80, John told me, had taught him to put newspaper against his skin before putting his clothes on to keep the cruel, high altitude cold out when doing late-fall field work. He had had some help, sure, but basically, the load had been put on his young shoulders.

At seventeen he had been getting by in school, running the farm and dating his future wife. So much for a carefree adolescence of experimentation; it had not happened, not for him. With his mother's urging and "to get a tax break", he says unashamedly, he and Joyce married four days before his twentieth birthday. Before he knew it or really thought about it much, they had their first two children, Sheila and Leland, a few years break and then two more, Michelle and Kent.

When the children were still little he had looked into going to school to learn a trade to get off the dead-end rented White farm, but just then a chance had opened up at Ray Schaper's place. It was three miles south of Churchill and the price had been right. He'd known it would mean an end to sharecropping and old machinery and they'd have a fresh start. Again, Mom influenced his decision.

He wasn't a bit proud of going along with her ideas for his life, he told me. Milking cows had been her life; it didn't have to have been his, but there hadn't been any other adult telling him otherwise. The day he bought the Schaper farm was the day he chained himself to the life of a dairyman. He chained himself and the whole family right along with him. Dairying did not allow for days off or vacations. It was an unending grind of up before dawn at 4:30, in the barn at 5:00, milking again at 4:00 in the afternoon until 7:00 in the evening, seven days a week and 365 days a year. Then there was the cleanup, the inspections, the calves, the insemination programs, veterinarian issues, grain and alfalfa crops and equipment upkeep. He had worked since he was a kid old enough to carry a pail full of milk and he kept on working harder than most men most of his life.

"...after many years of trial and error I finally got things about half way figured out on my own," he wrote. "...I finally thought I was doing the right thing. I had many dreams about efficiency, production and started setting goals, worked very hard to attain these goals and tried to become a success. It is financially impossible to jump in and out of a situation like a farm and the more goals I set the deeper I got in financially and the harder I had to work."

Like a diver from the jackknife position on the high board, he dove into things whole hog and quickly earned the reputation for being a "plunger" in the Dutch community. Big barns, big silos, first big star on top of the silo and big loans from the bank.

When the recession of the eighties hit and banks were looking for bigger profits, he had learned some nasty lessons. One was that bankers were no longer sympathetic to the ups and downs of family farming. One banker in particular had doubts about the dairy's survival and put the screws to the couple. He refused to finance the upcoming year's feed bill. It was the closest they ever came to begging somebody for leniency. Another lesson John learned during those hard times was never to reveal his disability. Bankers and business men did not like giving credit to "a cripple".

"After many years," he wrote, "I finally got to the point where I was able to stand back and say 'I am almost there.' The herd of cattle I had was something to be proud of, the new house was built, the silos were up, good line of machinery and on and on. The only thing left to do was pay for it all and be able to really call myself a success. Then the roof caved in. I, thirty-four years old, the guy with the biggest dairy in the valley, found out he had Alpha I. Then (I) found myself in the hospital with back surgery...and then it was time for another back operation. Now I have to depend on someone else to do my work which I can not accept. This was my operation and I was not about to turn it over to anyone else."

He earned the reputation for having been tough on his kids during those years too; but, despite some struggles, none were the worse for it from what he could tell. Out of the blue his oldest, Sheila, had given birth to a baby boy, Justin John. That was a huge adjustment for the family and it had taken him a good bit to adjust to all of a sudden being a grandparent as well as a parent. But, life moved on—as it does. He forgave Sheila and embraced Justin as his own. "It wasn't hard;" he wrote, "the little guy quickly won our hearts and love, and Joyce, the peach-kind-of-a-gal that she is, took care of Justin in the early years like she did the other kids."

Sheila, after high school, attended the Women in Transition Program at the university. There she took practical courses in computers and office management. She did well in her courses and landed a good job at Skyland. She could then move out on her own with Justin and be self-sufficient. At Skyland she managed the payroll for 700 people. "With those kinds of skills," he said with pride, "she won't have any trouble finding work if she ever has to go on the job market again." She now comes across as a self-assured woman, single parent, loyal family member and her personal life is her business. "I have to hand it to her," he said; "she, also, after all these years still keeps a hand in at the dairy by feeding the calves. She says it is her stress reduction program. If something happened to Joyce, I know that I could depend on Sheila; she would know what to do." She and well-adjusted, bright, college-bound Justin live within walking distance of the folks on Churchill. "Justin is good company. That kid already knows all about the computer and he will have a great job someday."

Leland, his hardworking, earnest, elder son is a dedicated husband to Lisa—daughter of Nelson and Bonnie Van Dyke—and a proud father of three: Brett, Kyle and Breanne, all really terrific kids. In fact, Lisa is pregnant again, so they are going on four. The family lives on the dairy. "Leland and I had our tug-of-wars," John said. "We were both stubborn as the day was long. We have a lot of traits in common; we are, also, frustrated by physical limitations and aren't about to talk about it with the other." When Leland's arm was mangled in the silo machinery, John told me, he flew with his son to Billings and in the hospital "I took a washcloth and washed the silage and grease off my boy's wounds." For a long time after that Sheila was Leland's right arm, and John had to give the kid a lot of credit. Leland switched from being right-handed to left-handed and the guy just plain found ways to function. Nowadays Leland is becoming his own man and John can trust him to get the job done. "Leland is a deacon in the church already," Bro said proudly. "Man, how fast these kids grew up!"

Michelle or Shelly graduated from Calvin College in Grand Rapids, Michigan before she married Shane Leum, son of Art and Hazel Leum from Belgrade. She was working part-time at the Help Center and as a waitress in Bair's Restaurant where she met Shane. Shane has good, steady work at the Belgrade Lumber Mill and now

Shelly is putting her social work degree to work with the Head Start program. "She never liked farm chores. Her thing is kids; she loves kids. She loves to talk, too, and," he said, "I can talk to her." She was always busy and pulled in lots of directions at once, but he likes her lightness and the fact that she and Shane live nearby. He had been scared to death that she would find someone away from home.

And then there is big, strapping, kind, soft-hearted Kent, his youngest. John remembered fondly the days when the kid got up at five in the morning to make basketball practice. He had given it 110 per cent effort and had been a good player as a result. "He has proved to me that he can be a hard worker," John said, "but Kent and his new wife, Dorothy—daughter of Doug and Carol Heavner in Manhattan—are young people. They like to enjoy life too." John wasn't worried. He was confident that the same dedication Kent showed for basketball would come for the dairy before long. And Kent's heart, John predicted, will balance out with his head, especially when he and Dorothy start to have a family. No doubt about it, Kent is a loving caring guy—in fact, the floral centerpiece in the coach was from him and Dorothy, they were thoughtful that way, and Kent was always there to help out his father in whatever way he could; you can't fault a guy for that. He would never forget that time when Kent hoisted him up into the large tandem truck so that he could ride out to the field with him and get a load of chopped hay nor when both of his sons hoisted him up into the tractor so that he could chop that last swathe of hay. What bittersweet moments those were for dear old Dad.

Sometimes, he said, personality differences between Kent and Leland cause work-related issues. He didn't ever go into detail. Both he and Joyce play their cards close-to-the-vest when it comes sharing family business. "It's like any business," he said. "There is always going to be some of that when you get two young bucks together."

In lean times both daughters-in-law willingly worked outside of the home to bring in extra income. Actually, Joyce, along with always doing the dairy bookwork, had cleaned houses and worked as a cook in the retirement home,too, bless her heart. And to save on clothing expenses, she had sewed dresses, skirts and suits for herself and the girls. Lisa had worked in a candy store and a pie store and she baked cakes for special occasions. Dorothy had worked at the Holiday Inn, mowed lawns and both worked grading potatoes.

Beyond hard work and toughness John had demanded organization and maintenance. Everything had to be in its place; it paid off in the long run. He was the kind of guy who looked over his shoulder one last time to make sure everything was right. John didn't go to the farm anymore; not if he could help it anyway. He couldn't stand to see that the boys had their own ideas and ways of doing things. These days they had tools laying everywhere. They would learn eventually, he knew. He had.

He had been tough, he would admit that, but as a family they had their good times too: the horseback rides he had enjoyed with the kids while checking the cattle in the Jackson Creek area, the many family outings on the lakes with the boat and water skiing, the teasing, the laughter, the fishing trips, the good feelings that came with all working together and having good meals and devotions together. He was very proud of his family unit and what they had accomplished together.

The dairy had been John's business with which to earn money and provide for his family, but it was never his bliss. His real passion had been to fly airplanes. As a kid, he told me, he used to stand out in the field, look up at the jets going by and dream about what it would be like to fly one. He had been successful with the dairy, no doubt about it. He and Joyce with uncommon persistence had made it successful. So successful that, when he had to admit that he could no longer do the hard physical work of it or be in the dust of it, he had enough money to pursue his dream and take flying lessons.

He had never studied anything as hard. Lift vector, drag, chord line, resultant force, angle of bank and load factor, trailing edge vortices and weather prognostic charts. He wrapped his head around all of it and proved to be up to the mental challenge. There was another great bonus. He loved having a mentor, a flight instructor, who cared about his progress. On June 12th of 1980 he mastered the written and flight requirements for the Piper PA-38 Tomahawk. He had finally earned the long-wished-for pilot's license and, wow, was he proud!

Thereafter, he loved nothing more than revving up the motor, pushing the throttle ahead, pulling back on the yoke and leaving the earth behind. When he was airborne all the worries stayed down below on the ground, far, far below. "It is so peaceful up there, you can't believe it," he said. "All of a sudden man isn't so important anymore. Guys who like to throw their weight around down there are just ants; not even ants. I can't even see those little buggers." He flew over the dairy and the Gallatin Valley, over the Bridger Mountains and beyond. Talk about total concentration, man, when he was flying he was in a zone! It was pure heaven. John Gillespie Magee Jr. of the Royal Canadian Air Force put it into a poem for pilots like John. "High Flight," composed in 1941 peaks in a religious crescendo near its ending:

> "I've topped the windswept heights with easy grace
> Where never lark, or even eagle flew.
> And, while with silent, lifting mind I've trod
> The high untrespassed sanctity of space,
> Put out my hand, and touched the face of God."

John took Joyce, his mom, me and my sisters, his kids and friends up, one at a time, to show us all what he could do. "You have to check off every item on this list," he'd say. "You don't want to get up there and discover that one of your flaps isn't working."

January of 1983 he achieved the next level and earned his instrument rating. He was ready for above-the-weather operations. The normal Piper engine could not handle the thinner high attitude air. He needed a turbine wheel attached to a compressor wheel, a turbocharger, in other words. His mentor and he found a sweet deal for a Piper PA-28R Cherokee Arrow III N22ME and each went in for half. That was huge! He owned his own plane, 22 Mike ECHO, and he could fly for the Civil Air Patrol. He had never felt smart especially in relation to his educated sisters who had been given the awards. He was more of a C student but when he flew for the Air Patrol, he felt smart, really, really smart.

One of his jobs with the Patrol was to plant a downed airplane in an undisclosed location for rescue drills. He also served as Finance Officer and earned the rank of Second Lieutenant. Not having been previously in the military, he had never known what it would feel like to be an officer in the line of command. One of the highlights in his life turned out to be the time that he walked onto Malstrom Air Force Base in Great Falls in uniform and, man, personnel everywhere saluted him. What a rush! By George, he'd puffed himself out like a peacock that day and rightly so.

He and Joyce flew as far as the state of Wisconsin and he was working on his commercial flying license when he had to stop. He could no longer pass the physical because of the lung thing. "It tears at my heart that I can't leave this earth anymore," he said. "I wouldn't need to pass a physical to fly a homebuilt or an ultralite but I'm too tall for those. I have promises all the time from guys that they'll take me up, but not a one of them has gotten the job done."

To compensate as best he could, he watched the celebrities fly into Belgrade Airport in their 727 and 737s. He drove himself to Osh Kosh, Wisconsin to an air show and with over a million other people saw the British Concord take off. In '91 in Arizona during Desert Storm, the first U.S.-led war against Iraq, he spent hours parked on the outskirts of William's Field Air Force Base in southeast Mesa. From there he watched training pilots take off in their F16s. At the last split second those babies rose up over the ten-foot, heavy-wire security fence, by which he was parked, and a guy could feel the ground shake under his feet. That noise shook more than his feet. It shook his soul too, and, though pledged for life as a devoted Calvinist, he'd have probably sold that shaken soul without a second thought for a chance to fly that powerful bird just one time. He'd gotten some great pictures but the wishing was another case of pissin' up a rope. All a guy got for it was having his nose rubbed in the fact that he would never have the chance.

John, sitting erect on the Honda in Sunlife, breezed by Soph's and my trailer, F-66, without turning his head. My brother had written me just two letters in the first 22 years I was away from home. The first one wasn't even a letter; it was a manila envelope filled with dried samples of alfalfa, wheat, barley, oats and a note which said simply, "So that you won't be so homesick." He knew who to get to me; I sobbed over that one. I remember as kids, when we first moved onto the farm by Manhattan and the folks would be gone in the evening, he and I in the dark—so the folks wouldn't know we were still awake—would be backwards in the big chair on our knees looking out over the back of the chair out the window down the three-quarter-mile lane hoping to see the headlights of the car turn in off the highway. We had each other for company in our fright. So, after I received my Alpha diagnosis in the early eighties, at my initiation, he and I regularly exchanged letters and cassette tapes for the next ten years. Again, so we could have each other for company in our fright. He was happy to have someone to talk to about coping with the disease, but we shared a lot of other stuff, too.

I remember him telling me about his fondness for *Opa* Heidema, and he had sent me a picture of a rocking chair that reminded him of sitting in such a chair on Grandpa's lap in Holland. About how he had written a story about his grandfather for an assignment in school and about how the teacher had accused him of copying it from someone else because it was "too good". He told me all about his and Joyce's trip to Holland, about how they with Steven and Pat had had a "rip snortin' good time," about feeling like *Oom* Piet was standing in for Dad when they had visited with each other in Thesinge and how he, John, had "broke(n) down several times" and that he and *Oom* Piet had shed tears together. He said that he was sorry that he had not gone back to Holland more often.

He told me that it was difficult for him when some of his friends "shunned" him because of the disease, but he also told me how he was meeting new people as a Bobcat Booster, to which he donated a steer every year, and as a board member of Crimestoppers in Bozeman. He sent me travel logs in which he would talk into the microphone as he drove. He would take a back road into town and tell me about such things as the old Teslow Grain Elevator where he had rolled grain with Levi Hedglin and Bud Bailey "who always had that terrible smelling breath", or about a family from the past or a crop he was passing. He'd tell me about having a piece of lemon meringue pie in the Western Café which he said would "probably be as close to an orgasm" as he'd have that day and, when he resumed talking into the tape after one of those stops, he talked about having sat with Pete Alberda that day. And about how they had talked about Pete's arthritis and about John's breathing problems. "His fifteen year-old had twins," John said, "and his wife, Bonnie, is helping to raise them like Joyce did with Justin, so Pete and I found out we have a lot in common. God had it planned so we could help each other along the way today," he said. He talked about his fears; about how coming back from his trip to Osh Kosh he had turned "every shade of blue and had the dickens scared out of him" because he couldn't get that hubcap off. About how the doctors were telling him to use his oxygen but that he couldn't "face other people using a bottle" yet. And he talked about his achievements. How he went to Denver alone for a week and about how he got on a bus with mostly "darkies" and went to a Broncos football game in Mile-Hi Stadium. About how it had brought a tear to his eye when he had to ask for a reserved spot by church. About when Joyce's dad died and that Peter R. had been like a father to him. And that he now had two fathers on the cemetery. About how he was doing in Pulmonary Rehab where he had to do steps. He said he was collecting money to get an escalator in there so he wouldn't have to do those steps anymore. He always had a great sense of humor.

He told me about beating out a member of the well-established Christie family and being elected by 300 dairymen in the state to be the Montana representative at the National Holstein Association in Indianapolis, Indiana. He told me all about his work with the Montana Dairyman's Association. First he was on an advisory committee, then a legislative committee then he was on the board, then the president. He had to set up the hotel arrangements and line up speakers. He talked about how he was active in the politics of the state milk industry, in pricing, pooling, and in a voluntary quota system. He said that Meadowgold and Darigold tried to underprice each other just to get the market share. And that it was driving the price of milk down and that consequently everyone was losing out.

"If a state-wide pool could go through," he said, "all producers will be paid the same. (If they overproduce they will get considerably less for those pounds of milk making it not worthwhile.) It will unify the producers which in turn will get the processing plants together. No new dairy will be able to start without buying someone else's quota."

He talked about how the Hutterites were a strong, united force against the state-wide pool idea but how after another year they voted for it.

"If a farmer doesn't make money, nobody in the country makes money," he often said. "Government should get out of it and they should let supply and demand take over."

And another of his favorites about farming was "maybe next year will see you through and get you on top."

He told me about the hired man who was stealing tools and who he wanted to get into a counseling situation rather than pressing charges against him. About the hired man who had kicked a cocaine habit and who was trying to get custody of two sons. And about the hired man who left the water hose in the milk tank overnight and who caused $700 of milk to have to go down the drain. How he had held back that guy's wages and even though they "had him dead to rights" the dairy had lost that lawsuit.

"My diction is not as perfect as yours," he said in one, "words of teachers are more refined." "My dear sister," he would start; once he said, "Dear Girl." He didn't like to "pony up" when he lost a bet to me and when he had to move along he would say, "Have to kick ass and move out," or "Better to commence to lay down a swath of rubber." He always ended the tapes with "Catch-ya later," "Love-ya" or "Toodle-loo."

We had a good relationship over those ten years of tapes going back and forth. I would visit Montana every few years and they were good too. Then we started to spend winters together in Arizona. That started in 1991. He and I would go off to get our infusions together and then we would have lunch out. It was my task to find new places and he went along with it. Sometimes we would go to a ritzy ditzy place in Scottsdale and have a glass of wine with lunch. He advised me on buying a Starwriter Canon Bubblejet word processor, like his, and taught me the basics. But, when the stuff hit the fan, I, according to him, turned into nothing but a big boil on his backside. Boy, had he been wrong about me, he said. He used to think that I had it made: free, an education, a career, respect, travel where and when I wanted. He'd actually envied me, he confessed. But like green wood on damp ground, I guess, I had become warped. That was his opinion anyway.

This "dang fool" (that would be referring to me) had gone ahead and put an over $500 air conditioner/heater unit into her Arizona room, even though, he had advised me not to. So? Who had appointed him my boss? All of a sudden I felt like one of his kids. That was just one thing; there were quite a few more mistakes I was making according to him. Sophia and I wanted to live without a clock, to eat when we were hungry and to sleep when we were sleepy "like a couple of derelicts".

Now she's stuck up north up there in Seattle in the snow, serves her right, he thought as he crossed U street and continued east on the upper end of F.

Last year at about this time "on the worst day of his life" on the very day that Joyce was starting her chemotherapy for the breast cancer he and I had sat in his van in front of F 66 and, again, according to him, I had come "unglued". That was not how I remembered it, of course, but he was adamant that it had been my fault and he would never forgive me for it, he said.

I just remember telling him that I felt left out and that I wanted him to let me be a part of what was going on. That he had stopped taking me to the infusions (ostensibly because of Joyce's appointments) and that he wasn't letting me help with anything.

He had told me in turn about himself and Joyce with their neighbors praying, holding hands, all down on their knees asking God to spare Joyce and he'd asked me point blank, "Have you ever experienced anything like that, Christians with Christians?" He figured I hadn't and strongly suspected I didn't want to.

"Do you ever read the Bible anymore? Do you even have one in your trailer?" he asked. "If you had ever held a newborn baby in your two hands like I have (and he had held his two hands up the way he had received his four newborns) you would know what a miracle that is," he'd said. "I feel sorry for you that you never had that in your life."

I raised my voice, yelled and swore at him that I didn't want or need his pity. He told me to get out of the van, I refused. I thought simple-mindedly that we should talk it out.

"Stop talking and thinking about the past, I'm always telling you. You don't move on; you go back to the past and wallow there," he'd said. "The best thing I've done is to stop taking you to get our Prolastin," he went on. "I wasted more hours than I care to count. I listened to you bash Rush Limbaugh (the conservative 620 AM KFYI talk show host that he liked) with your godless feminist horse manure and went with you to all those lunch places you picked out. Always using those big words you learned in college, analyzing me, big shot R.N., telling Joyce what she should do and giving her that book on breast cancer that scared her half to death."

I rebutted his accusations vociferously and he in turn was convinced it was my lifestyle that led me to "fighting like that". People like me, he said, were disturbed by what we did. He told me it was a bad sin. He'd had it with the craziness of us two, he said.

It was true and he had a point. Sophia and I had acted crazy. In those days, the early nineties without a support system, Sophia and I still had the occasional knockdown-drag out argument and, for the first and last time in my life, during one of those alienating times when I was filled with self-recrimination, I had gone to John and Joyce. I had opened up and asked for support from him, John, a family member. He had been concerned and said nice things like, "I accept you just the way you are." I believed him—desperate, obviously—and came out to him about Soph's and my relationship. That ranks high on the list of huge mistakes made in the world! The next day he told me that, "No, you two aren't *that* way." According to him we didn't look it and didn't act like it and so we weren't *it*, plain and simple.

It seems to me that not long after our family moved onto the farm by Manhattan and we sat in that big chair together, he and I as kids started fighting. We would push and shove, punch and kick. I would wax the kitchen floor; he would walk on it with his dirty boots and laugh about it. I would cry with frustration. I was full of envy in those days and competed with him every waking minute. When Mom had had enough of our shenanigans, she would throw us out of the house. He and I would wrestle out on the lawn; we'd try to put a scissor grip on one another. Guess who'd lose? He was taller and stronger and became more so every day, but I refused to quit. There was an amazing amount of energy expended in all that. I suppose we were vying for our parents' love—it was understood that they loved us, but it was seldom shown and never mentioned. No one said I love you. And I suppose our failure to get their love and attention led to taking out our frustrations on each other. Fighting each other became our way of handling the stress in the family.

More than 30 years later, when John had to come face to face with the possibility of losing Joyce to breast cancer, he was stressed to the max. And right at that inopportune, crucial time I vied for attention. Like unloved children, we reverted to our old destructive way of being and had the blowout in the van.

In retrospect, I should not have moved into the same RV resort with him in Arizona. He wanted to get away from family and community pressures and I interfered with that. Imagining that he and I could be even closer—than we were in the tapes and letters—brought me to Sunlife, but I was wrong and I should have left well enough alone. Having a chronic disease is stressful and adding family issues to that stress can be too much to handle.

I have four children, four grandchildren with more to come and a business to run, he thought as he rounded the corner of C and started down B street. *My dairy provides for four families and I haven't even counted how many people that is. Joyce handles all the bookkeeping, pays the taxes, makes out the w-2s, paychecks, insurance and everything. We solve the problems that come up. Always have.*

I provided for Joyce last year like I've done all these years. Nobody can ever say anything different. I drove her to every appointment even though there were days when I first had to get my infusion in Phoenix, go back to East Mesa and then drive to Mayo's way out past Fountain Hills and back. I drove a good 150 miles on some of those days. Nobody, especially not my sisters, ever are going to have to help me do what needs doing for my wife."

Tjaakje uses her oxygen everywhere now. She doesn't need it. I'm worse than she is. They are all up there in Seattle yakking about everybody and everything like they like to do. A mother and three sisters getting along with one another because of my efforts, he reflected bitterly. *The time I got Pat and Tjaakje together when they hadn't been talking to each other and it's always been my responsibility to deal with Mom. Tjaakje is two-faced, no way out of it. I spent hours and hours talking with her and with Mom separately. I defended Tjaakje too yet and then she and Mom start buddying up together. They all left me alone with Mom. They don't know how hard it has been all these years.*

Now I'm the black sheep of the family and that is just how I want it, he affirmed grimly as he pulled up to the center and raised his bike up onto the kick stand. He'd let his mind wander. Not like him. The sun was setting and the air had cooled considerably. *I should have taken that jacket,* he chided himself.

He walked too fast to the Computer Room, looking to passers-by for all intents and purposes to be a perfectly normal human being, and bent down to put his key in the lock. Bending down from his height was hard on the breathing. He straightened. He hadn't noticed before but his back was killing him. Tylenol #3 with codeine was like taking candy. It didn't touch it. The searing, teeth-gritting, sciatic pain grabbed down the back of his leg. As he sensed the welling rush of fear he stepped through the door, closed it behind him and lunged towards a nearby chair. He fell into it, grabbed the armrests and straightened hard his arms and torso.

"Oh, God, no! It's happening again!" his mind screamed as the death grip of the panic attack began to squeeze his chest and smother the breath out of him.

> "Hear, O Lord, when I cry with my voice: have mercy also upon me, and answer me." Psalm 27:7

Shallow breaths moved in and out of his frozen chest. He had no control over them. Palpitations, warning all systems of an all-out-fight-or-flight emergency, wobbled his heart around like a square of Jell-O on a freight train. Blood rushing to his vital organs totally made the strength disappear from his limbs. They were rubbery and shaking. He was woozy, dizzy and felt strange, unreal somehow.

The adrenaline coursing through his body suggested to his mind that, in fact, he might suffocate to death in this room alone. Alone! The room elongated and the walls closed in as his brain short-circuited. The lights were too bright. A wave of nausea engulfed him and he broke out in a cold sweat. Like an old man with severe palsy, he fumbled to get the Xanax from his pocket into his mouth.

The first such attack had come a number of years earlier when he he'd blown a tire on Highway 90 a ways before Livingston. Literally, hours had gone by and no one had stopped to help. Never before had the reality of his lung disease hit home like that. He could not change his own flat! It was getting dark and cold. Wham! His anxiety system was overwhelmed by the events. Just like that out of the clear blue the symptoms had hit him. He did not identify it as a panic attack at the time. He had never heard they even existed. He had thought, instead, that he was having a heart attack.

A compassionate farmer had come to him across the expanse of a whole field on a tractor to help him out; but that act of godsent kindness was not what changed John's life. Being of the glass-half-empty (as opposed to half-full) nature that he was and having the genetic electrochemical makeup in his brain that he had, what changed his life was the memory of those terrifying symptoms. They were forever seared into his cerebral patterns. Fear of a recurrence and fear of public embarrassment was what changed his life.

He figured that it was part of his disease, that Alphas suffered from the attacks and that a good number of them medicated themselves with liquor. He had seen them drinking at the conferences he had attended. His pulmonologist had said as much. I said that I only had hot flashes but he knew my attacks were starting. It was all about the accumulated stress of a lifetime taking a toll on a guy, about being stuck like a prisoner in four walls that kept closing in, about not being able to handle stress and frustration with hard physical work.

The episodes had been getting more frequent and severe ever since. Sometimes, in the middle of the night he would wake up with sweaty palms. Barely contained panic, back pain and only being able to lay on his right side robbed him of ever having a full night's sleep. He was up and down every two hours even with a couple of Halcions, his nightly sleep medication.

His life was now organized around, "What if I get a panic attack?" Fully charged cell phone with touch-tone button #1 for Joyce and #2 for 911, extra oxygen on board, always pills in the right pants pocket and plenty on the shelf, avoiding uncomfortable and risky circumstances and any long distance meant Joyce came along.

His worry, "What if Joyce dies before I do?" had led to an exhausted nervous system, the exhaustion triggered the panic and the panic reinforced the worries. He had been trapped in that viciously spinning cycle until Joyce, his rock of Gibraltar woman that she was, proved to him that all his what-ifs were groundless. She had been tough through it all, at peace, never doubting that the many prayers offered on her behalf and God would see her and them through. Their relationship and faith had been strengthened. His attacks had lessened after her recovery but, maddeningly, persisted.

Truth be told, his life was like a block of Swiss cheese: strong, self-made, successful, proud, macho-resilient with black holes of fear, panic and suffering. But the truth wasn't being told. He was hiding it as much as he could for as long as he could, and only Joyce would know the extent of his distress.

John had not always wanted to but he had toed the line his whole life and, like Job having all but the kitchen sink thrown at him, panic attacks were not going to drive him to renounce his God. No way. His body and mind might fail him but not his faith. If anything it made him draw closer to his Lord. God, he told himself, was obviously still testing and teaching him. That is what he believed and it gave him a measure of peace.

"So do not fear, for I am with you; do not be dismayed, for I am your God. I will strengthen you and help you. I will uphold you with my righteous right hand." Isaiah 41:10

What he could not admit, which a therapist might have told him, was that his inflexibility and habits or rituals in dealing with his feelings and the imperfections, uncertainties and paradoxes of life were a part of the equation. So were his high expectations, his shame as a man about what was happening to him and his inordinate fear of public humiliation. The very thought of exploring such would have made him start to hyperventilate, and rapid, shallow breathing would make the blood more alkaline and that would make the anxiety escalate. He, John Wayne or The Lone Ranger in Sunlife, wanted absolutely nothing to do with that kind of psychobabble. That was my balywick, not his.

"I love the Lord, because he hath heard my voice and my supplications. Because he hath inclined his ear unto me, therefore will I call upon him as long as I live. Psalm 116:1-2

Finally, the Xanax kicked in and his mechanisms returned to normal. He had been lucky. No one had come into the Computer Room. He checked his watch. Joyce would have dinner ready. He would know better next time to take his Xanax earlier, wear his jacket and not get caught up in his thinking. He got on the bike and headed home, a solitary silhouette against the southwestern sunset.[5]

Evening: *Het Onze Vader* and the Group Picture

Spirits were high as our group hustled to sit down for Pat's Saturday evening ham dinner. It was the first meal at which all were present. Brandon could hardly wait; he wanted to skip dinner and get to the gifts.

"Mother Heidema, Pat, Sandi and whoever else knows it, would you please say the Lord's Prayer in Hollandse?" asked Steven.

"*Ja*, sure," murmured Ann. "Will somebody help me?"

She bowed her head, clasped her hands and gathered her thoughts in a moment of silence. Then she, Pat and Sandi began the prayer that it is said Jesus taught to his disciples in his sermon on the mountain. It is commonly referred to as the Lord's Prayer or in Dutch *Het Onze Vader:*

"Onze Vader die in de hemel zijt,   (Our Father who art in heaven,
Uw naam worde geheiligd.   Hallowed be thy name,
Uw koningkrijk kome,   Thy kingdom come,
Uw wil geschiede,   Thy will be done,
op aarde, zoals in de   On earth, as it is in
hemel.   heaven.
Geef ons heden ons   Give us this day our

---

[5] Thankfully, John and I enjoyed a degree of reconciliation in our last years together. He and Joyce left Arizona for the last time in April of 2002. They left from Falcon Field in Mesa in a private plane flown by John's original flying mentor. John was well enough to appreciate what would be his last flight on earth. Panic attacks continued to plague him until he passed away on the 10th of January, 2003, at the age of 62. He had been at his home on Churchill for nine months before he died and had greatly enjoyed the love and company of his immediate family. At their last Christmas party together he sang with them his favorite song: "What a day that will be when my Jesus I shall see, And I look upon his face—the one who saved me by his grace. When He takes me by the hand and leads me thro' the Promised Land; What a day, glorious day that will be!" He is survived by the aforementioned family members and six additional grandchildren: Keith and Kelsey of Leland and Lisa, Colten and Mariah of Shane and Michelle and Logan, Madyson and Carson of Kent and Dorothy.

Sweeping Away the Sand

dagelijks brood;	daily bread;
En vergeef ons onze	And forgive us our
schulden,	debts,
Zooals ook wij vergeven onze	As we forgive
schuldenaren;	our debtors;
En leid ons niet in	And lead us not into
verzoeking,	temptation,
maar verlos ons van de booze.	but deliver us from evil.
Want van U is het konenkrijk,	For thine is the kingdom,
en de kracht,	and the power,
en de heerlijkheid,	and the glory,
tot in eeuwigheid.	forever and forever.
Amen."	Amen.)

"And," Sophia supplemented, "thank you, God, for bringing Sandi safely over the pass, finally."

"Right on!" chorused Sandi.

"This is our second Christmas dinner", counted Brandon.

"During our first Christmas dinner," Pat began, "we were trying to think of those skits, Sandi, that all of you kids did at John and Joyce's. The only one I could remember was the bum on the park bench. What were some of the others?"

"One skit," Sandi recalled instantly, "had four kids on hands and knees like each was a tire on a car." She paused briefly to find the file in her brain. "It's kind of vague; somehow the pretend car had automatic headlights. Oh, yes, I remember! The front people raised and lowered their heads for that. The other feature was the automatic windshield wipers. The front two tires each had a mouthful of water and would spray it on the glasses of a fifth person on hands and knees in the center, who would then, of course, automatically wipe them off.

"Then there was the desert scene with the glass of water sitting across the room. Each kid drags himself on his belly slowly on the pretend desert floor desperately trying to get to the water saying, 'Water ... water,' but dies before reaching the glass. The last kid is finally able to reach it, but instead of taking a drink like everyone expects, he pulls out a tooth brush and begins to brush his teeth!"

"Oh, right," I exclaimed, "that one's coming back to me now that you say it. I remember little Michelle trying to do just what the older kids were doing. It was very cute and funny,"

"I remember something with an elevator. What was that?" questioned Marge.

"That one is my personal favorite," Sandi responded laughing heartily. "An elevator operator pushes buttons and as the imaginary doors open, says, 'Fifth floor—Toys.' Someone enters carrying toys and says,' Basement, please, and hurry.' Then it is 'Fourth floor—Sporting Goods,' and of course the person enters with some kind of sporting equipment. He says, 'Basement, please, and hurry.' 'Third floor—Lingerie,' well, you get the idea. Each person is distinctive with what they are wearing and what they have bought but all are a little tense and restless as the elevator fills up. Finally, 'Basement—long pregnant pause on the part of the elevator operator—Bathrooms,' and everyone heaves a sigh of relief and rushes off."

"It was so funny with those little kids doing that!" Pat affirmed laughing.

"*Ja*," Ann added, "I can remember it too now."

"Okaaay, that's probably enough on the skit stories for now," suggested Arlyce knowing full well that her sister would stop only when she had exhausted her memory of skits known to mankind and not a moment before.

"Oh, sure, and I have to go to the bathroom. Thanks a lot, Sandi," complained Sophia good-naturedly.

"Sorry, Soph and Arlyce, but I just thought of another one, too!" Sandi was on a roll and loving it.

"Oh, no," groaned Arlyce.

"There is a railroad station and a family of hillbillies comes in. The father has a sign around his neck which says 'Paw' and the mother has 'Maw' and the kids—a long line of them—are lined up behind her from tall to short. Paw asks the station manager in a slow drawl, 'Any trains coming from the west today?'"No, no trains from the west today' says the station manager. Paw nudges Maw and says, 'No trains coming from the west today.' Maw passes it on to the first kid and it gets passed down one by one in the same fashion. Then Paw asks the station manager in the same slow drawl, 'Any trains coming from the east today?' 'No, no trains coming from the east today.' Paw nudges Maw and Maw passes it to the first kid and on down the line. Paw follows the same with north and south. After the last repeat of the message by the last kid, Paw says, 'Well then, I guess we can cross the tracks!'"

"Oh, puh-lease," Arlyce agonized.

Ann was amazed by her smart granddaughter. "How do you remember all those things, kid?" she asked. "I wish I could remember like that."

"And," Sandi continued, "I also remember Leland playing the trumpet for us in some kind of uniform, it seems."

"John put on his Civil Air Patrol uniform once, I remember that," said Marge.

"Yes, he was so proud of that uniform," I concurred. "We took pictures. He was really heavy then from all that Mexican medicine."

"That's right," said Pat, "and Leland played the trumpet. I wonder if he ever does anymore. Do you know, *Moeke*?"

"No, I don't know, dear. I don't think so; he is too busy with all the cows that those boys milk."

"I knew Sandi would remember the skits," Pat exclaimed. "All right, is everybody about finished? It looks like it. Now then, B.J., now it is time to open the presents! Let's go into the living room; we'll have our dessert there later. Maybe Arun will wake up when he hears us."

"I'll go get him," offered Anil.

And what a party it was! To start things off, Pat surprised everyone and gave identical gifts to Anil and Sophia. "These are extra," she crowed, "I just had to do it! You'll see why in a minute."

Anil and Sophia opened their gifts simultaneously and each found a beautiful, green apron. They were identical. Pat explained proudly, "When I spotted the material with all the colorful vegetables, I just knew it was meant for you two!" With arms around waists and shoulders the threesome—the two wearing their aprons with Pat squeezed in between—posed for a happy snapshot.

Brandon bubbled with excitement as he took an unwrapped, large metal detector—the result of Doug's morning shopping trip—out of the shopping bag. He tried it out on rings, watches and everything metal in the room, and that night he dreamed of coins and precious metals flowing over earth's crust from lost treasure boxes. There was no doubt in his mind; in just a matter of time he would be extravagantly rich!

Sandi liked her 2000 piece Springbok puzzle from B.J. very much. It had a lovely picture of brightly colored hot-air balloons floating in the air with their images reflected in a lake below. "Springbok," said the veteran puzzler, "is great. The pieces always fit together so well."

Sophia received everything that she had written on her wish list from Sandi: A Mickey Mouse baseball cap, a rubber stamp, Thorlo socks, wrist weights and a Radio Shack video Black Jack game.

As Sophia opened the last of all her presents Mom nudged me with her elbow—we were sitting next to one another on the couch—and whispered, *"Dat het wel meer den vijf-en-twintig dollar kost. Dat wait ik wel* (That cost more than twenty-five dollars. I do know that.)"

I secretly winced and whispered back, "Probably."

"Ik zul nait noar di luisterd hemmen (I should not have listened to you)!" Mother grumbled.

I knew she was getting nervous. It would soon be Steve's turn to open his present from her and she wanted him to be pleased. Luckily, both of us were distracted when Arun, who seemed more interested in his old, than his new, gifts, came by with his "Toot" for us to see.

Eventually, everyone had a good laugh when Anil and I tried on our head warmers from Marge. I looked like a veiled Muslim woman and Anil could have easily played the part of the gangster. Marge also generously gave each of us a box of delicious candy from Montana. The music teacher had been selling the candy; proceeds were going for the Rudyard school band, she said.

Pat was pleased with her mirrored cosmetic tray and bathe-away-aches-and-pains packets. I gave Arlyce a ring from Tumbleweed Traders made by an Apache Native American. Ann received a small waffle iron and a subscription to "Good Housekeeping" while Doug's subscription was to "Motor Trends" along with a non-glare screen for the computer monitor. To Ann's huge relief Steve loved his pictorial book on the Northwest and his gift certificate to the bookstore.

We cooed and clucked our pleasure and gratitude like a flock of pigeons scuttling after pieces of bread in the city plaza and followed those utterances with hoots, hullabaloos and a hardy round of applause for the great organizing work Sandi had done. It was Sandi, Marge said, who had efficiently contacted everyone, solicited their wish list and conducted the name drawing. "That is a lot, a lot of work," she underscored. Three hip, hip, hurrahs in a row, everyone!

"Now," I proposed, as it was clear that we had reached the grand finale of the evening and that in a matter of minutes people would begin scattering about, "now would probably be a good time for a group picture." And, in doing so, in saying that one sentence—I immediately realized with no small amount of satisfaction—I regained my mother's approval and forgiveness.

"Oh, yes, everybody, a group picture," exclaimed Ann pushing herself up from the couch. "That is a good idea, Lottie. Let's do it! Where shall we stand or shall we sit maybe?"

Suggestions were made and tried and when all had settled, someone called out, "Say Merry Christmas!"

The button was pushed and the group chorused, "Merry Christmas!" as the shutter snapped.

"Okay, everybody ready for apple pie and coffee?"

Later, while the rest of us cleaned away wrapping paper, ribbons, boxes, and dishes, Sophia massaged the feet of Arlyce on the long couch. Each leaned back against an opposing arm of the couch and stretched their legs lengthwise on the cushions between. Arlyce's legs were elevated with a pillow, putting her feet in good position for Sophia's hands.

Arlyce looks exhausted, I thought as I unashamedly eavesdropped.

She had not slept well on the floor the night before, Arlyce was saying, as Sophia deftly located the sore spots and worked out the stress. "It wasn't the floor," Arlyce clarified, "I am used to that," and then, I noticed, she just stopped talking. The rain tapped lightly against the window as if the massage therapist were playing a nature relaxation tape recording.

Chapter 21
Pancakes to Celebrate

The reverse could also be said, of course; that my point of view, my beliefs, have shaped my experiences and, thereby, limited my scope.

Standing with nothing on but one knee-high stocking and white cotton panties Ann raised her arms and slowly, very carefully maneuvered the sleeveless, pink nightgown over her French twist. Then, one at a time, awkwardly worked her arms into the sleeve holes of the gown and let it flow familiarly down to her ankles. She lowered herself heavily onto the side of the bed, leaned forward and tried once, twice and a third time to put her index finger under the tight-fitting Job's compression stocking. A breath. Once more. Again, unsuccessful.

"*Och verhip toch! Ellendig ding* (Darn it! Miserable thing)!" she muttered aloud.

Showing her fierce determination, she bent her knee and pulled her foot firmly up onto the bed. She lifted her pink gown back over her ample white thigh, and really bearing down she worked a couple of fingers under the elastic fabric. With a few more grunts and groans she manipulated the nutmeg-colored, therapeutic stocking down the remainder of her leg and finally off her foot. Then, angrily, she threw the stiff, stubborn thing to the end of the bed.

Ann hated the stocking and she hated the ugliness of her legs. Venous stasis or pooled blood in the veins, due to the breakdown of so many tiny valves, made the blue veins bulge up and down her legs like so many swollen rivers and tributaries after a sudden spring thaw. Years of this stagnant pooling in the tissues had resulted in iron deposits in the dermis. Those were the large, dark brown patches on her shins and spider-veined, thick ankles. There was an even darker spot where the ulcer had been.

Given Ann's lifelong activities there were lots of explanations for the distended leg veins and poor peripheral circulation. First of all, with knees sharply bent, Ann had squatted on a three-legged stool under those milk cows for many of her formative years. Second, she had given birth to four children, three of them at home, when long periods of convalescence in bed were still fashionable. Third, throughout her adult life she had stood in small spaces for long periods of time: in the kitchen, in the garden, as the checkout clerk and pie baker in the grocery store and as a nurse's aid in the hospital. Last, add to that her being a typical hefty Dutch woman who had worn tight fitting-corsets and loved to cross her legs at the ankles and you will understand why it was a testimony to her genetic heritage that her veins had even one enduring valve left in them! Thank goodness, one leg was still a little better than the other.

Anymore, since her painful experiences with a blood clot and leg ulcers, she never left her bedroom without her custom-fit Job's stocking on the one leg and firm support pantyhose on both. Ann reached over to the bedside stand for the tube of prescription cream and began working it into the hardened skin of the previously ulcerated area. Ever so briefly she paused to inspect her foot. Other than their sheer determination to outlast this tough old woman and carry her to her grave, which was without a doubt deserving of a gold medal in itself, there was little to admire about those feet.

They, too, had begun life with the Friesian Holsteins and more than once, dancing toe-to-toe with the hobbled beasts, a split hoof had landed on a couple of Ann's tender toes. It would be exaggerating to say her feet would probably fit comfortably into a dried-up, twisted, old leather shoe that had spent a good long time abandoned in the muck at the bottom of a ditch somewhere, but not by much.

"Badly in need of a trip to the foot doctor," Ann sighed as she rubbed the tender bunions. She did not dare to come near the calluses and thickened ingrown nails with a scissors any more.

She rose from the bed and padded into the bathroom. There she took out her durable old dentures, brushed them, placed them in a glass of water and reflected briefly on their history.

Forty-eight years earlier—in her first year in the States—she was suffering from a bad toothache. Because she could hardly speak or understand English at the time, Uncle Bill made arrangements for her to see the only dentist in Manhattan, a Dr. Coglan. Ann had no idea what had been negotiated between the two men and no idea of the dentist's reputation when she walked into the dentist's office the next week.

Coglan, she discovered instantly, worked with neither a receptionist nor assistant and had breath that reeked of alcohol. There were few preliminaries. He motioned her into the old fashioned mint green dental chair with black padding, slapped a white cotton bib on her chest and set to work.

In this one shocking and torturous session without any Novocain or nitrous oxide (laughing) gas he pulled all of her teeth! It was not easy for dentist or patient. He pulled with all his might; Ann clung to the arm rests with all of hers. Blood and drool ran down Ann's chin and neck. In fact, blood was everywhere. It was on his white coat and hands (dentists did not wear gloves in those days), on her bib and dress, on his green chair, on his floor and on his shoes.

It was his intention, of course, to transfer each extracted tooth with the clamp from her mouth to the instrument table; but, in trying to do so, he dropped several of the teeth unceremoniously to the floor instead. His hands were shaking. Once the teeth were all pulled out, he went down on one knee and then clumsily crawled on hands and knees to pick up the fallen ones! He was still on the floor on all fours when Ann, bloody, white bib pressed to her mouth, fled out the door. Slurring his words badly Dr. Coglan called after her.

"Yo hav-a com baaack. Ness week."

There just was no other choice; even we kids had to go to Dr. Coglan for years to come. So, Ann went back the next week. Dr. Coglan, exhaling alcoholic fumes as before, took impressions. And, again, beyond belief, teeth fell out of the mold and the shameless dentist searched for them on the floor!

Perhaps as compensation from the queen of tooth fairies for having to undergo such a horrendous ordeal, Ann healed well. For three months she went toothless; then he put in her new $125.00

set of dentures and they fit beautifully. She had lost her familial trait of slightly separated and protruding front teeth and her mouth and smile looked stiff, but no more toothaches.

Now, 48 years later, her fake teeth are still white, thanks to a bit of Clorox bleach now and again, and only one tooth—not that long ago, in fact—ever came loose from the dental plate. That tooth was easily reglued in only a 20 minute office visit. Remarkable. In so many years there has been no need for any other adjustments.

Dr. Coglan, less successful than Ann in his efforts to escape his torture chamber of another sort, long ago was laid to rest in Meadow View Cemetery which abutted our farm three miles south of Manhattan. Standing by his gravestone, in those days, she would shake her head and wonder how she had survived that ordeal.

If Ann had been in her retirement home apartment on this evening, instead of in the Cok home, she would have put her dentures in her trusty "chopper hopper." The dome cover of this familiar pink and white ceramic container forms the top half of a friendly-looking, gray-haired grandmother wearing wire-rim glasses and a lime-green scarf over her pink flannel nightgown. Ann bought that "chopper hopper" for her new set of dentures at Keene's Hardware in Manhattan 48 years ago, and with the exception of when she is on vacation, she has used it every day since.

After the dentures were nestled into their glass for their overnight soak, Ann removed her glasses and laid them on the countertop. She then unrolled two feet of toilet paper and carefully folded the length of it into several thicknesses. Using gray-colored bobby pins, she tacked the paper in place on one side of her head in front of her ear, squinting and tilting her head slightly as she leaned in to the mirror to better see what she was doing. Then she brought the paper around the back to hold the French twist securely in place and tacked it again in front of her ear on the other side.

Ann replaced her glasses over the pins and toilet paper then paused and took a good look at her image in the mirror. Mouth sunken in without the teeth, plenty of wrinkles, brownish patches and liver spots here and there on her overly exposed, sun-weathered face, stubby, grey-blonde, irregular eye brows and seemingly no lashes (they were so light and short), piercing blue eyes with a hint of fear in the pupils and the toilet paper turban.

"Hai, hai, wel bis du toch? (Dear, dear, who are you)?" she asked the image with only slight affection.

She lifted a sprayed-stiff wave of thin hair back from her forehead and leaned in closer to carefully inspect the small white scars, the taut skin and the hairline underneath. She was lucky to not have far worse.

One day she and Margaret were involved in a dangerous accident on their way back from bringing me to the airport at Billings. We had missed the flight in Belgrade and I had begged her, demanded her actually, to drive on to Billings. She should not have; she should have put her foot down and said, "Absolutely not." The roads had been icy all the way. I had made my flight, but on their drive back, a wooden tailgate that had been lying loose on a flatbed truck just ahead of them, had started to slide. For a split-second Ann had seen the tailgate careening in mid air; then, with eyes squeezed shut and foot squeezing the brake, she had felt the wooden missile slam full force into her windshield. The impact shattered glass into her and Margaret's laps, hair, clothes and skin.

Mom showed great presence of mind to keep the car under control and bring it to the side of the road without further accidents being caused. By the grace of God, as she believes, the tailgate was deflected by the frame of the windshield. It could have come murderously slicing into the interior of the car! The unidentified, careless truck driver never looked back. Decades later now, slivers of glass, still imbedded in Ann's forehead, are causing tiny areas of skin cancer. Periodically the areas have to be excised. One of those times the area of excision was necessarily more extensive and Ann received a sort of unplanned face-lift to the top half of her face.

She lowered the forelock and looked at herself again. *I used to love to hear my mother say, "Hes ja wel zoon mooi heller gezicht* (You have such a nice, bright face)," she thought wistfully. *How I would love to hear my mother's voice say that again.*

She washed her hands and her thoughts continued. *Mother visited with us on the farm here in the States for a whole year in 1950. That was really something. How I would love to be with my mother and my sisters like my girls are now. The other ones in this house all have a mother, husbands and sisters on these special days; I have no one. My family is far away.*

A familiar blend of envy, loneliness and sadness filled and pressed against Ann's chest. She took the towel from the rack and continued her inner dialogue. *Wina calls me sometimes. It is nice to hear her voice and to talk with her.*

Wina, Ann's youngest sister by 16 years, made a visit to the states, too, once. Being a tall, well-endowed, high-spirited woman with extraordinarily erect posture and a hearty laugh, Wina made quite an impression on everyone. She is talkative like Ann and the two have maintained a good long distance relationship via the telephone.[6]

Dienie is mie ja nou niks weerd (Dienie is now not any good to me)." Ann's face and neck tightened. She moved faster as she dried her hands vigorously and returned the towel to the rack.

Dienie from the start was wound up too tight, Ann thought, as she strenuously worked lotion into her hands and up and down on her long-boned, loose-skinned arms. Her movements softened, however, as she imagined again hearing her mother calling to the girls to get out of bed in the early morning back on the *boerderij* (farm).

"Anje?" Mother would call from the bottom of the stairs.
"Jaaa."
"Martje?"
"Jaaa."
"Trui?"
Nothing.
"Trui?"
A long pause and then a drawn out, "Jaaaaa."
"Dienie?"

Whup! Maar zo was Dienie al to ber uit. Dat was Dienie (Whup! Just like that Dienie was out of bed. That was Dienie).

Ann's second-to-the-youngest sister and only other sibling to emigrate from the Netherlands does not live that far away from Ann. She lives in Canada just up north across the border in Calgary, Alberta. Dienie is not far away from Ann as the crow flies; but, unfortunately, the two are worlds apart when it comes to seeing eye to eye.

---

[6] In 1999 Wina de Vries Elzes was awarded the coveted House of Orange special medal for her dedicated volunteer work with the alcohol and drug addicted homeless of the city of Groningen. She is fearless in her concern for the street people. To this day she bicycles through their streets, brings them food and mothers them into shelters. She is a remarkable presence among them.

Dienie, always irrepressible, in mid-life sadly lost her grasp on sanity. Genetics was a major contributing factor but there were other factors too. Her marriage to Hein Werkema, from day one a disaster, had finally broken apart; but divorce for Dienie was a total anathema to her belief system. The conflict was unbearable for her. And her second son, Gary—Klaas was the eldest, Diane and Patty the daughters—choosing to rely on faith and refusing treatment of any sort, died of leukemia. He had been a young husband and father in his early twenties. The events were devastating to Dienie's fragile personality.

She suffered a classic menopausal, schizophrenic split from reality. When not properly medicated, Dienie thinks of herself as the Queen of Heaven, and from that lofty vantage point she has plenty of critiques and agendas to take up with her older sister and mother figure, Ann.

Ann will have none of it. Especially, Ann wants none of it on Churchill in her community ever again. Viewing Dienie as spiteful as much as sick, Dienie's stridence and religious zealousness has been an embarrassment for Ann. Dienie will call Ann. If it is a good call, Ann will talk; if not, she hangs up the phone.

"And Trui," Ann murmured aloud, "it was nice to call her too sometimes but now she is not so good anymore." Trui, six years younger, has not visited the States. She has three daughters, Pieta, Klaziena and Marga, and it is Marga who has visited the States. Compared to her sisters, Ann, Dienie and Wina (and often to their annoyance), it is Trui's nature to operate at a much slower speed. Trui, until recently, was affectionately considered the family newspaper: she kept track of everything and everybody. Lately, however, she was disturbingly forgetful and unsteady.[7]

Anne massaged a little Mary Kay cream bought from Lisa into her face. She was not one ever to use makeup. A morning wash with soap and water and a little moisturizing cream, that was her routine. To liven herself up throughout the day she would give her cheeks a vigorous friction rub.

As she smoothed the cream under her eyes, Ann remembered what her mother had always said, *"Even't gezicht goud wrieven* (Just give the face a good rub). *Den liekt 't wel beter* (Then it looks better)."

---

[7] Trui continued to decline after this writing and passed away in 1999.)

Sweeping Away the Sand

My mother gone now for years and Martje, my other sister, has been so long dead now already, Ann thought with deepening sadness. *Martje, she was my buddy when we were kids.*

Ann switched off the light in the bathroom and stepped into the hallway. There she paused in the semidarkness. *Are you children asleep?* she wondered. *No, Tjaakje's light under the door across the hallway is still on. She is probably reading.*

She could hear Steve and Pat talking quietly on the first level. *That is the way they are, doing last-minute cleanup and talking things over to be ready for tomorrow,* Ann thought as the dull pain of longing swept through her again.

Like an amputee feeling phantom limb pain in the area of the missing limb, Ann experienced the pain of her missing partner in the essence of her being. So often, the all-encompassing pain had threatened to bring her to her knees. To stand up to it took sheer force of will. The absence of her loving husband pulled her down, but the memory of her tall, proud father kept her standing. When it came to will, everyone agreed, Ann had it in spades. She was the toughest of them all.

"Sophia *snurkt al* (Sophia snores already)," Ann muttered as she continued on into her bedroom. "*Zal kin 't beste sloepen* (She can sleep the best)."

Anne left the door ajar. At the window she pushed aside the curtains and peered into the night hoping to see if there was still a light on in the motor home. The roof over the portico made it impossible to see the motor home but she could not see that the portico was there. It all looked dark.

"Good, she said softly, "the Langel's are getting a good night's sleep for a change. That's good. They always keep B.J. up too late. That's not good."

Ann got into a sitting position against the headboard in her bed and found the day's meditation in the devotional guide:

Can Christians Find Happiness Today?

Psalm 68:2-3, "...as wax melteth before the fire, so let the wicked perish at the presence of God. But let the righteous be glad; let them rejoice before God; yea, let them exceedingly rejoice."

Tjaakje C. Heidema

Can Christians Find Happiness Today? In the times
when the Psalmist was...

Ann's heart was not in her reading tonight; and, as if drawn by
an unseen force, her mind went back to her buddy, to her sister
who had been closest in age, Martje. When Ann and had been in
the States for only a short time, a traveling salesman had come by
and Ann had ordered three framed—oval, about eight by fourteen
inches—tinted photographs of her father, mother and sister, Martje.
She never wanted to forget her buddy. As if talking to a devoted
listener at the foot of her bed, Ann mentally recounted her
memories.

Martje and me, I remember, *when we were young we would have to
check the cows sometimes at night. Just the two of us, we would go back into the
barn where the cows were, you know. Some would move a little, or all of a
sudden. One would make a noise or some other noise. It would be pretty dark
and it was a little scary for me. Ik was oldste ja. Ik zol toch nait bang weden (I
was the oldest. I should not be afraid). But I was more scared than Martje in a
way. She would just have fun with it.*

*Martje was such a strong-willed girl and so smart. That girl was smart. I
was, too; we were both good students. At home, too, she could make such
beautiful things with her sewing and so. Ik zal wel zeggen dat zai was echt
creatief (I will say that she was very creative). And she was pretty, tall and very
pretty.*

*But Martje could get so upset and mad too. She would fight so with my
parents. I didn't dare to. I didn't want to. I loved and respected my parents. But
Martje sometimes would hold to her own ideas. She wanted nothing to do with
milking the cows and so forth. Sometimes, she would not come out of her room
and only Jan, my brother, could talk her out of it.*

*We did not have hugs and touching from our parents. Martje, I think was
the kind who needed that. 'Ik hol van die (I love you)' was just never said. We
would get just a handshake or a quick kiss on the lips. When there were
arguments or things mother didn't want to talk about, she would say, 'Goi zand
der over (throw sand over it)!' That would stop the talking.*

Ann renewed her grip on the devotional booklet. She didn't
like where her thoughts were headed. *"Mouten moar gain olle koien to
sloat ouit hollen* (literally translated this means that it is better not to
take any old cows out of the ditch, but it is comparable to sayings
such as "let sleeping dogs lie" or "let bygones be bygones"), *moeke*

zul ook wel zeggen (mother would also say)."

She needed to take herself in hand, put an end to all this *flauwekul* (nonsense) and finish reading so she could get to sleep:

> Is it still possible in this world of the nineties to extend the hand with the cup of water? Jesus, in the gospel of Mark, talks about losing one's saltness...

Martje liked the boy she was engaged to very much. His name was Paul Boomker and she was planning to marry him. She was preparing for it. It was een geweldige teleurstelling voor mijn zus (a tremendous disappointment for my sister) when this boyfriend called off the wedding. We had already had the engagement party for her, Ann recalled, as she resignedly lowered the booklet down to her lap. *Martje didn't understand. Nobody could understand why he did that. He never said why that I know of, anyway.*

It was like Ann had run into a patch of Canadian thistles in the potato field. To really make any headway with these stubborn, thorny thoughts it might just be better if she changed from her cloth gloves to the leather ones, sat down with the patch and pulled out one thought at a time. She removed her glasses and rubbed her tired eyes.

Martje never got over the breakup, Ann reported to the listener in thought. *And then, our father died at almost the same time. It was too much for her all at once. Martje started to have lots more problems, and she tried to get help with it, too. When I was married, I would have her at my house in Thaisin sometimes. Jan Piet and me would have tea with Martje in the koamertje (parlor) in the afternoon. Sometimes, even for a few weeks at a time, she would stay, and she was pretty okay. Jan Piet didn't mind that she was there; I liked it, too. I thought it would help her to be away from Baflo from everybody and everything. I think it did help some.*

The pictures in Ann's mind were as vivid as if the events had taken place only yesterday. Her glasses and the booklet lay forgotten on the covers in her lap.

But, then Pia (Pat) was born, of course, and later my miscarriage and then my son, Jan (John). It wasn't so easy for me to go away then or to have company. And Martje's problems didn't just go away when she would be was with us. I couldn't have her there so much of the time. It was hard.

She couldn't be with my mother either. Martje was getting worse. It was terrible to watch but not to be able to do something. One time she smashed the glass all to pieces in Mother's French doors. That was at the boerderij. They were pretty, leaded pane glass. Full length of the doors! Martje could get so mad at my mother. She could always get mad, that's true. But when it got so bad, she was sick then, you know. She had too much strength. It would take three or four men to put her in a car when she knew that they would take her to the hospital again.[8]

Och, then, I can hardly stand to think about it, I would go to see her in the asylum. That was terrible. It was terrible, very terrible, for her to be in there. She was so against it. It was terrible for me, too, to see her there so with all those strange people. And then, oorlog der ook nog bie (war along with it, too, yet). Ann squirmed from the discomfort of remembering.

It was not so easy in wartime always to go places on a bike. You would worry about being stopped and asked questions. You had to have papers with you always. Patients too, in asylums, would be moved from one place to another so the Germans could use the buildings. We would not always know where she was. Martje got so thin and pale after a while. She would not come out of the asylum anymore. Then, sometime, she just stopped talking. She never said another word.

Ann took a deep breath before she continued. *I would talk to her by myself. I think she knew I was there and that it was her sister there by her. But she would never say anything to me again! That was the hardest.* Ann shook her head to clear away the heart-rending scenes.

"Ik wait ja wel beter (I know better)," she reprimanded herself aloud, and sniffed her nose.

She did know better than to think so much about Martje. So she seldom did. It always tore her heart out. She put her glasses back on, and tried again to pull herself together to read. Where had she left off?

Here, I'll just start here, she thought.

We can renew ourselves and our faith if we but make
Christ a part of our every waking moments..."

---

[8] This time in history predates the discovery of psychotropic drugs by about 20 years. Antipsychotics, antidepressants and major tranquilizers were not available to the mental health personnel. Treatment consisted primarily of confinement, restraint, punishment and shock, all of which may have subdued the patient for a time but allowed the disease to progress untouched. From the description of Martje's behaviors, it is evident that Martje was struggling with an acute schizophrenic reaction which over time progressed to a chronic catatonic state.

There was one more piece to her memories of Martje, and her mind stubbornly insisted that she go over it. Ann relented.

It was the end of the war. I will never forget it. People were suddenly out in the street in front of our house. Everyone was celebrating! Singing and talking with one another which had not happened for so, so long.

I said to Jan Piet, "Wias wel wat ik doun goan (Know what I am going to do)? I am going to make some pancakes for Martje and take them to her today! She loves pancakes!"

So I started to make big pancakes. I made pancakes and I made more pancakes. Jan Piet said finally, "You don't think you have about enough pancakes by now?"

I had a stack of pancakes at least a foot high. It was something. I wrapped them all up good en op fiets doar ging ik (and on my bike there I went) to the Dennenoord Stichting (Dennenoord Asylum).

I pedaled and pedaled for miles and miles, 15 kilometers to Assen or was it near Drente? I can't remember exactly, but I do remember that it was a very long ways, maybe nine or ten miles. But I didn't care. I had my pancakes, the war was over and I was very excited.

Hours later, tired but thinking how much Martje would like the pancakes, I asked permission to see my beloved sister.

As Ann allowed the memory to unfold, she felt the age-old grief welling up in her chest. The feelings that she worked so hard to keep away from were now surfacing.

"Why am I thinking about this?" she asked herself angrily.

The reproof, like a sandbag thrown in to block the swell after the levee has been breached, came too late. Tears overflowed her lower lids and fell on her cheeks. She wiped them away.

Permission was granted and I was let into a dark, large ward. It was so noisy and the people all were coming towards me. I was scared, I can tell you. They were starved, you see. The Germans had not let them have enough food for months and months. There was not much food for anybody in the country in the last months and weeks especially in the city, but these people had it worse, much worse.

With their hungry faces and dark eyes they saw my package and maybe they could smell the pancakes, I don't know. Maybe they thought that there could maybe be food in the package I had under my arm. They started to pull at my arm and the package; I held it tight but it came open. One after another grabbed a pancake. I kept walking and trying to keep them away, but I could see it was not going good. There was no help for me. There was no one there to help.

And, do you know, they took every pancake I had! I stood there with empty hands. All the people who didn't get one were looking at me. I just couldn't go on. I turned around and went back home. I think I cried all the way home on the bike.

I don't remember if I ever saw her again. I don't know. Maybe Martje had tuberculosis, too, by that time; so many of those people in asylums did. My dear sister died pretty soon after that. She lived to be only 31 years old and I have missed her.

Ann's mouth and chin trembled. Her shoulders shook for a few seconds as she let the tears come. She reached for a couple of tissues, lifted her glasses and with one hand softly wiped away her tears. Then she blew her nose and heaved a big sigh.

"Mijn geliefde suster, Martje (My dearest sister, Martje)," she said.

Here I am, this old lady with all these young people in their beds. An old lady with toilet paper on her head who must stop this gezoes (silly talk), she chided herself, trying her best to force a better humor. *It is way past my time to go to sleep too.*

Ann laid the booklet aside, blew her nose once more, firmly clasped her hands in prayer, closed her eyes and bent her head. With characteristic intensity she prayed in her native tongue.

"Heilige Vader (Heavenly Father)..."

She prayed softly aloud asking for strength to stand tall in the family and strength to be proud of being alive and being a Christian.

"...in *het naam van de Vader, de Zoon and de Heilige Geest* (in the name of the Father, the Son and the Holy Spirit. Amen."

Chapter 22
Epiphanies along the Way

Allowing, even encouraging, experience to shape and change my point of view/beliefs and vice versa is not a process honored by many in my family.

It was almost midnight and I was still propped up with two pillows at my back in the master bedroom. I stopped reading and studied my book, *Death Comes for the Archbishop*, by the great American woman writer, Willa Cather.

Well, the version that Ms. Cather has of the ghostly figure that Juan Diego saw on Tepeyac Hill in Mexico and how Bishop Zumarraga came to build the shrine to Our Lady of Guadalupe in that place, I grumbled in thought, *sure is a disappointing, white-washed version of what I've read before (Cather 46-49). I had thought Cather was more aware than that.*

I picked up my thick, well used journal, the latest of about eight such that I have filled over the years, and thumbed through its pages.

Not that long ago, I remembered, I had read *Longing for Darkness: Tara and the Black Madonna, A Ten Year Journey* in which the author, China Galland, had quoted Eduardo Galeano on the subject. He, as I recalled, had some very different ideas of who the apparition had been.

I found the journal entry and, according to my notes, Galeano in *Memory of Fire* stated that Tepeyac Hill had been a site for the Aztec worship of the earth goddess, Tonantzin. The Indians, Galeano says, loved Tonantzin and they called her "our mother". He went on to accuse the Roman Catholic Archbishop Zumarraga of destroying some twenty thousand Aztec temples and idols in Mexico which had been built in honor of the earth goddess. (The selfsame Bishop Zumarraga, also according to Galeano, was the keeper of the branding iron that stamped the Indians' faces with the names of their proprietors.) Even though, Galeano said, the ghostly sighting that Juan Diego had seen on Tepeyac Hill had spoken to Diego in Nahuatl, the Aztec tongue, it was Bishop Zumarraga who had decided that she had not been Tonantzin but Quadalupe, the Dark Madonna from Spain, and had built the shrine to Our Lady of Quadalupe (Galland 247-248).

The Bishop made a calculated switch and either Ms. Cather didn't know any of that, or worse she chose not to write about it, I complained.

At this point you may be wondering why and how I came to be interested in this obscure subject. First of all, such sleuthing about in religious politics is a hobby of mine; however, this particular story came about through another hobby. Two of my hobbies dovetailed, in other words. Let me explain.

I learned to work with stained glass with the help of my neighbor in Mesa, Wilma Griffee. Wilma has done lots of stained glass and she was willing to teach me. For my first project I had looked through Wilma's patterns and had chosen a mosaic of The Lady of Guadalupe. I decided that the icon would make a good gift for Elinor Bethke, my long time friend from graduate school. We attended the University of Colorado together from 1968 to 1970 and have stayed well connected through the years. She and her husband, John, live in Monte Vista, Colorado but we get together when she comes to visit her father who lives in Sun City West.

It happens that Elinor is neither a woman of color nor a Catholic but she does live in the San Luis Valley in Colorado alongside many Mexican Americans. It is common for her to see a Madonna in the lawns and windows of her neighbors. Elinor, in turn, has become particularly intrigued not by the common Madonna but, more specifically, the black Madonna. I was so curious about my friend's quirky interest that, when I picked out the Madonna pattern with Wilma, I decided to explore the phenomenon. I went to Mesa's Main Public Library on Center Street, and to my complete surprise I found a wealth of pictures and the above mentioned book by Galland. For weeks, I vicariously traveled the globe with Ms. Galland finding black figurines around the globe and discovering that, historically and currently, she is worshipped in a variety of forms in a variety of religions. Who knew?

Uncovering the fact that my previous studies coincidentally crossed paths with and contradicted the material in this Cather book, was fascinating to me. That type of discovery, I must admit, stirs the same excitement in me as did reading a Hardy Boys book under the covers with a flashlight as a kid. One day in high school I was exploring one thing or another and I ended up sneaking into a Christian Science Reading Room in Bozeman. There I read a Mary Baker Eddy text about Christian Science and metaphysical healing. I was astounded. Other than seeing the African or South American "pagans" and "heathens" in the missionary movies in school, it had never occurred to me in those days that there were ways, other than Christian Reformed, of looking at things. I was admonished for that sneak peak outside-of- the-box in a special one-to-one session with Reverend Tadema, but obviously, as you have just read, his words did not put a stop to my sleuthing out the mysteries in religions.

I read from another Galland quote that I had copied into my journal:

> "Mary is also God: unacknowledged, female and dark. She is the Mother God. God...is both female and male, both dark and light and neither male nor female...God the Mother is just as real and as present today as any other human conception of a power which no human term can fully describe.
>
> Saints, poets, mystics, philosophers, believers, and theologians throughout the ages have wrestled with the dilemma of description. The language of paradox seems the most accurate: God is both and neither/nor, both is and is not. The mind is pushed beyond conceptual limits...Without (the language of paradox) we fall too easily into polarization, duality; we imagine that there is an "other". It is our mistaken notion of the *other* that threatens to destroy us...
>
> But Mary does not belong just to certain belief systems. She belongs to everyone who longs for a richer, more vital conception of a power greater than ourselves ...the experience of God can become much fuller by exploring the feminine side of God (Galland 158-160)."

297

Overcome with a coughing spell at that point, I returned my journal and book to the bedside stand and took some deliberate, slow, deep breathes. I removed one of the pillows, eased down, reached up to switch off the light and covered up with the blankets. In the cool, semi-darkness I rolled familiarly on my side, pulled up my knees and cradled my face with one hand.

Thank you, Great Spirit, Mother God, Whoever or Whatever you may be, I began, and was keenly aware in the same moment that, almost within reach, were those in my family who would consider my words as dismissive or even *spotten* (mockery). I use the feminine in relation to God sometimes because it helps me to imagine a more receptive deity, me being a woman; however, my development of that imagined female deity remains very vague.

How is it, I wondered for the umpteenth time in my life, halting my attempt to pray, *that I have come to such a singular, almost agnostic, place in my beliefs?* Singular in my family, that is. Not so unusual in some other circles, I have learned, much to my relief and after much searching.

I pushed the never-fading, always-urgent question aside and continued, *Thank you for this opportunity to be with my family again, with Mom, and all the others. Thank you for enough strength and resources, thank you for continued life. Thank you for dear Beej.*

My thoughts were interrupted as I coughed more and became annoyed with the persistent bronchial irritation. I didn't want to admit that I had bronchitis again and that I should begin to take the antibiotic that I always had on hand. Instead, I reached for a Maine Fisherman's Friend lozenge and listened to the muffled, monotonous litany of the frog. It had resumed its croaking after a couple of quiet nights. *Weirdest darn thing,* I thought.

Back I went, inevitably, over the peaks and through the valleys of my torturous journey of faith. Given free reign, my editing mind gleefully hits "Select All" and brings the polished scenarios up on my cerebral map of memories. Then mind places the fancied wooden, rubber-tipped pointer on the specifics for review.

Here, the pointer indicates, was young Charlotte's happiness on a Hobo Hike with the Pioneer Girls.

Yes, I remember it well! I responded excitedly. *You know I am like a junkie being offered a free fix, don't you? Take me through it all again! Pioneer Girls? Yes, past where Dutch Kimns lived on the gravel road outside of*

Manhattan, about ten of us shyly smiling and excited eight-year-old girls walked single file on a path through a field of dried grass. It was a hot day. Each of us was holding a short, leafless twig over one shoulder. There was a bundle in a red and white bandana tied to the end of each twig. Inside the bundle was a single wiener wrapped in a strip of bacon. We entered the quiet, cool woods and came to a riverbank. I remember that the water level was very low and there was a sand bank in the center of the river bed. On the soft, sandy grass by the peacefully flowing waters we had a wiener roast. My first wiener roast ever! How neat, was that? I love wiener roasts! The leaders had brought the buns and everything else needed. Afterwards, we sat in a circle and sang songs. They were songs I had never heard before, but I learned them quickly and could sort of sing along.

The day after that happy day there was your confusion and unhappiness, the pointer tapped, when *Moeke* said that she would not let you go to any other Pioneer Girl events.

That's right. I have not forgotten it. Why was that again?

Well, as you might recall, the pointer responded, *Moeke* had been told by someone that Pioneer Girls was not a Christian group, or was it not the right kind of Christian group? Anyway, that was that, *Moeke* said.

Here, the pointer underlined, were the magical, safe times in Vacation Bible School with Mrs. Kuiper in the little church in Manhattan.

Yes, some of my favorite times as a kid! There the colorful stories of the Bible sprang to life with cutouts on the flannel board. Everybody, even the teachers, colored pictures of Noah and Moses, Jesus in white robes, rainbows and lambs and memorized Bible verses. I loved all that.

"Swords up!"

We stretched so high and held our closed Bibles up in the air as far as we possibly could.

"II Kings Chapter 17 verse 39," the teacher would call out. No one could move. There would be a long pause until everyone was very quiet.

"Charge!" the teacher shouted.

Genesis, Exodus, Leviticus, Numbers, Deuteronomy, Joshua, Judges, Kings. I and II Kings. Flip the pages. Find the chapter. Down the page to the verse and jump up!

"II Kings Chapter 17 verse 39. 'But the Lord your God ye shall fear; and he shall deliver you out of the hand of all your enemies!'"

"Correct!"

Oh, yes! I knew my books of the Bible. I was the overall best in the two weeks of sword drills one year and won the zippered Bible! How we loved to stand tall, push forward our chests, march in place with noisy steps and sing at the top of our lungs, "Onward Christian Soldiers, marching as to war, with the cross of Jesus going on before..."

A few years later, the pointer indicated, unimpressed with my theatrics, tragedy struck early in the fall, just after you had started junior high school, in the old building where all of the respected high school students were.

Right, I sighed, *the all-consuming fire burned down not only the much loved school building and my desk but my precious, irreplaceable, zippered Bible too. Gone! Poof! Gone for good were the Bible and a piece of my self.*

There, the pointer signified, was the conversation, upon which you eavesdropped. It was between your mother and father about your father getting into a fist fight and punching out the American man, Red Cheney, because he had stolen the irrigation water from upstream overnight.

Yes, I felt scared about that and remember wondering things such as: Where had God been? Pa was a righteous man. Could not God have stopped his fist like He had stopped Abraham's in midair when he was going to stab his son, Isaac, to death? Would Pa be in trouble now? How bad was it?

You felt the same fear and wondered the same things over here, my imaginary pointer moved only slightly, when grape-sized hailstones tapped ferociously and relentlessly on the kitchen windows.

Right, yes, I remember it clearly. The grain in the fields was just ripe enough so that the hailstones would knock off the heads. I knew that much. Pa stood by the kitchen window looking out for the longest time. His face looked hard and his fists where clenched. It looked to me like Pa might want to punch God like he had punched Red Cheney. I believed that God was making it hail, you understand.

And again here, over here, you faced another wrenching dilemma about God's whereabouts and intentions when the phone rang and you and your dusty, exhausted family heard about another terrible fire.

Yes, that was a tough one. We were sitting around the kitchen table for a very late dinner, and had to hear that the just-completed, huge, fresh haystack was going up in flames.

"Stacking day" was a difficult day on the farm and it involved every member of the family. That particular day had been no exception. John, shirtless with his blonde crew cut and no more than thirteen years old, if that much, had driven the John Deere tractor all day long. It was his job to pick up the dried windrows of alfalfa on the buck rake, go to the stack, fit together the wooden teeth of the rake with the teeth of the stacker, push the load off onto the stacker, pull back with an empty buck rake and go for a new load. Sometimes, when he wasn't paying attention, he would snap one of the eight-feet-long wooden teeth on either buck rake or stacker. *Pa* would have to replace it and he would fuss at John for wasting so much time. That had not happened on this day. Things had gone pretty well.

Pat, four years older than John, had driven the truck with the attached wire cable. The heavy cable pulled the rickety stacker upright and dumped the load of hay onto the stack. True, there were short down times when she had to wait for John to bring another load, and sometimes she could even squeeze in a paragraph or two from her Grace Livingston Hill romance novel. But, in reality, it was a stressful, tricky job. Each time she had to drive the truck at just the precise speed and distance: slow enough so the cable would not break, yet briskly enough so the load would flip towards the center of the stack. When she was in her groove and things were going well, she could strategically flip that load farther towards the back or closer to the front of the stack, wherever *Pa* wanted it. However, when she didn't have the knack and things were going wrong, Pa got mad and Pat became a nervous wreck. Then sometimes she drove too far or too fast and the cable snapped. Ah, big problem! Tension city.

Pa, bless his heart, in the heat of the summer day always with cumbersome, tiring footing and nothing but a pitchfork, had to straighten the back-breaking loads and fashion the hot, prickly alfalfa into a beautiful, oblong, compact haystack. He gobbled down salt pills and drank in huge gulps to keep from becoming dehydrated. His shirt was always drenched with sweat, and his sun-darkened face was marked with rivulets of dust and sweat.

Moeke, Margaret and I in the old, light brown Chevy bounced over ruts in the field to bring food and drinks: coffee in the morning at ten o'clock, cold lemon and orange drink with tons of sugar in the afternoon about three-thirty. Even though it was hot, there was nothing like the aroma of fresh hay mingling with that of coffee from the heavy Stanley thermos and the spices of the buttered brown bread, unwrapped from wax paper. Forget inlaid, gold streets and celestial choirs; coffee time out in the field was a slice of heaven for me. As a family we sat in the shade to relax, refuel and talk while *Pa* smoked a Pall Mall.

The talk was about the sky—was anything moving up there? how fast? were there afternoon thunder clouds building?—and the quality of the hay—had it dried enough so that the stack would not heat up too much? was there any mildew in it? were there enough nutritious leaves left on the stalks? My parents made plans—how long would they continue? would they try to finish tonight or start fresh again in mid-morning after the dampness from the dew had dried? That day *Pa* decided they would work late and try to finish.

When break was over I envied Pat and John, oh, so very much. They could work outdoors with Dad all day long; I had to go back home and help Mom indoors. I had to help with dishes, cooking, canning, cleaning and looking after Margaret. I couldn't wait until I would get a chance to drive that truck.

It was late that evening, the pointer tapped insistently as if annoyed within my brain. It was about ten o'clock—

Yes, yes, I am getting to it. There it was, the family masterpiece with the stacker still in place, off in the distance in the black, black night, writhing and waving like a demented dinosaur that had been doused with gasoline and set aflame. There was nothing we could do but watch in horror. Could it have been a spark from the John Deere or from a passing freight train? The hay had been dry, Pa was certain of that; so spontaneous combustion was out, and he was always very careful with his cigarettes and matches.

I had been taught every day of my life to that point that God was all powerful, everywhere at every moment, seeing and hearing everything and that he was a just God. Everyone, including me, had worked so hard, praying the whole time that rain would hold off until the job was done. God must have seen and heard us. How was this just?

Typically—although I do not remember the specifics that followed this event—there was a scene of my parents having another edgy discussion about what do you suppose? Money, of course, what else? It was always about not enough money. They talked in short clipped sentences about loans and not being able to make a payment to the Whites or to Uncle Bill and about having to tell them face to face. *Pa*, dark, pessimistic, over-whelmed with burdens, smoking, Mom shoring him up, anxious, minimizing, toughing it out, *"Misschain is't wel nait zo slim, jonge."* (Maybe it's not so bad, bud.) *Wie zeilen der wel deur kommen.* (We'll get through it). They would wash up, put on clean clothes and go to Manhattan to the bank or to a meeting with Rose White or to Butte to see Lester and Polly White.

The pointer wasted no time. That voice, that pointer in the brain is so relentless, is it not? Here, over here, tap-tap-tap in the pleasure category, it indicated, is your unbridled joy and amazement when you realized that you had ridden the big palomino.

Oh, yes, and bareback too! Full speed across two fields until he tired! Not until I fell off or reined him in, but until he tired. Now that was a coming into the light, an epiphany, a sudden perception of the essential! I had been ordered not to ride that horse, and at first, when he took off, I thought I might get killed. Then, I tasted strength, courage and freedom. I have taken that ride so many times again in my imagination.

And there was your angry frustration and moral confusion when typically your mother let John take the bigger piece.

You would have to bring that up. I'll never forget it. Here's how it went every single time.

"What would you have done?" Moeke would ask me when I complained.

"I would take the little piece like you say we're supposed to," I would whine in return.

"Zo, dat hest doe nou ja. Ist nait zo? Mos der nait over jammerin. Ik wil der nait meer van heuren!" (So that is what you have now, isn't it? Don't moan about it. I don't want to hear any more about it!)

On my own initiative I continued. *I remember the self-pity and loathing I felt, too, when I sobbed uncontrollably to Mom up in my bedroom, "Pat is the oldest, John is a boy and Margaret is the youngest. Who am I? Who am I to you?"*

And, Mom's answer, "Hai, hai, dat is ja vreselijk. Zo mos doe nait weer proaten (My, my, that is terrible. You must never talk like that again)!

Here at the age of ten you are so sad when Pat left home and here at thirteen you are frantic when *Moeke* came home with a terrible head cold. She had been in Galen, Montana with your father. The pointer circled the memory several times; it always did that.

I see that scene like it was yesterday. With tears and sniffles, Mom told

John and me what the doctor had said about Pa's sickness, "Tis kanker, kinder, tis kanker." (It's cancer, children; it's cancer.)

John and I boiled water, poured it in a basin and put a teaspoon of Vicks in the steaming water. We put the basin in front of Moeke, and insisted that she put a towel over her head and lean over the basin to inhale the fumes. What if she got sick, too? Moeke had to plead with us to stop.

"Het is te hait, kinder! Ik mout der ouit! (It is too hot, children! I have to get out!)"

After that fateful evening, when my childhood came to a screeching halt, no matter how good I was, and I was as good as I could possibly be, how much I worked, and I worked harder than I ever had, how much I read in my Bible, how much I prayed believing God when He said, "Ask and ye shall receive," I could not turn the process around. A year and a half went by as I watched my beloved father suffer and waste away.

In the summer of 1958 I was a vulnerable adolescent. Not only because I was fifteen but because I was recovering from encephalitis. A day towards the end of my father's life I sat by his bedside. He was terribly thin. His simple, gold-band wedding ring fell loosely down to the knuckle of his finger. The normally strong, suntanned, callused hands were white and frail, his eyes sunken and closed. Even in sleep his hands clutched the ever-present, squashed tissue box. He was unshaven; he had been too tired to have it done that morning. Cold sweat glistened on his white, hollow cheeks and in his eyelashes. It trickled down his temple. His wet, thin, dark hair was plastered to his head, showing no signs of having been combed only a short while before, and his pajama top, the one with white and green stripes that I ironed so often, was getting wet and wrinkled already. As I watched him take each noisy breath, his eyes opened. They were much too big and much too bright.

"Come here," he instructed me weakly. With one shaky hand he made a signaling gesture across his body.

I went to stand by the other side of the bed.

"Moes dat draaien (You have to turn that)," he rasped.

With a great quavering effort, he rose up, sweat pouring off his pale face. His arm and hand shook as he took hold of my upper arm, moved it toward the large green oxygen tank and desperately urged me to turn it.

He started to cough; then, he made a circling motion with his arm and repeated it. Stupefied, I imitated the motion and recognized it. It was like turning the wheel on the ditch digger. The faster I made the circling motion the more he relaxed. He fell back down completely spent and was again asleep. I stood in shock and shame, so glad that no one had walked into the room. Then I felt ashamed for being selfish.

That night, as I did every night, I kneeled by my bed to pray, but no words came with which to plead. Like a free, high-spirited horse finally accepting a rider, I had been broken. I crawled into bed and sobbed for what seemed like hours.

Finally, I lay spent. I stared out the uncovered window, and it must have been a full moon bed because I watched huge, puffy, white clouds move across the black sky. Several clouds came together slowly, silently, and formed a hand. Then the cumulus hand extended towards me. Startled at first I drew back, but then I relaxed and felt comforted. *Pa* died the following week.

You felt betrayed when he died. The pointer was still on task.

Yes, inconceivable to me—though not surprising because they had been saying it all along—the adults were saying that it was God's will. I didn't want to hear it, and I most certainly was not going to condone it. If it were true, I wanted no part of Him, and on top of that I was not going to be fooled like that ever again. From everything I had heard, believed and sung about at home, church and Christian school I was pretty sure that I had built my spiritual house on solid rock. But, like the foolish man in the song who built his house upon the sand, when the rain came down and the floods came up, my house fell flat. I was drowning and no one had prepared me for that possibility.

And yet, the pointer mapped out, three years later on a Sunday before leaving for college you stood in First Church publicly professing your commitment to the doctrine of the Christian Reformed Church.

Yes, I know. I did.

"Do you believe in God, the Father, Almighty maker of heaven end earth?"

"I do."

"Do you believe in Jesus Christ as your own personal savior and Lord?"

"I do."

But I was wooden, numb. I don't mind telling you that I walked away from that ceremony with an already mouse-bitten burlap sack of faith on my shoulder.

Ten years later, the pointer indicated, after you finally emerged from your schooling, first in Michigan then in Colorado, there were only a few kernels left in the corners of that sack.

True enough; one kernel represented the billowy white cloud (hand) in the night sky. I never have let go of that personal little vision or miracle. And a few kernels represented the beauty and spiritual stillness that I could still find in nature.

With those seeds in safekeeping, I mended my sack, one stitch at a time, and began to add kernels of precious little epiphanies along the way.

There have always been special moments of truth for you, the pointer insisted. There was, for instance, the stranger, the elderly lady, on the train when you first left home who reached up her hand to touch your face.

I remember. "What a beautiful complexion you have, dear," she said. This stranger told me that something about me was beautiful. I so needed that. Loss, grief and deeply buried anger had left me feeling ugly and unworthy.

There was Mrs. Nichols, the patient who died on Christmas Eve in 1963 when you were in nurses training.

Yes, she left me with a brave, peaceful, and mindful example of dying. "Thank you for staying with me today," she whispered tenderly. She showed me how to live and die with a generous spirit and she included me. Mom had not included me the evening or night that Dad died. Margaret and I were with Al and Pieka when the telephone call came.

There was the stranger at Shop and Save grocery who helped you select the right sausage just after your tenure at the university had been denied and you were devastated.

I'll never forget that! In a fugue-like state for several minutes, I came to, hearing a voice beside me say, "This one, dear, take this one. Take it." A short woman was insistently pushing one of the sausages into my hand and pressing her body close against mine. "You'll like it, dear. I know you will. It will be fine," she said.

The earth breathed a big cleansing breath with her words and I shifted from fear to fascination. "Yes, yes, I'll be fine," I said. Uh, I mean the sausage will be fine. Thank you. Thank you so much."

And there is Sophia with whom to share your life.

Yes, yes, what an awesome gift she has been! Though our lifestyle is still rejected by the church community and though I can more easily say what I do not believe than what I believe, I am sometimes certain that I am loved and that

Sophia is really an angel sent to be with me. I would most likely not be alive without her or stuck in a nursing home somewhere.

I remember one, I said eagerly, beating the pointer to the punch. *Last year at Christmas time, I rode on an open wagon bed sitting on and leaning against hay bales. Beautiful, large, black Percheron horses with their harnesses creaking were pulling a group of us residents through the streets of Sunlife. I sang Christmas carols with the mostly familiar people and took in the many multi-colored lights against the clear black of the night. Following a carol, after a quiet lull, there came the tiny, perfect voice (like the reed in an instrument) of the ninety-year-old woman singing "O' Noche Santa" (Oh Holy Night). The words, not understandable to me and thus not a distraction, spoke poignantly of the woman's courage and spirit, of light and dark and of persons mingling with us as if spirit-sent to soften our hearts within our wounded chests.*

One last moment for emphasis, tapped the pointer. Those little girls back at Sunlife a few days ago, remember?

I stirred and heaved a huge sigh. This habitual, mental track of mine is so well worn that there are potholes in my psyche. I obsess about it; I realize this.

Again, at another time, I thought, *like an addict after the effect wears off, I'll want to go over it all again, and for what effect really? Justification? Reassurance? Understanding? Understanding, I guess. It is who I am. I always have this need to understand how I got from Point A to Point B.*

I used to have a stack of baseball cards of some of the biggest names that ever played the game: Whitey Ford, Mickey Mantle, Duke Snyder, Yogi Berra, Warren Spahn, Sandi Koufax, Ernie Banks, Willie Mays, Ted Williams on and on. I loved baseball in my adolescence. In fact, listening to the "Game of the Week" with Dizzy Dean and Mel Allen on Saturdays was the only thing that made washing the woodwork weekly in the kitchen somewhat tolerable. I loved the Yankees and I loved collecting and trading the cards. Then one day on Churchill I stood at the burn barrel in the backyard and tossed the cards into the fire. I was too much of a tomboy Mom said. She didn't want members of the community to start saying things about me. It was time to start acting more like a girl should act. I watched for a few seconds as the flames embraced the cards then turned and walked to the house. I have so wished that I had not done that! As with all the scenarios that I have just reviewed, the events stand as they are, and looking back does not change them; it only explains what I became because of them. Now, among other things, I am determinedly more of a tomboy than I ever was. I revel in putting on my carpenter pants, loading up the special loop with my hammer and filling my pockets with nails and screws and working right outside where all the neighbors can see me. Me and my faith or lack thereof are always a work in progress.

I placed the phantom pointer in its tray at the bottom of my mythical map and gratefully, as though redeemed through the sheer amount of effort alone, fell into a deep sleep.

Chapter 23
As the Kaleidoscope Turns

Some are not only able but consider it a matter of faith to keep experience and viewpoint quite separate. In other words, they trust their beliefs irrespective of experience.

L ottie! Lottie, pick up the phone!" Pat burst into the master bedroom, short house coat over sweats flying in the breeze. She was wide-eyed and her heart was racing.

Pat has a murmur, an arrhythmia, in her heart for which she has been medicated for years and years. She also has a benign nodule quietly growing in her thyroid. Long ago, to slow the growth, the natural workings of her thyroid gland were intentionally shut down by synthetic thyroid pills. Now and then, I think, her doses could use a little tweaking.

It was Sunday morning about eight-fifteen. Everyone, including Pat, had slept in after the festivities and reflections of the previous evening and everyone, just five minutes ago, had been abruptly awakened by the loud ringing of the telephone.

Pat found me sitting up in bed using my inhalers. The bronchodilator and anti-inflammatory inhalants are essential; I am no longer able to function without them. Asthma and bronchitis are secondary problems to the emphysema but no less troubling. Invariably, they flare up at times of infection.

"*Oom* Piet is on the phone!" exclaimed Pat. "*Oom* Piet! He heard about Seattle's snowstorm on T.V. in Holland! Can you believe it? He wants to know if we're all right! This is such a riot!" Pat laughed elatedly holding her hand over her heart.

"Mom's talking to him right now. Is this phone hooked up? Yes. Here he is. Just say a few words." Pat pushed the telephone towards me.

"No, oh, please, I can't do this," I spluttered. My weak pleas, however, betrayed my ambivalence. I did want to talk with him but I didn't know if I could.

Pat thrust the phone into my hand. "Go ahead," she urged.

I acquiesced. "Hello, *Oom* Piet? *Dit* is Tjaakje."

I strained to hear and understand *Oom* Piet's words. Pat hurried back downstairs to get on the extension.

Oom Piet is our father's half-brother. Whereas Dad was tall and lanky, Piet is thickset and a half-foot shorter. Their different body types clearly mirror the differences that were in their mothers: Dad's mother was Trientje Dijk; Piet's mother was Heina Smit.

Piet married Wiets Hellinga just before our family left for America and the newly-wedded couple moved into our house. Fifty years later they still live there and hardly anything has changed.

That brick, family home on plot number 1277 in Thesinge was built in 1848 by Jan Roelf van Bruggen (1810) and Rachel Jans Pesman (1819). The van Bruggens gave birth to two daughters, Tjaakje and Emke. Daughter, Tjaakje van Bruggen, married Pieter Heidema.

An interesting bit of history in this regard is that Lodewijk Napoleon, Bonaparte's brother, sometime before 1810 in order to tax and collect revenues from the peoples of the low countries, required that everyone take a surname, a last name. It was decreed that these new last names take the place of keeping track by saying Jan the son of Pieter who was the son of Jan Pieter etcetera.

In this case Tjaakje van Bruggen or—literally translated— Tjaakje "from the bridge" married Pieter Heidema, "the man from the heather." It is a rather romantic image to see the woman from the bridge running towards the man in a field of blooming, reddish-purple heather, don't you think?

Tjaakje and Pieter Heidema eventually moved into the family home and had five sons. Jan, their oldest, who inherited the family business of grain brokering and shipping in Thesinge, married Trientje Dijk (Dyk) after she returned from America in 1906. Their first child was born in 1907 and they named her Tjaakje Fijlina. She was followed by Jan Pieter in 1908 and Fijlina in 1913. Sadly, mother Trientje was never well after giving birth to Fijlina and died in April of the following year, 1914. Trientje was a month short of becoming 32 years old. What a shock for that young family. Jan Heidema married a second time to Heina Smit and had the one son, Pieter Heidema *(Oom* Piet) in 1922.

Tjaakje Fijlina—who I am named after—had diabetes. She did not marry and had no children. At the age of 29 in 1936 she became ill with a severe cold and was not able to eat properly. She died within a matter of hours from insulin shock. (Tjaakje died a year before Mom's father, Klaas de Vries died (1937) which meant my parents, Jan Piet and Anje, wore their *raubant*—black armband signifying mourning—for two solid years. That was the custom in those days.)

Fijlina (Lien) married Klaas de Boer. They settled in Ten Boer where they lived the rest of their lives and had two daughters, Tini (pronounced Teenie) and Wina. Lien, along with severe eczema, has had an amazingly high blood pressure all her life. It registers as high as 210/150 and no medicines ever work! Both conditions are genetic; her grandmother, Fijlina (van Dijken) Dyk, who lived in America, also had what is medically known as essential benign hypertension.

As siblings will do, Piet has a favorite grumble about his sister: *"Lien is altiet houg hartige* (Lien is always snobby)," Piet will complain, *"omdat her moe en Dijk waz* (because her mother was a Dyk)." (Presumably, there must have been some class or respect distance between the Dijk and the Smit names in Holland which Lien could rub in at times. That was the custom after all.)

In 1958 from February until August Lien left behind her husband and daughters to come to America to be with her brother, Jan Piet, who was dying, and our family. Not long ago out of the clear blue *Tante* Lien called me. In the course of our conversation *Tante* Lien told me about a dream that *Pa* had recounted sometime during the last weeks of his life.

He had dreamt, she said, that he was climbing a high mountain and that Jesus was standing at the top. As he neared the end then, *Tante* Lien said, *"Moe vragt him, 'Is Jesus dar nou ook (Moe* is short for *Moeder* meaning mother and refers in this case to my mother, Ann, who is asking, 'Is Jesus there now too)?'"

"'Ja!' roept hij ('Yes!' he called out). I can still hear him, she said.[9]

---

[9] Fijlina Heidema-de Boer passed away on February 1,2001. She was preceded in death by her husband, Klaas, and her youngest daughter, Wina, who had succumbed to breast cancer.

Tjaakje C. Heidema

Piet and Wiets had three children: Jan, Pieter and Heina. Wiets, a quiet-mannered loving soul, perfectly offsets her hot-tempered, often stressed-out husband. Piet took over the family grain-brokering and insurance business, but his work was soon phased out in favor of other evolving methods. In its place, along with becoming a board member of the bank and the bookkeeper of the church finances, Piet became the head inspector and registrar of the genealogy or blood lines of the *Warmbloed Paard Associatie* (Warmblood Horse Breeder's Association) of the Netherlands. He is very well-acquainted with breeders, commissioners and veterinarians throughout the country and performs as a well-known, much respected judge at the horse shows.

For his work he has been "*geridderd in de orde van Oranje Nassau* (inducted into the order of the House of Orange of Nassau)" and given its special medal. In addition to this expertise he is known for his plain speaking ability. Where one might say that a particular horse tends to show best in a position that is more popular in France—meaning it leans a bit to the left—Piet will simply say, "'*t Peerd is schaif* (the horse is crooked)."

Oom Piet took Margaret and myself, on our separate visits to Holland, to a horse show in which he was the presiding judge. Everyone deferred to him as he thoughtfully strolled around the horses with his hands behind his back—just like Dad always did—before he gave the final word.

The inherited love of horses in some family members, therefore, comes from both sides of our family. *Oom* Jan on the de Vries side and *Oom* Piet on the Heidema side. In the new generation both Michelle and Kent with their families like to ride horseback up into the mountains, different landscape but similar genes.

"*Ja*, from Arizona *ver tien doag'n,* ah, *voor tien dagen* (for 10 days)."

I stumbled awkwardly through my conversation with *Oom* Piet. Some words were in English, some in *Gronigs,* the defunct dialect, others in proper *Hollandse* and some words belonged to no recorded language. They were combinations of English and Dutch in what is known as *Yankee Dutch.*

"*Ik ben orig goud. Ik ben wel wat slow,* aah, *langzomlijk, moar anders ist nait te slem. Slecht, ja, not too slecht. Hou ist mit you en Tante Wiets? (*I am pretty good. I am somewhat slow but otherwise it is not too bad. How is it with you and Aunt Wiets)?"

When the telephone conversation was ended, Ann came into my bedroom and sat on the side of the bed.

"Wat is dit toch waat (This is really something)," she exclaimed. *"Ik kin der oost nait over kom'n (I* can hardly get over it). Seattle *wier woudt bepraat ein Holland* (Seattle weather is being talked about in Holland)!"

Pat joined us in a few minutes and sat on the other side of the bed. We shared every word of what *Oom* Piet had said to each of us and the news was excitedly rehashed a second time.[10]

Brandon came in and wishing to participate gave the report from the Langel quarter. Steven stood in the doorway waiting for an opening in the conversation. When a lull at last ensued he announced, "There will be no one going to church on this Sunday."

"What?" Ann whipped her head around to the left to see Steven.

"The services at the First Seattle Christian Reformed Church due to the severe weather conditions have been canceled," reiterated Steven.

"Now that is really something!" Ann said aghast at the development. "Here in Seattle, no church on Sunday."

"Wow," said Pat. That has never happened before!"

It was indeed likely that there would be few if any church services throughout the entire metropolitan area. Travel advisories strongly urged everyone to stay at home. The few streets that had been passable with the snowpack were now impassable due to heavy slush covering a solid sheet of ice. The mountain passes were closed again and hordes of people were stranded at the airport.

Pat suddenly decided to e-mail a quick letter to John and Joyce. She jumped up and started towards Steve's office. Brandon and Steve turned to go and Ann followed them to the dining room to have breakfast.

"There's so much to tell them!" Pat said to me reappearing in the doorway. I had not budged from my position in the bed. "The last time we e-mailed was on Christmas day. How is it going between you and John anyway? I haven't had a chance to ask you

---

[10] Piet Heidema, the last living uncle in the family living in Holland, died on September 6, 2002. It was just a little over a year after his devoted wife, Wiets, died. The home which had been in the family for 150 years had been sold to someone outside of the family a few years prior to Piet and Wiets' deaths

before."

"I hardly ever see him anymore," I sighed deeply. "The only time I do is when I invite myself over for tea. They just never initiate anything."

"When he talks about Harry and Shirley being like brother and sister to them, I'm glad for him and for them, but I just want to say, what's wrong with the sisters you have? It upsets me too," said Pat.

"Trust me, you don't want to know what he thinks is wrong with you. According to him I totally botched up our relationship; like he's perfect or something."

"Well, they could do something with you."

"They were at the Computer Club table for the Thanksgiving Day dinner like usual. I said 'Happy Thanksgiving' to them but it isn't something he would ever make an effort to do. Joyce would but he wouldn't. It's like I don't exist anymore, or like I'm not family or doesn't want people to know that I am, or something. I still think we should do something with family on holidays, but that's not the way he thinks, I guess. His family is his kids not me. It hurts. I've pretty much given up."

"Well, don't do that."

"I mean in the sense of wanting anything from him, from a brother, you know. We're superficial with each other now. I confronted him when I should have been stroking his ego. For example, just a small thing, I pointed out to him once that I always gave him something for his birthday and that he didn't do that in return. I asked him if he would make it a mutual thing and he point-blank said, no, he wouldn't, and when I asked him if he wanted to do anything with me at all he couldn't think of a thing. I try to forget about it but it really breaks my heart, you know?"

"I know; it's really sad. Maybe things will change some day."

"Or not," I grumbled as Pat disappeared around the corner.

Filled to the brim with Sandi's belongings, Christmas wrappings and sleeping bag there was no floor space left in Steve's office. Pat walked on the sleeping bag and pushed aside a few bags so she could sit down at the computer.

By the time I finished my shower and dressed, it was close to lunchtime. I went down the stairs and saw that the table had been cleared of breakfast food and the dining room was empty. I went on to the kitchen to see what was happening.

Sweeping Away the Sand

Arlyce and Anil, huddled together at the movable island counter in the center of the room, were intently focused on one another and looked quite serious. Behind the twosome, faithful and forbearing Steven—what a trooper!—was gathering up the trash. Unobtrusively, he had already emptied the dishwasher and put away the dishes from the night before. Then refilled and rerun the dishwasher with the breakfast dishes. To the right at the table Ann was talking on the telephone to Michelle. She was animatedly telling Shelly everything that had transpired in Seattle and at the same time was getting the latest scoop on the Heidema kids, Montana weather and Jim DeJong's health.

Looking beyond Mom to the outdoors I could see the dejected-looking snowman. The continuing rain was quickly transforming it into a formless, faceless lump. Green M&Ms that had been its eyes and the orange carrot-nose had already dropped off onto the deck. The twigs that had been its arms hung limp, slowly sliding out of their sockets. The baseball cap advertising Deep Sea Fishing in Westport, Washington, had disappeared, rescued most likely by its owner.

I walked past Ann who gave a quick wave and looked into the living room. Arun and Brandon, Brandon having laid aside his saxophone, were playing shuffle board which for some reason had been placed on the long couch in the living room. It was at a perfect height for Arun who was doing a lot of clapping, chattering and running back and forth to his parents.

I turned around to go to the family room and intercepted Marge who was walking through with some neatly folded clothes and towels. Upon whispered inquiry Marge informed me that Arlyce and Anil were planning the evening's hot meal which would be Indian style. Yummm, we concurred and smiled broadly like mimes on a street corner.

It reminds me of the time I went to Michigan to be with Marge for the Thanksgiving holiday. We sat in the theater, watched the Laurel and Hardy clips and mentioned how much Dad had enjoyed the hilarious twosome on television. There we were, two sad souls wishing we had a Laurel or Hardy in our lives to make us laugh again.

Back in Seattle Marge whispered a quick scenario in my ear. Anil and Arlyce, she said, were originally going to have everyone

315

over for an Indian meal in their own home on this date but thinking that the weather might be a problem they had brought the food items with them to the Cok home on Friday evening.

"Ahah," I said, nonverbally smiling my comprehension as well.

"But," continued Marge, "they don't have some of the very important seasonings."

"Oh."

Earlier, she went on to tell me after we ducked into the laundry room, Anil had thought about trying to go home. He had driven Max, the Nissan Maxima, out of the driveway but in seconds had run stuck in the cul de sac. Neither Steve nor Doug had been able to budge it. The wheels had spun fruitlessly on the waterlogged snow and ice. Now both of the Coumar cars, Cressie and Max, were stuck and out of commission.

"Oh, oh."

She and Doug, Marge said, were taking advantage of the downtime to take showers. She needed to get the towels up to Doug on the second floor and off she went.

I continued on. In the family room Sandi, dressed in royal blue spandex shorts with a navy T-shirt from Glacier Park, and Sophia in her black sweatpants and gray T-shirt also from Glacier Park were doing aerobics to a video. Both were pumping elbows and knees like a couple of oil derricks gone berserk.

Suddenly, a decision had been made. Anil, it was said, despite the terrible weather, the pouring, slashing rain and treacherous, icy paths, would walk to the home of a presumably Indian man in the neighborhood. Those who had seen the man come and go were pretty sure anyway that he was from India. No one had ever spoken to him but he looked somewhat like Anil and he appeared friendly. It had been concluded that Anil would forthrightly ask to borrow spices from him. A fellow Indian, it was surmised, would likely have the essential herbs and spices like a Greek would have olive oil and lemons or a Dutch person would have sugar and butter.

Eagerly awaited, a chilled, wet Anil soon came back in from the garage triumphant with cumin, coriander and turmeric in plastic baggies tucked inside his jacket!

"What did he say?" "Was he surprised?" "Did he look shocked?"

The questions rang out as those of us within earshot gathered to hear the story and update Pat who was just coming in on the tail end.

"He was dressed in his pajamas!" proclaimed Anil laughing heartily as he wiped the rain from his face with his hand. "I said to him, 'I have a very unusual request. Sorry to ask you but I would like some help from you.' He looked somewhat frightened and very concerned when I said that." Anil laughed again.

"Wouldn't you be if this strange man is saying this to you on your doorstep on a day like this and there is no car in sight? The man probably thought you wanted money or were gong to rob him or something. What did he say then?" queried Sandi who was embellishing the drama with her personal presentiments.

"He said, 'Tell me, tell me.'"

"Oh, that was a nice thing to say. He must not have been too concerned," offered Arlyce taking the spices from him so that he could take off his wet jacket.

"I told him I have all these people to feed and I want to borrow some spices. He looked relieved," continued Anil. Everyone laughed.

"Then he took me in to the kitchen. He got some sandwich bags and the spice rack. I took the spices I needed."

"Did you talk about anything else?" wondered Pat.

"We talked about being from India but we are from very different parts of the country so we could only share in English. We had nothing else in common. I am cold!"

Anil shivered and then blurted out, "I don't have any shorts on!"

Everyone burst out with laughter.

"That's not so bad," Pat jested. "If your pants fall down while you are cooking, your new apron will cover you!"

That brought more laughter.

"What would be worse is if we run out of diapers for Arun, and that is about to happen" added Arlyce.

At that the group dissolved as with the rotation of a kaleidoscope into other activities. The aerobics transformed into a line doing the Macarena dance. Pat, having had trouble with the computer and the e-mailing, began instead to place leftovers on the dining room table for a do-it-yourself-when-you-feel-like-it lunch and the cooks returned to their task.

After having a bite to eat I brought a deck of cards to the kitchen table where Ann was sitting writing in her diary and sat down beside her. When Mom finished writing, I offered to teach her how to play solitaire.

"No," responded Ann decisively, "I do not want to learn to play solitaire."

"Nuh," I exclaimed puzzled by her strong and unexpected resistance. "I thought you said that Marion Drew plays solitaire all the time; I just assumed that you, too, might like to know how to play it."

"No, you are not going to push this old lady away into a corner and put cards in front of her to keep her quiet," asserted my mother strongly.

"Of course not; that is not why I am doing this," I rejoined in protest as I pressed on and laid out the cards.

Obviously, I was rubbing her fur the wrong way and, when rubbed that way, old contentious feelings quickly surface. As a middle child growing up, I was strong-willed and rebellious. Though I have been much tempered by life's paradoxical realities, I still am like that to some extent. I also have always had an unquenchably fierce drive for independence and make the mistake of thinking that others have the same.

Ann, first born, was much more of a pleaser in her family. She held her parents and their privileged position in society in deepest regard. In fact, she has never ever said a bad thing about them. She expects the same in turn from me.

At cross-purposes as mother and daughter we have fought our share of verbal battles over time, but nonetheless have achieved a degree of respect for one another in more recent years. As Mom has aged and as my lung condition takes its toll, the plight of each of us has become more similar; we can commiserate as travelers on a common path.

"There was an old lady in the care wing of the hospital and that is what they did to her," Ann revealed. "They just pushed her in the corner and put cards in front of her."

As it happened Doug walked by and corrected a few errors that I was making in the rows of cards that I had laid out in front of us. He lingered at Ann's side. Pat came by and mentioned that she and Steve played solitaire all the time on the computer. It did not take much more. Ann, with Doug's guidance, was moving cards around at will. I recognized my cue to exit stage right and vanished into the living room.

There was no preaching that Sunday at the Cok home and no offertory was taken. But there certainly was communion; in the small c sense of the word, that is. And later in the afternoon there most definitely was a full-fledged choir. Steven played the piano, and as often as he could manage to play the piano and sing he came in with his well-seasoned tenor. Pat, sitting to his right also on the piano bench, sang, turned pages and found requested songs. Next to Pat was Ann. She clasped her hands, lifted her head and, like a yellow canary in rapture, sang pure soprano. Marge, Sandi and I stood behind the others with our arms encircling one another's waists and sang as if our lives depended on it.

Song after song was played and sung. Pat commented that the alto and bass, usually sung by the absent brother and sister-in-law, floundered in places. But the weakness deterred no one. We surrendered our personal pent-up energies to inspiring harmony and sang on. Lots of favorites were found in *The Old Fashioned Revival Hour* hymn book, the lime-green one with the black plastic, spiral binding: "Out of the ivory palaces into a world of woe", "By the sea of crystal all the saints in glory stand, myriads in number drawn from every land", "Just as I am without one plea", "I come to the garden alone while the dew is still on the roses ... and He walks with me and He talkes with me ... and the joy I feel as I tarry there none other has ever known."

"That was Jan Piet's favorite," said Ann of the last song. We three daughters affirmed that we knew that and those of us who had the memory stored within, recalled Jan Piet bravely singing aloud Dutch Psalms in the Bozeman Deaconess Hospital. Coughing, spitting sputum into a white tissue, he had sung on as death came ever more near, "Faith of our fathers living still in spite of dungeon, fire and sword" and in spite of cancer, said the image.

"Sweet hour of prayer that calls me from a world of care", "Constantly abiding Jesus is mine, constantly abiding rapture divine. He'll never leave me lonely, whispers, oh, so kind, 'I will never leave you,' Jesus is mine", and on it went. Plus, of course, there were the Christmas carols.

B.J., taking an uncommon time of rest, lay on the couch and

319

covered his ears with his arms in mock desperation as Sophia took pictures of the choir and then of him. In the third verse of about the twentieth song Sophia who, because of her Greek Orthodox upbringing, recognized none of the oldies stole away upstairs and caught some of the wild card, football playoff game on television.

Finally, we ran out of songs to sing and our last notes echoed off into the ethers. Within minutes, like an aviary after sunset, peaceful quiet settled in throughout the house. It was time for the Sunday afternoon, Christian Reformed nap. Tantalizing aromas wafted into the family room where Sandi was quietly set up the projector for her slides and into the living room where Marge was reading and hoping that the mad, deeply traumatized horse, Pilgrim, in *The Horse Whisperer* could learn to trust again.

Given the right circumstances, she reflected, *I could probably have been a horse whisperer. I would have loved that.*

Across the room Brandon, halfway through *Monster Blood II*, one of R.L. Stine's popular Goosebumps series, felt the hair on his neck move and the shiver go through his body. He loved it when that happened. *This is a terrific book,* he thought.

And the cook—assured that the meal would turn out a success after all and that he had a few undisturbed moments with his able assistant—relaxed, took Arlyce into his arms and kissed her on the lips. First lightly, then feeling her welcoming response, kissed her more deeply and savored the aromatic flavor of coriander that he found there.

An hour or two later after the scrumptiously satisfying dinner of chicken curry, *avil* (yogurt and vegetable dish), *satnbar* (like a South Indian stew), beans with coconut and mustard seeds and rice and more rice, and after Sandi had shown scintillating scenes from the island and the warm waters of the Gulf of California, which looked oh, so very inviting on this cold evening, Anil, Arlyce, Arun and Steve bravely bundled up to set out for the Coumar home in the red pickup.

It wasn't long before Pat heard again the muffled motor sound coming from the garage.

"Steve's home," she called.

Pat had talked to Steve a couple of times on the cellular since he had left and had reported already that Steve had not even tried to drive all the way to the Coumar house. He had stopped and parked at the bottom of the hill. He and Anil had piled the Coumar belongings, including their Christmas presents which had been stuffed into a garbage bag, onto a sled. Anil had carried Arun, and Steve and Arlyce had pulled the sled up to the house. The slushy, wet snow had come up to their knees but the Coumar family was safely back home at last. All but Cressie and Max, they would have to wait just a little longer before they, too, could come home.

Steve came into the family room, stood on the rug and wiped his hand over the top of his wet head. Some of the family stood, others sat and listened attentively like hideaways in a tornado shelter listening to what was left of the world as we once knew it.

"It's like riding on a washboard," reported Steve. "The streets are very bumpy from the ice but some of the snow is gone. There is a lot of water in places now. I'm glad to be back here." He reached down to undo his tennis shoe laces. His feet were soaking wet.

"We better get to bed, everybody. Pat has to work in the morning," I announced.

"Well, let's talk a minute about plans for tomorrow, okay? Do you think people can go out, Cok?" asked Pat.

"Maybe, if it's not flooding too much."

Doug bounced his fist on B.J.'s head and B.J. turned around to punch Doug's arm. The two scuffled backwards towards the kitchen.

"I hope we can go out," said Marge frowning at her two guys. "I think those two have a bad case of cabin fever; they're not used to staying in like this."

"Me either!" chimed in Ann. "Especially not on a Sunday!"

Chapter 24
Recess Time In-between Storms

To echo the author Thomas Wolfe in his autobiographical book, Look Homeward, Angel, *"It was my innocent wish to represent differing views without malice or prejudice."*

Like kids pouring out of school at recess time, our family poured out of the Cok home on Monday morning. It was the thirtieth of December, five days after the first snow had started, and at last there was a break in the storms.

Steven brought Pat to work. Awakened by the noise of the garage door rising and the pickup going, the Langels came out of their small home. Colter, naturally, bounded around. He was thrilled to be out in the early hour. Sandi, too, worried now about all the calories she had been eating, came out of the house and stretched to warm up for an early run. She was soon followed by Sophia and me wearing our sporty, new leisure suits. We were going off with Steven to 24 Hour Fitness where he regularly worked out to strengthen his shoulder muscles. Ann, finding no one in the house, leaned out of the door to see what all was happening.

Not everyone in the region awoke to such banal circumstances, however; far from it, in fact. "In the aftermath of two snowstorms and heavy rains, Seattle-area residents faced mudslides and sinkholes that damaged houses, washed out roads and sunk the tarmac of a gas station," the *Seattle Times* reported.

One scene, according to the *Times*, illustrated the tensions of dealing with mudslides. "All day, along a narrow, secluded lane, residents and city engineers waited for precarious slopes to collapse...and they did. Muddy streams periodically raced downhill, eating away at the saturated soil, leaving more than one expensive house sitting at the edge of an unstable cliff."

Nearby, on Ballinger Way in Lake Forest Park, a Shell gas station was sinking as a creek ate away a tunnel underneath it. Four cars of a Seattle-bound Burlington Northern Santa Fe freight train had derailed, the reporters said, after the tracks apparently separated in the softened soil. Two of the cars had turned over.

A 100-foot-wide wall of mud covered all four lanes of Highway 12 into Aberdeen. Yakima County was feeling the effect of its more- than-a-foot-of-snow. A warehouse collapsed producing a potentially dangerous cloud of ammonia gas.

Weather-related deaths in the region had climbed to at least twelve. A man was killed when a tree fell and crushed the roof of his car. His thirteen year-old son was in serious condition. A couple who planned to hunt ducks on the icy Columbia River was feared drowned and a traffic fatality was attributed to the weather in Skagit County. Flood warnings were in effect for as many as eleven rivers forcing the evacuation of hundreds of homes. The Red Cross, it was reported, had opened a shelter at the North Bend Senior Center.

Taking one thing with another, on the plus side, air traffic was moving better and many stranded travelers were finally reaching their destination. The bus service, too, was resuming more normally. Chains had been put on tires and 24-hour staffing had dug out the many sidelined buses. The commute in to work on the freeways was said to be slow and steady but some secondary roads and streets were still treacherous.

And, as ill luck would have it, the siege of the Northwest by unusual winter weather was not yet over. Forecasters predicted yet another major assault. An abnormal amount of heavy rain, they said, was expected for the following day, New Year's Eve. This time it was to be accompanied by strong winds. That was definitely not good news. With the ground fully saturated, they warned, the area could expect more flooding, mudslide damage and power outages.

Contrary to our expectations, Steven, having sleuthed out a route after he had dropped Pat off at the office, called her on the cellular to say we could make a trip to the mall. "Before the next storm hits," he said.

Pat called Sandi at about half-past-eleven and laid out the

scenario. "Okay, it's all set. You'll take two vehicles and go to the mall. Put some of the food that we've been keeping cool in the garage in the back of the car. Just in case. And be sure to put in a blanket with some wool hats and gloves."

"Mom, I don't think..." Sandi started to reason.

"Just do it, all right? Even if you think I'm being overly cautious. I can get off at noon. It's not very busy here, so one vehicle can come get me. We'll have Chinese food for lunch at the Mandarin Gate. After that, we'll go to Arlyce for tea. Anil was able to get in to work today so he won't be able to be there. Have to go back to work now. Bye."

Once in the mall our group, as if on cue, fanned out separately in all directions. It must have been that each of us craved a fix of anonymity, anonymity that would give a few blessed minutes of psychic relief. Relief, for instance, from maintaining vigilance over old fears, jealousies and insecurities that can so easily get sparked by a simple word or innuendo in a family. Relief from being back in the crucible in which one's mettle, one's very identity and form, is constantly in danger of being melted right back into the amorphous family soup from which emerged. And relief, one can surmise, from pushing down disappointment.

Hopes, expectations and self-acclaim had grown, you see, when our respective parties had been distant one from another for the length of a year or more. In that hiatus our devious, defensive minds had cleverly created versions of self, of the absent family members and of family life that were more ideal, more simpatico with the creator's, the self's, wishes than was true in reality.

Those fictitious hopes, expectations and that self-acclaim had been coming face-to-face, day after day with our human foibles. Quirks, failings, peculiarities, defects, and annoying habits were all being magnified in our prolonged, close quarters. In other words, we were just plain getting on each other's nerves. As in winter the power of the growth season slows and dissipates with the coming of cold nights, so too, the power of our hopes, expectations and self-acclaim was dissipating with the cooling of the familial ardor.

With the collective mental mechanisms shutting down, the inner volcanic steam was building. Were one to erupt, disappointment could flow unheeded from the core. Psychological debris, mud, fire and ash, dirty and dangerous, could harden and change the family landscape forever. Forever! This was the fear, was it not?

My former therapist, Joy—what a wonderful name for a therapist wouldn't you agree?—said that we often set ourselves up to be disappointed by the internal choices we make. The farther removed our expectations are from reality, the greater the risk of disillusionment. She stressed that we make choices, choices about what we think, what we expect and even about what we feel.

Be that as it may, making logical sense out of my brief flight in the mall was not of any interest to me right then. My brain, frankly, was mush and in the midst of strangers, alone and unknown, I allowed the emotions and tears to well up. I gave in to feeling my overwhelming tiredness. I knew it was the tiredness of having bronchitis and of pretending I was better than I was. I pretended I was fine so I didn't have to see the fear and the sadness about my condition in the family members' faces, so that I could give Sophia a break from the constant monitoring that is her lot as a caretaker and so that I could stay involved and still be relevant. It takes a lot of energy to pretend. I pushed my cheap infant stroller with the portable oxygen tank lying in it into Penney's and shielded myself best I could with the racks of clothes in the women's department. I took out a tissue, wiped my eyes, blew my nose and then found a restroom.

I was tempted to let out more of my emotions, to challenge the stoical norm. *But you have really done that one time too many,* I chided myself. *You do not want to blow it this time.* True, I needed to recoup, to avoid having red eyes and a red nose and to choose to think of how well things were going. To choose to feel satisfied with what was. *Oh, sigh, why couldn't I have grown up Italian or Jewish?* I thought ruefully. *Italians think nothing of raising their voices and spilling their guts. The Dutch build dykes to hold back the tide but the Jews have a whole public wailing wall.* Double sigh.

"Oh, gosh, I thought that was a real baby in your stroller when I first looked at it! Does your baby have a name?" an inane woman babbled as I washed my hands.

"That was *SO* funny!" she said to her friend on the way out of the restroom.

"Oh, God, why me?" I muttered.

B.J., being twelve, was the first to want family attention thus bringing the brief healing time of obscurity to a close. More than attention, he wanted some adult cash. Already, he had an eye on a ring that he might want to buy from one of the center aisle kiosks. He found Doug and began his best sales pitch.

Ann, worried when she could not see a familiar person, went looking for one. She found Sophia in the Hallmark store checking out Christmas cards and wrappings that were on sale. Ann put her hand through the crook of Sophia's arm and held on. The two, after strolling a while longer, found me sitting on a bench seemingly content to watch the passing people.

"There are some great sales on Christmas cards and wrapping, Tjaak, maybe we could..."

I cut her off abruptly, yet pleadingly. "Don't even go there, Soph, please. Remember, we have presents to take back."

"I was afraid you'd say that without even hearing me out," protested Sophia.

If Sophia were picked to be one of an elite corps like in the old war movies she would, without a doubt, be given the role of Scavenger. Back and forth to Maine and Arizona we have lugged an old green suitcase. In Maine it is loaded down with garden produce: carrots, beets and onions that Sophia cannot bear to leave behind. In Arizona special deals on vitamins, herbs, and spices from the popular Apache Junction health food store, The Good Earth, find their way into the suitcase. They join a "few items" from Hajji Baba, the Middle Eastern store in Tempe, The Body Shop at Superstition Mall and The Country Store at Sunlife or Viewpoint.

"Now, don't fight, girls," cautioned Ann whose ears, like Figgy's, can hear a conflict a mile away.

"We're not fighting, *Moeke*," Sophia assured her as we made our way back to the entrance of Nordstrom's for a latte. "I just say things sometimes. Greeks are like that. Tjaakje takes it too seriously."

I rolled my eyes but said nothing further because I saw Steven approaching from the other direction.

"Come, Lottie, what kind of latte shall we have this time?" asked Ann. "I love lattes!"

Marge, the one who had been doing some serious distancing and shopping, was the last to rejoin the group. Living in Rudyard, she does not have the opportunity to shop in a mall as often as the rest of us do, and B.J. at this age outgrows his clothes so quickly.

As we enjoyed our mocha lattes Ann said wistfully, "I wish this would not came to an end. I hate to think of it. Wouldn't it be nice if we could do this more often?"

"Yeah, it would," answered Marge slowly as guilt for not telling the total truth like a rat gnawed at the edge of her conscience.

Actually, I think Mom and Pat are not loners but the rest of us are. Dad was, too. A big part of it, I think, is that we are shy. Mom says she is shy, too, but she doesn't often show it.

After lunch B.J., Sophia and I went to see Glenn Close as Cruela in the movie "101 Dalmatians", while Ann, Pat and Marge shopped some more at the mall. When we reunited we made one last stop at Larry's, the import grocery. Sophia went in to buy a pint of fresh oysters which we had promised to take back to Mesa for the Griffees.

It surprised all of us that it was already very dark when we finished tea and were finally back in the car ready to return home. Without meaning to, we had all lingered a bit too long. First, we had chatted with Arlyce and played with Arun, and then Steve and Doug had gone to pull Cressie out of the snow bank with the pickup. That had taken a while, but at least she was now parked out of harm's way in the parking lot of QVC. We headed home in both the pickup and Explorer and were immediately ensnared in slow-moving, end-of-day traffic.

There was snow piled up on the sides of the streets. Here and there coal black water, which reflected the street and car lights, was pooled or flowing swiftly next to the equally dark pavement. The rain from the next storm had started sooner that predicted; it was already coming down very heavily. Black pavement glistened like something from the Twilight Zone as ripples of water, swept by the wind, repeatedly crossed it. Shortcuts, under the weather circumstances, Steven warned Sandi via the cellular, were out of the question.

"I hope we make it!" gasped Pat at a particularly perilous intersection.

"At least we won't be hungry if we get stranded. Anybody feel like eating or singing?" asked Sophia.

"No, not right now," retorted Ann sternly. Tension was written across her face. "We have to be careful."

Tjaakje C. Heidema

The cars moved slowly along. Suddenly, out of the dark from across the street loomed the figure of a woman. The bigger-than-life solitary soul was standing in the downpour and in Statue-of-Liberty-like fashion she held jumper cables high in the air.

"Oh, look," cried Sophia, "Can't we help her?"

"Shall I try to turn around?" Sandi called out.

"Sure!" "Yes!" voices chorused.

"Can we? Really?" asked Ann.

Despite Sandi's best efforts, by the time she could maneuver the Eggplant Mobile into position the woman had mercifully been rescued by a male Good Samaritan.

"That's better;" Sandi said, "we didn't really want to get wet anyway."

A few blocks later an impatient male in a yellow pickup started to push Sandi's buttons. He was obviously oblivious to the harrowing conditions around him and was doggedly tailgating the Explorer. Marge, sitting in the tight space behind the back seat, watched the pickup driver through the rear window. She could see from his tight-jawed expression that he was not just kidding. She found her cell phone and pretended to be talking and giving the man's license plate numbers. The tailgater, as if magically able to hear the conversation, backed off.

"Way to go, Marge!" called Sandi.

"Great idea!" Sophia chorused.

"Wow, that really worked on him," Marge beamed.

The wind was steadily picking up velocity. Black tops of huge pine trees swayed from side to side and here and there on sodden lawns lay large, broken branches from the previous snow storm. Sandi strained to see as rain lashed against the windshield.

"Can you believe this? In Seattle!" exclaimed Ann who was unable to make out forms in the glaring darkness.

"I'd hate to be driving in this alone," said Pat. "I'd be dead scared. I am now practically. I hate this section of Lake Forest Avenue. You can't see a thing. There are so many accidents here."

Everyone was quiet for a minute and then Sandi said, "We're doing fine, Mom. You don't have to worry so much. We're almost home."

"Home sweet home," echoed Ann with a wistful sigh.

328

Chapter 25
Holland and the Sea

Until nearly the end I viewed myself from a distance and used third person pronouns for myself. I was afraid to claim ownership.

U pon entering the kitchen I could see Ann sitting alone in the family room with a gloomy expression. "What's the matter with Mom?" I asked Pat.

"I have no idea," she responded. "She didn't say a word; just went in there without saying anything."

It was late the following morning on Tuesday, New Year's Eve. Ann was crocheting around a small hand towel and watching the television news. Most of Seattle was coping with varying degrees of flooding. A large roof sheltering boats in dry dock on the Edmonds Marina had completely collapsed. A house had slid down a hill and was teetering on the very edge of Interstate 5. Vast areas in the Northwest, in the state of Oregon as well as Washington, and in the city of Portland were covered by the deluge.

Ann was all too familiar with the impact that water can have on people's lives. In spite of the fact that she had always been a landlubber and a person who turned green the instant she sensed the movement of waves, the struggle against the sea was bred into her as it was into every Dutchman. Knowledge of the character of water as both friend and foe has been solemnly handed down through the centuries in the Netherlands.

Amazingly, one half of the Netherlands 13,104 square miles are lower than sea level! Passengers who land on the concrete platform at *Schipol*, the international airport at Amsterdam, are reminded of this remarkable fact by the words on the control tower: "Aerodrome level 13' below sea level". That is thirteen feet, not inches lower than the sea. Imagine, standing on land and looking up to see a thirteen-foot-high wall of water with a ship floating at the top! There are even lower lying areas that are as much as twenty-feet below sea level.

In Holland there is a nursery rhyme the first line of which is "Amsterdam, that large city, is built on piles". Houses in Amsterdam and Amstel, a smaller city next to Amsterdam, are all built on hundreds of thousands of piles. The royal palace actually stands on 13,659 piles (Miller 75)! The pilings are wood and wood has the property of staying intact and not rotting under water. If the subsoil water level should ever fall, that is, flow to a lower area, the tops of the pilings would be above water. If that were to happen, they would begin to rot spelling disaster for entire cities.

By 1200 A.D. the sea had claimed an estimated 100,000 lives. In 1287 that number was increased by another 50,000. In those earlier days, when a flood threatened, "Dike Peace," as it was called was automatically instituted. "Dike Peace" meant that all arguments and feuds were forgotten. Any person who broke the peace was killed and his body was used to patch a damaged dike, a harsh but necessary action taken by historically peace-loving people.

Holland is a small country that is the most densely populated country in the world. Jan Piet or *Pa* used to say that the Netherlands is one-thirteenth the size of Montana but has thirteen times as many people. Across Holland's northern and western borders lies Germany and across the south is Belgium; so as far back as the Middle Ages, as the number of inhabitants increased, the people Dutch looked to the east, to the sea to expand. Through clever control of water levels of both the sea and the freshwater rivers, the Rhine and the Meuse, the Dutch have been able to increase their acreage. Every square yard wrested from the greedy, grasping sea is a result of clear and hard reasoning enterprise which has evolved over the centuries.

The Romans began the first systematic work of building primitive dikes from 58 B.C. to 400 A.D. After the Romans the Frisians piled up dirt and clay into mounds called *terpen*. The *terpen* were high enough to stay out of water at high tide. On these they built houses, barns and eventually towns (Steffen 11-12).

By the late 1200s the windmill was being built. Plentiful wind turned the sails, which turned a scooper. The scooper lifted the water and hurled it across a dam. When the water was removed, another windmill would be built at a higher level and the draining repeated.

In these modern times of the twentieth century the Netherlands Central Organization for Applied Physics Research with its corps of engineers works everything out in workshops and laboratories. The first step in claiming land from the sea is to determine where to build a dam, better known in Holland as a dike. The ground is studied. The precise course of currents and tidal movements is predicted and measured. This step may involve thousands of calculations and take years. If the dike is meant to stop high-water levels with powerful sea breakers and heavy gales, the top wall, of course, has to be higher and wider than at places where calmer water has to be kept back. Once the location is determined, it is marked by posts. The construction must begin in the spring, and by late fall work on the dike must be advanced enough to ward off destruction from winter storms.

Between the rows of posts that have been placed for location, a gully is formed by dredging away soft subsoil in the middle and dropping it on either side. When more firm ground is reached, boulder-clay, which does not absorb water, is dumped into the gully by hopper-barges. Hopper-barges are more or less square vessels with a bottom that has flaps to allow for dumping of the load. Sand is washed over each layer of boulder-clay to fill in spaces (33-35).

As the floor of the gully rises the embankments are also supported with boulder-clay. Pilings are driven in for toe structure. To protect the embankments from attack by the restless water, huge mattresses or wattle mats made of poles intertwined with twigs, reeds and branches are lowered underwater on either side. These mattresses are weighed down with rubble such as a mass of rock pieces. Above the water thick bundles of sticks are bound together and tied to one another into what is called fascine matting. This matting is staked down and covered with more rubble. Finally this layer is covered by basalt (a hard, dense volcanic rock) and brick.

The sea has a weak side. This is when the high tide is at its lowest level or, in other words, when there is the least rise and fall of water. This is known as neap tide. In contrast, spring tide is when the high tide is at its highest. Neap tide comes twice a month, in the first and third quarters of the moon. Also during both neap and spring tides, four times per 24 hours, every day, ebb or flow comes to a standstill when the course is reversed. Putting the two together means this: at neap tide when the sea is at a standstill it is vulnerable. This is its weak side (7-8).

The fleet of boats—in one such instance the fleet consisted of 27 dredgers, 13 cranes and transporters, 60 tugs and 132 barges (21)—and workers stand by ready to go into action. At the precise moment that the weak side of the sea presents itself, the strong side of humanity applies its utmost exertion. It is at this time that the dike is finally and festively closed. After it has been properly closed, a road will most likely be built along the top of the dike.

Circular dikes are built creating artificial islands. Channels for conducting water across a dike or from a canal are made with reinforced concrete and carried on reinforced concrete piles. They are called sluices. The sluices are controlled with double-heavy steel gates, one on the sea side, one on the reservoir or river side. These gates open with low tide letting water drain, and close with the pressure of high tide keeping the salt water out. In this way water drains from a large area.

The enormity of some of these projects is astounding. Power stations and concrete factories are built on site to support the work. Ships convey raw materials. *Telpher* line, which is an overhead rail, carries suspended hoppers that dump 360 tons per hour. Gigantic cranes are especially built for the project. Engine rooms are built from where the gates are hydraulically operated.

To further remove sea water from the land, ditches and canals are built. Though the classic presence of the windmills still outlines the Dutch landscape, they are monuments to the past. Electrical pumps now move the water from a lower to a higher level.

Saltwater lakes and swamps, even seas, are drained. Whole islands cease to exist. Fisheries are eliminated. An example is the *Afsluitdijk* (Close-off Dike) which is 20 miles long and almost 100 yards wide. Where formerly there was the *Zuider Zee* (Zuider Sea), there is now a major highway connecting northern Holland with the eastern coast. 560,000 acres of new land was won with this dike and 300,000 acres of fresh water called *Ijsselmeer* (Ijssel Lake) was created. The Netherlands has with its many projects enlarged its territory by more than ten percent!

Amongst foreigners there is a myth about Peter, a Dutch boy, who all through a long, dark night held his thumb in a hole in a dike to save a town. This is pure fiction and an absurdity created by Mary Mapes Dodge in *Hans Brinker and the Silver Skates*. Some men in the tourist trade decided to capitalize on this American tale. They had a statue made of a young lad. Complete with wooden shoes, thumb and dike, it can be found in Spaarndam. This piece of bronze is meaningless to the Dutch and is shunned as an outrage by them. It distorts reality and minimizes the many sacrifices and great suffering of the people (17-18).

The sea does not give up her land willingly and fights to get it back. Floods happen and conquered land is lost. The latest of these disastrous floods happened in 1953 when the full moon at spring tide conspired with the 100-miles-per-hour wind to create higher and higher waves. Not able to withstand the twelve-foot wall of raging water, the dikes broke at hundreds of places, sending people up trees and onto rooftops. 1,800 people and 50,000 cows, horses, pigs and sheep drowned. 50,000 homes were under water and 130 towns were demolished. The vengeful sea repossessed 360,000 acres of fertile land (37-38).

This blow was felt across the world. Jan Piet, Anje and we kids listened to it in horror on the world news on the radio in America. Later we read about it and saw the devastating pictures in the newspapers that our relatives sent. None of our immediate relatives had been in danger, praise God; nonetheless, all Dutch people grieved the loss of members of the Dutch family.

In response to this latest onslaught by the sea, the Dutch began their counterattack and executed a 25-year plan that resulted in shortening the 1100 mile coastline by 435 miles. That means less chance of flooding, less loss of life and fertile soil. As long as there is the mighty sea to struggle against and as long as there is a sea bed to claim, the stubborn Dutch will continue along these lines (38-41).

However, the story does not end here. Turning a seabed into fertile soil requires a similar patient, persistent approach. The land areas from reclamation are called polders. Sand, silt and boulders during thousands of years of pressure from the seawater are compressed into a rich boulder-clay known as diluvial clay. This clay plus a fertile loam are found after the water is drained.

Reed is sown to impede the growth of other tough, and, therefore, undesirable vegetation. The reed also helps to ventilate the soil and so promotes evaporation. In this way damp ground dries out faster. The reed can be removed fairly easily. By growing certain successive crops, the sea salt in the waterways and soil is reduced and eventually reaches normal levels. The result is a rich soil for crops and grazing land to support Holland's many dairies.

Not until the third generations do the reclaimed lands start to pay. For every farm that is developed into 30, 60, 90 or 120-acre plots many candidates apply. Knowledge, skill and capital are the criteria. After investing so much to prepare this precious land, care is taken so that it does not get into the hands of unqualified people.

Along with selecting certain farmers for new polders, others are selected, too, adding a certain number of doctors, storekeepers, bakers and others in the mix. They even build in an old look with streets at strange angles and highways with interesting curves. "God made the world but the Dutch made Holland," said Descartes, the French philosopher.

The salt in the sea is as much a force as the sea itself. A fact of life in our times is the melting of the polar ice cap which causes the level of the sea to rise and the land to shrink. The nether lands are shrinking at a rate of one-and-a-half feet per century. In four decades the tongue of salt near Rotterdam has moved inland ten additional miles! Salt with its chlorine content is poisonous to plant life. It threatens agriculture and market-gardening. In dairy farming if there is too much salt in the grass and water the milk-yield diminishes strongly. Too much chlorine in milk or water makes it unsuitable for human consumption.

Salty seawater seeps under dunes and dikes. It enters through locks, sluices, reservoirs and canals. Twice a day millions of cubic feet of salt water flows into the country. The water also returns to the sea twice daily but much of the salt is left behind. The best way that the Dutch have found to combat this problem is to add fresh water. Rainfall which is about 28 inches annually is collected. Dams in rivers restrain and redistribute fresh water coming down from the mountains of Europe via the Rhine River. Trees, too, are a precious resource. The government owns most of them. Each tree that dies or gets burned is replaced with a new one (49-53).

"Luctor et emergo", I struggle and emerge. This is a Latin motto that used to be on Dutch coins. In a coat of arms from Zeeland the Dutch lion breasts the waves, and, so too, in her own way, Anje

struggles to keep her head above water on this morning. She watches the disasters on the television as her own sea of discontent pounds against her dike built of faith and determination. She is tired of staving off the gales of envy and waves of loneliness. Yearning has engulfed her and the poisonous salt of despair reaches ever further into her bones and organs.

I am old, children. Do you know that I am old? The question clanks back and forth against the thinning walls of her skull. Today, Ann is ending another year and is blessed to begin a new one. How is it then, in the midst of her children and grandchildren on this day that she feels so terribly abandoned and alone? She is as always awash between cultures, between time periods, past and future. Everyone has someone; she has no one. Yet, ironically, she despises and thinks with dread about the rapidly approaching time when she will have to tear herself away from this family wherein she experiences this poignant painful loneliness.

For almost forty years she has grieved her soul mate on this New Year's Eve day. *Will Jan Piet be there when I die and go to heaven? Will it be like it was before and even better?* On this day, like dry land in the Seattle area, the sustaining answer of yes, the oft-repeated answer of hope is out of her reach. She watches sadly as rain pours and houses slide from their foundations.

"Mom, why don't you go into the living room while I vacuum," Pat suggested. "This room is filthy! Do you mind?"

"No, dear, I don't mind."

Ann gathered her things and Pat clicked the remote control making the desolate images disappear.

Chapter 26
Cool Stories

One day the anonymity of the third person perspective felt deceitful. I changed my chapters to the first person and was blissfully happy about it.

"Tjaakje, tell me some of those cool stories you told me once. Will you?" pleaded Brandon. "I am so bored!"

B.J. was on his knees on the living room carpeting and annoyingly flipping an occasional brick down the *sjoelbak* that was still lying on the long couch. I was sitting on the short couch peeling and cutting into wedges a few red apples on a plate in my lap.

"You mean the one about the man who lived on the other side of the pasture across Camp Creek who had the long-barreled rifle?" I responded nonchalantly. "The man who had one good eye and the socket sunken way in on the other one because someone had shot his eye out, is that one?"

"Oh, Lottie, what are you talking about now?" asked Ann tersely as she entered the room.

"Yeah, that's the one! That's the one! Tell me, okay?" pressed B.J. eagerly.

"The one where Sharon Brouwer and I went onto his property and broke into his old shed where there were a ton of old comic books? And then this one-eyed guy with the sunken socket all of a sudden was standing there with his shot-gun telling us he could smell us and asking us what we were doing on his land? You mean that one, Beej?"

"Yes, come on, Tjaakje, tell it right like you did the first time," B.J. pressed.

"Or do you want the one where John and I hid in the porch cupboard? When we emptied the stuff like brown pear cores, dried bread crusts and crumpled-up wax paper out of our lunch buckets onto the kitchen floor, messed up the rugs and tipped over the kitchen chairs to make it look like there had been a struggle and a kidnapping? And when our parents came home and started worrying and were going to call the police and when we jumped out of the cupboard all laughing and everything and they didn't think it was a bit funny? And when we had to go to bed without supper? That one?"

"Oh, that's a good one. Tell it again! Better this time, please! Come on, Tjaakje." B.J. had come to stand in front of me and was hitting me softly on my arm.

"Listen, Beej, I might have a better idea. Since you already know those stories, I think you need a new one. *Oma* (Grandma) has some great stories. Don't you, Mom?"

"I guess so. If you think so anyway." Ann settled herself into one of the easy chairs and reached across for a wedge of apple.

"Tell him the one about you and *Vrouw* van Ketten in wartime. That's a good one."

"*Ja?* O.K. Well, B.J., how shall I start? We lived in the Netherlands, in the old country in wartime. There were German soldiers in Thesinge in our town, our village, who tried to get young boys, the seventeen and eighteen-year-old boys."

"Why?" asked B.J. He had slid to the floor and was leaning back against the couch.

Marge and Sandi strolled in and decided to join the group. Marge squeezed in next to the *sjoelbak*; Sandi sat on the short couch with me.

"Start over, please, would you, Grandma? So I can get in on the beginning," requested Sandi.

I quickly reiterated what Mom had said, then urged her to go on with the story.

"Well, one evening I was going upstairs in our house.

I don't know why exactly. Get something maybe. The window on top of the stairway was covered, darkened with a dark shade so that no light could get out. Everybody was ordered to do that. There were no lights outside either. Everything was always dark during wartime. The window upstairs behind the shade was open; it was summertime. I heard some noise. A man's voice said that the German soldiers were by the neighbors. I quick told my husband. You see, the voice out there was our policeman. Hoekstra was his name. We were in contact with Hoekstra a lot. He was on our side really but he had to be in service with the Germans. The Germans didn't know he was on our side."

Ann sat up straight. She held her hands up. They were tightly clasped with fingers interlaced. At times she twisted them back and forth or wrung her hands like she was applying hand lotion.

"My husband, your grandfather, grabbed his bike with the *surrogaat* tires."

"What kind of tires?" queried Sandi.

"*Surrogaat.* They had just a strip of rubber. Some people didn't even have rubber but used other things. There was no air in the tire. There was no other kind of tires that we could buy then in wartime. My husband hurried to *klunder,* an area on the edge of the village that he could get to on a cinder path, to warn as many families as he knew who were hiding young men or boys."

Pat had come in and was perched on the piano bench. Ann continued.

"I went out of the house to tell my neighbor lady *Vrouw* van Ketten and she was already standing in the street. She told me that the soldiers had taken her husband and one of the two boys that they were hiding, put them in the vehicle and took them away off to Groningen, the city. Together we started walking into Thesinge to do the same as my husband, to warn families.

"Didn't you say once that *Vrouw* van Ketten had bare feet and that her feet were so black?" I interrupted.

Ann laughed. "*Ja, Vrouw* van Ketten had bare feet but they were not dirty. That was *Vrouw* Omkes, one of the families whose door we knocked on, the lady who came to the door. Later on *Vrouw* van Ketten and I would talk and laugh about that lady's terrible black toenails. I will never forget them!" She laughed some more.

"Go on with the story please, *Oma,*" begged Brandon.

"Okay, dear. As we two ladies walked in the dark we could hear the German soldiers sneaking around the *bosjes,* bushes. We talked it over what to do if they would find us. You see we had a curfew from the Germans and we were not supposed to be out on the

338

streets after it became night time. We whispered to one another and I said to her, 'You start crying. *Dou moar net zo als dou helemaal van streek bis.'*"

"Tell me what that means!" B.J. cried in earnest.

"Just act like you are completely upset," offered Pat.

"Just say you are completely upset," repeated Ann," and I will say to them, if we are stopped, that I am helping my friend to get home."

Ann's dark mood of the morning had vanished. She was a great storyteller. Through wrinkled and fragile skin, one could see the bright, shining, young student sitting alertly poised in her chair holding the attention of her audience. There was something so classy about how she conducted herself. The way she sat with her back so straight, proud, feet together, hands clasped. A girl of breeding, one could have said.

Perhaps she was a rare testimony to the benefits of not being overly educated. She had no cynicism. She did not speak with a political voice. She still was the eager school student, the teacher's pet. She struggled over finding the right English word and it was her struggle that added tension and drama to the story. She reached and hoped to pull out a word that she may have read or heard that would fit. In those moments there was a pureness about her. One could glimpse a light in her, a path of glory untouched by the horrors of the war of which she spoke.

"After a while we went back to *Vrouw* van Ketten's home," she continued. "Oh, oh! There was not a drawer untouched in her house, everything was upset!" Ann clapped her hands together loudly one time. "And the picture of the Queen, Queen Wilhelmina from Holland, was stepped on, and in a million pieces. It was! On the floor! I couldn't believe it, children!"

Our small group was spellbound; she continued.

"The second boy had run into the fields, not been found yet. So, you can imagine. Two German soldiers stayed with *Vrouw* van Ketten to wait for him to come home. She said to me to go home, go home and she would take good care of the two soldiers."

"Later she told me then. She made them first pretty comfortable by heating up the stove nice and warm, and a little warmer, and offered them a drink of alcohol. They drink. *Ja*, a little more and still a little more, and a little warmer and pretty soon

339

those two are falling fast asleep."

"Then she very quiet, so quietly, put Jim, that was the boy's name, she put Jim's clothes and necessities ready setting by the back door. So when he came at dawn, by the back door she whispered to him not to come in. He was cold and wet and shivering, but, go, go where he came from. Go back!"

"*Ja* then. The soldiers woke up in the morning, shocked, ashamed and they left for town."

"What happened to her husband and the boy the Germans took?" asked Sandi.

"He, her husband van Ketten, was lucky to come home again in a couple of days. But the boy they kept. He had to go to the camps in Germany. The other one, Jim de Gooyer, that one in the field, came by us the next day. He stayed in our bedroom in the daytime and in nighttime he was in the hay and we occupied the bedroom. For three weeks we took care of him. Then we found another place for him in the province of Utrecht."

"Do you think that Hoekstra was warning you that night on purpose?" inquired Pat. "I sure don't remember this."

"*Ja*, sure," answered Ann. "He was talking louder out in the street so we maybe would hear him."

"What would they do with the boys if they caught them?" asked Brandon who had been listening attentively.

"I don't know so much about that. I think make them work for them and go in their army. And if they don't want to do that then they maybe keep them in the camps and clean the toilets and so."

"Didn't Dad have a radio he wasn't supposed to have?" Pat asked.

"*Ja*. He had a radio and he listened to it. You remember that correctly."

"Knowing that he listened to it when he wasn't supposed to really scared me," Pat added.

Pat's early childhood had been cruelly twisted during the five years of the Nazi occupation in the Netherlands and in Thesinge. For instance, there were the times when people were not permitted to use electricity. On those dark nights she had watched scary shadows moving on the walls. They were created by the flickering of the flame in the *tootlampke (oil* lamp) but she had never been quite certain of their harmlessness.

Sweeping Away the Sand

At first, after Pat had come to the United States, she would curl up in terror behind a couch and scream at the sound of thunder. It reminded her of the drone of the German *Luftwaffe* that flew overhead at night. The planes had usually been on their way to London, but, sometimes, there were bombings in Groningen, the closest large Dutch city only ten miles away. And rarely, but it happened, a bomb exploded nearby.

It had been Jan Piet and Anje's custom during the air raids to take us children from our beds, where we had been sleeping fully clothed in warm things, and to hustle us off to the connecting barn. Built with bigger beams the barn was presumed to be safer but one could not be certain of that either. Pat had huddled with our family in the dark, cold cow stall and tried to sleep on a bed of hay until it was quiet overhead. She remembers the sound of the horse stomping his hoof on the concrete floor and feeling the boards next to her move when the horse moved.

She also remembers very well that the body of a classmate's brother was found in the basement after a bomb hit. Everybody talked about it.

Such unrelenting fear in a helpless child takes its toll. So many years later, her unconscious still asks, where will the bomb fall tonight? What more horrible thing might happen?

In addition to her fear of thunder, she has an inordinate fear of flying. Despite taking a class to learn to counter her anxiety and despite taking tranquilizers when she goes aloft, she is still plagued with the phobia.

"Wasn't there something about a little boy getting killed once and Dad had to go out to find him?" asked Pat trying to recall days that she, for the most part, had successfully blocked from her memory.

"Oh, that was so, so terrible, too terrible," said Ann slowly shaking her head and getting a faraway look in her eyes.

"There was a bomb that hit a house. The couple and a little girl were not hurt but their little boy was gone. Some men, your father too, your grandfather had to go with buckets walking over a field to pick up bits and pieces of this little boy's body. Oh, your father was so, so sick over that. That was terrible. Awful." Ann shook her head back and forth again to ward off the pictures and sounds.

"Tell them about the time the Gestapo when they-" I thought

better of finishing my sentence and leaned forward instead to whisper it to Mom.

"Oh, those German soldiers. *Och, och.*"

Fifty years after the experiences and Ann's brain still ticked out alert messages when she said those words. She felt some of the resulting adrenaline rush and made the most of it. With a shiver, she pressed her elbows into her sides, hands up, clasped even more tightly together.

For a few moments she looked a bit like a bridled horse held in check by a tight rein: the quiver, the stiffening, the intensity in her mouth and eyes, the jaw thrust forward and teeth clinched. She let out a slightly seething breath, closed her eyes and shook her head with disbelief and rage. The onlookers could easily imagine this woman taking on a deserving Nazi barehanded and leaving him in a rumpled pile with some major injuries. Time had erased nothing. It had instead created space in which the anger fermented year after year.

"Germans! I want nothing to do with them! People don't know what all they did. One night, it was about bedtime at my mother's home on the farm in Baflo," she began. "They were having coffee, my mother and my younger sisters and Tjaard and the boys that they were hiding. So as not to have so many cups and saucers on the table, they washed the coffee cups of the boys and put them all back in the cupboard as soon as they were empty. That is what they always did."

"My mother felt a little nervous then that night and she said to the boys that she thought it was time for them to go to the back to their hiding place. She hurried them a little and so they left. They were gone just out the door and *maar zo* (just like that). *Patz* (Crash)!!"

Ann's hands flew up, one a little higher than the other as if to shield her face and body. The group flinched with her sudden movements. Oh, she was so good at this.

"*De raam splintered!* The window splintered," Ann exclaimed. "A soldier's long, big, black boot stepped through the glass right into the room! And, then the whole man stepped in too, right through the kitchen window!"

Brandon's mouth stood open as he watched *Oma*. He was wide-eyed as he tried to imagine what stepping through a window might be like.

"He stepped right through the window from the outside?" he reiterated.

"Yes, dear, right from the outside. There was glass everywhere!"

"What did he do then?" asked Brandon. "What did he say?"

"The man, the German solder was very mad. He wanted to know, 'Where are you hiding them? Where are the boys? We know they are here!'"

Sandi stretched her arm far out towards one or the other as she doled out wedges of apple. Marge watched B.J.'s reaction closely. These war stories had been scary fairy tales for Marge a time or two when she was young. We other kids, her siblings, had coaxed our reluctant parents years ago into telling the stories. Now, it was B.J.'s turn to hear them. She was glad he was a little older than she had been.

"What did they say? Did they tell him? Were they scared?" B.J.'s voice was urgent.

"Sure, they were scared. Of course. But they did not let on where they were. They stayed calm and said, 'Boys, what boys? What are you talking about? We know nothing of boys.'"

"Wow," exclaimed Brandon and then whistled impressively through his front teeth.

"Then the man, and there were others too now that had come in the doors and window, they looked over everything. Everything, everything! They pulled the *boederij* apart."

"Did they find the boys?" asked Sandi.

"No. They did not find the boys. So many times they looked, thirteen times they came and turned it all upside down and they never found the boys. There was a stall in the barn that had lots of old, broken, dusty things in it from over the years, like harnesses, milking stools, milk cans and so forth. Underneath those things were some loose boards that covered a small space. The boys crawled in the space on their stomachs and pulled everything back over them. The Germans never figured it out."

"There were soldiers that stayed in our house too," said Pat. "At the end of the war there were two Canadian soldiers who stayed with us. Right, *Moeke?* I remember their big packs, helmets and guns laying on the floor."

"That is true. I can't believe that you remember these things,

Pat. We better stop now. If you ask me to say more, children, we will be here all night and we better not do that."

"I want to be a pilot in a war time", ventured Brandon.

"Honey, no, don't ever say that." Ann implored. "You don't know what you are talking about. War is terrible. I hope you never have to be in war."

"Well, this has been interesting but it's time to move on, everybody," announced Pat as she stood up. "I came in here to tell you that we're having leftovers again. I put them on the table and the table is set so I think we're ready to go, okay?"

"Yes, I'm starved!" exclaimed Sophia who had just come into the room. "I came down and it was so quiet down here. I wondered what you all were doing."

Trailing behind the rest as we filed out of the room, B.J. wrapped his arm around his grandmother's waist and her arm encircled his shoulders.

"I liked those stories, *Oma*. They were so-o-o cool,"

"*Ja*? You liked them, dear?"

"Oh, yeah. They were scary. I loved them."

Chapter 27
Ollie Bollen

The name Tjaakje, someone told me, may be a derivative of the French Huguenot name of Isaac, the son of Abraham. The Huguenots went to Germany to seek religious freedom. Such is the complexity of Europe, the world, our families and each of us.

P at pushed the telephone off-button and quickly reported what she had learned. "Verna says the church service is at seven-thirty so we have to hurry. It is a communion service and it will take a little longer than usual. Mom, are you ready? It's raining cats and dogs out so we have to allow some extra time to get there. I've taken the last of the leftovers from the hood of the car in the garage and from the refrigerator and put them on the table so, everybody, just help yourselves. If you need to add some vegetables or applesauce just get them from the freezer. Steven, did you get the fan out of the attic yet? Eileen's deep-fat fryer is on the table in the kitchen. Can you people think of anything else you might need?"

"We need to have the Dutch recipe book," I said as I tried fruitlessly to wind up obstinate tubing in order to get it out of the flow of traffic coming towards the dining room.

"Would it be better to wind that up in a figure eight? It might not get so twisted," suggested Steve.

"Someone in the oxygen supply business has come up with this swivel which is supposed to help keep this tubing from twisting. I've tried the figure eight thing but, you know, it doesn't seem to make a difference."

"Which one, Lottie?"

"What?"

"Which cookbook do you use? The green or the yellow one?" urged Pat.

"I use the blue and white one. It's pretty thin. You know the one I'm talking about?"

"Oh, that one. I never use that one. I wouldn't have any idea where that one is. It's got to be here somewhere."

Pat put a kitchen chair against the stove then stood on the chair to look behind the row of well-used cookbooks.

"We didn't think of yeast," she gasped. Do you need yeast?"

"No, we don't need yeast."

Sophia, seeing that some of the food needed to be heated, was making trips back and forth between us two to the microwave.

Steven, Sandi and Ann, having been robbed of their church services on Sunday, stood ready and eager to go to the New Year's Eve service.

"May we all have a *zalig uiteinde* (blessed year's end)," said Ann in a rare quiet moment.

Pat found the correct cookbook and as soon as they were out of the door the rest had a quick bite to eat. Then we sprang into action. It was time to make the *ollie bollen* (the traditional Dutch New Year's Eve fritters with currants)!

Margaret, following the designated recipe, prepared the dough. It wasn't the first time she had made *ollie bollen* and when she put her mind to it she also made a very tasty *krientje brej* (a dessert made with barley, currants, sugar and a red wine or raspberry jello). She could cook but it just wasn't her thing. Especially not when there were those around who liked to cook.

"In Maine the first time Tjaakje made *ollie bollen* something wasn't right. They tasted terrible," recalled Sophia who was emptying bottles of vegetable oil into the deep-fat fryer as well as another deep pan on the stove. "Even the seagulls that eat everything wouldn't touch them."

I was peeling and dicing a couple of Granny Smith apples at the kitchen table. They would be added to the dough along with the currants.

"That was the first time I ever tried to make *ollie bollen* without Mom around," I admitted. "It was a disaster."

After a few minutes Doug set up and started the big fan in the kitchen, directing the air out towards the opened slider. Rain could be heard pelting down onto the deck.

"About time for you to go in the other room," he counseled me. "I can start to smell the oil, probably not too good for you to stay in here."

"Oh, boo hoo, Tjaakje, I'll come visit you," wailed B.J. dramatically as he threw his arms around me.

"Don't disappear, okay, Douglas?" enjoined Marge. "We're going to need you at the pan on the stove. Sophia can't do both of them."

Marge folded the apple pieces and currants in with the dough and then plopped a spoonful of the mixture into the hot oil. It sizzled festively. After half a minute or so she reached in with a spoon and nudged the *ollie boll*. It flipped over to its other side. When both sides were a little more than golden brown she removed it. The fritter had puffed up to about the size of an egg but with a more irregular shape. It even had an interesting tentacle. She cut the *ollie boll* in half to see if the interior was cooked and took it to the dining room to coat it with powdered sugar. Then she handed it to Sophia who did the taste test.

"Excellent!" announced Soph.

Soon both fryers were in full operation and browned *ollie bollen* draining on paper towels in a 9 by 13 cake pan were being shuttled by Brandon from the kitchen to the dining room. I coated each with a layer of powdered sugar and placed it on a plate. B.J. brought the full plates back to the kitchen table.

"Hellllooo, we're back!"

"Already?!" Marge and Sophia chimed in unison.

"Oooo, it smells good in here!"

"How's it going everybody?"

The churchgoers in their finery filed back into the kitchen.

"We were late! Verna was wrong! Church started at seven. We walked in half way through the service! I was so embarrassed!" squealed Pat.

Fingers reached for *ollie bollen as* their owners talked. A fine dusting of powdered sugar fell onto bibs and lapels. Soon all of us were congregated at the kitchen table, some standing, some sitting.

"Ummm, delicious!"

"Its great to have traditions, isn't it?" said Sophia.

"I'll start a pot of coffee," offered Pat.

"I've had about twenty of them already," boasted B.J.

"Anil called. He would like us to go there for a pasta lunch tomorrow," I chimed in as I licked a finger. "I didn't make it definite. We'll have to call him later when we decide what we're planning for tomorrow, okay?"

Sophia handed me a napkin.

"You know what I really need, Soph, is a *schuddeldouk*," I said. "My hands are all sticky."

"You know what a *schuddeldouk* is, Sophia?" asked Ann.

"Oh, sure, *Moeke*," answered Sophia. "I couldn't live with Tjaakje and not know what a *schuddeldouk* is."

"On the farm when they were kids John and Tjaakje were always throwing the *schuddeldouk* at each other. Those two! We couldn't make them stop."

"It took careful strategy," I explained. "You had to make sure that you were the one who had the *schuddeldouk* right next to your hand when Dad prayed. Then as soon as he said, 'Amen,' you had to sail that thing. I remember once John let loose of it and you, Mom, had just opened the refrigerator. It whizzed over my head and into something in the frig behind me. You didn't think that was too funny."

"Oh, no. That was not funny. It was always some kind of trouble with you two, I know that." There was a pause.

"It would have been nice if John and Joyce could have been here too, huh?" added Ann.

We nodded our silent agreement.

The churchgoers decided to change clothes then and on their way up the stairs Ann added, "We should do something for John's birthday. It is coming up pretty soon, you know. January 2 is the day."

The mess of making the *ollie bollen* was cleared up and we reconvened in the family room for coffee and a few spirited rounds of *sjoelin*. A few minutes before the magical moment of midnight Steve turned up the volume on the television set. In unison we excitedly counted down the seconds with Dick Clark and all the people in Times Square.

"Three! Two! One! Zero!"

The ball hit the mark and there were exuberant hugs and kisses all around.

348

"Happy New Year!"

"Gelukkig Niewjaar! Ik bin toch zo bliet dat ik heir bin mit u allemaal!
(I am so happy that I am here with all of you!)"

"Yuk, I hate all this slobbering!" protested Brandon.

"Oh, B.J., I forgot you!" cried Sandi planting yet another kiss
on his face.

"Good grief," he spluttered. "Stop, already!"

"One more game?" asked Ann hopefully.

Chapter 28
It's CHIPS but It's Not Potato Chips

Historic ethnicity, geography, religion and culture are woven into the design of my fabric.

O ld MacDonald had a farm ei, ei o...," Arlyce washed her hands and wrists to the jaunty beat in her mind until she came to the end of the verse. Then she rinsed thoroughly, shook her hands free of the excess water and dried them carefully on a paper towel. Studies at the Cancer Hospital and Institute of Puget Sound (C.H.I.P.S.), known as "Chips" to those who had connections to it, had shown that hand washing in-between patients for the length of time it took to sing "Old MacDonald" was highly effective in reducing spread of microorganisms. Another study along the same line had concluded that face masks were ineffective after just fifteen minutes. They were rarely used anymore. Sometimes, this conscientious nurse still felt naked or guilty of a crime when working with a patient without wearing a mask.

Double- and triple-checking, Arlyce, trim and professional-looking in white uniform, took a last look at the settings on the intravenous pump at the bedside. She was extremely careful not to touch anything, then walked hastily to another bed on the far side of the large, open room, visually checking a couple of other patients in recliners as she went by. *Orrie might be about ready to go home,* she thought. He was, fortunately, not having any ill effects from the drugs, as had been expected.

Covered with several white, flannel, bed blankets, the bald-headed woman in the bed was still having chills. Her body was visibly shaking. Arlyce reached for the digital thermometer. The fever could be part of the rash that had brought this patient in or it could be the first sign of a much bigger problem. As yet, she was an FUO, fever of undetermined origin. Sometimes an FUO could go from bad to much worse in a matter of minutes and Arlyce, a veteran in bone marrow transplantation nursing, knew to keep a close eye.

When she was first employed by the Institute she had spent many years in the in-hospital aspect. Now she was in the new outpatient clinic where she had been for over a year. With all that experience under her belt she was a respected presence and voice amongst staff. Arlyce was confident but she was never comfortable; she knew there was way too much on the line to allow comfort.

Patients in her outpatient unit first underwent high dose chemotherapy and then total body irradiation. Both strategies were last resort attempts to kill cancer cells before the ruthless cells killed the patient. Unfortunately, the drastic assault on the immune system killed not only the abnormal cells but healthy cells too. Without the healthy, defensive cells standing guard, so to speak, the person was vulnerable to all sorts of opportunistic bacterial and viral infections.

The next step in the process was to start the immune system up again. Patients were categorized as either allogeneic or autologous. The allogeneic were given the bone marrow from a relative or a non-relative donor. This donated, healthy bone marrow given intravenously would reproduce healthy cells able to destroy harmful substances including, hopefully, any remaining cancer cells.

The potential was great but—ever to be free again from cancer—the allogeneic had a second ordeal to overcome. Donor bone marrow might or might not accept its new body. It was unpredictable. All donor recipients, therefore, had to take immunosuppressive drugs to minimize the chances of the body being rejected by the new cells. Unfortunately, the drugs were still far from foolproof. Like a high school football game between neighboring teams, Graft versus Host, the rivalry was intense.

The autologous, in contrast, had a portion of their own bone marrow and stem cells harvested and stored at a time of remission prior to the chemotherapy treatments. Those stored cells then were returned to the patient after the treatments. That meant the autologous did not have the rejection worry. Instead, they had the reintroduction-of-cancer worry. Harvested cells could still harbor the obnoxiously aggressive cancerous cells.

These two scenarios, allogeneic and autologous, presented then a plethora of medical and nursing challenges both in diagnosing and in treating. Nurses spending more time than the doctors in observing the subtleties, often sorted out the processes and patterns.

Hattie, a fifty-year-old nurse administrator from Wisconsin with the diagnosis of multiple myeloma, was allogeneic and had been through all of this before. It was her second transplant. Not many patients wanted to come back for another round of uncertainty, mouth sores, nausea, vomiting, cramping, extreme fatigue, depression and whatever else. It took a very strong will to live through it and an even stronger one to do it twice.

"Pr-r-rett-ty bad timing on th-h-is one," Hattie chattered. "New-ww Year's E-ve. W-w-we should p-p-party but I've got such a headache." She could barely get the words out as the chills took hold of her.

Her face, moon-shaped and puffy from the immunosuppressive drugs and with a greenish-yellow cast from the chemotherapy, was uncommonly flushed. Her eyes were a little glassy and filled with inner torment. They betrayed the brave exterior.

Inevitably, Arlyce knew—and she could hear it in Hattie's voice—when a patient was weakened by a fever, the demons rushed in. There was the ever present guilt over wrecking a special evening for her family, the self-doubt about the decision to put everyone through this again and the tremendous dread welling up over what this episode of fever meant. The demons would fight with one another to be the one to undermine this tough woman's resolve. Hattie's long-time husband, Eric, and a grown daughter sat nearby in straight chairs, shoulders sagging discouragingly, not able in their despair to offer the much needed encouragement.

Sometimes "in the valley of the shadow," when a point of exhaustion was reached, Arlyce had seen hope slip quietly away. It was the nature of things. But, in a sizeable number of the exhausted "Chips" patients, nature would be forcibly reversed. That was the technology of things.

"Your temperature is down just a little," Arlyce reassured her patient, "so we're going in the right direction. Let's hope it keeps coming down, Hattie. That will ease your headache and, you know, there may still be a little time to party."

Doctors, especially in the oncology setting, talked the language of statistics and percentages. Nurses counterbalanced with intangibles. Hope, courage and belief were the intangibles.

Arlyce knew Hattie was a hardy survivor, tough as nails. Vital to her making it, was the fact that she had a solid, active support group, only part of which was her immediate family. She had four grown daughters, a couple of grandchildren and lots of friends. All loved and adored Hattie. She was a tall, large-boned woman who, when healthy—Arlyce had seen the pictures—had shoulder length, thick glistening black hair, a beautiful, expressive face and enchanting brown eyes. Even in these circumstances Arlyce had seen her exude intelligence, boldness and curiosity. Plus, she had a great sense of humor and, in better times, a wonderful, hearty laugh. Hattie had a lot going for her. This was a bad series of downs; that's all. It wasn't the ball game.

Of course, Arlyce had thought the same thing about the dock worker from New Jersey. He had been special, a crusty sort of guy. That was the word that came to her mind when she thought of him. She liked it, the word that is. Crusty, a tough guy protecting a soft heart. They, the tough guy and the nurse, had discovered a common bond. They were each married to a person from Kerala, India. How likely was that coincidence to ever happen? They had a commonality to talk about and in a different world it would have been nice for the couples to have become friends. As a token of appreciation he had given her a gift, a small gold necklace from India.

The dock worker hated what his life had become. So much so, in fact, that he had ended it by hanging himself. Not on the unit or anything. It wasn't like that but, still, his suicide had been a shock to Arlyce. It was so violent and, at the same time, pretty apropos for a crusty sort of guy.

Who could fault him? Filling a man with poison and radioactively frying him until there was not a hair left on his body pretty well stripped away every layer of dignity that had taken him a lifetime to build. Gone just like that, all those layers. And the path he had gotten on to? It never would circle back to where he'd started it. He had already been changed forever.

"Is your little granddaughter visiting with you?" Arlyce asked as she carefully inspected the reddened, raised areas on Hattie's arms.

Seeing Hattie's daughter had created a question in Arlyce's mind and she was being a detective now. Children were carriers of lots of intriguing microorganisms. Maybe immune-compromised Hattie had picked up something from the child. Patients were urged to keep their distance from children during susceptible times. But this being Hattie's second time around and, thinking life was ever so fragile, she might have bent the rules and held the child.

"Yes, she is so wonderful," answered Hattie. "Di-d-ddd that little boy that w-w-was in here ma-kkk-e it?"

Arlyce knew who she meant, little Nicholai, the precious four-year-old child from Greece. He and his parents, while they had been in the unit, had won the hearts of everyone.

Nicholai's support group had made extra large, campaign style buttons for the staff to wear. They showed the two characters, Pooh and Rabbit from A.A. Milne's *Winnie the Pooh,* holding hands and several sentences from Chapter VII "In Which Kanga and Baby Roo Come to the Forest, and Piglet Has a Bath:

"It is hard to be brave," said Piglet..."when you're only a
    Very Small Animal..."
Rabbit said, "It is because you are a very small animal that
    you will be Useful in the adventure before us."
Piglet was so excited at the idea of being useful...he forgot
    to be frightened anymore..."
(Milne p.94)

Arlyce looked into Hattie's eyes and then softly shook her head, no. Instantly Hattie's eyes filled with tears. Darn it, she had been so stubbornly determined not to cry over the holidays but, upon hearing this sad news, the dam of her resolve gave way and the reservoir of held-back tears emptied out onto her cheeks. It was time for a good cry.

"Oh, G-G-God," she sniffled reaching for the tissue box and pulling out a handful.

"I'm sorry, Hattie," Arlyce said as she stroked Hattie's head, "I'll show you what they sent us from his memorial service when you're feeling a little better, okay?" She placed her hand on Hattie's shoulder for a few more seconds and squeezed ever so lightly.

Painful as it had been for Hattie to hear about the child's death,

Arlyce could see that the tears—not self-pitying tears for Hattie herself but for the boy's family—were washing the demons out. Compassion for another, not something she as a nurse could inject or infuse in a person but something she had witnessed time and again, was a great healer of the soul.

The transfer from the inpatient unit to the new outpatient unit had at first intimidated Arlyce. In this location she was a trailblazer, the first contact for outpatients getting into trouble and a primary decision-maker. That independent aspect of responsibility was so different from the beehive, team-atmosphere of the inpatient unit. Once she adapted, however, she found that she liked it better.

Particularly the deaths, she had found with relief, were easier to take because she was not as intimately involved with the physical care and nurturing of the patients. In the inpatient unit some of the patients during particularly vulnerable phases were kept in laminar air-flow rooms. The rooms were bubble-like spaces intended to keep the person completely isolated. Nurses worked through arms of clear plastic and became the umbilical cord and placenta for these infantilized, dependent souls. Deaths in those circumstances brought on burnout or worse, post-traumatic stress syndrome, in staff. A nurse, as Arlyce well knew, might never forget the haunted eyes, the face or the torture she had helped to inflict.

It would be better to believe, as many did, that little Nicholai was safely in heaven, like the song in his memorial bulletin said:

"For to his angels he's given a command
to guard you in all of your ways; upon their hands, they
   will bear you up,
lest you dash your foot against a stone.
And he will raise you up on eagle's wings,
bear you on the breath of dawn..." (Michael Joncas)

Arlyce knew that it was Anil's path to quiet the mind, to go beyond ego and to experience the great nothingness, to observe the process. She, on the other hand, questioned if full involvement, sometimes head over heels involvement, in things and people was not what living was about, then what? Asking the question was as far as she went. What she did not want to do at this time in her life was to think about spirituality in concrete, doctrinal terms. She wanted to be open and genuine and to share another's sense of the moment. It was not easy to look death in the face without flinching but that is what she asked of herself. Looking, seeing and letting spirit be nurtured by truth, kindness, love and caring, not by thinking, wishful or otherwise, or not thinking.

The telephone rang at the desk and Doctor Crowe, reading a chart next to it, never stirred. Arlyce washed her hands at Hattie's bedside and walked to the central station. She made the decision: another patient was coming in. While still at the desk she read an order that Dr. Bowen had left on a chart. He wanted antibiotics added to an intravenous. She felt a gnawing in her stomach then and realized it was past time to let the other nurse have a supper break so that she, too, could have a turn later.

After a half-hour when Shaun, the nurse from the medical pool, came back from his break, Arlyce quickly went into the lounge next to the unit to eat her sandwich and call home. There were just a few minutes left before Arun's bedtime.

She said good night to Arun then talked with Anil. It was one of their rituals.

"Were you able to connect with your patient, Michael? No, I really mean Michael's mother, don't I? Were you able to connect with her this afternoon like you had hoped to do?" she asked between bites of food.

"Yes," responded Anil. "She had many questions. She was satisfied with my answers and did not mention a lawsuit. The student will be all right, I think."

"Oh, I'm glad."

"I spoke with Aunt Lottie on the telephone earlier," he continued. "The folks and Grandma are in church. The others are making oily balls. Do you know what oily balls are?" asked Anil quizzically.

Graphic images leapt to mind and Arlyce put her head back and laughed uncontrollably for a few seconds. Then, sensing that Anil was not amused she explained, "Oily balls are *ollie bollen*. They are food. It is a Dutch thing. They are made from dough that has currants and small pieces of apple in it. Large spoonfuls of dough are deep fried and then covered with powdered sugar. American people call them fritters, I think. They are delicious, a tradition on New Year's Eve carried over from Holland. I wish I could have some."

"I spoke with Aunt Lottie for everyone to come for pasta tomorrow," Anil continued. "She will speak with the others. I felt her to be hesitating."

Arlyce yearned to laugh about oily balls again. Given Hattie's sadness, administering chemo for deadly cancers, the student's attempted suicide, events all juxtaposed with holidays and family tensions, it had felt really good to have a belly laugh about oily balls. Instead, she gave way to heaviness. There were just times when Anil could be so serious and sensitive. He didn't let anything go. If someone offended him, he jumped in with both feet and confronted people. If he detected hesitance, he took notice. In many ways, she admired those very traits and so wished she had more such gumption. But there were times when his intensity tired her.

It isn't just Anil, she thought, *it's me being sensitive. Me and all women with children, even without, who are always juggling interests, proposing compromises, making sacrifices and sorting things out. Couldn't Dr. Crowe just have picked up the phone once, for instance, instead of being oblivious?*

She had been able to be more empathetic and available for Anil when it was just the two of them. A number of past incidents in his work and in life in general had undercurrents of racism directed at Anil, her, too, and she was learning more than she had thought she would need to about ingrained bigotry in people and in herself. Sometimes, the intolerance was not an undercurrent at all but came, rather, as a full force wave of hatred that smacked up against her. Those left her drenched with shame to be Caucasian in America. Anil, she knew, had to deal with layers of prejudice that she would never know nor encounter and because of that she almost always gave him the benefit of the doubt. Yet, there were times when, in her opinion, it was the best policy not to dig more deeply but to be practical. This was one of those times, she decided.

"Do we have everything we need if they do come, Baboo?" Arlyce inquired.

"Yes. We will deal with it in the morning," he replied.

"I'll see you at midnight. Don't be asleep, okay? I love you."

"Me and my oily balls will be here. I love you, too," Anil responded and laughed along with Arlyce this time. The heaviness vanished and she wished she were there with him.

The remainder of her shift passed quickly and towards the end of it she happily sent Hattie and her family home. Her hunch had been correct: Hattie had contracted something from the grandchild and, luckily, once the bug was pinpointed, it had been easy to treat. By eleven-thirty all the patients had been dispersed either to the inpatient unit or discharged and the charts were up-to-date. She checked the medication cart and computer one last time, made sure she had done all the preparations for the morning shift, put on her coat, shut off the lights, locked the unit door and stepped into the elevator.

"Happy New Year!" she called as she passed the security guard on the main floor, then she pushed her way through the front door and exited the building.

Once out, she stopped and stood for a few seconds under the protective roof extension. *It's still raining so hard but I don't mind,* she thought. *It's refreshing.* She took in deep breaths of the cool night air. As she crossed the street to her car, the wind blew huge drops of rain directly into her face. *That feels so-o-o-o-o good!*

It'd be great if I could go for an invigorating run or a swim like I used to. I'd love to do something really physical.

She and Sandi had been on Watson Groen's basketball team at the same time and they had been great. They had gone all the way to State finals in Spokane. She had been a strong swimmer and a lifeguard, too. Well, she could not walk, run, play basketball or swim tonight. Not at almost midnight, not when her husband expected her and not when her child would awaken at six in the morning. However, there was the chance that Anil would still be awake.

In the car Arlyce locked the doors, started the engine and turned on the windshield wipers. Alone and free for the upcoming dark and mostly abandoned miles between downtown Seattle and home, she happily pretended to be that carefree adolescent again. She turned on the radio and cranked up the volume as she pulled out of the parking lot. Once on the street, much like her favorite, endangered, maniacal, screeching, siamang gibbon (ape) at the zoo often did from his perch at the top of a tree, she bee-bopped deliciously in her seat, and with equal gusto and abandon, she joined the "Pet Shop Boys" in their version of the call of the wild. *Life, what a gift!* she thought as she opened her window a little to let in the cool rain.

Chapter 29
See You in Mexico!

Gluing past to present, place to place and event to meaning in my particular way has brought me the knowledge of belonging and a resulting measure of peace.

P at emerged from a vivid, black and white dream with a pressing sense that she was needed. She raised her tousled, groggy head an inch off the pillow to see the clock on the mantle. There were deep lines pressed into the side of her face and the tissue was puffy around her eyes. She looked and felt tired; sleep had not erased her bone weariness. It was 4:30 a.m. She dropped back heavily onto the pillow choosing to be grateful for a couple more hours of sleep rather than to wonder why she was needed. Steven was still asleep beside her. She pressed her back against his and pulled up her knees.

Then the sounds of wind swirling around in the labyrinth of her exposed ear, registered on the cerebral cortex by way of the acoustic nerve and thoughts formulated. They were such: *The wind has died down some but it is still gusting and raining. We probably will not have any trouble getting to Arlyce and Anil today but, just the same, I wish the wind would stop. There are broken tree limbs ready to come crashing down, whole trees are even being uprooted along streets. It is so dangerous.*

Bingo! She was awake. *The weather these days,* she thought, *how many has it been by now?* Pat counted on her fingers beginning with the day after Christmas. *Seven.* For seven whole days the weather had been like a boisterous cousin disruptively setting the tone.

But why aren't I sleeping? I'm losing precious minutes of my two hours. She compulsively opened her eyes and raised up to look at the clock again. *Still 4:30; a couple of minutes must have gone by? And it is pretty light out. Wait a minute!* Pat sat straight up. *It is too cold in the room, too. The electricity must have gone off!*

"Steven!"

Steve woke with a start and, hearing Pat's voice and her news, hw hurriedly pulled on his clothes and a jacket, reached for the flashlight and went outside to waken Doug. Above all else, the family would need heat. Doug's supply of gas was not that great but the generator would give them some hours. No one could tell just how many. He might have to start the fireplaces. Lottie would be bothered by the smoke but they might not have a choice.

Upstairs in the master bedroom I was buried under the covers when I was awakened by what I thought was a heavy thump next to my bed. *What in heaven's name was that?* Without lowering the covers I pulled over towards the left side of the bed and looked down. There was the quart jar of spiced crab apples lying on its side on the rug. *Thank goodness, it looks intact.* It was still wrapped in the bubble wrap which must have been what saved it. *Phew, lucked out this time.* I could hear the wind blowing outside. *The vibrations from the wind must have moved it,* I deduced, as I turned myself around to get a glance at the clock. It was only 4:30 but almost light out. The bedroom was cold. I turned over and burrowed deeper into the warmth.

Before Sandi became conscious, she frowned. *What was that infernal beeping?* It was above her head and it had awakened her. She could see that it was only 4:30. *Why would the computer be acting up at this hour?* She rose up to look at the screen; her dad always had it running with a screen saver. The humming of the fan in the monitor had not bothered her but this beeping was making her very irritated, very fast.

She went up on her knees and clicked the mouse. Nothing. She couldn't take it anymore. She pushed the On/Off switch. It would be a hard shutdown for the computer but at least it wouldn't bother her anymore.

She crawled back into the sleeping bag and tried to sleep. No luck. Aargh!

At breakfast everyone was bundled up in sweaters and sweats. Sophia was wearing gloves; I was wearing a wool hat. The guys, as a generous concession, had decided it would be all right to run the coffee pot and toaster along with the furnace. Hot coffee had never tasted better. It was far from toasty warm in the house but it was tolerable.

"I've got to say," Sophia began and waited until everyone was looking at her expectantly. She slowly, deliberately wiped her mouth with the napkin, then continued. "I am very grateful for all that you have done during this stay. You, Pat, and Steven have worked every minute and you have been wonderful. I just want to say that now you are really overdoing it." She paused lengthily again. Pat stopped mid-chew to listen. "All I wanted was a little bit of snow just to remind me of what I was missing," Sophia said thoughtfully. "Believe me; I have had enough of your winter weather! I remember! I remember!" she exclaimed forcefully.

"Oh," laughed Ann, "I wondered what she had to tell us when she started like that!"

"She has had enough, everybody," called Sandi in jest. "Just turn the power back on!"

"That's right!" exclaimed Pat. "I forgot. You're the one who started all of this, Sophia!"

Pat squeezed Sophia's shoulders as she went behind her chair into the kitchen to get the jam.

"It's all your fault, Sophia," chimed in B.J.

"This is what I think we should do," said Pat walking back into the dining room. "We called and Arlyce and Anil have power. I think we should go there for the pasta lunch and plan to take everything that we would need for tonight's *hutspot* dinner to Arlyce and Anil just in case our power is not back on. We can go over there pretty soon; they are expecting us."

"I'll make a salad and we can bring that," volunteered Sophia.

Before long, the three bundles of kale, five pounds of potatoes, one half-cup of barley, the jar of spiced apples, the pan of *krentjebrei* and we bundled up refugees from the Cok home were on our way to the Coumar home. The rain was steadily coming down. So far, in this latest storm, the overworked meteorologist said, two inches of rain had fallen. Water was forming, not pools, but ponds in low areas. Twigs, branches and whole trees were downed in sodden, snow-blotched lawns along the way. All traffic signal lights were dead, making inter-sections four way stops for the sparse traffic.

We were unloading midst much chatter at the two-story Coumar home when Sophia suddenly realized that her salad had been left behind.

"It was so beautiful too," wailed Sandi.

In a quick, disjointed confab it was determined that, under the circumstances, a trip back to the Cok home for the salad was not warranted and we all agreed that we would do just fine with what the Courmars had to offer.

Since we had an early breakfast, we thought we might as well have an early lunch, too. So before noontime already, the lovely, heaping bowlful of pasta that Anil had prepared was totally gone.

"The frog was quiet again this morning," I interjected into the post-lunch-but-still-sitting-at-the-table conversation.

"What?" asked Ann.

"I've been hearing a frog croak over at Steve and Pat's house. It was croaking when we first came. During the snow it stopped. It was croaking again for a couple of nights or so but not this morning."

"That's crazy," said Pat. "I haven't heard any frog! We never hear frogs, do we, Steven?"

"No, no frogs," said Steve unequivocally.

"There is enough water for frogs to be here," commented Doug dryly.

"I've heard the frog," offered Margaret. "I've heard it and I've seen it."

"Really, you saw a frog?" queried Ann. "I don't believe it."

"Yes, it is a real big one and it croaks every time you walk by it."

"Oh!" exclaimed Sandi.

It was clear to all that a light bulb had gone on in Sandi's brain,

"It's one of those fake ones," she proclaimed.

"Yep, pretty phony," said Marge.

"I thought it sounded crazy," murmured Ann.

"I was sure fooled," I said disgustedly and then expanded. "I hate those noisy, fake things. They're stupid. Pretty soon we'll have a fake skunk spraying us with some obnoxious perfume."

"Cute, Tjaakje," praised Brandon. "Maybe we'll have a horse farting."

I smiled and nodded at the boy's playfulness.

"Brandon," warned Marge.

Brandon and I rolled our eyes at one another.

"I have decided not to go back tonight like I planned," announced Sandi, mercifully changing the subject before I got Beej into more trouble. "I will be leaving in the very early morning. They say the rain will have stopped by then."

"Don't leave us, don't leave us," mocked B.J. in a melodramatic, sqeaky-high voice.

"Well, I guess, we will have to start for home on Friday, said Marge.

"Oh, no, don't all say that," pleaded Ann. "Sandi and the girls are leaving already tomorrow and then you on Friday too?"

"Aunt Francis died and Doug would like to be at the funeral," informed Marge. "We got a phone call last night. It's kind of strange."

"What do you mean, strange? How old a woman was she?" asked Pat.

"Well, she was pretty old. I think she was 88 or so. Wasn't she, Doug?"

"I guess so; I don't really know for sure," he responded.

"What was strange?" I pressed.

"Well," began Marge, "Aunt Francis knew details of the murder of her daughter at the hands of her granddaughter's boyfriend. Like how she was murdered and so, things that she never told anybody."

"Wow, that sounds like a Mary Higgins story!" exclaimed Pat.

"You girls and your Mary Higgins books. Maybe, I should read one once so I know what all you are reading about," muttered Ann.

"No, seriously," continued Marge, "nobody has been arrested for the murder and somebody knows something, but they are not saying. It's possible that the ex-husband of Aunt Francis' daughter was in on it."

"How did this person die?" asked Anil.

"Well," said Doug slowly, "somebody set the place on fire with her in it. There was something fishy about it."

"Let me get this straight," asserted Sophia. "This woman, Aunt Francis, 88 years-old was burned in a fire and they think her ex-husband had something to do with it?"

"No, Aunt Francis died a day or two ago but not in a fire. Her daughter was murdered in a fire longer ago. How long ago was this?" Sandi asked.

"Last summer," replied Marge.

"So the possibly murdered woman's mother has now died and the death may be suspicious, too," clarified Sandi.

"I still don't have it straight," said a puzzled Sophia. "Did the younger daughter or granddaughter know these guys were going to kill her mother and now maybe her grandmother?" asked Sophia.

"She may have," said Marge.

"In tiny Rudyard? People know that somebody murdered a person but nothing is being done about it? Wow!" I exclaimed.

"Aunt Francis told me some things and you kind of wonder who will be next," added Marge somberly.

"Oh, dear," said Arlyce, "this really does sound serious."

"It could be," said Marge calmly.

"Does anybody know that Aunt Francis talked to you?" Sandi hastened to inquire.

"Maybe," responded Marge.

"You'll have to find out if Aunt Francis died of natural causes," suggested Steven sensibly.

"I'm sure an autopsy won't be done," said Marge.

"I'll protect you, Mom," said Brandon. "I'll take a rifle and stand by the door and shoot anybody that comes near you."

"You will do no such thing!" insisted Marge in a shocked tone. "Two dead people are more than enough."

"And, you say, then, that you are leaving tomorrow? I don't want to hear that," reiterated Ann who could put murder aside but not her concerns about being left.

"No, Friday, *Oma*. Not tomorrow," corrected B.J.

Arun had no more patience with sitting at the table and was given permission to leave to play with his hot wheels and the two-story, toy parking garage in the middle of the living room. Soon after, Anil said he would show Steven and Brandon the flight simulator on the computer and they went down the hall to Anil's office. Arlyce and Sandi went out for a brisk walk and talk in the rain, the amount of which coming down had lessened some, and Doug, Pat and Marge prepared for a game of Hand and Foot as soon as a fourth would join them. Sophia went into the bedroom for a nap and Mom and I began to peel the potatoes for the *maus* dinner.

"I think you have way too much kale, Tjaakje," Mom, the veteran of *hutspot*, asserted.

"I don't think so," I replied hesitantly and immediately wished that I could have sounded more confident. I have been making *maus* for many years and have a certain way I like it: less potatoes, more kale, more flavor, in my opinion. But I had not been making *maus* for twelve people, and therein lay the rub. Can she be right? I wondered.

"Well, I'll let you do it your way," she conceded.

"I just remembered," I said, "that I have a birthday card for John in my bag. I bought it at the mall the other day. Would you please get it out, Pat? I thought it might be nice for each person to write a little something in it and I'll give it to him tomorrow when we get back to Mesa."

"That's a good idea, Lottie," Pat said as she looked for and found the card.

"*Ja*, they are by themselves there in Mesa and we are all here together. It is too bad, hey, that they could not be here too," chafed Ann as she made a long, glum face.

"I think they like it that way, Moeke," I demurred.

"There are always two parts of the family. They in their world and you are here in Seattle. I wish sometimes we could all be together but that is not to be," our aging matriarch lamented sadly.

Steven came from the back room and joined Arun on the floor. I got up to fill the pan of potatoes with water and, since it was not quite time to start them on the stove, I decided to have a visit with Anil who was now alone in his office.

"I have not had a chance before this to have a minute alone with you, Anil," I declared as I entered his room and sank into a chair. I paused to catch my breath before continuing. "Is this an all-right time to chat?'

"Sure," he responded.

"I have wanted to say to you in person that I was sorry for your loss of your father. I know that is an important milestone in a person's life. Are you doing okay with it?"

"There are times when I have felt very empty, very sad," Anil responded forthrightly.

"I can well imagine," I commiserated.

"Sad feelings are good to have for such a thing in one's life," remarked Anil, "I would not want it any other way. I have thought a lot about him and how we were to each other. I am also going to therapy to work out some of my confusion."

"I admire you for that, Anil. It takes courage."

"You, Lottie, how are you?"

"I have talked with you on the phone about John. I worry about all the pills that he uses and I am afraid for him down the line, you know."

"You must remember that he is a responsible adult and makes his own choices."

"Yes, true. We are superficial with one another now which is better than nothing, I guess. I am no longer telling him to do things that he does not want to hear. That is progress, I suppose."

"That is about John. How are you?"

I laughed nervously, "I did veer away from myself, didn't I?"

I paused to reflect and Anil waited.

"Sophia and I are thinking more and more about selling our home in Maine. It is sad for me to realize that I am not as able as time goes on and that changes need to be made. I need a one-story home, I need not to travel in airports with oxygen anymore and I want to be closer to family, but the decision to leave Maine is very hard for Sophia to make. Maine is her home state and she has friends there that go back to childhood."

I paused again and Anil remained silent.

"It is such a relentless thing, this disease. It just keeps making me face losses. I get worn-down with that part. The flip side, though, is that it also makes me grateful for all that I still have and can do. I will enjoy being closer to family."

"I have a couple of tapes that may interest you," offered Anil. "It is about dying, and you may not like that, but it is also about living. It is a talk given by Ram Dass. Are you familiar with him?"

"Yes, I am. I used his book, *How Can I Help?*, in one of the classes that I taught."

"Would you be interested in the tapes?" asked Anil directly.

"Absolutely," I enthused falsely. *Yeah, right,* I muttered internally, *I want to read about dying just about as much as I want to read about the activities of a tape worm in humans. Not! Yes, yes, I will. It is a good idea and I wouldn't want to die ignorant. What does Ram Dass know about dying that I don't know? That's the hooker and that is why I'll probably listen to the tapes, but I really would rather, if you must know the truth, talk to someone who's been through it.*

"I would like it if you moved to Seattle," said Anil breaking into my personal, cynical moment.

"Thanks," I replied. We'll see what happens."

Sophia came out of the bedroom from across the hallway and upon seeing Anil asked, "Would now be a good time to do your feet, Anil?"

Before Anil could respond I said, "I have to start my work in the kitchen so I have to go. You guys go ahead."

Anil came out to sit on the funky over-stuffed couch and Sophia went to prepare the special, warm, sudsy, foot-soak solution. His were the last remaining pair of feet to be soaked and massaged and she had, indeed, met her goal. Words are not Sophia's forte; she is more confident with touch and, by unobtrusively carrying out a time-honored Middle Eastern tradition, Sophia had in her unique fashion served and touched each individual.

As I finished mashing the potatoes and kale together, Mom made one last suggestion: "Nog even es goud der rujeren (Stir it good once more)," she said. It wasn't long before all of the *maus,* spiced apples and *krentjebrei* disappeared from sight into the mouths of the how-could-they-be-hungry-already-again!?-group. The power was at last reported to have come back on in the Cok neighborhood and it was almost time to disperse.

"Before we part for the evening..." began Arlyce.

"We would like to give a gift to Grandma," finished Anil.

"Me?" asked Ann, looking both surprised and immensely pleased.

"Yes, you, Grandma," said Arlyce. "Anil has made something which we hope will be very special for you."

"You may have seen me taking video pictures these days and today?" ventured Anil.

"Yes," responded Ann with anticipation in her voice.

"Well, I have made a video for you to have of what we have been doing these days and you can play it over again when you want to remember it."

"Oh, my dear children," celebrated Ann as she clapped her hands. "You did that for me! Thank you very much. I am so happy that we could all be together for this."

"Okay, we have to go now," intervened Sophia, cutting off any possibility of long-winded speeches. "Tjaakje and I have to pack yet. It will be a big day for us tomorrow."

"We'll watch the video at our house after everybody is gone,

Moeke," said Pat.

"That sounds good," replied Mom. "I guess we will be left to take down the tree and the decorations, Pat. I am glad that I do not have to leave until Tuesday. Maybe, Monday we can go shopping," she hinted broadly.

"I am way too exhausted to go shopping," replied Pat slouching down in her chair for added emphasis. "Arlyce will have to take you."

"Maybe Monday you will feel different," countered Ann.

Our group spread hugs all around in the good-byes to the Coumars and piled back into the cars.

"Hey," someone shouted, "it is not snowing or raining!"

"No wind either," called another. "It sure is cold, though."

"How about let's get together in a warmer, drier place next time," Sophia suggested.

"How about Mexico?" I rejoined.

"Okay, Mexico it is!" shouted Sandi.

"See you in Mexico!" voices called back and forth and arms waved as the cars backed out of the driveway under a clear sky.

"Love you!"

"Love you too!"

"Mexico? Really? That may be a little too far for me," debated Ann as the group headed for home.

SELECTED BIBLIOGRAPHY

Anderson, Ken. *Hitler and the Occult.* New York: Prometheus Books, 1995.

Anthony, Martin M. and Swinson, Richard P. *Phobic Disorders and Panic in Adults: A Guide to Assessment and Treatment.* Washington D.C.: American Psychological Association, 2000.

Asscher-Pinkhof, Clara (Translated by Teresa Edelstein and Inez Smidt) *Star Children.* Detroit: Wayne State University Press, 1986.

Blumenthal, W. Michael. *The Invisible Wall: Germans and Jews, A personal exploration.* Washington D.C.: Counterpoint, A member of Perseus Books, 1998.

Cather, Willa (Copyright by W. Cather in *1927*). *Death Comes for the Archbishop.* New York: Alfred A. Knopf, 1950.

Cheneviere, Alain (Translated by Lisa Davidson). *My Future Ramachandra in India.* Minneapolis: Lerner Publications CO., 1996.

Clark, Mary Higgins. *Moonlight Becomes You. New York: Simon* & Schuster, 1996.

de Jong, Louis. *The Netherlands and Nazi Germany.* Cambrige: Harvard University Press, 1990.

De Mannen Van Overste Wastenecker: De geschiedenis van de B.S. In Noord-Hollands Noorderkwartier. N.V. Drukkerij V/H C. De Boer Jr. / Den Helder 1947.

Ebon, Martin. *Saint Nicholas: Life and Legend.* New York: Harper and Row, 1975.

Fradin, Dennis B. (Copyright by Regensteiner Publishing Enterprises, Inc.) *Enchantment of the World: The Netherlands.* Chicago: Children's Press, 1983.

Frankel Ph.D., Bernard and Kranz, Rachel. *Straight Talk about Teenage Suicide.* New York: Facts on File, Inc., 1994.

Galland, China. *Longing for Darkness: Tara and the Black Madonna, a Ten Year Journey.* New York: Viking Press, 1990.

Goldhagen, Daniel Jonah. *Hitler's Willing Executioners: Ordinary Germans and the Holocaust.* New York: Alfred A Knopf, 1996.

Hackett, John Winthrop. *I Was a Stranger.* Boston: Houghton Mifflin Co., 1977 (American Edition 1978).

Heitzman, James and Worden, Robert L. Editors. *India: a country study.* Washington D.C.: Federal Research Division, Library of Congress.

Holland, Cecelia. *The Sea Beggars.* New York: Alfred A. Knopf. 1982.

Ippisch, Hanneke. *Sky.* New York: (Pub. By Troll Communications L.L.C. 1996) Reprinted by Simon & Schuster Children's Publishing Division, 1998.

James, William. *The Varieties of Religious Experience.* New York: Penquin Classics, 1986 (First published in 1902).

Knopp, Guido and Remy, Maurice Phillip. *The Rise and Fall of Adolf Hitler.* Film Series, Volumes 1-6.

Krishnamurti, J. (Edited by Lee, R. E. Mark.) *The Book of Life: Daily Meditations with Krishnamurti.* New York: Harper Collins, 1995.

Leininger, Madeleine M. *Nursing and Anthropology: Two Worlds to Blend.* New York: John Wiley & Sons Inc., 1970.

Mac Pherson, Malcolm C. *The Blood of His Servants: The True Story of One Man's Search For His Family's Friend and Executioner.* New York: New York Times Book Co., 1984.

Miller, Olive Beaupre' Editor. *Tales Told in Holland.* Chicago: The Book House for Children, 1926.

Milne, A. A. *Winnie-The-Pooh.* New York: E.P. Dutton, 1926 (Copyright Renewal, 1954 Dutton Children's Books, Penquin Putnam Inc.).

Morris, Jan. *Fifty Years of Europe: An Album.* New York: Villard Books, a division of Random House, 1997.

Mulisch, Harry. *The Assault.* (Translated from the Dutch by Claire Nicolas White). New York: Pantheon Books, 1985. (Originally published in 1982 as *De Aanslag* by Bij de Bezige).

Nicholas, Evan. *The Horse Whisperer.* New York: Delacorte Press, 1995.

Root M.D., Benjamin. *Understanding Panic and Other Anxiety Disorders.* Jackson: University Press of Mississippi, 2000.

Schaap, James C. *Our Family Album: The Unfinished Story of the Christian Reformed Church.* Grand Rapids: CRC Publications, 1998.

Schama, Simon. *Embarrassment of Riches.* New York: Alfrd A. Knopf, 1987.

Smith, Janet Grosshandler. *Coping When a Parent Dies.* New York: Rosen Publishing Group, 1995.

Steffen, Wim K. and Noordam, B.W. *When the Tide Turns: The Netherlands' Struggle Against the Water.* The Hague: N.V. Uitgeverij W. Van Hoeve, 1963

Walkerman, Elyce. *Father Loss: Daughters Discuss the Man That Got Away.* New York: Doubleday & Co., 1984.

Weisel, Mindy Editor. *Daughters of Absence.* Herndon: Capital Books, Inc. 2000.

Woolf, Linda M. "Survival and Resistance: The Netherlands Under Nazi Occupation." Paper presented at the United States Holocaust Memorial Museum, April 6, 1999. http://www.webster.edu/~woolflm/Netherlands.html

Printed in the United States
99375LV00003B/73-75/A